THIRD W[...]

Cognitive Behavioural Coaching

Contextual, Behavioural and Neuroscience Approaches for Evidence Based Coaches

**Edited by
Jonathan Passmore
and Sarah Leach**

Third Wave Cognitive Behavioural Coaching

© Pavilion Publishing & Media

The authors have asserted their rights in accordance with the Copyright, Designs and Patents Act (1988) to be identified as the authors of this work.

Published by:
Pavilion Publishing and Media Ltd
Blue Sky Offices
25 Cecil Pashley Way
Shoreham by Sea
West Sussex
BN43 5FF

Tel: 01273 434 943
Email: info@pavpub.com
Web: www.pavpub.com

Published 2022

A catalogue record for this book is available from the British Library.

ISBN: 978-1-803880-00-6

Pavilion Publishing and Media is a leading publisher of books, training materials and digital content in mental health, social care and allied fields. Pavilion and its imprints offer must-have knowledge and innovative learning solutions underpinned by sound research and professional values.

Editor: Jonathan Passmore and Sarah Leach
Production editor: Mike Benge, Pavilion Publishing and Media Ltd
Cover design: Phil Morash, Pavilion Publishing and Media Ltd
Page layout and typesetting: Phil Morash, Pavilion Publishing and Media Ltd
Printing: CMP Digital Print Solutions

About the Editors

Jonathan Passmore DOccPsych is a chartered psychologist, an accredited coach and holds five degrees. He has published widely, including 30 + books, 50 + book chapters and over 100 scientific papers. His titles include *The Coaches Handbook* (2021), *Becoming a Coach* (2020), *Mastery in Coaching* (2015), *CoachMe* (2022), *Succeeding as a Coach* (2021) and *WeCoach!* (2021). He is listed in the Global Gurus and Thinkers50 coaches list of thought leaders and has won multiple awards for his work. He is the Chair of the British Psychological Society Division of Coaching Psychology (2021-2022) He has held senior roles in the public, private and not-for-profit sectors, including for OPM, IBM and PricewaterhouseCoopers. He is Professor of Coaching and Behavioural Change, Henley Business School, UK and Senior Vice President Coaching for CoachHub.

Sarah Leach is a lecturer in coaching at Henley Business School, the founder and executive career and life coach at Stride Coaching & Consulting, and published author. In addition to this title, Sarah has published book chapters in titles such as *The Coaches Handbook* (2021), *Succeeding as a Coach* (2021) and *WeCoach!* (2021). Sarah has a corporate background in the utility sector, holding senior roles in leading and enabling business change.

Foreword

Without change, we die. The human organism must refresh itself from cellular mitochondria to our behavioral repertoire to adapt to changes in our environment. Is the pace of change more rapid than ever before in human history? I doubt it. Ask people in leadership positions from 1475 to 1525, or 1750 to 1850, or 1914 to 1945. Although the specific forms of change may differ, what confronts our very existence is a process of continually adapting or innovating to adjust or create a new world.

From the ancient Chinese and Greek philosophers, the curiosity of humans as to how and why we change has preoccupied and even haunted us. For example, who can fathom the teenage mind? Why do people persist in habits that damage their bodies, minds and relationships? If we really believed our lives were predetermined, we would have little incentive to adapt or attempt to improve the conditions of our lives. The most casual observer notes that people do not change and adapt to the same degree or at the same time. Some people seem to thrive and others languish. Why?

This new book by Passmore and Leach is a compilation of various approaches to behavior change. The authors review theories they use. They review the empirical research and provide exciting exercises for reflection or experimenting with possible change.

In a sense, this book is a crosswalk between psychotherapeutic approaches and coaching. It traces the key thinkers from Pavlov to Ellis to Perls and Rogers, and even cognitive behavioral therapy to more recent approaches like mindfulness. But there is more here than new buzz words to impress friends at future dinner parties, they provide us with ways to compare the approaches presented with others not represented in this book, or new and emerging approaches that will appear in future books.

Our 30 years of longitudinal outcome studies, fMRI and hormonal studies of the mechanisms of change make it clear that we have multiple paths to new behavior and habits. We can be inspired by hope, vision and a dream. We can experiment with specific new actions to prepare, adapt or merely to please others. We can build our relationships in healthy ways or atrophy in isolation and loneliness. Sadly, our research also shows that trying to fix someone else, batter them with feedback about their ineptitude or lack of progress, harangue them with specific goals to aspire to reach all invoke neural and hormonal states that close the person to new ideas and other people. In other words, they do the opposite to what we intended or hoped to do.

As you read each chapter and explore each exercise, ask yourself:

1. Does it invoke or affirm a person's (or client's) dreams for the future, their sense of purpose and meaning of life?
2. Does it encourage or actually renew the helper or change agent or coach?
3. Does it invoke and support actual changes in day-to-day behavior?
4. Does it help to build more resonant relationships between helper and client and others?

Richard E Boyatzis, PhD

August, 2021

Contents

About the Contributors

Tim Anstiss MD is a doctor, coach and trainer, specialising in behaviour change and wellbeing improvement. He has trained thousands of healthcare professionals in motivational interviewing and health coaching and has been involved in a number of national and international health behaviour change initiatives. Tim is a member of a visiting faculty at the Henley Centre for Coaching, Henley Business School (University of Reading, UK).

Simon Barnes has been practising mindfulness meditation for 20 years. The personal benefits he felt inspired him to become a mindfulness teacher. He gained a Masters in Mindfulness with Bangor University, and trained with Breathworks and the Mindfulness in Schools project. Recently, Simon was among the first to complete Oxford University's Mindfulness in the Workplace programme and he teaches mindfulness to diverse groups, including in corporate settings and healthcare settings.

Iain McCormick PhD trained as a clinical psychologist in forensic settings, and subsequently became a field psychologist during a long Antarctic traverse, studying work stress for his PhD. He has coached and consulted for 35 years in Canada, Hong Kong and New Zealand. He lives in Auckland with his wife and two sons.

Katherine Finlay PhD is a chartered psychologist and psychology lecturer at the University of Reading, UK. Katherine's research work specializes in the application of health psychology and behaviour change to the management of chronic health conditions. Katherine has considerable expertise in intervention-development and is regularly employed on grants, and in research and consultancy roles as a trainer in motivational interviewing. She learnt motivational interviewing in Cardiff from its originators, Stephen Rollnick and Bill Miller.

Matthew Pugh is a clinical psychologist, CBT psychotherapist, advanced Schema therapist, voice dialogue facilitator, single session therapist, and leading chairwork practitioner and trainer. He has written numerous articles and book chapters on chairwork, and is the author of *Cognitive Behavioural Chairwork: Distinctive Features* (2020). He is a member of visiting faculty at the Henley Centre for Coaching, Henley Business School (University of Reading, UK).

Patricia Riddell, PhD is a Professor of Applied Neuroscience in the School of Psychology and Clinical Language Sciences at the University of Reading. She has published widely in coaching and leadership including *The Neuroscience of Leadership Coaching*. She is a member of faculty at the Henley Centre for Coaching, Henley Business School (University of Reading, UK).

Reinhard Stelter PhD (Psych) is Professor of Coaching Psychology at the University of Copenhagen and visiting professor at Copenhagen Business

School. An accredited coaching psychologist (ISCP) in his own practice, Honorary Vice President of the ISCP and founding fellow of the Institute of Coaching at Harvard.

Rob Willson is a cognitive behavioural therapist, trainer, researcher and author, based in London, UK. He has a keen interest in the relationship between therapy and coaching and is a member of visiting faculty at the Henley Centre for Coaching, Henley Business School (University of Reading, UK). He has authored a number of books including *Cognitive Behavioural Therapy for Dummies* (2019) and *Overcoming Obsessive Compulsive Disorder* (2021), and numerous book chapters including for *The Coaches Handbook* (2021).

PART ONE:
First Wave

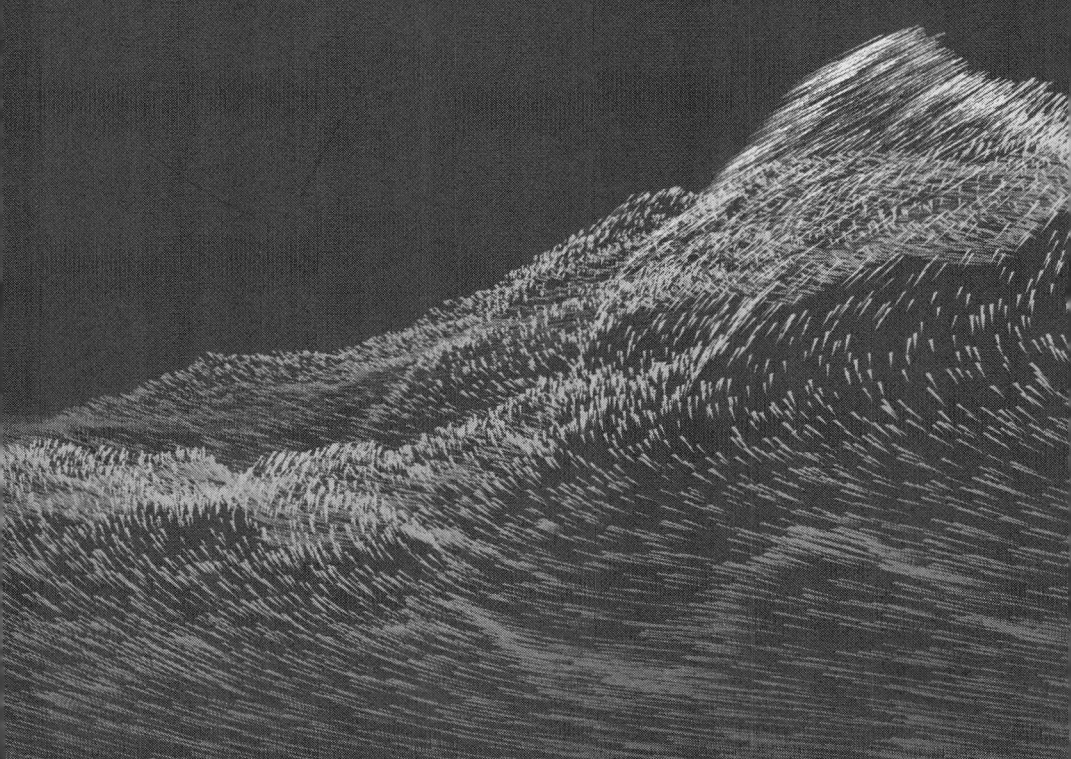

Introduction: First wave behavioural approaches

Jonathan Passmore and Sarah Leach

Cognitive behavioural therapy (CBT) is a psychologically rooted intervention which aims to deliver behavioural change. It is used in the UK by the National Health Service, and commonly used across the world by counsellors and health professionals seeking to support their clients in making and sustaining behavioural change. In health and wellbeing work CBT has become the intervention of choice for presenting topics such as mild depression and some forms of phobia, and has developed an impressive evidence base over the past few decades.

CBT is based on a combination of the basic principles from behavioural and cognitive psychology. It is different from many approaches used to deliver behavioural change. For example, psychodynamic approaches may focus on working with the client to explore and surface repressed memories which act to sustain unhelpful or destructive behaviours, or person centred approaches which focus on enabling the client to create the best conditions allowing them to flourish. In contrast, the cognitive behavioural approach focuses on exploring the clients' 'problem', helping clients understand the relationship between their behaviours, thoughts, and their emotions, while also adopting an 'action-oriented' approach.

The emergence of cognitive behavioural approaches can be seen as a reaction to other schools of thought, particularly the psychodynamic school that emerged in the late 19th Century, based on the work of writers such as Sigmund Freud and Carl Jung, and their focus on diagnosis through analysis. The cognitive behavioural schools rejected this in a belief that it was not possible to step into the black box of the mind, to understand the human unconscious, but inferences could only be made through observation of behaviour.

The first steps in this journey began with the emergence of the behaviouralists school, and the work of psychologists such as Ivan Pavlov (1927), whose work on dogs has been much reviewed and criticised (Adams, 2020). While Pavlov and later behaviourists accepted the importance of heredity in determining behaviour, they argued that behavioural changes could be learnt through environmental interventions, punishments and rewards.

Pavlov's work led to the emergence of what is known as 'classical conditioning', where the presentation of an external stimuli leads to, or triggers, a specific behaviour. In this case, the dogs 'learnt' to salivate at the ringing of a bell, through an association with the presentation of food, when the bell was being rung.

Subsequent work by researchers such as J. B Watson (1913), B.F. Skinner (1957 and 1974) and Edward Thorndike (1927), led to the 'Law of Effect'. This argued that behaviours could be strengthened or weakened by the use of consequences for the specific behaviour. Skinner's own contribution of behavioural radicalism was to suggest that covert behaviours, including cognitions and emotions, were subject to the same controlling variables. His work on pigeons, rats and other animals confirmed that animals could be trained to perform tasks through the offer of rewards (or punishments).

These ideas coincided with the emergence of personnel management and a greater focus on individual performance and work, and how enhancements can be made through time and motion study, training and development and job design. It may not be surprising that these ideas from behavioural psychology have underpinned much of our thinking in personnel and human resources for the past 70 or more years.

In this section we will explore in more depth the behavioural school of psychology, and its application in coaching, with a focus on behavioural change for coachees. In Chapter 1, Behavioural Coaching, we will specifically look at the emergence of early coaching models such as GROW, and how others have developed other behavioural-based approaches which can be highly effective to help clients develop the skills or competences required to perform their workplace role or a specific task.

References

Adams, M. (2020) The kingdom of dogs, *The Psychologist*, **33** (6) June, pp. 76–79.

Pavlov, I. P. (1927) *Conditioned Reflexes: An Investigation of the physiological activity of the cerebral cortext*. Translated by G V Anrep. London: Oxford University Press.

Skinner, B. F. (1957) *Verbal Behaviour*. New York: Appleton.

Skinner, B.F. (1974) *About Behaviourism*. London: Jonathan Cape.

Thorndike, E. L. (1927) The Law of Effect, *The American Journal of Psychology*, **39** (1/4), Dec pp. 212-222.

Watson, J. B. (1913) Psychology as the behaviorist views it. *Psychological Review*, **20**, pp158–77.

Chapter 1
Behavioural Coaching: Theory, research and practice

by Sarah Leach

Introduction

The first wave of cognitive behavioural coaching is more commonly labelled 'behavioural coaching'. Behavioural approaches form the foundation of both second and third wave cognitive behavioural approaches, and the techniques drawn from this approach are still used widely by many coaches without realising they are rooted within the behaviourist tradition (Peel, 2005).

Behavioural approaches began to develop through the work of Watson, Thorndike, Pavlov, and Skinner in the early to mid-20th Century (Eldridge & Dembkowski, 2013). Their research with animals examined how behaviour changed because of different stimuli or triggers. The behaviourists explored the idea of learning through association (*classical conditioning*), through rewards and punishments (*operant conditioning*) and through social processes (*social learning*). Albert Banduras's social learning theory built on and developed these ideas and we can find behavioural-based coaching approaches that still underpin much of our human resource management practices in organisations today (Eldridge & Dembkowski, 2013).

In this chapter I explore the theory of behavioural coaching, starting with the work of the behaviourists. I look at some of the research on the development of behavioural psychology, acknowledging there has been a limited amount of work done on the impact of behavioural coaching itself. I go on to take a closer look at behavioural coaching in practice, sharing some tools and techniques that you might find useful as coaching practitioners and leaders. Finally, I recommend several key texts for further reading and some reflective questions for you to consider for your own development.

Theoretical foundations

The theory of behavioural coaching originated from the work of psychologists Pavlov and Skinner who, through working with animals, identified ways in which humans learnt and therefore behaved. They identified three primary ways:

1. The first through association or *classical conditioning*
2. The second through being rewarded or punished for a particular behaviour, known as *operant conditioning*
3. The third through *social processes.*

(Passmore, 2007)

Albert Bandura extended this thinking through his social learning theory, exploring the idea of human learning at both the conscious and unconscious level. These behaviourist ideas were developed alongside modern management practises of the time, which looked to psychologists for inspirational ideas on improving efficiency and increasing the adoption of modern manufacturing techniques (Passmore & Sinclair, 2020). This led to Taylor's scientific management (Taylor, 1911), the root of many human resource practices developed over the last century.

Behaviourists argued that human behaviour was a result of conditioning, typically through the process of reinforcement. If you learn that behaving in a certain way causes something good to happen, you will likely continue to behave in that way, particularly if it is positively rewarded or reinforced. The opposite is also true. If you behave in a certain way and it is ignored or punished, you might learn not to do it again. We now know, through research into neuroscience, that past experiences inform future behaviour (Brown & Brown, 2012, p7):

> *'The skill of coaching from a brain perspective is facilitating change in a client in such a way as to get the brain working with new pathways in order to establish and maintain new ways of being [including new behaviours].'*

At a very simplistic level the brain lays down new neural pathways and, therefore, new ways of being and behaving as you learn, discover, and experience new connections, triggers, and responses. In observing patterns of behaviour in response to certain triggers, the behaviourists began to better understand the connection between stimulus and response and how it could be changed. In other words, how certain experiences determine certain behaviours.

Classical conditioning

Pavlov (1927), with his classic conditioning model, discovered he could change a dog's natural behavioural patterns. The dog would naturally salivate only on seeing food (*unconditioned stimuli*). Pavlov introduced a neutral stimulus (an intervention with no previous association to food), a ringing bell, every time the food arrived. Over time the dog began to salivate based on the sound of the bell alone, a conditioned response. In this example of classical conditioning, Pavlov was looking for ways to break the connection between the original stimuli and the response, replacing it with another in this instance, to change behaviour. This example also emphasises what we know today about the importance of practice, repetition, and reinforcement in creating new habits, routines and structures that enable behavioural change (Whitten, 2014). On this basis, Whitten (2014) argued that behavioural skills can be practised, such as developing the skill of assertiveness by experimenting with contributing at meetings for example. This exposure to new experiences and practise of new skills, repeatedly over time, enables behavioural change.

Watson started to adapt Pavlov's ideas and attempted to show how respondent conditioning could also explain the behaviour of humans (Jensen, 2019) and was the first to start talking about behaviouralism as the study of observable human behaviour (Watson, 1913) – 'observable' being the important word here. Watson suggested that complex habits could be broken down 'into a series of interlinked conditioned responses' (Eldridge & Dembkowski, 2013, p299). In his book *Behaviourism* Watson proposed that the stimulus-response reflex was the root of all human behaviour (Jensen, 2019) and that human behaviour could be measured in an observable way, much like dogs or rats! Many coaching approaches draw on these ideas and focus on observable behaviours or competencies as the single most importance aspect of coaching, client learning or change, the ICF competencies being just one example of this.

Thorndike, Watson's contemporary, also believed in the connection between stimulus and response in human learning. In 1911 he developed the 'Law of Effect' which stated that behaviours rewarded tended to be repeated, whilst behaviours that went unnoticed or were punished tended to weaken (Peel, 2005, pp20–21). He refined his thinking regarding the 'Law of Effect' further in the 1930s to reflect the fact that punishment could lead to avoidance of the situation or created anxiety and fear, rather than just weakening the stimulus-response connection (Peel, 2005).

Operant conditioning

Skinner built on the work of Pavlov, Watson, and Thorndike, distinguishing between two types of behaviour. The first being *respondent behaviour*, typical of classical conditioning as identified by Pavlov, the second being *operant behaviour* which focused on behaviour-environment relationships (Jensen, 2019). Skinner worked with rats and pigeons, looking at the differences in behaviour associated with rewarding or punishing specific behaviour and discovered operant conditioning. Skinner suggests the process of operant conditioning occurs when a new behaviour is learned, perhaps through trial and error, and then rewarded by a successful outcome. This reinforces the new behaviour and encourages repetition. In his book *The Behaviour of Organisms: An experimental analysis* Skinner theorized that:

> '*operant conditioning in the form of reinforcements and punishments leads to an association between a behaviour and its consequence*'.

(Rholetter, 2019, Abstract)

Riding a bike or playing football could fall into this category (Eldridge & Dembkowski, 2013). In learning to pedal a bike you realise you can keep the bike upright and moving forwards, and so continue to pedal, getting better and better each time.

Skinner also suggested that punishment could be used to drive the desired behaviour, either by providing a punishment directly after the behaviour or by removing a positive reinforcement (Passmore, 2007). For example, if targets are missed at work, the associated bonus might not be given, or if a child misbehaves, screen time is restricted by their parents. It is the consequence that reinforces the behaviour, either strengthening it or weakening it (Jensen, 2019). Phobias, substance abuse problems and obsessive-compulsive disorders for example, have all been treated by modifying behaviour through operant conditioning (Rholetter, 2019). In operant conditioning a third party or 'teacher' determines the rules and the mechanism by which to reward or punish behaviour that does not follow the rules. For example, in coaching an employee may hear stories of people being promoted at work for behaving in a certain way or being rewarded at work for a specific output, or cultural rituals that suggest if someone speaks out, they are not considered to be a team player. Individuals, as well as the systems and cultures we live and work in, can play a significant role in the context of operant conditioning, and it is something that, as coaches, we need to be mindful of when thinking about effective behavioural change.

Superstitious behaviour would also sit in this category. For example, it is common to witness sports men and women performing a 'ritual' before competing. Superstitions are an example of how we think and feel determining how we behave. Skinner did not deny the role of the brain in understanding behaviour but was unable to observe the impact. However, he continued to explore other aspects of behaviour, as described in his book *Verbal Behaviour* (Skinner, 1957), including more complex behaviour-environment relationships, and he was the first to attempt to extend stimulus response models to cognitive human processes (Eldridge & Debkowski, 2013; Moore, 2011). For example, teachers asking a student to think through the solution and then providing an environment where their thinking is praised or rewarded with high scores (Jensen, 2019). At this stage Skinner classified his work as radical behaviourism, *'the philosophy of a science of behaviour treated as a subject matter in its own right apart from internal explanations, mental or physiological'* (Skinner, 1989, p122). Critics of behaviourism were of the view that reducing all human behaviour, particularly complex human behaviour, to a stimulus response relationship was too simplistic. It took no account of any processing occurring internally (Eldridge & Debkowski, 2013).

Social learning theory

In response to such criticism, Bandura developed his social learning theory, integrating some of the thinking from cognitive approaches which talked about behaviour resulting from beliefs, values, and memories, in addition to the impact of external stimulus (Eldridge & Debkowski, 2013). Social learning is about understanding what we can learn from others, how they are rewarded or punished, by observing the behaviour of role models or mentors (Passmore, 2007). This is a common approach applied in behavioural-based coaching. The coach might explore with clients the possible consequences of a particular behaviour based on the observation and knowledge of others who have had similar experiences, as well as drawing on their own experiences.

Bandura also introduced the concept of self-efficacy and its significant influence on understanding behavioural change and coaching (Eldridge & Debkowski, 2013). He started to notice two divergent trends appearing in behavioural change thinking – one that human behaviour was acquired and regulated by cognitive processes, the other that successful performance-based outcomes were driving behavioural change (Bandura, 1977). Bandura's hypothesis examined whether,

> *'expectations of personal efficacy determine whether coping behaviour will be initiated, how much effort will be expended and how long it will be sustained in the face of obstacles and aversive experiences'.*

(Bandura, 1977, p191)

He concluded that the higher your perceived self-efficacy the more likely the individual is to succeed at changing their behaviour. Skiffington and Zeus (2003) also note the influence of constructivist thought on behavioural coaching. In other words, how individuals make their own meaning of the world around them and how heavily influenced behavioural coaching is by the systems in which we operate, and organisational and social psychology more generally (Skiffington & Zeus, 2003).

A century later and the popularity and influence of the behavioural approach in coaching is still strong (Passmore *et al*, 2017). This is particularly true of workplaces around the world where managers and purchasers of coaching want to see tangible and observable (behavioural) outcomes from the coaching process (Leach, 2021). It is important to note the relatively recent influence of the human potential movement during the 1980s on behavioural workplace coaching and leadership development – specifically Tim Galewey's *Inner Game of Tennis* (1986) and Whitmore, Alexander, and Fine's development of the GROW model (Leach, 2021; Whitmore, 2017; Alexander, 2016) – developed by observing and reflecting on coaching conversations with senior executives and the associated behavioural changes. The world of business coaching at this time was highly influenced by research in sports psychology that reinforced the importance of goal setting, finding your flow, and having high levels of motivation and commitment, in enabling behavioural change (Skiffington & Zeus, 2003).

More recently Dryden (2018) has written about the importance of understanding what role behaviour plays in the existence and maintenance of the client's problem, distinguishing between impulsive behaviour and behaviour that is intended to remove painful feelings or avoid something else. Dryden (2018) also points out the importance of noticing action tendencies, such as an urge to act, versus overt behaviour. As an example, you might be working with impulsive clients about the need to take a step back, re-focus and breathe before acting; or helping clients to notice the urge to act or behave in a certain way and using that urge to address their underlying thoughts and/or behave in a way which more consistently aligns with their values.

Research evidence

As with other coaching approaches based on therapeutic and psychological theory, there has been a limited amount of research done to assess the impact of behavioural coaching. The lack of studies that specifically reference behavioural coaching makes it difficult to ascertain whether behavioural coaching might be better suited to addressing certain topics compared with other approaches such as cognitive behavioural approaches. However, it continues to be widely used across many sectors to enable behavioural change.

A small number of studies have focused on the measurement of goal attainment (Eldridge & Demkowski, 2013). A comparative study completed by Anthony Grant (2001) looked at the effects of cognitive, behavioural, and cognitive behavioural coaching with students. His study focused on how these three coaching approaches impacted upon academic performance and study skills, as well as mental health, self-consciousness, and self-concept, with three different cohorts of students and a control group. Those receiving only cognitive coaching reported improved study skills and a positive impact on approaches to learning, as well as reduced levels of anxiety and depression. Although academic performance declined in comparison to the control group. Those receiving only behavioural coaching, showed lower study related anxiety and an increase in academic performance. The group receiving cognitive behavioural coaching also reported lower anxiety levels and an improvement in academic performance, in addition to enhanced study skills, improved self-regulation and self-concept. As such, Grant concluded that the combination of both cognitive and behavioural coaching was more impactful, and thus more effective at improving performance and well-being (Leach, 2021).

Behavioural-based approaches continue to be used in the management of anxieties, for example a client who becomes anxious at the thought of delivering a presentation. A more recent example of managing anxiety links Pavlov's findings to PTSD, where:

> 'neutral cues can take on great salience when they predict a threat to survival. In anxiety disorders such as posttraumatic stress disorder (PTSD), this type of conditioned fear fails to extinguish... for decades after the danger has passed.'

(VanElzakker *et al*, 2014, p3)

In the field of health and clinical psychology there have been other studies looking at the effectiveness of behavioural therapy on depression (Jacobson *et al*, 1996) and on anorexia (Channon *et al*, 1989) for example, both of which suggested that behavioural therapies alone were just as effective as cognitive behavioural therapies in treating these conditions. Following on from Jacobson's findings a new therapy for depression known as 'behavioural activation' was developed (Kennerley *et al*, 2007).

Several neuroscientific studies have looked at negative and positive prediction errors (Schultz, 2016; Schultz & Dickinson, 2000) that have reinforced the thinking around reward and punishment, and thus operant conditioning. Neurons in the brain appear to 'code prediction errors in relation to rewards, punishments, external stimuli and behavioural reactions' (Schultz & Dickinson, 2000, p473) therefore impacting behavioural learning, the processing of sensory information and the short-term control of behaviour. When the reward received is greater than the reward expected there is a positive prediction error, and when the reward received is less than expected there is a negative prediction error. These experiences impact the way our brain 'codes' prediction errors, altering our behaviour accordingly. This could be as simple as the negative impact of arriving late to a work meeting and, as a result, being given all the actions, or receiving a thank you card in the post for going the extra mile with a customer.

Behavioural approaches are commonly used in career coaching, which is often goal and action oriented, where progress can be measured and observed. Ibarra (2004) talks about the 'Test & Learn' approach which starts with action, followed by analysis, leading to other actions, creating a cycle of testing and learning where individuals create experiments or try out new experiences to explore possible selves. Much like operant conditioning, if the experience is positive, it might be repeated and/or learnt from and re-applied again in the context of career planning and development. Bandura's self-efficacy theory has heavily influenced career theory too. Lent *et al* (2017) looked at the sources of self-efficacy and outcome expectations for career exploration and decision-making, finding that sources of self-efficacy were linked to goals indirectly but mastery and positive affect both significantly impacted levels of decidedness in career decisions.

Passmore and Rehman (2021), in exploring coaching as a learning methodology, suggested that behavioural coaching was most effective in the development of behavioural skills. In a study by Allison and Ayllon (1980) which used a behavioural coaching strategy to aid the learning of specific sports skills with 23 participants, it was found that performance increased along with an appropriate use of skills by an average of 50%. As a result of this study Passmore and Rehman (2021) went on to suggest that a behavioural coaching approach might be successful in driver training which involves learning a motor skill. However, they also acknowledged the importance of cognition and emotion in driver decision-making. In two RCT studies (Passmore & Rehman, 2012; Passmore & Velez, 2012) the researchers provided some evidence of the potential benefits of driver coaching in improving outcomes (appropriate learnt behaviours) and reducing learning time (Passmore & Rehman, 2012), but that such benefits were only gained over time, and cannot be achieved in short one-or two-hour interventions (Passmore & Velez, 2012). Other qualitative studies (Passmore & Townsend, 2012) explored the perceptions of coaching on driver training and highlighted the personal focus as a key component.

Hutton *et al* (2002) have highlighted a positive effect of changing negative behaviours by using feedback, which one could argue is like Ibarra's 'Test & Learn' approach (2004), where feedback is part of the post experience analysis, leading to further adjustments in behaviour.

The work of Olivero, Bane and Kopelman (1996) was the first reported attempt at examining the influence of coaching in a public sector municipal agency. A conventional training programme for managers was delivered to 31 people followed by an 8-week programme of one-to-one coaching delivered by internal coaches. Action research was asked to look at the influence of coaching on embedding the training into workplace behaviour change. This study found an 88% increase in productivity after coaching, in comparison to a 22.4% increase after training alone. However, this research has considerable weaknesses in its methodology, but the paper has been frequently cited since its publication as evidence of the value of coaching.

Practice

Skiffington and Zeus (2003) talk about behavioural coaching as enabling a client to move through the four stages of change:

Stage 1: The Reflective Stage

At this stage individuals are not intending to make a change soon. They may be aware that an issue exists but are not necessarily committed to changing their behaviour yet.

Stage 2: The Preparation Stage

At this stage there is an intention to act. The individual may have set a goal, developed an action plan, and even experimented with or rehearsed a few new skills and strategies to enable the change.

Stage 3: The Action Stage

It is at this stage that the action plan is put in place, and behavioural changes can start to be measured and evaluated.

Stage 4: The Maintenance Stage

At this stage the individual is focused on maintaining the new behaviour, embedding the change so that it becomes a regular habit or established way of being and behaving.

Based on scientific principles and research methodologies, behavioural therapies allow for the effects of an intervention to be measured through personal observation or more detailed micro analysis, rather than just personality profiling (Skiffington & Zeus, 2003). The behavioural approaches tend to focus on the problem and generate an action-orientated approach to finding a solution. As we have discovered over recent years, behaviour does not stand in isolation from cognition and emotion. They are integrally related (Dryden, 2018). As a result, when a client thinks about changing their behaviour, they will have an associated thought and a feeling about these future acts which may help or hinder their progress (Dryden, 2018). It is important as a coach to remember the client's cognitive, emotive and behavioural responses and how these are linked if maximum progress is to be made. Having said that, working on behavioural changes in relative isolation with the help of some of the following tools and techniques can and will aid small but significant steps in progress and may also enable tiny shifts in cognitive and emotive responses without realising.

Dryden (2018, p20) notes *'Behaviour plays a very important part in both PF-CEBC and DF-CEBC'*, where PF-CEBC is problem-focused cognitive-emotive behavioural coaching and DF-CEBC is development-focused cognitive-emotive behavioural coaching. Later chapters will explore how 'the role of the CBC coach is to combine solution-focused behavioural methods with cognitive strategies and awareness' (Whitten, 2014, p151).

Coaching examples

In the following examples I will offer five ways we can bring alive behavioural approaches in coaching. These include a brief exploration of the GROW model, the role of goal setting, questions, role modelling and behavioural rehearsal.

1. GROW model

GROW, developed in the 1980s by John Whitmore, Graham Alexander and Alan Fine, is probably the most well-known behavioural model used widely by coach practitioners as the basic building block of any great coaching conversation. It was developed from noticing underlying patterns in the structure of conversations with senior executives (Alexander & Renshaw, 2005). Scoular (2011) has a lovely way of describing GROW, comparing it to an accordion that expands in and out as the topic and time available demands. Similarly, Alexander (2016) talks about not becoming too obsessed with the structure of GROW, allowing the conversation to remain fluid and natural within this framework.

Figure 1.1: The GROW model (Leach, 2021, p177)

In practice, GROW starts with a 'T' for topic (see Figure 1.1, above), or T-GROW (Passmore & Sinclair, 2020). Something is identified by the client that they want to discuss. Responsibility for the topic and the coaching **Goal** (the '**G**' in GROW) sits firmly with the client (Bossons *et al*, 2012). Determining a coaching goal and specific outcome for the session can take time and it's important to get clarity on both. As Whitmore (2017, p63) states 'we tend to get what we focus on' and, so, the greater control and clarity over the goal, the more likely a successful outcome. Without a clear goal, the conversation can lose direction and purpose (Leach, 2021).

R stands for '**Reality**' and presents an opportunity to explore the current situation. Whitmore (2017) talks about this phase as enabling objectivity. In other words, raising awareness of things as they really are, including both internal and external influences and potential barriers to change. It is common for clients to become stuck here. So deeply attached to their own story that important practical and emotional things can be hidden from view (Leach, 2021), like a horse with blinkers on. It's often those things we can't see, or are unaware of, that hinder our progress or even control us.

The next step is identifying and exploring **Options** (the '**O**' in GROW) to move forward. Here, the coach is using open questions and other tools and techniques, as required, to facilitate the client's learning. Collaborative brainstorming techniques can also be useful at this stage to generate a wide-ranging set of viable options, being mindful that the coach offers ideas without attachment or intention of directing the client (Leach, 2021). The coach supports the client in evaluating each option, allowing the client to be in full control of the evaluation criteria (Scoular, 2011). This also ensures the focus and energy is on the client and their own learning and wisdom, not that of the coach (Starr, 2016).

Once the options have been evaluated, so the coach moves to stage 4 – **W**, **Wrap-up** or **Way forward**. This step is focused on taking action and forward momentum. Not only should the coach be looking to help define what steps the client will take, but how motivated they are to do it. Many of the tools common to motivational interviewing, such as the scaling question and listening out for 'change talk', can be helpful here (Anstiss & Passmore, 2013). It's important for the coach to facilitate a degree of granularity about what the client is going to do and by when, bringing a degree of toughness to the conversation in an attempt to activate the client's will (Whitmore, 2017). Supporting the client in evaluating the implications associated with each action, and any other practicalities or other obstacles that might hinder progress, should be explored at this point (Alexander, 2016).

More recent research by Panchal and Riddell (2020) suggests that, despite the popularity of the GROW model, behavioural change can be slow. By integrating elements of HAPA, Health Action Process Approach (Schwarzer, 2008), which considers both the initiation of change, for example planning for the change, as well as the actions associated with making the change happen, the GROW model has been found to be:

> *'more effective since proactive elicitation of strategies to overcome potential obstacles and recover from setbacks led to more successful initiation and completion of goals'.*

(Panchal & Riddell, 2020, p12)

2. Goal-focused coaching and action plans

As coaches, we are told of the importance of getting clear on the coaching goal, the goal of the coaching overall and the goal of the session, a process which is reiterated over and over in many models of coaching, including GROW. The use of goals in coaching, however, is somewhat controversial, including arguments around forcing the process to be overly linear, the possibility of the goal acting as a barrier to dealing with issues as they arise in the coaching conversation, or inadvertently forcing clients to pursue an inappropriate goal or a goal that might be easy to measure but insignificant in the overall context (Grant, 2021). However, in his chapter 'An integrated model of goal-focused coaching', Grant (2021) describes a new model of goal-focused coaching to enable change and suggests preliminary research 'highlights the vital role that coaches' goal-focused skills play in determining successful coaching outcomes' (Grant, 2021, p116).

Goal-setting methods such as SMART, PURE or CLEAR goals can be used, see Figure 1.2 (Leach, 2021) and do support goal theory. However, Grant (2021) argues there may be a need for a more sophisticated approach with a deeper understanding of the multifaceted nature of goals. In Grant's model the client's self-regulation cycle is key to the process and ultimately goal attainment – as depicted in Figures 1.3 and 1.4 below – where each stage overlaps with the next facilitating forward momentum. Like other behavioural techniques, success is measured by observable changes, where actions are monitored and evaluated, and feedback is generated as the client moves through the self-regulation process. Grant (2021, p132) suggests that 'the coach may need to find ways to develop action plans that focus on observable, easily monitored behaviours'.

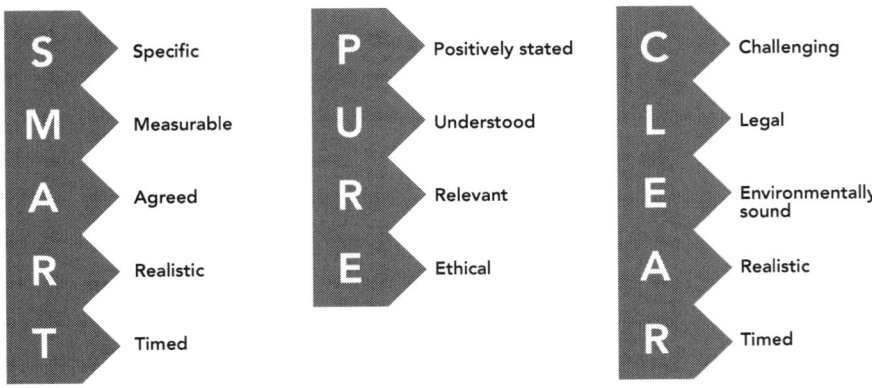

Figure 1.2: Goal-setting methods (Leach, 2021, p179)

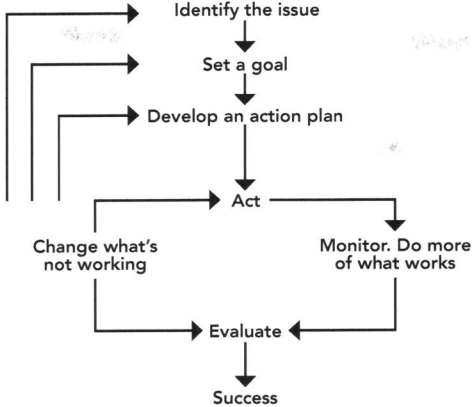

Figure 1.3: Generic model of goal-directed self-regulation (Grant, 2021, p119)

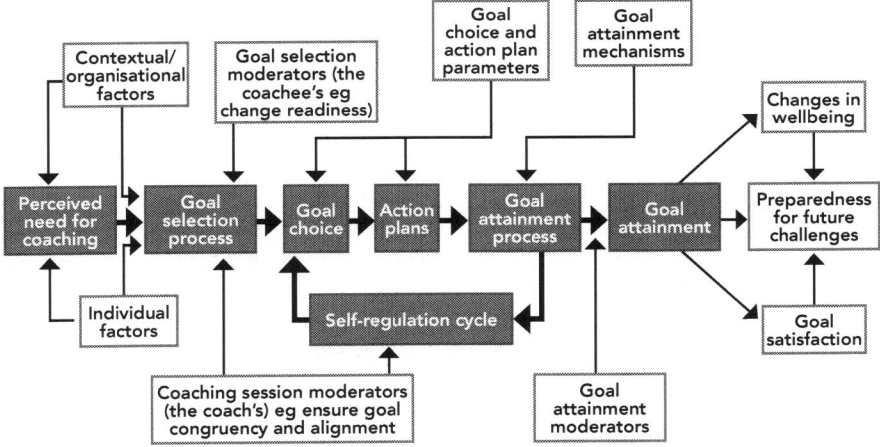

Figure 1.4: Integrative model of coach-facilitated goal attainment (Grant, 2021, p129 [adapted])

A similar self-regulation process is also used in the Co-active coaching approach, which talks about forwarding the action (taking action towards a defined goal) and deepening the learning (monitoring what's working and changing what's not). In fact, 'it's the cycle of action and learning over time that leads to sustained and effective change' (Kimsey-House *et al*, 2011, p78). As Kimsey-House *et al* (2011, p13) point out,

> *'learning generates new resourcefulness, expanded possibilities and stronger muscles for change'*

Learning is also an equal and complementary force to taking action, hence the co-active phrase of 'Forward and Deepen' – forward the action and deepen the learning. So, as coach, you will need to discuss ways in which your client can monitor the effect of their behaviour and changes to it, so they can learn from implementing their action plan and modify as appropriate. Some of the following questions might help:

- What are you expecting to see change because of taking this action and by when?
- What does success look like?
- How will you be able to measure it?
- What observable changes will you notice?
- What indicators will you be looking for along the way?
- How will you know if the change is not having the desired impact?

Action plans are a critical tool in enabling behavioural change in this way. Here the key is to make sure the plan can be integrated into the rest of their life (Dryden, 2018), to make implementation as easy as possible. As coach you may explore with your client the options available and any other potential blockers. For example, does your client have the skills, knowledge and experience required to implement the action plan? What other support, help or resources might they need? Could they develop the skills required to enable the plan?

Action and learning are what the client experiences, whilst it is the job of the coach to create the space and conditions to enable them to forward the action and deepen the learning (Kimsey-House *et al*, 2011).

3. Socratic questions and enquiries

In both GROW and goal-focused coaching, it is likely that most coaches will draw on Socratic questions to enable forward momentum and to help build the motivation for change. Named after the ancient Greek philosopher Socrates, Socratic questions involve:

'asking a logical series of questions that test assumptions until they reach the point of reductio ad absurdum'

(Clutterbuck, 2021)

In other words – they are no longer useful or are absurd!

Socratic questions are useful because they can enable greater understanding of the desired behavioural change and Socratic methods can involve behavioural experiments or tests, a common component of cognitive behavioural coaching (Kennerly *et al*, 2017). When dealing with a client who has a fear of failure, for instance, you may use Socratic questions to explore the rationale for a behavioural experiment:

- What might happen if you faced your fear?
- What might the effect of doing that be?

- What is the evidence for that?
- Could there be any alternatives?
- How would you feel if you were able to confront your fear?

This might lead onto further questions that shape a potential action or behavioural test:

- How might we test this out?
- What would help you to complete this task?
- Is there anything you want to do in preparation?
- How are you going to know if it's successful?

Working with the client to scenario-plan for failure or modest success might also be wise:

- What might be the worst-case scenario in taking this action?
- How could you prepare yourself for that eventuality?
- What could you learn from this perspective?

The Socractic method reflects a process covering four stages as described by Padesky (1996):

Stage 1: Concrete questioning, structured and designed to gather information

Stage 2: Empathic listening providing non-judgmental attention to what is being said and how

Stage 3: Summarising what the client has said to check understanding, the underlying premise of the hypotheses, to clarify information or reiterate a point made

Stage 4: Synthesising or analysing the questions to either expand an idea or refine key information

In applying these skills, the coach enables the client to review all relevant information before making a conscious choice about the action they want to take.

4. Role modelling and future self

Another simple yet powerful technique to enable behavioural change is to ask your client to find an example of someone they would like to emulate in some way, a role model who inspires them and/or demonstrates a skill or behaviour they'd like to develop. As coach you must be mindful of facilitating this conversation carefully so as you build, rather than erode, confidence in your client. It's not about the client finding someone whose life or character they'd rather have but focusing on finding an example of someone who has been successful at cultivating the skills, knowledge, habits, or behaviours of one or two things they are thinking about changing. It could be delivering presentations for example, or sticking to a regular exercise regime. The key is to help them explore what it is their role model does differently and how they might learn from the role model's experiences, and then find a strategy to enable a similar change in a way that suits the client. This is commonly used as a technique in motivational interviewing for instance, as is exploring possible future selves (Anstiss & Passmore, 2013).

You can combine the idea of using role modelling with 'imaginary conversations' and 'future self' for an even more powerful impact. Once a role model has been identified, real or fictional (often clients find it easier to connect with characters in books or films), the coach invites them to sit down and have a conversation with that person about their current dilemma. Adapted from techniques used by Julia Yates (2019) and the balance coaching approach by Kimsey-House *et al* (2011), the coach asks the client to imagine the advice their role model would offer. The coach's role here is to use their creative and courageous coaching skills to help the client expand their thinking, prompting them to physically embody their role model to evoke greater awareness. In coming back to the present moment, the coach facilitates a conversation to help understand and deepen the learning from the details of the advice given:

- What is the most valuable piece of advice you've received?
- What new thoughts or ideas have appeared as a result of this conversation?
- What might not be useful or relevant to you?
- In what ways might you act on this advice?

Of course, if the role model is a person the client knows or can be introduced to, the coach might explore the opportunities of being able to speak to them in real life, supporting the client in preparing for such a conversation.

Similarly, the coach might invite a client to imagine their future self, having made the changes demonstrated by their role model and/or explored in the imaginary conversation, by using either visualisation techniques and/or asking them to write a letter from the future. Julie Flower (2021, p437) positions this as a tool 'to help clients explore, articulate and build commitment towards a goal or future vision'. Used within or outside of the coaching session, the following steps are recommended (Flower, 2021):

- The client decides upon a timeframe for their letter, depending on what they want to achieve.
- The client writes a letter and places in an envelope.
- The letter can be free form. However, the coach would prompt the client to consider the following, much like the questions for a visualisation exercise:
  - What is happening in the future since the change has been made?
  - How does it feel?
  - Is there anyone or anything else involved?

- What have you learned along the way?
- What did you have to overcome?
- What are you able to do now?
- What might be next?

■ The letter is kept by the client, who may choose to share it with their coach, and the coach facilitates a conversation regarding the learning from the exercise.

■ This exercise would finish by asking the client how, in the future, they might use the letter.

5. Rehearsal and relaxation techniques

Hyperarousal can interfere with how you behave, as we discovered with Pavlov's dog and his ability to salivate. Similarly, anxiety based on previous events can trigger instant behaviour patterns (Whitten, 2014). These behaviours take over before the client has had a chance to understand what is happening. Learning to plan responses to difficult situations can help switch off unhelpful spontaneous behavioural responses. This is closely connected to the way you think about the situation which is more cognitive behavioural coaching than behavioural coaching. However, developing and rehearsing constructive thoughts and behaviours can help to re-programme the mind–body response so that when met with a similar situation the client can make a more conscious choice to react or behave differently. The other thing to be mindful of is that humans are habitual creatures and, when stressed, tend to revert to old patterns of behaviour (Whitten, 2014).

In working with the client on a range of different scenarios that trigger hyperarousal, stress, or anxiety, as coach you can help the client to plan for 'known' behavioural responses. For example, if presentations cause a client to panic and forget their words, strategies can be developed to help decrease the impact of such events in advance. For example, visualisation techniques which focus on a successful delivery, role play, practising the presentation in front of a smaller friendlier audience, asking a trusted colleague to review the presentation before hand, learning positive body language techniques to aid delivery such as ways to stand to enhance your impact (Shaw, 2019), or finding your 'dragon's tail' as Goyder puts it (2014, p31). This is another visualisation exercise where the coach encourages the client to imagine having a long, weighty dragon's tail that falls out and away from the base of their spine. In asking the client to feel the weight of the tail, as it curls out behind them, it can encourage a feeling of physical stability as well as increasing a feeling of presence and therefore confidence as they visualise the tail filling the room.

Finding ways clients can integrate relaxation techniques immediately before such events and in the moment are also helpful. Breathing techniques help to manage anxiety and panic during stress or high performing situations for example. O'Morain (2014, p168) talks about 'ten pockets of time', little, tiny pockets of time that in using breathing or mindfulness techniques you can reduce stress and regain your presence. For example, arriving a couple of minutes early to a meeting and taking those few minutes whilst everyone else arrives to focus on the breath and being present; counting to 5 before responding to a difficult question or asking for a quick toilet break to allow you to recompose. Numerous psychological studies have reinforced the benefits of mindfulness practices as part of everyday life, as well as helping us in the moment (Williams & Penman, 2011).

Conclusion

The most recent research has asserted how important the link is between thoughts, feelings and behaviours, as described in 2nd and 3rd wave approaches to cognitive behavioural therapy and coaching. However, you can have an impact as a coach, and your client can make forward momentum and build confidence, just by focusing on the behavioural aspects. In fact, physically taking some kind of action is known to be a key stage of the adult learning cycle as described by Lewin and Kolb (Kennerley et al, 2017). Making a behavioural change can have an impact on how you think and feel, as well as the other way round. They are interacting systems, not necessarily a linear process (Kennerley et al, 2017). Today, the behaviourists' theories are criticised for being too simplistic, however there is much to be said for keeping it simple!

Five questions for further reflection

1. **How much of an influence does behavioural coaching have on your coaching practice?**

You can see the roots of behavioural psychology in many coaching practices today, no matter how small. Whether in asking a powerful Socratic question or doing chair work to explore a troublesome relationship, for example, I would argue that most coaches are trying to support their clients in enabling effective and sustainable behavioural change, extending the ideas of the behaviourists in the way in which they go about it.

2. **What types of presenting problems can you impact by focusing on behavioural change?**

If you think about the presenting issues your clients bring to a coaching conversation, you can frequently recognise issues surrounding confidence, resilience, anxiety, stress, and productive habits for example, all of which can be addressed to a greater or lesser extent by behavioural approaches.

3. What do you observe are the easiest behaviours and most difficult behaviours for your clients to change?

We all know it takes time to change, time to adapt unconscious behaviours that are ingrained in our everyday lives, behaviours that we now know are intrinsically linked to how we think and feel. Behavioural change can be hard. Starting small and linking behavioural change to existing habits and routines can be a great place to start. For example, establishing a mindfulness practice whilst brushing your teeth in the morning, as opposed to setting out to run a marathon in three months, when you have only ever managed to walk to the corner shop.

4. Which tools and techniques do you find most helpful in enabling behavioural change and why?

There are some tools and techniques that we are naturally drawn to; others, we avoid or hesitate over – yet what do our clients really need? Socratic questions will always be an essential part of a coach's toolkit and highly effective at enabling behavioural change, yet role modelling or mindfulness techniques might feel a stretch too far for some. If it is the role of the coach to enable the client's best thinking, we need to experiment with a wide range of approaches to find the ones that work best. Tools and techniques that create a new perspective, a new way of thinking, provide for a different experience or exposure to something new, helps our clients learn and stretch, just as it does for ourselves.

5. What action would you like to take to further your learning in this area?

As coaches, it is important to keep learning and practising, breaking down old and new approaches, tools, and techniques, and seeing how you can enhance your practice as a result. As the environmental context within which we operate continues to change and evolve, often at a rapid pace, so we too must amend, adapt, and extend our practice to accommodate the needs of our clients. The world today requires a very different response to the world of the behaviourists in the early 1920s, but we can still learn a great deal from them.

Suggested reading

Alexander, G. (2016) Behavioural coaching. In: J. Passmore (Ed.) *Excellence in Coaching: The Industry Guide*, 3rd ed. London: Kogan Page, pp99–111.

Bandura, A. (1977) Self-efficacy: Towards a unifying theory of behavioural change. *Psychological Review*, **84** (2) 191–215.

Eldridge, F. & Demkowski, S. (2013). Behavioural Coaching. In: J. Passmore, D. Peterson and T. Freire (Eds.) *The Wiley Blackwell Handbook of the Psychology of Coaching and Mentoring*. Chichester; Wiley, pp298–318.

Peel, D. (2005) The significance of behavioural learning theory to the development of effective coaching practice. *International Journal of Evidence Based Coaching and Mentoring*, 3 (1) 18–28.

Skiffington, S. & Zeus, P. (2003) *Behavioral Coaching*. NSW, Australia: McGraw-Hill.

References

Alexander, G. (2016) Behavioural Coaching. In: J. Passmore (Ed.) *Excellence in Coaching: The Industry Guide*, 3rd ed. London: Kogan Page, pp99–111.

Alexander, G. & Renshaw, B. (2005) *Super Coaching: The missing ingredient for high performance*, London: Random House Business Books.

Allison, M. G. & Ayllon, T. (1980) Behavioural coaching in the development of skills in football, gymnastics and tennis. *Journal of Applied Behaviour Analysis*, **13** (2) 297–314. https://doi.org/10.1901/jaba.1980.13-297.

Anstiss, T. & Passmore, J. (2013) Motivational Interviewing Approach. In: J. Passmore, D. Peterson and T. Freire (Eds) *The Wiley Blackwell Handbook of the Psychology of Coaching and Mentoring*. Chichester: Wiley, pp339–364.

Bandura, A. (1977) Self-efficacy: Towards a unifying theory of behavioural change. *Psychological Review*, **84** (2) 191–215.

Bossons, P., Kourdi, J. & Sartain, D. (2012) *Coaching Essentials: Practical proven techniques for world-class executive coaching*, 2nd ed. London: Bloomsbury.

Brown, P. & Brown, V. (2012) *Neuropsychology for Coaches: Understanding the Basics*. Maidenhead: Open University Press.

Channon, S. De Silva, P., Hemlsey, D. & Perkins, R. (1989) A controlled trial of cognitive-behavioural and behavioural treatment of anorexia nervosa. *Behavioural Research Therapy*, **27** (5) 529–535.

Clutterbuck, D. (2021) Questions in Coaching. In: J. Passmore (Ed.) *The Coaches Handbook: The Complete Practitioner Guide for Professional Coaches*, Abingdon: Routledge, pp92–103.

Dryden, W. (2018) *Cognitive-emotive-behavioural coaching: A flexible and pluralistic approach*, Abingdon: Routledge.

Eldridge, F. & Demkowski, S. (2013) Behavioural Coaching. In: J. Passmore, D. Peterson and T. Freire (Eds) *The Wiley Blackwell Handbook of the Psychology of Coaching and Mentoring*. Chichester; Wiley, pp298–318.

Flower, J. (2020) Fifteen Tools and Techniques for Coaches. In: J. Passmore (Ed.) *The Coaches Handbook: The Complete Practitioner Guide for Professional Coaches*. Abingdon: Routledge, pp427–442.

Galewey, W. T. (1986) *The Inner Game of Tennis*. London: Pan.

Goyder, C. (2014) *Gravitas: Communicate with confidence, influence and authority*. London: Vermillion.

Grant, A.M. (2001) *Coaching for enhanced performance: Comparing Cognitive and Behavioural Coaching approaches*. Paper presented to the 3rd International Spearman Seminar Sydney.

Grant, A.M. (2021) An Integrated Model of Goal-Focused Coaching: An Evidence-Based Framework for Teaching and Practice. In: J. Passmore and D. Tee (Eds) *Coaching Researched: A coaching Psychology Reader for Practitioners and Researchers*. New Jersey: Wiley, pp115–139.

Hutton, K.A., Sibley, C. G., Harper, D. N. & Hunt, M. (2002) Modifying driver behaviour with passenger feedback. Transportation Research Part F, 4: 257-269. https://doi.org/10/1016/S1369-8478(01)00027-4.

Ibarra, H. (2004). *Working Identity: Unconventional strategies for reinventing your career*. Boston, CA: The One Page Business Plan Company.

Jacobson, N. S., Dobson, K. S., Truax, P. A. et al (1996) A component analysis of cognitive-behavioral treatment for depression. *Journal of Consulting and Clinical Psychology*, **64** (2) 295–304.

Jensen, R. (2019) Behaviourism. [Online] Salem Press Encyclopedia of Health, Available at: http://search.ebscohost.com/login.aspx?direct = true&db = ers&AN = 93871802&site = eds-live [Accessed: 29 July 2021].

Kennerly, H., Kirk, J. & Westbrook, D. (2017) *An Introduction to Cognitive Behaviour Therapy: Skills and applications*, 3rd ed, London: Sage.

Kimsey-House, H., Kimsey-House, K., Sandahl, P. & Whitworth, L. (2011) *Co-Active Coaching: Changing Business Transforming Lives*. Boston: Nicholas Brealey Publishing.

Leach, S. (2021) Behavioural Coaching: The GROW model. In: J. Passmore (Ed.) *The Coaches Handbook: The Complete Practitioner Guide for Professional Coaches*. Abingdon: Routledge, pp176–186.

Lent, R.W., Ireland, G.W., Penn, L.T., Morris, T. R. & Sappington, R. (2017) Sources of self-efficacy and outcome expectations for career exploration and decision making: A test of the social cognitive model of career self-management. *Journal of Vocational Behavior*, **99**, pp107–117.

Moore, J. (2011) Behaviourism, *The Psychological Record*, **6**, pp449–464.

Olivero, G., Bane, K., & Kopelman, R.E. (1997). Executive coaching as a transfer of training tool: Effects on productivity in a public agency. *Public Personnel Management*, **26** (4) 461–469.

O'Morain, P. (2014) *Mindfulness On The Go*. Great Britain: Yellow Kite.

Padesky, C. (1996) Guided discovery using Socratic dialogue (DVD). Huntingdon Beach, CA: Centre for Cognitive Therapy. Available from www.padesky.com.

Panchal, S. & Riddell, P. (2020) The GROWS model: Extending the GROW coaching model to support behavioural change, *Coaching Psychologist*, **16** (2) 12–24.

Passmore, J. (2007) Behavioural coaching. In: S. Palmer and A. Whybrow (Eds) *The Handbook of Coaching Psychology*, London: Brunner-Routledge, pp99–107.

Passmore, J. & Sinclair, T. (2020) *Becoming a Coach: The essential ICF guide*. West Sussex: Pavilion Publishing and Media Ltd.

Passmore, J. Brown, H. Csigas, Z. et al (2017) *The State of Play in Coaching & Mentoring: Executive Report*. Henley on Thames: Henley Business School-EMCC. ISBN 978-1-912473-00-7. Retrieved on 1 November 2020 from: https://www.researchgate.net/publication/321361866_The_State_of_Play_in_European_Coaching_and_Mentoring Accessed 7 July 2021.

Passmore, J. & Rehman, H. (2012) Coaching as a learning methodology – a mixed methods study in driver development – a Randomised Controlled Trial and thematic analysis. *International Coaching Psychology Review*, **7** (2) 166–184.

Passmore, J. & Townsend, C. (2012) The role of coaching in police driver training – An IPA study of coaching in a blue light environment. *An International Journal of Police Strategies*, **35** (4) 785–800. https://doi:10.1108/13639511211275698

Passmore, J. & Velez, M. J. (2012) Coaching Fleet drivers – a randomized controlled trial (RCT) of 'short coaching' interventions to improve driver safety in fleet drivers. *The Coaching Psychologist*. **8**(1), 20–26.

Pavlov, I. (1927) *Conditioned Reflexes*. Oxford: Oxford University Press.

Peel, D. (2005) The significance of behavioural learning theory to the development of effective coaching practice. *International Journal of Evidence Based Coaching and Mentoring*, **3** (1) 18–28.

Rholetter, W. (2019) Operant Conditioning [Online] *Salem Press Encyclopedia*. Available at http://search.ebscohost.com/login.aspx?direct = true&db = ers&AN = 89677602&site = eds-live [Accessed 29th July 2021]

Schultz, W (2016) Dopamine reward prediction-error signalling: A two component response. *Nature Reivews: Neuroscience*, **17** (3) 183–95.

Schultz, W. & Dickinson, A. (2000) Neuronal coding of prediction errors. *Annual Review of Neuroscience*, **23**, pp473–500.

Schwarzer, R. (2008) Modeling Health Behavior Change: how to predict and modify the adoption and maintenance of health behaviors. *Applied Psychology: An International Review*, **57** (1) 1–29. Doi: 10.1111/j.1464-0597.2007.00325.

Scoular, A. (2011) *Business Coaching*, Harlow: Pearson Education Limited.

Shaw, G. (2019). *The Speaker's Coach: 60 secrets to make your talk, speech or presentation amazing.* Harlow: Pearson Education Limited.

Skiffington, S. and Zeus, P. (2003) *Behavioral Coaching*. NSW, Australia: McGraw-Hill.

Skinner, B. F. (1957) *Verbal Behaviour*. New York: Appleton.

Skinner, B.F. (1974) *About Behaviourism*. London: Jonathan Cape.

Skinner, B. F. (1989) *Recent Issues in the Analysis of Behavior*. Columbus OH: Merrill.

Starr, J. (2016) *The Coaching Manual: The definitive guide to the process, principles and skills of personal coaching*, 4th ed. Harlow: Pearson Education Limited.

Taylor, F. (1911) *The Principles of Scientific Management*. New York: Harper & Row.

VanElzakker, M.B., Dahlgren, M. K., David, F., Dubois, S. & Shin, L. M. (2014) From Pavlov to PTSD: The extinction of conditioned fear in rodents, humans, and anxiety disorders. *Neurobiology of Learning and Memory*, 113, pp3–18.

Watson, J. B. (1913) Psychology as the behaviorist views it. *Psychological Review*, **20**, pp158–77.

Whitmore, J. (2017) *Coaching for Performance: GROWing human potential and purpose. The Principles and Practice of Coaching and Leadership*, 5th ed. London: Nicholas Brealey Publications.

Whitten, H. (2014) Cognitive behavioural coaching. In: J. Passmore (Ed.) *Mastery In Coaching: A complete psychological toolkit for advanced coaching*. London: Kogan Page Limited, pp151–189.

Williams, M. & Penman, D. (2011). *Mindfulness: A practical guide to finding peace in a frantic world*. Great Britain: Piatkus.

Yates, J. (2019) *The Career Coaching Toolkit*. Abingdon: Routledge.

PART TWO:
Second Wave

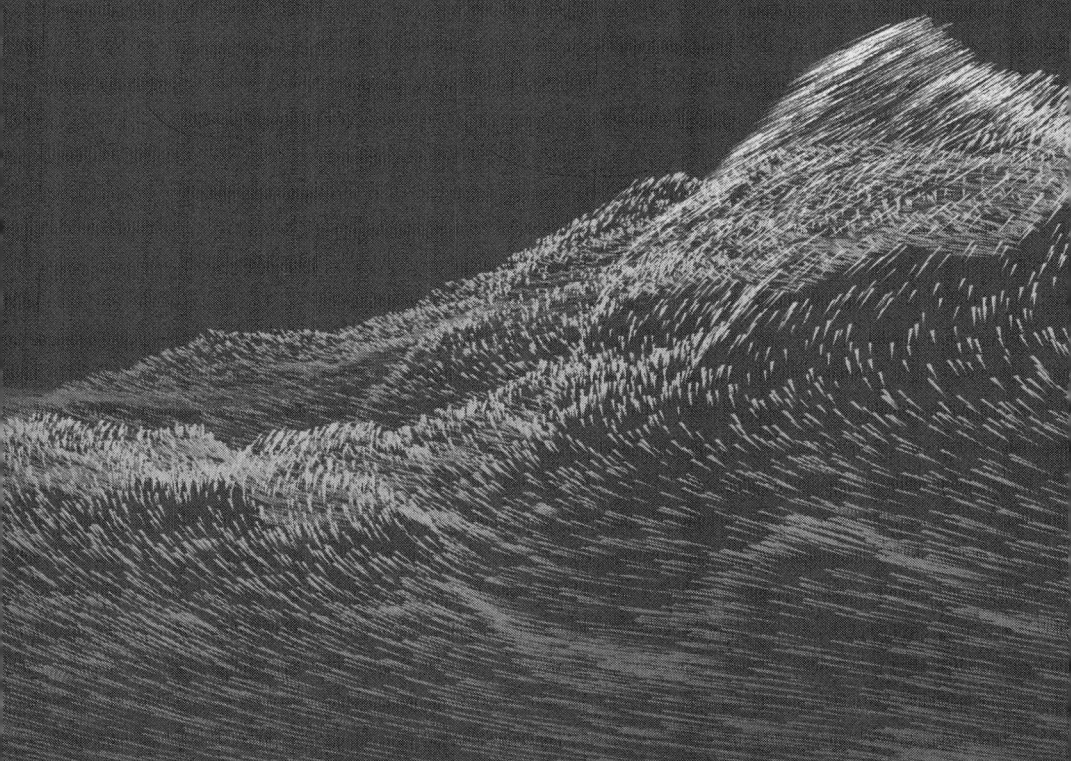

Introduction: Second wave cognitive behavioural approaches

Jonathan Passmore and Sarah Leach

The second wave of cognitive behavioural approaches arose out of work on cognitive models of human behaviour that occurred in the 1960s and was in turn a break from the behaviouralists' school which had been dominant during the period 1920–1950s and its view that unobservable mental processes, 'the black box of the mind', was outside the scope of scientific enquiry, as such enquiry would need to rely on inference or hypothesis.

Cognitive psychology emerged from the work of researchers exploring the development of language and their interface with computing and cybernetics. This work continues today in the form of quantum computing, machine learning and the development of artificial intelligence which is behind everything from automated cars to internet search engines and search facilities on entertainment platforms such as Netflix, and HR coaching platforms such as CoachHub. They have also informed work in the area of human performance from memory to language and perception to metacognition.

Aaron Beck (1976) drew on these ideas in his formulation of cognitive therapy, working with clients with depression. He came to the view it was the way that his clients perceived, interpreted, and attributed meaning to events which was both the cause of their distress and their road to salvation.

Cognitive therapy is based on a model of human cognition which sees thoughts, feelings and behaviour as connected: a trinity of humanity. Individuals can move forward by recognising the interconnection of their thoughts, feelings, and behaviours, by noticing and challenging unhelpful behaviour and their inaccurate or illogical thoughts as well as developing new, more evidence-based or helpful cognitive processes to create a new way of thinking, feeling, and responding to their environmental triggers which may cause them distress.

In parallel, Albert Ellis, an American psychologist, created *rational emotive behavioural theory*. This started life as *rational theory* in the mid-1950s. Ellis believed, like Beck, that individuals often created self-defeating strategies through their irrational core beliefs and by challenging these through rational analysis and cognitively restricting clients could develop new more rational constructs of themselves. Ellis drew these ideas together in his book, *Rational Emotive Therapy* (1962).

Others have added to the thinking within this second wave, including Alfred Adler (eg 1927 and 1964) and Arnold Lazarus (1976), who developed multi-modal therapy (MMT). In this approach the therapist explores the client's BASIC ID (Behaviour, Affect, Sensation, Imagery, Cognition, Interpersonal Relationships, and Drugs/Biology).

As with many of these approaches aimed at the original domain of therapy, we have seen them transferred to the world of coaching by writers such as Michael Neenan, Stephen Palmer and Windy Dryden (eg Neenen & Dryden, 2020; Neenan & Palmer, 2021) who have written extensively about these ideas and how they can be adapted to non-clinical populations and presenting issues.

CBT has come to dominate the evidence-based therapy and is the recommended treatment of various mental health models in the UK by the National Institute for Clinical Excellence (NICE). This includes interventions to support coachees with depression (NICE, 2009), obsessive-compulsive disorder (NICE, 2005), panic disorder and generalised anxiety disorder (NICE, 2011). In the arena of coaching, cognitive behavioural coaching has emerged as one of the two dominant approaches (with solution focused) partly because of its evidence base (see Palmer & Williams, 2013).

References

Adler, A. (1927) *The Practice and Theory of Individual Psychology*, Abingdon: Routledge

Adler, A. (1964) *The Individual Psychology of Alfred Adler*. H. L. Ansbacher and R. R. Ansbacher (Eds.). New York: Harper Torchbooks

Beck, A.T. (1976) *Cognitive Therapy and the Emotional Disorders*. New York: International Universities Press.

Ellis, A. (1962) *Reason and Emotion in Psychotherapy*. New York, NY: Citadel Press

Lazarus, A. (1976) *Multimodal Behavioral Therapy*. New York: Springer.

Neenan, M. & Dryden, W. (2020) *Cognitive Behavioural Coaching: A guide to problem-solving and personal development*. Abingdon: Routledge.

Neenan, M. & Palmer, S. (2021) *Cognitive Behavioural Coaching in Practice: An evidence based approach*. Abingdon: Routledge.

NICE (2005) *Treating Obsessive Compulsive Disorder, OCD and body dysmorphic disorder (bdd) in adults, children and young-people: Clinical guideline* (CG31). National Institute for Clinical Excellence. Retrieved on 10 July 2021 from https://www.nice.org.uk/guidance/cg31/resources/ treating-obsessivecompulsive-disorder-ocd-and-body-dysmorphic-disorder-bdd-in-adults-children-and-young-people-pdf-194882077

NICE (2009) *Depression in adults: recognition and management. Clinical guideline* (CG90). National Institute for Clinical Excellence. Retrieved on 10 July 2021 from https://www.nice.org.uk/guidance/CG90

NICE (2011) *Generalised anxiety disorder and panic disorder in adults: management.* Clinical guideline (CG113). National Institute for Clinical Excellence. Retrieved on 10 July 2021 from https:// www.nice.org.uk/guidance/CG113

Palmer, S. & Williams, H. (2013) Cognitive behavioural approaches. In: J. Passmore, D. Peterson and T. Freire (Eds) *The Wiley Blackwell Handbook of the Psychology of Coaching and Mentoring*. Chichester: Wiley, pp319–338.

Chapter 2
Cognitive Behavioural Coaching: Theory, research and practice

Rob Willson

Introduction

The origins of the cognitive behavioural approach can be traced back to the 1950s (Wolpe, 1958) but the cognitive behavioural tradition in the 2020s is still evolving. At the time of writing, we are said to be in the 3rd wave of CBT. The first wave being behaviour therapy, the second the 'cognitive' revolution, the third being more mindfulness and acceptance-based approaches (Hayes, 2004). There will, no doubt, be further 'waves' but it's important to bear in mind that newer does not necessarily mean more effective. As we will see below, the evidence supporting the cognitive behavioural approach has been a signature strength for many years.

This chapter focuses on what might be loosely described as 'traditional' or 'second wave' cognitive behavioural coaching (CBC); coaching that largely follows the principles and practices of the 'original' cognitive behavioural models. Albert Ellis originated rational emotive behaviour therapy (REBT) (Ellis, 1962) and Aaron T. Beck outlined cognitive therapy (1976); CBC presented here is based on developments of their original ideas.

The application of a cognitive behavioural approach in what might be called a 'coaching context' is certainly nothing new; in 1967 Albert Ellis and Milton Blum devised a group training programme, based on REBT principles, aimed at improving staff and management relations. Their approach focused on eliminating fears of failure, how to be more tolerant and less hostile, self-acceptance, and developing high frustration tolerance. It's easy to see how these concepts would still be relevant in coaching today.

Theoretical foundations

The foundation of cognitive behavioural theory can be traced back to the first century, to Stoic philosopher Epictetus. He posited (Epictetus, 2008):

'people are not disturbed by things but by the view they take of them.'

CBC theory places meaning at the heart of the approach – that the meaning an event has to us has a pivotal effect on our response. The model proposes that the way we humans view ourselves, the world, and other people is shaped by our early experiences, and that patterns of behaviour help to maintain these 'core' beliefs. In recent years, greater emphasis has been placed on the role of mental behaviour such as worry, ruminating and self-focused attention (e.g. Harvey *et al*, 2004).

One of the simplest ways to express CBC theory is the ABC model (see Figure 2.1, below):

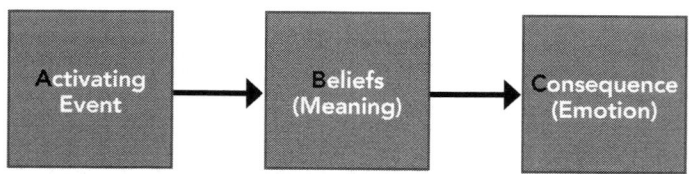

Figure 2.1: ABC model

The beauty of the ABC model is its simplicity and clarity. However, to some, it can seem to oversimplify human emotion. In my experience, it can also encourage novice practitioners to overemphasise the role of using verbal methods to help clients change their thinking. If emotional and thinking change is to happen, it's critical to push for behavioural change.

The Hot Cross Bun Model

The 'hot cross bun' shows the interaction between our thoughts, emotions, behaviours and physiology (Figure 2.2). In CBC, all of these areas are potential targets for change and part of cognitive behavioural theory is that a positive effect on one area will lead to a positive effect on others. It also takes into account the contribution of the world we live in. In the hot cross bun model, 'environment' refers to anything that acts upon the individual and is a 'trigger' for thoughts and emotional responses. This might be a task, a relationship, an interaction with a colleague, a team, the workplace, home, and so on.

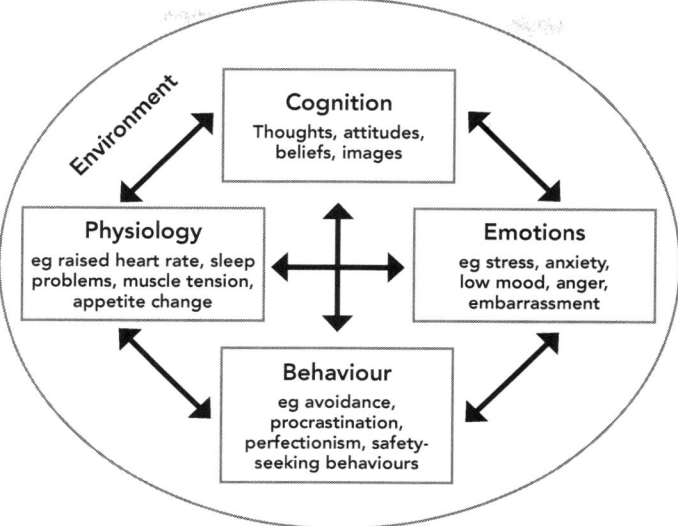

Figure 2.2: 'Hot Cross Bun' model

Three levels of meaning

Judith Beck (1995) outlines different levels of meaning as part of the cognitive model. At the most superficial level are 'automatic thoughts' that pop into the person's head; at the deepest are 'core beliefs' (sometimes called 'Schema') that are fundamental views of self, world, and others. A third, intermediate set of meanings are referred to as rules or 'assumptions'. All these levels can be targeted in CBC, but automatic thought (see 'Cognitive bias modification', below) are generally understood to be the most accessible and amenable to change.

Research evidence

CBT is the most extensively scientifically supported of all psychotherapies. Many hundreds of randomised controlled trials (RCTs) of CBT, for both mental and physical health problems, have been conducted. There also been numerous systematic review and meta-analyses of these RCTs. To provide a further level of evidence, reviews of these systematic reviews and meta-analyses have been carried out.

Butler *et al* (2006) review meta-analyses on CBT for clinical problems and found large effect sizes for depression, generalized anxiety disorder, panic disorder (with or without agoraphobia), social anxiety disorder, posttraumatic stress disorder, and childhood depression and anxiety. They found moderate effect sizes for marital distress, anger, childhood somatic disorders and chronic pain.

In 2012, Hoffman *et al* reviewed 106 of 269 meta-analyses of CBT for a variety of conditions. They found that CBT was more effective for occupational stress than other interventions, in particular when therapy was focused upon psycho-social outcomes (Hofmann *et al*, 2012).

More recently, Fordham *et al* (2021) conducted a far-reaching meta-review of systematic reviews and panoramic meta-analysis on the evidence for CBT in 'any condition, population or context'. They included 423 systematic reviews of RCTs of CBT for both mental and physical conditions (Fordham *et al*, 2021). The sheer scope of this article gives an idea of the truly vast amount of empirical support for CBT. No other approach to therapy, or indeed coaching, comes close.

The direct evidence for CBC is certainly more limited but does continue to grow. Importantly, one of the conclusions from Fordham *et al* (2021) is that the evidence for the effectiveness of CBT, across so many conditions and contexts, suggests that it is likely to be effective in areas in which there is not yet supporting evidence. This is positive news for cognitive behavioural coaches, who are widening the application of cognitive behavioural principles and techniques. The table below highlights some key studies on CBT and CBC that are of particular relevance to coaching.

Table 2.1: Summary of research

Study	Summary
Çavuşoğlu (2019)	CA systematic review of the efficiency of CBT on work-related mental health problems, showing a positive impact on mental wellbeing.
Edwards & Newton (1994)	A qualitative assessment showing positive results of stress-management focused 'Cognitive CoachingSM Training'.
Edwards & Newton (1995)	A quasi-experimental design showing beneficial effects of Cognitive CoachingSM on Teacher efficacy and empowerment.
Gardiner et al (2013)	Found that CBC reduced GP stress levels and lowered their desire to escape rural general practice.
Grant (2003)	An exploratory study finding impact of life CBC on goal attainment, meta-cognition, and mental health.
Grant et al (2009)	An RCT Executive coaching enhances goal attainment, resilience and workplace wellbeing.

Table 2.1: Summary of research (Cont'd)

Study	Summary
Green *et al* (2006)	An RCT finding that cognitive-behavioural, solution-focused life coaching enhanced goal striving, wellbeing, and hope.
Hofmann & Smits (2008)	A meta-analysis of randomized placebo-controlled trials of cognitive-behavioural therapy for adult anxiety disorders.
Joyce *et al* (2016)	A systematic meta-review of workplace interventions for common mental disorders, finding strong evidence for CBT-based stress management.
Junker *et al* (2020)	A randomised controlled field study of the effect of cognitive-behavioural stress management coaching. Found evidence to support that CBC is effective in helping individuals stay goal focused and develop strategies to deal with stress.
Libri & Kemp (2006)	A withing subject, single case design found that a cognitive behavioural executive coaching program improved a male executive's sales performance, core self-evaluation, and global self-ratings of his performance.
Ogba *et al* (2019)	Study evaluating effectiveness of a 12-week 90-minute group CBC (SPACE) programme in a sample of 65 Nigerian school administrators. Found a significant decrease in perceived stress and stress symptoms compared to wait-list controls.
Onyishi *et al* (2021)	An RCT concluding that rational emotive occupational health coaching was helpful for subjective wellbeing among police officers and people working under chronically stressful conditions.
Morley *et al* (1999)	Systematic review and meta-analysis of randomized controlled trials of cognitive behaviour therapy and behaviour therapy for chronic pain in adults, excluding headache.
Ratiu *et al* (2016)	A pre-post test study of a CBC program for 23 mid-level managers. Found an increase in coaching skills, assertive communication skills and motivation of subordinates.
Tan *et al* (2014)	A systematic review and meta-analysis of nine RCTs of interventions aimed at preventing the development of depression in the workplace concludes that there is more evidence for the effectiveness of CBT-based programs than for other interventions.

Practice

Having outlined CBC theory and research evidence above, this section will focus on some main elements of CBC practice. I will introduce Socratic questioning, which is a key competency across all areas of CBC practice. An overview of building a cognitive behavioural conceptualisation for a client's problem will be given. This can help the client understand how their problem is maintained, as well as guiding them towards an intervention. I will also give an introduction to 'cognitive bias modification', which is a core principle in helping clients change the way they think. What often logically follows from the more cerebral process of changing thinking is some form of behavioural change or 'experiment', which I outline below. Lastly, I cover the practice of negotiating what is often referred to as 'homework' in CBC – the work the client puts in between sessions and very often where change really happens.

To give this a little more context, below is a list of some of the core characteristics of CBC practice:

- The coaching relationship is collaborative.
- Client and coach set an agenda for what they want to cover in the session.
- The coach actively listens to the client and regularly summarises the coaching conversation.
- The coach is explicit about the cognitive behavioural model and sees part of the aim of coaching as training the client to become their own coach.
- The coach aims to keep coaching focus towards explicitly agreed goals.
- The coach focuses on helping the client change unhelpful meanings and behaviour.
- The coach largely uses Socratic questions in 'guided discovery' to help the client uncover unhelpful thoughts, analyse them, and construct more helpful alternatives.
- The coach encourages the client to make written notes of key discoveries and learning.
- The coach makes use of drawings, mental imagery, metaphors and role play to help keep learning active.
- The coach will often guide the client toward some form of out-of-session behavioural experiment or practice.
- Client and coach review together the outcome of the experiment or practice at the next session to facilitate learning.

Socractic questioning

Using Socratic questions is a key skill, helping clients to consider their thoughts and behaviour *for themselves* rather than telling them. To help with this we use a process called 'guided discovery' using Socratic questions. Socratic questioning has been the subject of considerable discussion within the literature on CBT (Padesky, 1993; Kazantzis *et al*, 2014) and in coaching (Neenan, 2009). The aim is to help the client to learn, remember, and build trust in their own capacity for thinking helpfully and creatively in the service of solving problems. There is some empirical support for the assertion that using Socratic questions improves outcome (Braun *et al*, 2015). Below are some examples of Socratic questions that can used at different stages of CBC.

Helping clients elicit their thoughts, images and behaviour

- What's going through (or went through) your mind?
- Did you see anything in your mind's eye?
- What did (event/trigger) mean to you?
- What did you do when (event/trigger) happened?
- What was your response?

Helping clients consider their thoughts

- What's the effect of thinking this way?
- What's the evidence for...?
- Could there be any alternatives (eg ways of interpreting an experience)?
- What are the costs and benefits of this (thought, belief or interpretation)?
- How might someone else view the situation?
- When you're away from the situation what do you think?
- What might you think a year from now?
- How does this fit with...?
- How do you put ____ (thought) together with _____ (evidence)?
- Is there anything you might tend to overlook?
- Now you have stepped back and looked at the situation, what do you make of your original conclusion?

Helping clients consider the effect of alternative thoughts/beliefs/interpretations

- What's the effect of thinking this new way?
- How does this alternatve perspective make you feel?
- Now you know (new information/interpretation) how do you feel?
- What are the costs and benefits of this (new thought, belief or interpretation)?

Building a plan for out-of-session practice

- How could we find out more?
- What do you think would happen if (you changed X behaviour)?
- How could we put this (thought, theory, assumption) to the test?
- How might you practise thinking or acting to help build on this?

When not to be Socratic

It's important to know when to stop using Socratic questioning, when:

- The client is confused or overly stressed by the process.
- The client does not have the information available to them needed to answer the question.
- Session time is running short, and a quick didactic explanation may be more pragmatic.

You can then switch to an example, a metaphor, or a simple explanation, and ask what they think and feel about the point you have made.

Building a cognitive behavioural conceptualisation

Like any good form of problem solving, CBC recognises that an attempt to solve a problem can only ever be any good if the way we define the problem is effective. In CBC, the theory as to what is maintaining the problem, and thus guide us to what to change to solve the problem, is called a formulation. Abel *et al* (2016) found evidence to support the widely held assumption that formulation may lead to better client outcome.

Formulations can be incredibly simple and just put into a few words. For example, 'I think the reason you haven't yet overcome your fear of dogs is because you always avoid them as much as you can and this means you've not yet given yourself a chance to get used to them', a simple diagram of a vicious circle, and all the way up to and including complex visual diagrams that can be reminiscent of complex circuits.

However, I've heard Albert Ellis criticise complex CBT formulation as an exercise in 'clever therapist', and favoured his simpler ABC formulation of emotional problems. Needless to say, it's generally a good idea to use the simplest and clearest formulation that will offer an adequate working hunch on how the client's problem is maintained. The 'hot cross bun model' (Figure 2.2) can provide a very useful structure for collaboratively building a formulation with many clients.

Cognitive bias modification

The concept that human beings can be prone to unhelpful thinking (as well as helpful thinking) is central to CBC (Beck, 1976; Ellis, 1962). A core strategy is to help clients become more aware of their cognitive biases – sometimes called 'cognitive distortions' or 'thinking errors'. Once we are more aware of the unrealistic, illogical and (most importantly) unhelpful thoughts we have, we have an opportunity to correct for them. Below, I'll introduce a form of 'thought record' that can be very helpful in this endeavour. First, I'll outline key thinking errors that can be helpful to share with clients, alongside some useful responses to these.

Catastrophising

Catastrophising means jumping to a worst-case conclusion based on limited evidence. Catastrophising is jumping to the conclusion that an error at work will mean career suicide or a minor disagreement as loss of reputation. Catastrophic thoughts can often present in the form of vivid images, as well as verbal thoughts.

Here are some options to help clients who engage with catastrophic thinking:

- Normalising – sharing common examples of catastrophic thoughts.
- Practising detached observation – treating catastrophic thoughts like they are passing events in your mind.
- Interpreting catastrophic thinking as alarm signals, but like a faulty car alarm an anxious brain can be too easily triggered. We then can choose to let these thoughts take care of themselves rather than act on them.
- Considering alternative explanations for an event – for example, boss looks grumpy because they had a bad night's sleep, not because they are planning to sack you.
- Increasing tolerance of uncertainty – helping clients to see the value of sticking with 'maybe' or 'I just don't know' instead of assuming the worst.

All-or-nothing thinking

All-or-nothing or black-or-white thinking is extreme and can result in unhelpfully extreme emotions and behaviours. For example, something's either perfect or no good. People are either responsibility-free or totally to blame for a problem. A core technique to use with clients is a continuum – like a thermometer. The continuum helps with thinking in degrees, not extremes. A further alternative to all-or-nothing thinking is 'both-and' thinking, for example I can BOTH make a mistake AND still think of myself as competent.

Fortune-telling

This, of course, means making predictions about the future and this type of thinking is very much influenced by our mood. Invite clients to think of the difference in the thoughts they have about the future depending on whether they are excited, down, or anxious. It can be helpful to understand that some thoughts are a bit like sweaty palms – an output of how we feel, a product of our mind, not a window into the future. Invite them to consider alternatives instead of assuming predictions about the future are true. As we shall see below, a core part of CBC is to encourage the testing out of predictions. It can often be important to help people understand that their (distressing) past experiences may be exceptions, and as such make poor guides to what will happen in the future.

Mindreading

Mindreading means jumping to conclusions about what others are thinking. A common bias is to assume that others are thinking critical or disapproving things about us. It can be helpful for clients to learn to spot this kind of negative automatic thought and to consider alternative interpretations of someone's gaze, facial expression, or behaviour.

Emotional reasoning

Emotional reasoning refers to assuming that how we feel tells us something significant about the world. For example, a client feeling vague sense of dread and assuming that there must be something bad about to happen. However, human emotions can be especially unreliable as guides to reality when we are emotionally distressed. Again, helping clients practise spotting this thinking error and becoming more sceptical of their conclusions can be helpful.

Overgeneralising

Overgeneralising is the error of drawing global conclusions from one or more events. It can include thoughts like 'things always…', 'my team never…', 'people are…', or 'the world is…'. It can be helpful to encourage clients to deliberately look for evidence that is an exception to their overgeneralising. For example, this might aid a client in moving from the 'people always….' to the less extreme 'people sometimes….'.

Labelling

Labels, and the process of labelling people and events, are everywhere. For example, those who tend to be self-critical may label themselves as 'worthless', 'inferior', or 'inadequate'.

Clients may label other people as 'no good' or 'useless', and thus are more likely to become angry with them. Or perhaps they label the world as 'unsafe' or 'totally unfair'. The error here is that they are globally rating things that are too complex for a definitive label. The following are examples of labelling:

- You read a distressing article in the newspaper about a rise in crime in your city. The article activates your belief that you live in a thoroughly dangerous place, which contributes to you feeling anxious about going out.
- You receive one piece of negative feedback from a colleague, and you start to feel low and label yourself as a failure.
- You become angry when someone cuts in front of you in a traffic queue. You label the other driver as a total loser for his bad driving.

Our aim is to help clients avoid labelling themselves, other people, and the world around and instead consider varying degrees and complexity. The world isn't a dangerous place but rather a place that has many different aspects with varying degrees of safety and risk. Celebrate complexities. All human beings are unique, multifaceted, and ever-changing. To label ourselves as failures on the strength of one failing is an extreme form of overgeneralising. Likewise, other people are just as complex and unique as us.

The classic big 'I', little 'I' picture (Figure 2.3) can be a great way of illustrating the point. The big 'I' represents the whole of us, the little 'I' just one aspect. The part is not the whole no matter how great or terrible.

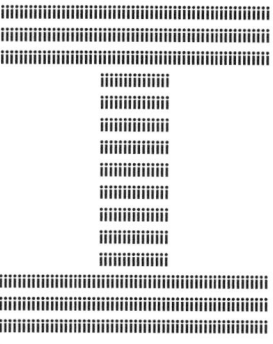

Figure 2.3: Big 'I', Little 'I'

Demands

The inflexibility of the demands (musts, should etc) we human beings place on ourselves, the world around us, and other people often means we don't adapt to reality as well as we could.

Holding *flexible preferences* about ourselves, other people, and the world in general is the healthy alternative to inflexible rules and demands. CBC aims to help clients to retain their standards, ideals, wishes, wants and preferences, and ditch their rigid demands about how they, others, and the world 'have to' be.

Mental filtering

Mental filtering is a bias in the way we process information, in which we acknowledge only information that fits with a belief we hold. The process is much like a filter on a camera lens that allows in only certain kinds of light. Information that doesn't fit tends to be ignored. If a client thinks any of the following, they are making the 'mental filtering' thinking error:

- If a client believes they are 'not good enough' they are likely to focus on mistakes at work and overlook successes and achievements. This will mean they often feel disappointed about your lack of achievement, but this is largely the result of not paying attention to successes.

- If the client believes they are 'unlikeable', they will tend to notice each time a colleague is late to call back or seems too busy to see them. Further, they tend to disregard the ways in which people act warmly towards them, thus sustaining their view that they're unlikeable.

To combat mental filtering, help clients to look more closely at situations in which they feel down. Deliberately collecting evidence that contradicts their negative thoughts can help to correct this information-processing bias. For example, helping clients to keep track of and notice friends behaving warmly towards them over a period of a week.

Disqualifying the positive

Disqualifying the positive is also related to the prejudice model above and describes the way clients can dismiss a positive event or can transform it into a negative event in our minds. For example, a client disqualifies the positive by seeing themselves as an 'imposter' or a 'fraud'. They process a work promotion by thinking, 'This doesn't count, because anyone could get this sort of thing'. Instead of feeling pleased, this results in a feeling of disappointment.

It's important for clients to become aware of responses to positive 'data'. We can help them to practice acknowledging and accepting positive feedback and acknowledging good points about themself, others, and the world. For example, they could override workplace disappointment by recognising that *they* got a promotion last year. And that the promotion was a result of their hard work which was acknowledged by their manager.

Low frustration tolerance

Low frustration tolerance refers to the error of assuming that when something's difficult to tolerate, it's 'intolerable'. This can lead to magnifying discomfort and to problems building up due to not tolerating temporary discomfort when it is in our interest to do so for longer-term benefit. For example, a client might procrastinate on tasks, thinking, 'It's just too much hassle. I'll do it later when I feel more in the mood.'

The best way to overcome low frustration tolerance is to foster an alternative attitude of high frustration tolerance. This means thinking things like 'I can stand it' or 'It's hard to bear but not unbearable'. We can help clients achieve this way of thinking by encouraging them to do things that are uncomfortable or unpleasant if it is in their interest to do so. For example, they can commit to work on assignments even if they are not in a good mood, face that challenging client, or resist the short-term gratification of unhealthy food.

Personalising

Personalising involves interpreting events as being related to us personally and overlooking other factors. This can lead to emotional difficulties, such as feeling hurt easily or feeling unnecessarily guilty. For example, a client feels hurt when a colleague leaves the office after saying only a hurried 'hello'. They think, 'She was obviously trying to avoid talking to me. I must have offended her somehow.'

We can help clients address this issue of personalising by considering alternative explanations that don't revolve around them. It might be helpful to encourage them, for instance, to imagine what else may contribute to the outcome they are assuming personal responsibility for.

Working on cognitive biases using the 'ABC form'

The ABC form, sometimes called a 'dysfunctional thought record' or 'DTR', is in many ways CBC in a nutshell. Thought records are a core technique in cognitive behavioural approaches (Greenberger & Padesky, 2015) and have some empirical support as a stand-alone intervention (Pheng & Yaacob, 2018). Working through an ABC form as part of self-coaching and with clients can be an effective framework for learning the CBC approach. An example is given below (Figure 2.4).

Activating Event (Trigger).	Beliefs, thoughts, and attitudes about A.	Consequences of AxB on your emotions and behaviours.	Dispute (question and examine) any unhelpful thoughts/ beliefs (from B) and generate alternatives.	Effect of alternative thoughts and beliefs (D).
Briefly write down what triggered your emotions (eg, event, situation, sensation, memory, image)	Write down what went through you mind, or what A meant to you. B's can be about you, others, the world, the past, or the future.	Write down what emotion you felt and how you acted when you felt this emotion.	Write an alternative for *each*, using supporting arguments and evidence.	Write down how you feel and wish to act as consequence of your alternatives at D.
		Emotions eg, depression, guilt, hurt, anger, shame, jealousy, envy, anxiety. Rate intensity 0–100. Behaviour eg, avoidance/ safety-seeking behaviour eg, procrastination, checking.		**Emotions** Re-rate 0–100. List any healthy alternative emotion eg sadness, regret, concern. Alternative behaviour or experiment eg facing situation, increased activity, assertion

Figure 2.4: ABC form

Using the form above, client and coach can work though an example of a problem area together. The client can then be given some blank forms to practice with in their own time, when they notice an unhelpful emotional and/or behavioural response. Notice that the start point for the ABC form is not thoughts or trigger, but the client's emotion and/or behaviour 'C' ('consequence'). This is because not only is 'C' often the most noticeable element to the client, it is emotional and behavioural change that is the goal of thinking change in CBC. After teaching the ABC form, the coach can often take a truly 'coaching' role in supporting and encouraging the client in working though their emotional and behavioural challenges using the ABCDE process and helping to trouble-shoot any stuck-points.

Behavioural experiments

Actions, of course, speak louder than words. Aaron Beck, founder of cognitive therapy, encourages a therapeutic perspective where client and therapist work on 'being scientific together'. Beck (1976) emphasises that testing your thoughts in reality, rather than simply talking about them, underpins change. Bennet-Levy *et al* (2004) offer an excellent overview of the application of behavioural experiments in a variety of clinical problems.

In CBC, behavioural experiments can be used in the following ways:

- To test the validity of a thought or belief the client holds about them self, other people, or the world.
- To test the validity of an alternative thought or belief.
- To discover the effects that mental or behavioural activities have on the client's difficulties.
- To gather evidence in order to clarify the nature of your problem.
- Testing prediction – for example, taking a risk on outcome or ability to cope.
- Contrasting effect of old and new behaviour.
- Testing the effect of dropping a safety behaviour.
- Change in focus of attention.
- Trying out a new attitude.
- Duration and or intensity of emotion.
- Testing different interpersonal style.
- Testing the effect of difference in the way eat/move/sleep.

Coaches can share the following four steps to devise a behavioural experiment:

1. Describe the problem

Invite the client to write down the nature of their problem and include their *safety behaviours*. In other words, things they do to try to prevent their feared catastrophe in their own words and make a note of how the problem negatively affects their life.

2. Formulate your prediction

Help them explore and decide what they think will happen if they try out a new way of thinking or behaving in real life.

3. Execute an experiment

Help them think of a way of putting a new belief or behaviour to the test in a real-life situation. It works best to try to devise more than one way to test out your prediction.

4. Examine the results

Look to see whether the prediction came true. If it didn't, check out with them what they learned from the results of the experiment.

The coach can help them rate the degree to which they believe a prediction will come true on a percentage between 0 and 100 at the start of the experiment. After they have completed the experiment and processed the results, invite them to re-rate the conviction in their original prediction.

Behavioural experiment example:

- Describe the problem

A client is afraid of people thinking negatively and of being shunned at work if they disagree with colleagues.

- Formulate a prediction

The client predicts 'If I express an opinion or disagree with my boss, they'll like me less and want to get rid of me.' Conviction in this idea is rated as 80 per cent.

- Execute an experiment

The client commits to raising some alternative ways of running a project at a meeting with their boss.

- Examine the results

The client found that their boss did not wholly agree on all of their ideas but was in fact pleased to hear more of their thoughts and encouraged more input.

Out-of-session client practice ('homework')

One of the distinctive features of CBC is client 'homework' or 'assignments' and there is strong evidence that homework compliance is a key ingredient in the successful outcome of CBT (Burns, 2000; Kazantzis *et al*, 2010; LeBeau *et al*, 2013). Just as much of the outcome in physiotherapy or personal training (or even sports coaching!) depends on work and practice in-between sessions, the same is often true in CBC.

However, some clients are not fond of the term 'homework' or 'assignment', and 'assigning homework' is not in-line with the collaborative spirit of CBC. The best way to approach homework, or out-of-session practice, is to help clients to develop an idea, choose a strategy that will help them to develop and build upon the work in session. First, ask them if it makes sense to take some further steps (eg 'How can we find out more?') and what they think would be a good way of building on the work from the session. If the client is unable to think of a good strategy, you can ask their permission to offer some ideas. Ideally, you would present more than one option for them to choose from, with a short explanation of your rationale.

Below is a list of some of the more common tasks that clients carry out outside of the session in CBC:

- Countering avoidance of certain tasks, activities, people, or places
- Scheduling activities, including work, rest, and recreation in a realistic and balanced way
- Dropping safety-seeking behaviours such as excessive checking tasks, reassurance-seeking, over-planning, perfectionism
- Practising identifying, evaluating, and replacing unhelpful thoughts
- Carrying out a behavioural experiment
- Using a 'positive data log' (Greenberger & Padesky, 2015) to deliberately record evidence that helps to challenge an old and unhelpful belief and supports a new more helpful belief
- Bibliotherapy – a CBC coach will usually have good knowledge of key recommended texts that are consistent with CBC principles (e.g. Burns, 1999; Dickson, 2012; Dryden, 2020)

In CBC, we encourage our clients to write down the agreed practice and the rationale for it. To optimise effectiveness of the tasks you agree with your clients, it's helpful to consider the following:

- What task frequency will be most helpful for the client?
- What duration and/or intensity of the activity will be most helpful for the client?
- Where should the client do the activity?

- Have you and the client started 'small' enough for the client to realistically be able to follow through on the task?

You can then further improve the chance of client success by helping them imagine carrying out the agreed coaching-related activity. This is often a good opportunity to check the client understands how to carry out the task and has the skills to do so. This can also be a good point to ask your client what obstacles they can anticipate (time, distractions, procrastination, lack of opportunity, avoidance of discomfort, and so on) and how they would want to tackle them. It can be helpful to 'sell' out-of-session practice as a no-lose endeavour. Whether the client does the task or not, if it goes well or goes badly, it all yields data – to the CBC coach this is all 'grist for the mill' – and we are bound to learn something.

Follow-up on your client's 'homework' with interest and curiosity. The aim is to help their efforts yield maximum benefit by drawing out key learning and discoveries, and thinking together about next steps.

Conclusion

The cognitive behavioural approach to coaching helps clients work towards their goals by helping them to break free from unhelpful patterns of thinking and behaviour. The approach is collaborative, active and goal focused. There is some good empirical support for the efficacy of CBC, for which one can draw further confidence due to vast amount of evidence supporting the efficacy of CBT.

Five questions for further reflection

1. How does CBC differ from CBT?

Broadly speaking, CBC is aimed at improving performance and wellbeing, whereas CBT is aimed at solving clinical problems and restoring normal functioning. There are inevitably going to be some overlaps as coaching clients (being human) will experience unhelpful emotions such as anxiety, depression, anger and shame – which are on a continuum with clinical problems. However, in clinical problems distress is more severe, the problem significantly interferes with important areas of functioning, and very often the person will be worrying, ruminating or engaging in an unhelpful behaviour for more than an hour a day.

2. With what types of clients and presenting issues might cognitive behavioural coaching be most helpful?

CBC is highly flexible and can be applied in a wide range of contexts and applied to a range of coaching challenges and dilemmas. CBC offers particular advantages to clients who are seeking a specific emotional and/

or behavioural change. Clients who prefer an explicit, pragmatic problem-solving style are often drawn to the approach.

3. **How do you encourage a client to engage in the practice that is often required in CBC?**

To help engage clients in the practice that is needed to get the most out of CBC:

a. keep the coaching session active whenever possible so that there is a natural link to being active outside of the session

b. use a natural, everyday analogy such as physiotherapy, tennis coaching, or personal training to help the client relate to the need for practice and 'training' outside of contact time with the coach

c. make sure that the client understands how practice you have agreed follows logically from the work in-session and that they are clear on how it will help them achieve their goal.

4. **How can coaches optimise their CBC sessions?**

Effective practice of CBC means holding in mind two, rather competing, principles. First is to avoid letting a session drift too far from the core principles of CBC, and keep the session focused. The second is to avoid applying the principles too rigidly so as to miss potential for a deeper connection and understanding of the client.

5. **What's the future of CBC?**

The future of CBC lies in the evidence base for CBC continuing to develop, whilst also benefiting from further research into CBT. There would also be value in cognitive behavioural therapists and coaches developing clearer pathways for cross-referral and collaboration for the benefit of clients. Future research on which of the many cognitive behavioural principles and techniques are most effective for clients seen in coaching contexts will also be fruitful. There is also the exciting potential for further use of technology such as virtual reality and apps to support both client and coach.

Suggested reading

Neenan, M. & Dryden, W. (2020) *Cognitive Behavioural Coaching: A guide to problem solving and personal development,* 3rd edition. Routledge: Oxon.

Branch R. & Willson, R. (2019) *Cognitive Behavioural Therapy for Dummies,* 3rd edition. London: Wiley & Sons Ltd.

Kennerley, H., Kirk, J. & Westbrook, D. (2017). *An Introduction to Cognitive Behaviour Therapy: Skills and Applications,* 3rd edition. London: SAGE Publications.

Greenberger, D. & Padesky, C.A. (2015) *Mind Over Mood,* 2nd edition. New York: Guilford Press.

Padesky, C. A. & Greenberger, D. (2012) *Clinician's Guide To Mind Over Mood.* New York: Guilford Press.

Beck, J. (1995) *Cognitive Therapy: Basics and Beyond.* New York: Guilford Press.

References

Abel, A., Hayes, A.M., Henley, W. & Kuyken, W. (2016) Sudden gains in cognitive-behavior therapy for treatment-resistant depression: Processes of change. *Journal of Consulting and Clinical Psychology*, **84** (8) 726–737. Available online at: https://doi.org/10.1037/ccp0000101 Accessed on 10 July 2021.

Beck, A.T. (1976) *Cognitive Therapy and the Emotional Disorders*. New York: International Universities Press.

Beck, J.S. (1995) *Cognitive Therapy: Basics and beyond*. New York: Guilford Press.

Bennett-Levy, J.E., Butler, G.E., Fennell, M.E., Hackman, A.E., Mueller, M.E. & Westbrook, D.E. (2004) *Oxford Guide to Behavioural Experiments in Cognitive Therapy*. Oxford: Oxford University Press.

Braun, J.D., Strunk, D.R., Sasso, K.E. & Cooper, A.A. (2015) Therapist use of Socratic questioning predicts session-to-session symptom change in cognitive therapy for depression. *Behaviour Research and Therapy*, **70**, 32–37.

Burns, D.D. & Spangler, D.L. (2000) Does psychotherapy homework lead to improvements in depression in cognitive-behavioral therapy or does improvement lead to increased homework compliance? *Journal of Consulting and Clinical Psychology*, **68** (1) 46–56. Available online at: https://pubmed.ncbi.nlm.nih.gov/10710839/ Accessed on 10 July 2021.

Burns, D.D. (1999) *The Feeling Good Handbook*. London: Penguin Books.

Butler, A.C., Chapman, J.E., Forman, E.M. & Beck, A.T. (2006) The empirical status of cognitive-behavioral therapy: A review of meta-analyses. *Clinical Psychology Review*, **26**, 17–31.

Çavuşoğlu, I. & Bekiroğullari, Z. (2019) Exploring the effects of cognitive behavioural therapy on the employees working in the companies: the efficiency of CBT on work-related mental health problems. *Uluslararası Yönetim İktisat ve İşletme Dergisi*, **15** (4) 1183–1200.

Dickson, A. (2012) *A Woman In Your Own Right: Assertiveness and you*. Quartet Books Limited.

Dryden, W. (2020) *Ten Steps to Positive Living*. Hachette UK.

Edwards, J.L. & Newton, R.R. (1994) *Qualitative Assessment of the Effects of Cognitive Coaching Training as Evidenced Through Teacher Portfolios and Journals*. (Research Rep. No. 1994–3). Evergreen, CO.

Edwards, J.L. & Newton, R.R. (1995) *The Effects of Cognitive Coaching on Teacher Efficacy and Empowerment*. Conference Paper: American Education Research Association.

Ellis, A. (1962) *Reason and Emotion in Psychotherapy*. McLean, VA: Carol Publishing Group

Ellis, A. & Blum, M.L. (1967) Rational training: A new method of facilitating management labor relations. *Psychological Reports*, **20**, 1267–84.

Epictetus (2008) *Discourses and Selected Writings*. London: Penguin Classics.

Fordham, B., Sugavanam, T., Edwards, K. et al (2021) The evidence for cognitive behavioural therapy in any condition, population or context: a meta-review of systematic reviews and panoramic meta-analysis. *Psychological Medicine*, **51** (1) 21–29. Available online at: https://doi.org/10.1017/S0033291720005292 Accessed 10 July 2021.

Gardiner, M., Kearns, H. & Tiggemann, M. (2013) Effectiveness of cognitive behavioural coaching in improving the well-being and retention of rural general practitioners. *Australian Journal of Rural Health*, **21** (3) 183–189.

Grant, A.M. (2001) 'Coaching for Enhanced Performance: Comparing cognitive and behavioral approaches to coaching.' Paper presented at the 3rd International 'Spearman Seminar: Extending Intelligence: Enhancement and new constructs'. Sydney, Australia. Retrieved July 16, 2009, from http:// www.psych.usyd.edu.au/coach/CBT_BT_CT_Spearman_ Conf_Paper.pdf. Available through Coaching Psychology Unit - Faculty of Science (sydney.edu.au) (10 July 2021)

Grant, A.M. (2003) The impact of life coaching on goal attainment, metacognition and mental health. *Social Behavior and Personality*, 31 (3) 253–64.

Grant, A.M., Curtayne, L. & Burton, G. (2009) Executive coaching enhances goal attainment, resilience and workplace wellbeing: A randomised controlled study. *Journal of Positive Psychology*, **4** (5) 396–407.

Green, L.S., Oades, L.G. & Grant, A.M. (2006) Cognitive-behavioral, solution-focused life coaching: enhancing goal striving, wellbeing, and hope. *Journal of Positive Psychology*, **1** (3) 142–149.

Greenberger, D. & Padesky, C.A. (2015) *Mind Over Mood: Change how you feel by changing the way you think.* New York: Guilford Publications.

Hayes, S.C. (2004) Acceptance and commitment therapy, relational frame theory, and the third wave of behavioral and cognitive therapies. *Behavior Therapy*, **35** (4) 639–665.

Hofmann, S.G. & Smits, J.A. (2008) Cognitive-behavioral therapy for adult anxiety disorders: A meta-analyses of randomized placebo-controlled trials. *Journal Clinical Psychiatry*, **69** (4) 621–32.

Hofmann, S.G., Asnaani, A., Vonk, I.J., Sawyer, A.T. & Fang, A. (2012) The efficacy of cognitive behavioral therapy: A review of meta-analyses. *Cognitive Therapy and Research*, **36** (5) 427–440.

Harvey, A. G., Watkins, E., Mansell, W. & Shafran, R. (2004). *Cognitive behavioural processes across psychological disorders: A transdiagnostic approach to research and treatment.* Oxford University Press, USA.

Joyce, S., Modini, M., Christensen, H., Mykletun, A., Bryant, R., Mitchell, P.B. & Harvey, S.B. (2016) Workplace interventions for common mental disorders: a systematic meta-review. *Psychological Medicine*, **46** (4) 683–697.

Junker, S., Pömmer, M. & Traut-Mattausch, E. (2020) The impact of cognitive-behavioural stress management coaching on changes in cognitive appraisal and the stress response: a field experiment. *Coaching: An International Journal of Theory, Research and Practice*, 1–18. https://doi.org/10.1080/17521882.2020.1831563

Kazantzis, N., Whittington, C. & Dattilio, F. (2010) Meta-analysis of homework effects in cognitive and behavioral therapy: a replication and extension. *Clinical Psychology: Science and Practice*, **17**, 144–156.

Kazantzis, N., Fairburn, C.G., Padesky, C.A., Reinecke, M. & Teesson, M. (2014) Unresolved issues regarding the research and practice of cognitive behavior therapy: the case of guided discovery using socratic questioning. *Behaviour Change*, **31** (1) 1–7.

LeBeau, R., Davies, C., Culver, N. & Craske, M. (2013) Homework compliance counts in cognitive-behavioral therapy, *Cognitive Behaviour Therapy*, **42** (3) 171–179.

Libri, V. and Kemp, T. (2006) Assessing efficacy of a cognitive behavioral executive coaching program. *International Coaching Psychology Review*, **1** (2) 9–20.

Morley, S., Eccleston, C., & Williams, A. (1999) Systematic review and meta-analysis of randomized controlled trials of cognitive behavior therapy and behavior therapy for chronic pain in adults, excluding headache. *International Association for the Study of Pain*, Elsevier Science B.V. pp1–13.

Neenan, M. (2009). Using Socratic questioning in coaching. *Journal of Rational-Emotive & Cognitive-Behavior Therapy*, **27** (4) 249–264.

Ogba, F.N., Onyishi, C.N., Ede, M.O., Ugwuanyi, C., Nwokeoma, B.N., Victor-Aigbodion, V., Eze, U.N., Omeke, F., Okorie, C.O. & Ossai, O.V. (2019) Effectiveness of SPACE model of cognitive behavioral coaching in management of occupational stress in a sample of school administrators in South-East Nigeria. *Journal of Rational-Emotive and Cognitive-Behavior Therapy*, 1–24.

Onyishi, C.N., Ede, M.O., Ossai, O.V. & Ugwuanyi, C.S. (2021) Rational emotive occupational health coaching in the management of police subjective wellbeing and work ability: A case of repeated measures. *Journal of Police and Criminal Psychology*, **36** (1) 96–111.

Padesky, C.A. (1993, September) 'Socratic questioning: Changing minds or guiding discovery.' In: *A keynote address delivered at the European Congress of Behavioural and Cognitive Therapies, London* (Vol. 24).

Padesky, C.A. & Greenberger, D. (2012) *Clinician's Guide To Mind Over Mood.* New York: Guilford Press.

Pheng, E.G. & Yaacob, N.R.N. (2018) 'Can dysfunctional thought record reduce postpartum depression?' In: *3rd ASEAN Conference on Psychology, Counselling, and Humanities (ACPCH 2017).* Dordrecht, The Netherlands: Atlantis Press.

Ratiu, L., David, O.A. & Baban, A. (2016) Developing managerial skills through coaching: Efficacy of a cognitive-behavioral coaching program. *Journal of Rational-Emotive and Cognitive Behavior Therapy*, **34** (4) 244–266.

Tan, L., Wang, M.J., Modini, M., Joyce, S., Mykletun, A., Christensen, H. & Harvey, S.B. (2014) Preventing the development of depression at work: a systematic review and meta-analysis of universal interventions in the workplace. *BMC medicine*, **12** (1) 1–11.

Wolpe, J. (1958) *Psychotherapy by Reciprocal Inhibition*. Stanford: Stanford University Press.

Chapter 3
Cognitive Behavioural Chairwork: Theory, research and practice

Matthew Pugh

Introduction

The cognitive behavioural approach encapsulates a broad intervention science that seeks to address the cognitive and behavioural factors associated with personal challenges and the achievement of meaningful goals (Kazantzis *et al*, 2018; Mennin *et al*, 2013). Consistent with the integrative ethos of cognitive behavioural therapy (CBT) (Beck, 1991), cognitive behavioural coaching (CBC) utilises a variety of multi-modal methods to achieve this aim (Palmer & Szymanska, 2019). Amongst these, experiential techniques such as 'chairwork' have gained a reputation for being particularly effective (Pugh, 2019a). This chapter will explore the theoretical basis of cognitive behavioural chairwork, its relevance to CBC with reference to the empirical literature, and its applications in coaching practice.

Theoretical foundations

Chairwork refers to an assembly of experiential methods that use chairs, positioning, movement, and dialogue to bring about change through facilitated, here-and-now interactions with parts of the self (Pugh *et al*, 2020). In its classical two-chair form, the individual places an empty chair several feet from their own and imagines that it holds either an aspect of the self (such as the 'inner critic'), another person (such as a parent or colleague), or a more abstract concept (such as a personal goal). Next, the individual speaks to the 'other' as if she, he, or it were physically present. After some time, the individual switches seats and responds from the perspective of the other. In this way, chairwork invites individuals to directly engage with – rather than describe and talk about – the issues they bring to coaching. This can be a powerful and sometimes transformative experience

(Pugh & Broome, 2020). However, two-chair methods represent just one of several forms of chairwork, as we shall see.

Chairwork originates from psychodrama (Moreno, 2008) but was popularised by Gestalt therapy (Perls, 1969) and has since been extensively researched in emotion-focused therapy (Elliott & Greenberg, 2021; Greenberg, 2015). Today, chairwork is practised in several coaching frameworks, including compassion-focused (Anstiss & Gilbert, 2014), integrative (Pugh & Broome, 2020), and cognitive behavioural approaches (Dryden, 2017), as well as representing a potential modality in its own right (Pugh, in press; Pugh & Bell, 2020). To unify its applications across coaching, individual therapy, and group psychotherapy settings, chairwork has recently been conceptualised as resting upon four fundamental 'pillars' relating to its principles, processes, procedures, and process-based facilitative skills: the building blocks of chairwork-centred coaching and psychotherapy (Pugh & Bell, 2020; Pugh *et al*, 2020).

Principles (SIT)

The principles of chairwork refer to its theoretical assumptions, many of which derive from *Dialogical Self Theory* (Hermans, 2002). Using the analogy of constructing a house, the principles of chairwork are like the mathematical and architectural concepts that inform a building's design.

Principle 1: Self-multiplicity

The first principle of chairwork is that the self contains multiple, semi-autonomous 'parts', 'voices', or 'I-positions'. Within CBT, these dynamic state-like components of personality are commonly referred to as modes (Beck, 1996) or minds-in-place (Teasdale, 1997). According to Dialogical Self Theory, I-positions extend beyond parts of the self (internal positions) and include representations of other individuals (external positions), as well as groups, institutions, and concepts (outside positions).

Principle 2: Information exchange

The second principle of chairwork is that I-positions exchange information and engage in 'dialogical relationships'. In other words, these parts of the self communicate and relate to one other. While this might seem like a strange idea, internal dialogue is a normal aspect of human experience (Alderson-Day & Fernyhough, 2015). Indeed, thoughts and feelings are often experienced as dialogical events that 'speak' to the self (eg, Konopka, Hermans, & Goncalves, 2019).

Principle 3: Transformation

The third principle of chairwork is that I-positions and their dialogical relationships create and shape our inner world. This leads to a further idea:

that the challenges which individuals bring to coaching can be understood not only as maladaptive patterns of thought, feeling, and behaviour (as is typical in CBC), but also in terms of problematic relationships between I-positions which perpetuate these cycles (Pugh & Broome, 2020).

Processes (SAT)

The processes of chairwork refer to ways in which its theoretical principles are operationalised during coaching. Returning to the analogy of building a house, we can think of these processes as the building blocks that give a building its shape and structure:

Process 1: Separation

Chairwork begins with identifying the I-positions that will form the focus of the intervention, naming these, and separating them by placing them in different chairs. While I-positions can be separated in other ways (eg, representing them with objects or figurines), chairs are advantageous because they will allow the client to embody and directly experience these parts of the self.

Process 2: Animation

The second process of chairwork involves bringing the client's I-positions to life so that interactions between them can occur in the here-and-now. I-positions are animated in two ways during chairwork: through either *embodiment* (the client changes seats and 'speaks as' an I-position) or *personification* (the client visualises an I-position in a concrete form, as if it were held in another chair).

Process 3: Talk

The final process of chairwork involves initiating an interaction between the selected I-positions to explore and resolve the client's complaint(s). These enactments take two essential forms: *horizontal procedures* in which I-positions talk to one another, to the coach, or the client, and *vertical procedures* in which I-positions are observed from a distanced perspective ('witnessing').

Procedures

Procedures refer to the various enactments that constitute chairwork (Table 3.1). Returning to the earlier analogy, procedures represent styles of building that can be constructed. However, it is important that coaches do not feel constrained by taxonomy: spontaneity and creativity lie at the heart of chairwork (Moreno, 2008), meaning that coaches can and should develop their own forms of chairwork.

Interviews

Interviews involve questioning the client in the role of an I-position: the client moves to a new space (either by changing chairs or shifting their occupied seat) and 'speaks as' the I-position. Through interviewing, 'action insights' (Kellerman, 1992) into the perspectives, motivations, and history of I-positions are acquired. Examples of interviews include:

- *Intrapersonal interviews* in which the client embodies a self-related part such as their 'inner critic' or 'inner champion'.
- *Interpersonal interviews* in which the client embodies another person such as friend, role-model, or stakeholder.
- *Interviewing the client as a personification* of personal or professional issues such as a goal, recurrent obstacle, or life event.

Dialogues

The best-known form of chairwork, dialogues allow two or more I-positions to speak with one another: the client moves back and forth between two chairs, speaking and responding from each perspective, so that parts of the self can converse. Examples of dialogues include:

- *Dialogues between parts of the self,* such as the side that wants to pursue a course of action (eg, getting married) and the part that does not
- *Dialogues with other persons* such as individuals towards whom the client holds lingering feelings such as unexpressed resentment ('unfinished business')
- *Dialogues with concepts* such as the client's company, community, or a culture.

Dramatisations

Dramatisations enable the client to re-visit past life scenes and experiment with future scenes through role-play. Given that dramatisations often involve multiple I-positions, the coach will often need to enact some of these roles on the client's behalf. Examples of dramatisations include:

- Enacting *past scenes* such as early life experiences to better understand why certain events transpired
- Enacting *present-day scenes* such as problematic interactions with others to assess the client's behaviour in-situ and develop insights into the responses of others
- Enacting *future scenes* in order to rehearse new behaviour skills (eg being assertive with others) and experiment with new ways of being.

Depictions

Depictions utilise chairs to map and measure aspects of the client's internal and external world. These spatial representations are useful during the early stages of coaching, helping to explore the client's challenges, goals, and context. Examples include:

- *Measurements,* such as how near or far the client is from achieving a goal, represented by an empty seat
- *Internal maps* depicting aspects of the client's intrapersonal world which are held in different chairs
- *External maps* representing the client's interpersonal world such as their relationships with other people, held in different seats.

Disclosures

Stories shape our identity and influence how we perceive and understand the world (Bruner, 2002). Disclosures use chairs to help the client externalise, recount, revise, and reorganize these self-narratives. This is a useful way to encourage emotional processing, identify themes that define the client's life, and highlight exceptions to problematic self-stories (Angus & Greenberg, 2011). Examples of disclosures include:

- *Novel disclosures,* in which the client uses a second chair to verbalise emotionally significant experiences which have not yet been shared ('silent stories')
- *Multi-storied disclosures,* in which new outcomes or exceptions to problem-saturated self-narratives ('same-old stories') are explored in different chairs
- *Expressive disclosures* in which the client uses a second chair to retell emotionally barren narratives ('empty stories') in a more candid, expressive manner.

Witnessing

While the enactments outlined so far aim to facilitate interactions with I-positions, witnessing enables the client to step back and observe parts of the self from a decentred perspective. These vertical procedures fulfil several functions such as supporting cognitive defusion and enhancing reflective processing (Pugh, in press). Witnessing also exploits the tendency to reason and regulate emotions more effectively from self-distanced positions (Kross & Ayduk, 2017). Witnessing is concretised by asking the client to stand during chairwork and adopt different meta- perspectives. These include:

- *Dispassionate witnessing* involving neutral and non-judgmental self-observation
- *Compassionate witnessing* involving supportive and care-focused self-observation.

Table 3.1: Core procedures in cognitive behavioural chairwork

Horizontal procedures	Description
Interviews	Questioning the client in the role of I-positions
Dialogues	Encounters and conversations between two or more I-positions
Dramatisations	Enacting scenes from the perspective of past, present, or future I-positions
Depictions	Mapping and measuring I-positions and their relationships
Disclosures	Recounting or revising the narratives of I-positions

Vertical procedures	Description
Compassionate witnessing	Compassionate observation of I-positions and task engagement
Dispassionate witnessing	Objective observation of I-positions and task engagement

Process skills

Process skills refer to moment-by-moment facilitative acts or 'micro-interventions' that coaches use to ensure that chairwork is as immersive, evocative, and meaningful for the client as possible (Pugh, 2019a; 2019b). Research suggests that process skills impact the uptake and effectiveness of chairwork (Muntigl *et al*, 2020) and so represent a vital aspect of its delivery. Returning to the construction metaphor one final time, process skills represent the mortar that binds the bricks (ie processes of chairwork) together, ensuring that the building's structure (ie the procedure being facilitated) is strong and robust. Examples of process skills include:

- *De-roling and roling:* Actions which indicate that a chair has taken on a role or is no longer involved in the enactment (Coach: 'Let's imagine that this seat holds your inner critic [*places an empty chair a few feet from the client*] – how do you picture that part of yourself?').
- *Doubling:* The coach offers the client first-person statements to repeat (or revise if they are inaccurate) to help express something unsaid, unknown, or unclear (Coach: 'If it feels right, try saying to your inner critic [*gestures to the empty chair*], "I can't go on with you hurting me like this" – does that fit with your experience?').

- *Psychosomatic enquiry:* The client is asked to put words to the non-verbal communications of I-positions, such as postures, gestures, and other silent statements (Coach: 'You're clenching your fist as you say that to your inner critic – what is your fist saying?').

- *Role consistency:* The client is encouraged to remain in role and speak only as the I-position they are embodying in a particular chair (Coach: 'Change seats and be the inner critic. [*Client changes seats*] Speaking as the critic in this chair, what do you say in response to hearing the pain you cause Matthew [*gestures to the client's former chair*]?').

- *Scene-setting:* Before commencing a dramatisation, the client describes, and imaginally re-enters the environment in which these interactions have, or will, take place (Coach: 'Let's recreate the conversation you had with your boss. [*Introduces a chair for the client's manager*] Before we begin, tell me – where is this conversation taking place? What does the room look like? What time is it? Who else is present?').

Theoretical relevance to cognitive behavioural coaching

What is the theoretical basis for incorporating chairwork into CBC? Models of information-processing, retrieval competition, and adult learning provide compelling rationales (Pugh, 2019b; Pugh & Margetts, 2020). Information-processing models such as the theory of Interacting Cognitive Subsystems (ICS; Teasdale & Barnard, 1993) identify two levels of meaning: 'intellectual beliefs' which are concerned with factual information but unrelated to emotional processes ('I know I am a successful coach…'), and 'emotional beliefs' which are associated with felt senses but are difficult to convey in words ('…yet somehow I still feel like a fraud'). ICS suggests that addressing the deeper, emotion-level beliefs underlying distress is often more productive than working at the level of intellectual beliefs, but requires more evocative and multisensory interventions. The implication of this is that experiential methods such as chairwork are a more productive medium for bringing about enduring heart-level, cognitive-affective change than discussion-based methods alone (eg, automatic thought recording) (Pugh, 2019b; Teasdale, 1997).

On the other hand, constructivist theories such as retrieval competition (Brewin, 2006) propose that multiple mental representations compete for retrieval from longer-term memory at any one time. The task of CBC, therefore, is not to modify negative mental representations (the belief 'I am a failure'), but to help individuals construct more adaptive mental representations (the belief, 'I am successful') which are preferentially retrieved in-situ. Crucially, these positive representations must be sufficiently vivid, distinctive, and memorable to win out at the point of retrieval competition. The novelty, intensity, and memorability of chairwork may mean it is a particularly effective way to construct these adaptive mental representations (Pugh, 2019a).

Finally, theories of adult learning (eg, Kolb, 1984) suggest that personal and professional development draws upon four interrelated processes:

- learning experiences (engaging in an activity)
- reflection (thinking about what happened during the activity)
- meaning-making (creating a model based on the experience), and
- experimentation (testing one's model through further activities).

If this is correct, coaching (and coaching supervision) would benefit greatly from including all four modes of learning, including active methods such as chairwork which provide compelling learning *experiences* (Pugh & Margetts, 2020).

Taken together, these theories suggest that experiential methods such as chairwork are advantageous in terms of the construction and retrieval of new knowledge, as well as addressing the implicit, heart-level meanings which cognitive-behavioural approaches are most concerned with. In other words, attempting to bring about change through conversation will go so far: effective coaching should incorporate the head (talking), the heart (experiencing), the hands (doing), and the hug (relating) (Pugh & Broome, 2020). However, theories of learning and cognition are just one of several frameworks for understanding the change processes underlying chairwork. For other perspectives, readers are encouraged to review the psychodrama (eg, Kushnir & Orkibi, 2021) and Gestalt / emotion-focused literature (eg, Greenberg & Malcolm, 2002).

Research evidence

Establishing the effectiveness of cognitive behavioural chairwork is challenging for two reasons. First, the sheer number of procedures that constitute chairwork makes it difficult to evaluate these interventions comprehensively. Second, research has tended to examine common and specific factors in psychotherapy and coaching, rather than specific interventions using dismantling or additive studies (Mulder *et al*, 2017). Nonetheless, sufficient evidence exists to hypothesise that cognitive behavioural chairwork is an effective method of intervention (Table 3.2).

Dramatisation (ie role-playing) procedures have undergone the most empirical testing in CBT and with positive results. Most notably, trial-based role-plays (de Oliveira, 2015) are proven to be an effective intervention for modifying negative core beliefs across diagnostic groups (eg, de Oliveira *et al*, 2012). Similarly, case studies suggest that 'rational role-play' is useful when working with entrenched cognitions (Cromarty & Marks, 1995; Newell & Shrubb, 1994). In comparison to other cognitive interventions, research suggests that cognitive restructuring combined with dramatisations, such as 'rational role-plays', are more effective than cognitive restructuring alone (Lipsky *et al*, 1980), and that trial-based role-plays outperform some 'standard' cognitive techniques such as automatic thought records and positive data logging (de Oliveira *et al*, 2012). Research examining the use of dialogue procedures in CBT is much more limited, with a single comparison study suggesting that empty-chair dialogues are just as effective as rational-emotive ABC chaining in reducing anger (Conoley *et al*, 1983). In addition, Elliott (1992) has presented a case study in which two-chair dialogues with the 'inner critic' were successfully incorporated into the cognitive-behavioural treatment of an individual struggling with procrastination and negative self-beliefs.

Other research has explored whether CBT is enhanced through the addition of emotion-focused chairwork (Thoma & Greenberg, 2015). These studies are predicated on the observation that CBT tends to deprioritise emotion exploration and experiencing (Goldfried *et al*, 1997; Wiser & Goldfried, 1993), even though emotional arousal is linked to better therapeutic outcomes (Watson & Bedard, 2006). Emotion-focused chairwork (which derives from Gestalt chairwork) appears to be an effective method for addressing a range of difficulties including self-criticism (Shahar *et al*, 2012), childhood trauma (Paivio *et al*, 2010), and indecision (Clarke & Greenberg, 1986). Moreover, emotion-focused chairwork appears to perform as well as popular cognitive-behavioural interventions such as cost-benefits analysis (Trachsel *et al*, 2012) and outperforms others such as problem-solving (Clarke & Greenberg, 1986). While studies combining CBT with emotion-focused chairwork suggest it is feasible and effective (Holtforth *et al*, 2012; Newman *et al*, 2008), it does not appear any more effective than 'standard' CBT (Holtforth *et al*, 2019; Newman *et al*, 2011).

Finally, qualitative studies have provided insights into the experience of chairwork and how it brings about change. Individuals describe chairwork as intense, emotionally demanding, sometimes awkward, yet ultimately helpful. Compared to other therapeutic tasks (eg, discussion and written exercises), chairwork is also distinguished by its immediacy, power, and emotionally engaging nature (Bell *et al*, 2020a; Bell *et al*, 2020b; Stiegler *et al*, 2018; Robinson *et al*, 2014). Individuals attribute positive outcomes in chairwork to increased self-complexity, self-compassion, and decentring from internal events, as well as the realism and 'felt truth' of cognitive-affective changes achieved through these methods (Bell *et al*, 2020b; Chadwick, 2003; Stiegler *et al*, 2018).

In summary, research suggests that cognitive behavioural chairwork is a promising intervention. Support exists for the use of dramatisation procedures and, to a lesser degree, dialogue procedures in CBT, including two-chair emotion-focused methods. Nonetheless, further empirical tests of cognitive behavioural chairwork are needed in CBT and CBC. In addition, the number of studies exploring chairwork is considerably smaller than more established interventions such as cognitive restructuring and imagery-based methods. The efficacy of interview-, depiction-, witness-, and disclosure-focused chairwork also remains unknown. However, evidence is beginning to accumulate outside of CBT (eg, Ling *et al*, 2021). Finally, change process research is needed to clarify *how* cognitive behavioural chairwork facilitates change (Greenberg, 2007) – are positive outcomes attributable to specific factors such as clients' level of emotional involvement during enactments, how these methods are facilitated, or a combination of both?

Before concluding this section, it should be noted that studies exploring the use of behavioural chairwork have not been included here. Research indicates that dramatisation procedures (eg, modelling and behavioural rehearsal) are an effective way to develop new behavioural skills such as assertiveness (see Speed *et al*, 2018) and appear to outperform passive training methods such as advice-giving (Lazarus, 1966). In addition, integrative treatments which combine cognitive behavioural interventions with chairwork procedures drawn from other psychotherapies (eg, Gestalt therapy) have not been discussed, although published findings are promising (eg, Butollo *et al*, 2014).

Table 3.2: Summary of research

Study	Summary
Bell *et al* (2020a)	Qualitative study explored the experience of compassion-focused therapy chairwork (dialogue procedure) for self-criticism (n = 12). Outcome: Participants described chairwork as more emotionally engaging than 'rational' cognitive interventions (eg, written tasks).
Bell *et al* (2000b)	Qualitative study explored the 'multiple selves' chairwork task (disclosure procedure) as used in compassion-focused therapy (n = 12). Outcome: Depressed clients described the task as accessible and helpful, particularly in terms of enhancing their self-compassion, self-coherence, and ability to de-centre.
Chadwick, P. (2003)	Paper included written feedback from individuals with psychosis (n = 2) regarding their experiences of chairwork (disclosure procedure). Outcome: chairwork was helpful in terms of supporting de-centring, increasing self-complexity, developing positive core beliefs that had 'felt truth'.

Table 3.2: Summary of research (cont'd)

Study	Summary
Clarke & Greenberg (1986)	Study compared the effects of Gestalt chairwork (dialogue procedure) (n = 16) against problem-solving (n = 16) in resolving indecision. Participants with a conflictual decision were seen for two sessions. Outcome: Gestalt chairwork was more effective than problem-solving in reducing indecision.
Coloney et al (1983)	Study compared the effects of chairwork (dialogue procedure), rational-emotive ABC chaining, and reflective listening in reducing anger in students (n = 61). Outcome: Empty-chair and ABC techniques were found to be equally effective in reducing anger, and more effective than reflective listening.
Cromarty & Marks (1995)	Case report describing the treatment of an individual with longstanding body dysmorphia which combined exposure, cognitive restructuring, and chairwork ('rational role-play'; dramatisation procedure). Outcome: Body dysmorphic beliefs remained unchanged following exposure and cognitive restructuring, but were significantly reducing after the addition of rational role-plays (two enactments over two sessions).
Delavechia et al (2016)	Study tested the effectiveness of a single-session multi-chair intervention ('trial-based thought record'; TBTR – dramatisation procedure) in modifying negative core in a mixed sample (n = 39). Outcome: TBRT resulted in significant reductions in the endorsement of core beliefs (approx.. 85% -> 18% belief rating) and improvements in mood. Effects were significantly greater when participants enacted different roles in different chairs, rather than remaining in the same chair.
de Oliveira, I.R. (2008)	Study tested the effectiveness of single-session use of the TBTR in modifying negative core in a mixed sample (n = 30). Outcome: Results indicated a significant reduction in the endorsement of negative core beliefs (approx. 76% -> 27% belief rating) and improvements in mood.
de Oliveira, I.R. et al (2011)	Compared the effectiveness of the TBTR (n = 17) against two 'standard' cognitive interventions (automatic thought records and positive data logs) (n = 19) in addressing social anxiety disorder. Treatments were provided over 12 sessions. Outcome: Both interventions were equally effective on most outcome measures, although the TBTR was advantageous in reducing fears of negative evaluation.

Table 3.2: Summary of research (cont'd)

Study	Summary
de Oliveira, I.R. et al (2012)	Study tested the effectiveness of single-session use of the TBTR in modifying negative core in a mixed sample (primarily depressed individuals) (n = 166). Outcome: TBTR achieved significant reductions in the endorsement of core beliefs (approx. 81% -> 20% belief rating) and improvements in mood.
Elliott (1992)	Presents a case study in which chairwork (dialogue procedure) was used to address procrastination and negative self-beliefs. Outcome: The author reports an immediate cessation of procrastination following the use of chairwork.
Holtforth et al (2012)	Study examined the effectiveness of exposure-based cognitive therapy (EBCT) which combines cognitive therapy (phase 1) with exposure-focused interventions (phase 2), including emotion-focused chairwork (dialogue procedures). 21 individuals with depression were treated over 20 sessions. Outcome: EBCT produced significant reductions in depression scores, which were predicted by the exposure-based phase of treatment.
Holtforth et al (2019)	RCT comparing CBT (n = 72) and EBCT (n = 79) for treating depression. Therapies were provided over 22 weeks. Outcome: Both therapies were found to be equally effective at the end of treatment and follow-up.
Lipsky et al (1980)	Compared outcomes for three rational emotive therapy (RET) conditions – RET alone, RET plus chairwork ('rational role play'; dramatisation procedure), and RET plus rational emotive imagery – in treating anxiety and adjustment disorders in adults. Outcome: RET alone outperformed relaxation in reducing symptoms of anxiety and depression, while RET plus role-play was significantly more effective than RET alone.
Newell & Shrubb (1994)	Presents two case studies in which exposure therapy for body dysmorphia was initially refused. Chairwork ('rational role play'; dramatisation procedure) was used as an alternative method of intervention. Outcome: Chairwork (number of enactments unclear) resulted in significant reductions in body dysmorphic beliefs and later uptake of exposure-based tasks.

Table 3.2: Summary of research (cont'd)

Study	Summary
Newman et al (2008)	Open trial evaluating the feasibility and efficacy of treating generalised anxiety disorder (GAD) with CBT combined with interpersonal/emotion-focused interventions (including emotion-focused chairwork; dialogue procedures) (n = 18). Outcome: CBT plus integrations significantly reduced GAD symptoms and produced a greater effect size than observed in standard CBT for GAD.
Newman et al (2011)	Randomised controlled trial comparing two treatments for GAD: CBT plus supportive listening (n = 40) versus CBT plus interpersonal/emotion-focused interventions (including emotion-focused chairwork; dialogue procedures) (n = 43). Outcome: Both treatments produced large effect sizes, with no significant differences post-treatment or at follow-up.
Paivio et al (2010)	Study compared two versions of emotion-focused therapy for trauma (EFTT): EFTT plus chairwork (dialogue procedures) (n = 20) and EFTT plus empathic exploration. Outcome: Improvements were equivalent in both treatments. However, EFTT plus chairwork was associated with higher rates of clinically significant change as well as higher attrition rates.
Robinson et al (2004)	Study examined group EFT for individuals with anxiety and depression (n = 10). Outcome: Qualitative feedback identified chairwork (dialogue procedures) as being the most powerful and helpful aspect of treatment.
Shahar et al (2012)	Study tested the effectiveness of emotion-focused chairwork (dialogue procedure) in reducing self-criticism. 10 participants were treated over 5 – 8 sessions. Outcome: Emotion-focused chairwork led to significant reductions in self-criticism, anxiety symptoms, and depression symptoms, as well as increases in self-compassion. Effect sizes were medium to large.
Stiegler et al (2018)	Qualitative study exploring experiences of emotion-focused chairwork (dialogue procedures) for self-criticism, following 10 – 14 treatment sessions. Outcome: Participants (n = 18) described chairwork as initially awkward, emotionally demanding, more 'real' than discussing their emotional experiences, and ultimately helpful.

Table 3.2: Summary of research (cont'd)	
Study	Summary
Stiegler et al (2018)	Study explored whether emotion-focused chairwork (dialogue procedure) added to the therapeutic effects of empathic attunement in emotion-focused therapy for anxiety and depression. Participants (n = 21) received 5 – 9 sessions focused on empathic attunement, followed by 5 sessions focused on chairwork. Outcome: Sessions incorporating chairwork had a greater impact on symptoms of anxiety and depression than the earlier sessions.
Trachsel et al (2012)	Two interventions for resolving partnership ambivalence were compared. Participants completed either written cost-benefits analysis (n = 25) or emotion-focused chairwork (dialogue procedure) (n = 25) over two sessions. Outcome: Both interventions were equally effective in resolving ambivalence.

Practice

Chairwork can augment most, if not all, within-session coaching tasks (Pugh, 2019a). The following section provides examples of chairwork that are applicable in routine courses of CBC. However, it is important that coaches maintain the 'frame' of CBC when using these methods, including collaborative empiricism, guided discovery, and a focus on cognitive-affective processes (Beck, 1991).

Examining self-defeating cognitions

Modifying negative automatic thoughts (NATs) which obstruct goal attainment and impair performance is a cornerstone of CBC (Palmer & Szymanska, 2019). Cognitive reappraisal through chairwork is approached in three phases.

- In phase one, the client presents evidence that supports their NAT in chair one, while the coach provides rebuttals in chair two, thereby exposing the client to valid counter-arguments and helping them internalise these new perspectives.

- Once skilled in formulating rejoinders, the client enacts both roles in phase two: a single piece of evidence supporting the NAT is presented by the client in chair one and then challenged (with the coach's support) in chair two.

- In the final and most provocative stage (sometimes referred to as 'playing devil's advocate'), the client presents healthy reappraisals in chair one while the coach defends the NAT in chair two[1]. Should the client become stuck at any point, roles are reversed or the dialogue is paused so that valid counter-arguments can be co-constructed.

According to the cognitive behavioural model, negative thinking patterns often derive from deeply held core beliefs relating to the self, others, and the world. Addressing core beliefs requires more intensive and sustained intervention than automatic thoughts due to their unconditional and entrenched nature. Based upon the analogy of a courtroom trial, de Oliveira (2015) has developed a complex yet compelling dramatisation for modifying negative core beliefs (referred to as 'self-accusations'), which involves the client playing several roles in different chairs, including defendant, the prosecution, defense, jury, and judge. Evidence supporting and disconfirming the client's core belief is submitted, refuted, and evaluated during multiple mock trials, resulting in changes in the negative self-belief.

Given that negative core beliefs are often resistant to change, helping individuals develop new, complex models of the self is sometimes more productive. Chadwick (2003) has outlined a disclosure-focused two-chair method for this purpose. First, the client changes seats and describes the lived experience of their negative core belief in chair one (Client: 'I always have been and always will be a failure in business'). Once this 'same-old' self-narrative has been expressed, the client moves to chair two and outlines exceptions to their negative core belief (Client: 'There have been moments in my career when I have succeeded in business'). After completing these disclosures, the client reflects on how both experiences of the self are equally valid and grounded in lived experiences. Rather than modifying negative core beliefs, this procedure lays the foundations for more positive self-appraisals and demonstrates that the client's self is complex, dynamic, and varied; in other words, the generalised 'same old story' about the self (stemming from negative core beliefs) is not the whole story.

Painful autobiographical events involving significant others (eg, parental criticism, bullying) often play a role in the formation of core beliefs (McNeel, 1999). Empty-chair dialogues allow the client to hold these individuals

accountable for their wrongdoings, reattribute blame for mistreatment, and work through lingering feelings such as anger, hurt, and grief ('unfinished business') (Thoma & Greenberg, 2015). Empty-chairwork begins with the client imagining the other is held in an empty seat and expressing their immediate emotional reactions. Once these feelings have been conveyed, the client changes seats and responds as the other. As the client switches

---

1 Assertive defence of the self (Padesky, 1997) is a variation of the devil's advocate procedure which is particularly helpful if the client's NATs relate to fears of negative evaluation (Client: 'My colleagues will think I'm weird if I look nervous during the meeting'). This dramatisation entails the coach enacting a critical individual who accuses the client in line with their fear (Coach: 'I can see you're anxious and I think it's weird'), while the client responds with assertive counter-arguments (Client: 'Actually, feeling anxious is normal').

between the chairs, expressing their healthy emotional responses (eg, sadness over losses, anger over violations) and associated needs (eg, for warmth, support, or appropriate boundaries), transformations in the other occur: figures who were viewed as threatening or uncaring usually begin to 'soften' into individuals who are empathic, flawed, and remorseful for their actions. Resolving unfinished business provides clients with a sense of unburdening, relief, and empowerment, but may require several dialogues to be fully worked through.

Changing cognitive processes

Worry, self-criticism, and other problematic cognitive processes can be highly performance-interfering. Positive metacognitive beliefs about the functionality of these processes often play a role in their maintenance (eg, 'worry helps me prepare', 'self-criticism helps me improve') (Gilbert *et al*, 2004). Inspired by the voice dialogue approach (Stone & Stone, 1989), intrapersonal interviews are a creative way to explore metacognitive beliefs and the functions of cognitive processes by speaking directly to these internal events. This experiential approach to functional analysis entails the client moving their chair to a different space and taking on the voice of a cognitive process (eg, speaking as the 'inner critic'). Next, the client-as-cognitive-process is respectfully and non-confrontationally interviewed in regard to its origins, triggers, intentions, and concerns. At the end of the interview, the client moves back to their original position and 'separates' from the cognitive process. In this way, intrapersonal interviews concretise the process of cognitive defusion (Hayes *et al*, 2016) and offer insights into how and why cognitive processes operate in the way they do.

Two-chair dialogues with cognitive processes are a helpful way to re-evaluate positive beliefs about cognitive processes. Suppose the client believes that self-criticism motivates the self. In this case, (s)he is asked to move to a second chair and (speaking to their former seat) berate themselves. After returning to their original chair, the client reflects on whether (s)he feels more or less encouraged after receiving these self-attacks (Pugh, 2019a). This enactment can be a powerful illustration of how cognitive processes negatively impact performance and well-being.

Greenberg and colleagues (1989) suggest that two-chair dialogues also encourage individuals to take responsibility for distressing cognitive processes, shifting from a position of passive recipient ('Worrying upsets me') to active agent ('I worry myself'). Moreover, dialogues with cognitive processes help individuals connect with the core emotional needs that can transform these experiences. For example, after criticising themselves from a second chair (Client-as-critic: 'You'll never succeed in life'), the client returns to their original chair and shares their emotional reactions to receiving these attacks (Client-as-self: 'I feel so hopeless and discouraged') and the needs associated with these feelings (Client-as-self: 'I need you [inner critic] to be more supportive of me'). Moving back to the chair of the cognitive process, two responses are then usually observed: either the cognitive process softens in reaction to the client's expressions of sadness and anger (Client-as-critic: 'I don't mean to cause you so much pain, I'm trying to help') or it remains indifferent (Client-as-critic: 'Stop being such a baby'). A positive outcome is still achievable if the cognitive process does not change during the dialogue: the client is encouraged to use their adaptive anger to set healthy boundaries with the part(s) that cause them distress (Client-as-self: 'If you're not going to help me, inner critic, then I am not going to listen to you') (Thoma & Greenberg, 2015)[2].

Reaching decisions and resolving ambivalence

Costs-benefits analysis is a popular method for evaluating the advantages and disadvantages of particular attitudes, cognitive processes, and courses of action. Chairwork enlivens the process of decision-making by working directly with the parts of the self that hold opposing viewpoints. For example, if the client has mixed feelings about changing careers, they can be interviewed in both roles: first, as the part which wants to take on a new job (chair one), followed by the part that does not (chair two). Returning to their original position (the 'centre'), the client is then able to separate from the two sides of the conflict and make a more informed decision from the central point, which balances the tensions of the opposing voices.

Decisional conflicts can also be resolved by facilitating a dialogue between the opposing perspectives (a procedure sometimes referred to as two-chair decisional balancing): the client moves to chair one and outlines the advantages of a particular course of action, followed by the disadvantages in chair two. As the client moves back-and-forth between the seats, responding and counter-responding from both perspectives, a decision is eventually reached. In the event of a stalemate, innovative perspectives can be introduced using a third chair (representing a past mentor, the client's best possible self, their personal values, etc), helping to tip the balance in favour of one side or the other.

It is not uncommon for individuals to feel ambivalent about addressing the issues that bring them to coaching. Afterall, change requires effort, persistence, and often a degree of risk-taking (Neenan & Dryden, 2020). The 'future selves' task (Pugh & Salter, 2018) is a two-stage chairwork exercise that aims to enhance motivation and commitment to change. In the first enactment, the client changes seats and embodies a future version of their

---

2   For extended discussion and detailed illustrations of emotion-focused two-chair dialogues, see Elliott and Greenberg (2021).

self who has continued to struggle with a complaint (Coach: 'Change seats and be Matt-in-five-years'-time who still procrastinates'). The coach then interviews this future self-regarding the impact this issue has had on key life domains (eg, career, relationships, health, finances, and so on). Towards the end of the interview, the future self is asked if it would like to offer advice to the client's current self (Coach: 'If you could go back in time and speak to Matt when he was thinking about working on his procrastination [*gestures to the client's original chair*], what guidance would you give him?'). The exercise is then repeated with the future self who has succeeded in bringing about change, thereby highlighting the benefits of addressing (rather than avoiding) current challenges.

Developing behavioural skills

Behavioural skills training (BST) aims to help individuals develop new behaviours or fine-tune existing skills. Typical targets for BST include assertive communication, negotiation, and public speaking. Contrasted role-plays (McNeilage & Adams, 1979) are a playful way to initiate BST and help the client unearth new behavioural skills through action-based guided discovery. This three-chair procedure involves the client enacting the extremes of new behaviour in order to identify an adaptive behavioural 'middle-ground'. For example, a client who wants to develop their assertiveness might begin by role-playing extremely passive communication in chair one, followed by highly aggressive communication in chair two, followed by an assertive middle-ground in chair three. This allows the client to evaluate the effectiveness of different styles of behaviour and develop idiosyncratic ways of being. In the later stages of BST (sometimes referred to as behavioural rehearsal), chairwork is used to sharpen behavioural skills through a combination of supportive instruction, dramatisation, and corrective feedback (Table 3.3).

Table 3.3: Stages of behaviour skills training ('I-MARCHED') (Pugh, 2019a)

1. *Instruction:* The coach describes the new behaviour and the steps it involves.
2. *Modelling:* The coach demonstrates the behaviour through role-play.
3. *Assess learning:* The coach checks the client's understanding of the behaviour.
4. *Rehearsal:* The client practices the new behaviour through role-play.
5. *Coaching:* Role-plays are paused to provide coaching and 'live' feedback as needed.
6. *Helpful feedback:* The coach praises the client's efforts and offers additional feedback.
7. *Edited rehearsal:* The behaviour is rehearsed again, incorporating corrective feedback.
8. *Develop homework:* New behaviours are reinforced through homework (eg, repetition).

Maintaining the coaching alliance

Cultivating a positive working alliance is central to CBC (Neenan, 2018; Passmore & Sinclair, 2020). Identifying and resolving tensions in the coaching relationship plays a vital role in maintaining this bond and can be a critical moment in coaching (Day *et al*, 2008). Transference refers to instances in which aspects of formative relationships are ascribed to the coaching relationship (Levy, 2009). For example, the client might expect the coach to respond critically to non-completion of a homework task, mirroring past experiences of parental criticism. In CBC, transference is understood to arise from the client's mental representations of the self-in-relation-to-others, which are triggered by cues in the coaching relationship (eg, a change in the coach's tone of voice) (Miranda & Andersen, 2007). Enacting transferences through chairwork is a powerful means to explore and resolve these reactions when they occur. To illustrate, the client who anticipates being criticised is asked to switch seats and enact the rejecting coach they initially expected ('playing the projection'; Levitsky & Perls, 1969) (Coach: 'Change seats and show me how you thought I would react when you said you hadn't completed the homework'). Next, the client contrasts these expectations with reality (Coach: 'Did you experience me as reacting in that way when you told me about not doing the task?'). Assuming that the client notices some discrepancy between their prediction and reality, links with other relationships are explored, thus helping the client to take back these projections (Coach: 'If you didn't experience me being critical of you for not completing the homework, where do those feelings and expectations come from? Did the critical coach you enacted a moment ago remind you of anyone else in your life?').

If ruptures do occur, these require direct and non-defensive acknowledgement, coupled with a collaborative exploration of how both parties contributed to the interaction ('metacommunication') (Muran *et al*, 2018). Exploring ruptures from a third-person perspective allows the coach and client to discuss these tensions in a non-confrontational manner and helps re-establish their connection (Roediger *et al*, 2018): both individuals stand up and look down on the chairs as joint bystanders, describing how and why the rupture occurred and how it can be resolved (Coach: 'It looks like the coach gave too much advice today [gestures to chair one] and now the client feels unheard [gestures to chair two]. What do you think would help these individuals bond again?').

Conclusion

Chairwork represents an exciting yet little explored frontier for CBC. Given the variety of interventions at their disposal, why should coaches consider adopting an experiential approach to their work? The basic premise of this chapter has been that coaching practice often prioritises talking over experiencing and doing. Consistent with cognitive and adult learning theories, this more passive way of working sometimes yields dissatisfactory outcomes. Chairwork offers a different medium for CBC, which is dynamic, memorable, and uniquely powerful. However, with this power comes responsibility: chairwork should not be applied indiscriminately and may require adaptation depending on clients' individual needs and preferences. In addition, these methods risk theatricalising clients' concerns if they are used flippantly or insensitively. Effective chairwork practice, therefore, requires care, reflectivity, and appropriate training and supervision.

Cognitive behavioural chairwork is also not without limitations. Research is needed to determine its effectiveness and drive further developments in this area of practice. Furthermore, experiential methods lie outside mainstream coaching practice and may not be a good fit for all clients. That said, a great many individuals will be surprised by how much they can achieve when they show us, rather than tell us, what brings them to coaching (Moreno, 2008).

Five questions for further reflection

1. Which clients and which presenting issues benefit the most from cognitive behavioural chairwork?

Chairwork is suitable for all individuals, but clients who are willing to work in a creative, expressive, and emotive way are likely to find it particularly useful. Individuals who have experienced limited gains using traditional (discussion-focused) methods might also find chairwork more productive. In terms of target issues, chairwork lends itself particularly well to conflicts (eg, indecisions, unfinished business, and problematic styles of self-relating such as self-criticism) and behaviour skills training.

2. What should the coach do if a client refuses to engage in chairwork?

Collaboration is central to coaching, so coaches should respect the decision to decline chairwork. After all, there are many other experiential methods that the client may be more willing to use (eg, imagery-focused techniques). That said, exploring why chairwork is unacceptable or intolerable will often bring to light important information about the client (eg, performance anxieties, fears of negative evaluation, or avoidance of emotion).

3. How can chairwork be used in work with teams and organisations?

Chairwork has a long history of applications in group settings (Goulding & Goulding, 1979; Levitsky & Perls, 1969; Moreno, 2008) and usually involves the group members supporting an individual in their work with the chair(s) or the entire group participating in an enactment. Chairwork can also be incorporated into team meetings. For example, an empty seat might be used to represent entities such as 'our brand', 'the customer', or 'key stakeholders' which team members give voice to. This can help introduce new perspectives into discussions and stimulate creative thinking (Neve-Hanquet & Crespel, 2020).

4. What are some of the potential uses of chairwork in supervision?

Chairwork has as many applications in coaching supervision as it does in coaching practice. Examples include using interviews to help the supervisee separate from I-positions that dominate their practice (eg, the 'fixer'); exploring difficult coaching sessions through dramatisation and re-enactment; and facilitating two-chair dialogues with I-positions that affect the coach's performance (eg, the 'imposter'). Be creative!

5. When working online, what adaptations does chairwork require?

Online chairwork is often just as productive as face-to-face chairwork but may require some adjustments (Pugh *et al*, 2020). Reverting to the principles and processes of chairwork can inform these changes. For example, suppose the client is working in a restricted space or has limited chairs available. In this situation, they might move their occupied seat into different spaces in front of their webcam to embody different I-positions. Alternatively, parts can be placed in empty chairs on the coaches' side of the interaction or concretised using small objects (see Pugh & Bell, 2020; Pugh *et al*, 2020, for examples).

References

Alderson-Day, B., & Fernyhough, C. (2015). Inner speech: development, cognitive functions, phenomenology, and neurobiology. *Psychological Bulletin*, **141**, 931-965.

Angus, L.E. & Greenberg, L.S. (2011) *Working With Narrative In Emotion-Focused Therapy: Changing stories, changing lives*. Washington, USA: American Psychological Association.

Anstiss, T. & Gilbert, P. (2014). Compassionate mind coaching. In: J. Passmore (Ed) *Mastery in Coaching: A complete psychological toolkit for advanced coaching*. London, UK: Kogan Page Publishers, pp225-252.

Beck, A.T. (1991) Cognitive therapy as the integrative therapy. *Journal of Psychotherapy Integration*, 1, 191-198. doi: 10.1037/h0101233.

Beck, A.T. (1996) Beyond belief: a theory of modes, personality, and psychopathology. In: P. Salkovskis (Ed.) *Frontiers of Cognitive Therapy*. New York, USA: Guilford Press, pp1-26.

Bell, T., Montague, J., Elander, J. & Gilbert, P. (2020a) "A definite feel-it moment": Embodiment, externalisation and emotion during chair-work in compassion-focused therapy. *Counselling and Psychotherapy Research*, **20**, 143-53. doi: 10.1002/capr.12248.

Bell, T., Montague, J., Elander, J. & Gilbert, P. (2020b) "Suddenly you are King Solomon": Multiplicity, transformation and integration in compassion focused therapy chairwork. *Journal of Psychotherapy Integration*. doi: 10.1037/int0000240.

Brewin, C. R. (2006) Understanding cognitive behaviour therapy: a retrieval competition account. *Behaviour Research and Therapy*, **44**, 765-784. doi: 10.1016/j.brat.2006.02.005.

Bruner, J. (2002) *Making Stories: Law, literature, life*. London, UK: Harvard University Press.

Butollo, W., König, J., Karl, R., Henkel, C. & Rosner, R. (2014) Feasibility and outcome of dialogical exposure therapy for posttraumatic stress disorder: A pilot study with 25 outpatients. *Psychotherapy Research*, **24**, 514-521. doi: 10.1080/10503307.2013.851424.

Chadwick, P. (2003) Two chairs, self-schemata and a person-based approach to psychosis. *Behavioural and Cognitive Psychotherapy*, **31**, 439-449. doi: 10.1017/S1352465803004053.

Clarke, K. M. & Greenberg, L. S. (1986) Differential effects of the Gestalt two-chair intervention and problem solving in resolving decisional conflict. *Journal of Counseling Psychology*, **33**, 11–15. doi: 10.1037/0022-0167.33.1.11.

Conoley, C.W., Conoley, J.C., McConnell, J.A. & Kimzey, C.E. (1983) The effect of the ABCs of rational emotive therapy the empty-chair techniques of Gestalt therapy on anger reduction. *Psychotherapy: Theory, Research and Practice*, **20**, 112–117. doi: 10.1037/h0088470.

Cromarty, P. & Marks, I. (1995) Does rational role-play enhance the outcome of exposure therapy? *British Journal of Psychiatry*, **167**, 399–402. doi: 10.1192/bjp.167.3.399.

Day, A., De Haan, E., Sills, C., Bertie, C. & Blass, E. (2008) Coaches' experiences of critical moments in the coaching. *International Coaching Psychology Review*, **3**, 207–218.

de Oliveira, I.R. (2015) *Trial-based cognitive therapy: A manual for clinicians*. East Sussex, UK: Routledge.

de Oliveira, I.R., Powell, V.B., Wenzel, A., Caldas, M., Seixas, C., Almeida, C. & Sudak, D. (2012) Efficacy of the trial-based thought record, a new cognitive therapy strategy designed to change core beliefs, in social phobia. *Journal of Clinical Pharmacy and Therapeutics*, **37**, 328–334. doi: 10.1111/j.1365-2710.2011.01299.x.

Dryden, W. (2017) *Very Brief Cognitive Behavioural Coaching (VBCBC)*. Oxon, UK: Routledge.

Elliott, J.E. (1992) Use of anthetic dialogue in eliciting and challenging dysfunctional beliefs. *Journal of Cognitive Psychotherapy*, **6**, 137–143.

Hermans, H.J.M. (2002) The dialogical self as a society of mind: Introduction. *Theory and Psychology*, **12**, 147–160. doi: 10.1177/0959354302122001.

Elliott, R. & Greenberg, L.S. (2021) *Emotion-Focused Counselling in Action*. London, UK: Sage.

Gilbert, P., Clarke, M., Hempel, S., Miles, J.N. & Irons, C. (2004) Criticizing and reassuring oneself: An exploration of forms, styles and reasons in female students. *British Journal of Clinical Psychology*, **43**, 31–50. doi: 10.1348/014466504772812959.

Goldfried, M.R., Castonguay, L.G., Hayes, A.M., Drozd, J.F. & Shapiro, D.A. (1997) A comparative analysis of the therapeutic focus in cognitive-behavioral and psychodynamic-interpersonal sessions. *Journal of Consulting and Clinical Psychology*, **65**, 740–748. doi: 10.1037/0022-006X.65.5.740.

Goulding, M.M. & Goulding, R.L. (1979) *Changing Lives Through Redecision Therapy*. New York, USA: Brunner/Mazel.

Greenberg, L.S. (2007) A guide to conducting a task analysis of psychotherapeutic change. *Psychotherapy Research*, **17**, 15–30. doi: 10.1080/10503300600720390.

Greenberg, L.S. (2015) *Emotion-Focused Therapy: Coaching clients to work through their feelings* (2nd edition) Washington, USA: American Psychological Association.

Greenberg, L.S. & Malcolm, W. (2002) Resolving unfinished business: Relating process to outcome. *Journal of Consulting and Clinical Psychology*, **70**, 406–416. doi: 10.1037/0022-006X.70.2.406.

Greenberg, L.S., Safran, J. & Rice, L. (1989) Experiential therapy: Its relation to cognitive therapy. In: A. Freeman, K.M. Simon and L.E. Beutler (Eds) *Comprehensive Handbook of Cognitive Therapy*. New York, USA: Plenum Press, pp169–187.

Hayes, S.C., Strosahl, K.D. & Wilson, K.G. (2016) *Acceptance and Commitment Therapy: The process and practice of mindful change* (2nd edition) New York, USA: Guilford Press.

Hermans, H.J.M. (2002) The dialogical self as a society of mind: Introduction. *Theory and Psychology*, **12**, 147–160. doi: 10.1177/0959354302122001.

Holtforth, M.G., Hayes, A.M., Sutter, M., Wilm, K., Schmied, E., Laurenceau, J.P. & Caspar, F. (2012) Fostering cognitive-emotional processing in the treatment of depression: A preliminary investigation in exposure-based cognitive therapy. *Psychotherapy and Psychosomatics*, **81**, 259–260. doi: doi.org/10.1159/000336813.

Holtforth, M.G., Krieger, T., Zimmermann, J., Altenstein-Yamanaka, D., Dörig, N., Meisch, L. & Hayes, A.M. (2019) A randomized-controlled trial of cognitive-behavioral therapy for depression with integrated techniques from emotion-focused and exposure therapies. *Psychotherapy Research*, **29**, 30–44. doi: 10.1080/10503307.2017.1397796.

Kazantzis, N., Luong, H.K., Usatoff, A. S., Impala, T., Yew, R.Y. & Hofmann, S.G. (2018) The processes of cognitive behavioral therapy: A review of meta-analyses. *Cognitive Therapy and Research*, **42**, 349–357. doi: 10.1007/s10608-018-9920-y.

Kellerman, P.F. (1992) *Focus on Psychodrama: The therapeutic aspects of psychodrama*. London, UK: Jessica Kingsley Publishers.

Kolb, D.A. (1984) *Experiential Learning: Experience as the source of learning and development*. Englewood Cliffs, USA: Prentice Hall.

Konopka, A., Hermans, H. J. M., Goncalves, M. M. (2019). *Handbook of dialogical self theory and psychotherapy: Bridging psychotherapeutic and cultural traditions*. Oxon, UK: Routledge.

Kross, E. & Ayduk, O. (2017) *Self-distancing: Theory, research, and current directions. Advances in Experimental Social Psychology*, **55**, 81–136. doi: 10.1016/bs.aesp.2016.10.002.

Kross, E. & Grossmann, I. (2012) Boosting wisdom: Distance from the self enhances wise reasoning, attitudes, and behavior. *Journal of Experimental Psychology: General*, **141**, 43–48. doi: 10.1037/a0024158.

Kushnir, A. & Orkibi, H. (2021) Concretization as a mechanism of change in psychodrama: Procedures and benefits. *Frontiers in Psychology*, **12**, 1–13. doi: 10.3389/fpsyg.2021.633069.

Lazarus, A. A. (1966) Behaviour rehearsal vs. non-directive therapy vs. advice in effecting behaviour change. *Behaviour Research and Therapy*, **4**, 209–212. doi: 10.1016/0005-7967(66)90068-4.

Levy, K.N. & Scala, J.W. (2012) Transference, transference interpretations, and transference-focused psychotherapies. *Psychotherapy*, **49**, 391–403. doi: 10.1037/a0029371.

Levitsky, A. & Perls, F. (1969) The rules and games of Gestalt therapy. In: H.M. Ruitenbeek (Ed.) *Group Therapy Today: Styles, methods, and techniques*. New York, USA: Atherton Press, pp221–230.

Ling, N.Y.C., Serpell, L., Burnett-Stuart, S. & Pugh, M. (2021) Interviewing anorexia: How do individuals with anorexia nervosa experience voice dialogue with their eating disorder voice? A qualitative analysis. *Clinical Psychology and Psychotherapy*. doi: 10.1002/cpp.2652.

Lipsky, M.J., Kassinove, H. & Miller, N.J. (1980) Effects of rational-emotive therapy, rational role reversal, and rational-emotive imagery on the emotional adjustment of community mental health center patients. *Journal of Consulting and Clinical Psychology*, **48**, 366–374. doi: 10.1037/0022-006X.48.3.366.

McNeilage, L.A. & Adams, K.A. (1979) The method of contrasted role-plays: An insight-orientated model for role-playing in assertiveness training groups. *Psychotherapy: Theory, Research and Practice*, **16**, 158–170. doi: 10.1037/h0086043.

McNeel, J.R. (1999) Redecision therapy as a process of new belief acquisition. *Journal of Redecision Therapy*, **1**, 103–115.

Mennin, D.S., Ellard, K.K., Fresco, D.M. & Gross, J.J. (2013) United we stand: Emphasizing commonalities across cognitive-behavioral therapies. *Behavior Therapy*, **44**, 234–248. doi: 10.1016/j.beth.2013.02.004.

Miranda, R. & Andersen, S.M. (2007) The therapeutic relationship: Implications from social cognition and transference. In: P. Gilbert and R.L. Leahy (Eds) *The Therapeutic Relationship in the Cognitive Behavioral Therapies*. Hove, UK: Routledge, pp63–89.

Moreno, J.L. (2008) *The Essential Moreno: Writings on psychodrama, group method, and spontaneity*. New Paltz, USA: Tusitala Publishing.

Mulder, R., Murray, G. & Rucklidge, J. (2017) Common versus specific factors in psychotherapy: opening the black box. *The Lancet Psychiatry*, **4**, 953–962. doi: 10.1016/S2215-0366(17)30100-1.

Muntigl, P., Horvath, A.O., Chubak, L. & Angus, L. (2020) Getting to "yes": Overcoming client reluctance to engage in chair work. *Frontiers in Psychology*, **11**, 1–16. doi: 10.3389/fpsyg.2020.582856.

Muran, J.C., Safran, J.D., Eubanks, C.F. & Gorman, B.S. (2018) The effect of alliance-focused training on a cognitive-behavioral therapy for personality disorders. *Journal of Consulting and Clinical Psychology*, **86**, 384–397. doi: 10.1037/ccp0000284.

Neenan, M. (2018) *Cognitive Behavioural Coaching: Distinctive features*. Oxon, UK: Routledge.

Neenan, M. & Dryden, W. (2020) *Cognitive Behavioural Coaching: A guide to problem-solving and personal development* (3rd edition). Oxon, UK: Routledge.

Newell, R. & Shrubb, S. (1994) Attitude change and behaviour therapy in body dysmorphic disorder: Two case reports. *Behavioural and Cognitive Psychotherapy*, **22**, 163–169. doi: 10.1017/S1352465800011942.

Neve-Hanquet, C. & Crespel, A. (2020) *Facilitating Collective Intelligence: A handbook for trainers, coaches, consultants and leaders*. Oxon, UK: Routledge.

Newman, M.G., Castonguay, L.G., Borkovec, T.D., Fisher, A.J. & Nordberg, S.S. (2008) An open trial of integrative therapy for generalized anxiety disorder. *Psychotherapy: Theory, Research, Practice, Training*, **45**, 135–147. doi:10.1037/0033-3204.45.2.135.

Newman, M.G., Castonguay, L.G., Borkovec, T.D., Fisher, A.J., Boswell, J.F., Szkodny, L.E. & Nordberg, S.S. (2011) A randomized controlled trial of cognitive-behavioral therapy for generalized anxiety disorder with integrated techniques from emotion-focused and interpersonal therapies. *Journal of Consulting and Clinical Psychology*, **79**, 171–181. doi:10.1037/a0022489.

Palmer, S. & Szymanska, K. (2019) Cognitive behavioural coaching: An integrative approach. In: S. Palmer and A. Whybrow (Eds) *Handbook of Coaching Psychology: A guided for practitioners* (2nd edition). Oxon, UK: Routledge, pp108–127.

Padesky, C.A. (1997) A more effective treatment focus for social phobia? *International Cognitive Therapy Newsletter* **11**, 1–3.

Paivio, S.C., Jarry, J.L., Chagigiorgis, H., Hall, I. & Ralston, M. (2010) Efficacy of two versions of emotion-focused therapy for resolving child abuse trauma. *Psychotherapy Research*, **20**, 353–366. doi: 10.1080/10503300903505274.

Passmore, J. & Sinclair, T. (2020) *Becoming a Coach: The essential ICF guide*. West Sussex, UK: Pavilion Publishing.

Perls, F.S. (1969) *Gestalt Therapy Verbatim*. Lafayette, USA: Real People.

Pugh, M. (2019a) *Cognitive Behavioural Chairwork: Distinctive features*. Oxon, UK: Routledge.

Pugh, M. (2019b) A little less talk, a little more action: A dialogical approach to cognitive therapy. *The Cognitive Behavioural Therapist*, e47, 1–24. doi: 10.1017/S1754470X19000333.

Pugh, M. (in press) Single session chairwork: Overview and case illustration of brief dialogical psychotherapy. *British Journal of Guidance and Counselling*.

Pugh, M. & Bell, T. (2020) Process-based chairwork: Applications and innovations in the time of COVID-19. *European Journal of Counselling Theory, Research, and Practice*, **4**, 1–8.

Pugh, M., Bell, T. & Dixon, A. (2020) Delivering tele-chairwork: A qualitative survey of expert therapists. *Psychotherapy Research*. doi: 10.1080/10503307.2020.1854486.

Pugh, M. & Broome, N. (2020) Dialogical coaching: An experiential approach to personal and professional development. *Consulting Psychology Journal: Practice and Research*, **72**, 223–241. doi: 10.1037/cpb0000162.

Pugh, M. & Margetts, A. (2020) Are you sitting (un)comfortably? Action-based supervision and supervisory drift. *The Cognitive Behaviour Therapist*, **13**, 1–19. doi: 10.1017/S1754470X20000185.

Pugh, M. & Salter, C. (2018) Motivational chairwork: An experiential approach to resolving ambivalence. *European Journal of Counselling Theory, Research and Practice*, **2**, 1–15.

Robinson A.L., McCague, E.A. & Whissell, C. (2014) "That chair work thing was great": A pilot study of group-based emotion-focused therapy for anxiety and depression. *Person-Centered and Experiential Psychotherapies*, **13**, 263–277. doi: 10.1080/14779757.2014.910131.

Roediger, E., Stevens, B.A. & Brockman, R. (2018) *Contextual Schema Therapy: An integrative approach to personality disorders, emotional dysregulation, and interpersonal functioning*. Oakland, USA: Context Press.

Speed, B.C., Goldstein, B.L. & Goldfried, M.R. (2018) Assertiveness training: A forgotten evidence-based treatment. *Clinical Psychology: Science and Practice*, **25**, 1–20. doi: 10.1111/cpsp.12216.

Shahar, B., Carlin, E.R., Engle, D.E., Hegde, J., Szepsenwol, O. & Arkowitz, H. (2012) A pilot investigation of emotion-focused two-chair dialogue intervention for self-criticism. *Clinical Psychology and Psychotherapy,* **19**, 496–507. doi: 10.1002/cpp.762.

Stiegler, J.R., Binder, P., Hjeltnes, A., Stige, S.H. & Schanche, E. (2018) 'It's heavy, intense, horrendous and nice': Clients' experiences in two-chair dialogues. *Person-Centred and Experiential Psychotherapies,* **17**, 1–21. doi: 10.1080/14779757.2018.1472138.

Stone, H. & Stone, S. (1989) *Embracing Our Selves: The voice dialogue manual.* Novato, USA: Nataraj Publishing.

Teasdale, J.D. (1997) The relationship between cognition and emotion: the mind-in-place in mood disorders. In: D.M. Clark & C.G. Fairburn (Eds) *The Science and Practice of Cognitive Behaviour Therapy.* Oxford, UK: Oxford University Press, pp67–93.

Teasdale, J.D. & Barnard, P.J. (1993) *Affect, Cognition and Change: Re-modelling depressive thought.* Hove, UK: Lawrence Erlbaum Associations.

Thoma, N.C. & Greenberg, L.S. (2015) Integrating emotion-focused therapy into cognitive-behavioral therapy. In: N.C. Thoma and D. McKay (Eds) *Working With Emotion In Cognitive-Behavioral Practice: Techniques for clinical practice.* New York, USA: Guilford Press, pp239–262.

Trachsel, M., Ferrari, L. & Holtforth, M.G. (2012) Resolving partnership ambivalence: A randomized controlled trial of very brief cognitive and experiential interventions with follow-up. *Canadian Journal of Counselling and Psychotherapy,* **46**, 239–258.

Watson, J.C. & Bedard, D.L. (2006) Clients' emotional processing in psychotherapy: A comparison between cognitive-behavioral and process-experiential therapies. *Journal of Consulting and Clinical Psychology,* **74**, 152–159. doi: 10.1037/0022-006X.74.1.152.

Wiser, S.L. & Goldfried, M.R. (1993) Comparative study of emotional experiencing in psychodynamic-interpersonal and cognitive-behavioral therapies. *Journal of Consulting and Clinical Psychology,* **61**, 892–895. doi: 10.1037/0022-006X.61.5.892.

PART THREE:
Third Wave

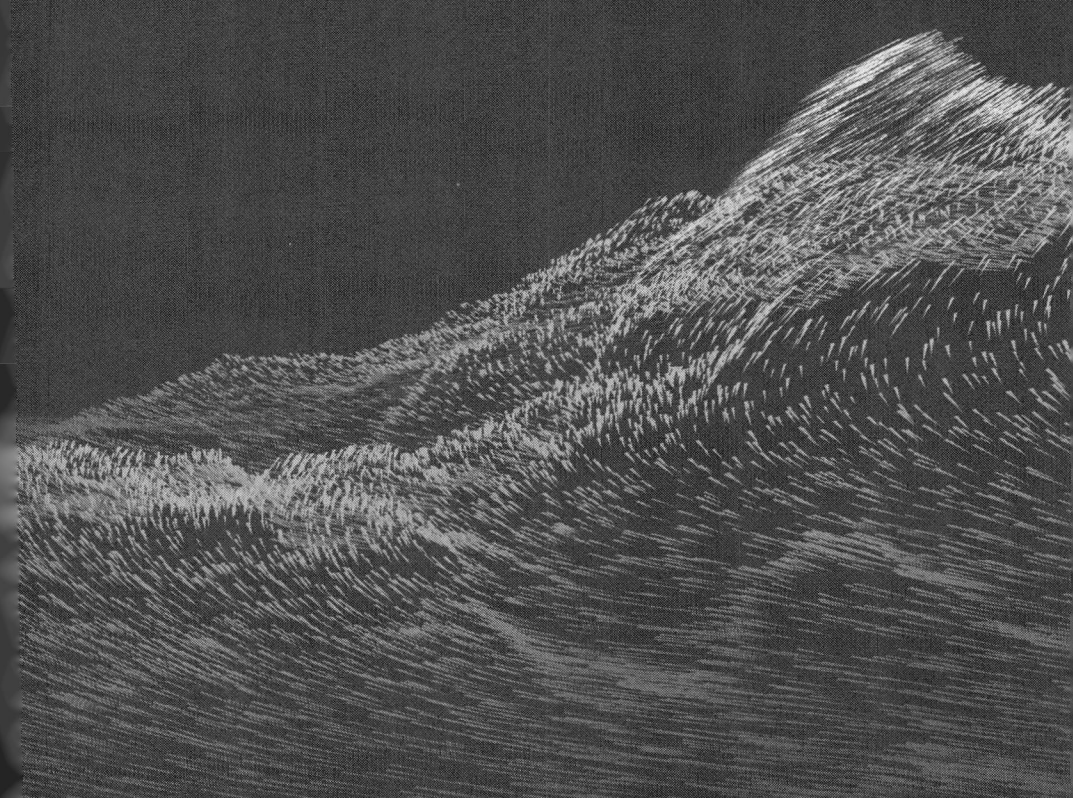

Introduction: Third wave cognitive behavioural approaches

Jonathan Passmore and Sarah Leach

As we have noted in Part One, first wave approaches were concerned with behaviour, in the belief it was impossible to step into and fully understand the black box of the mind. In the second wave the focus was on helping clients to recognise the connection between their behaviour, emotion and cognitions and then to support clients in challenging their unhelpful thinking, through analysis of how helpful, logical and evidenced based their original thinking was. The aim is to help clients develop a more rational approach to their thinking.

In turning to third wave approaches, the issue of definition becomes more complicated. Strictly speaking there is no clear consensus on what defines 'third wave CBT'. At a simple level, third wave CBT includes evidence-based therapies that have developed since the second wave approaches of Beck (1976), Ellis (1962) and Lazarus (1976). There is some degree of consensus regarding some of the therapies we can label third wave. For example, mindfulness-based CBT, acceptance and commitment therapy (ACT), schema therapy, meta-cognitive therapy, compassion-based therapy, and dialectic behavioural therapy (DBT) are all generally agreed upon as third wave therapies.

Table 3a Common third wave approaches	
Approach	Originator
Mindfulness-based cognitive behavioural therapy	Zindel Segal and Mark Williams
Mindfulness-based stress reduction programme	Jon Kabat-Zinn
Acceptance and commitment therapy (ACT)	Steven Hayes
Schema therapy	Jeffrey Young
Meta-cognitive therapy	Adrian Wells
Dialectic behavioural therapy (DBT)	Marsha Linehan
Compassion-focused therapy (CFT)	Paul Gilbert

There are also a range of other therapy interventions which are sometimes referred to as third wave approaches but are less popular or are on the periphery of third wave approaches. These may include approaches such as extended behavioural activation (eBA) and functional analytic psychotherapy (FAP).

Given this variety of approaches within the third wave, offering a single definition has proved hard. One aspect of third wave CBT approaches is their greater focus on the client's overall life, and whether they are thriving and flourishing, rather than looking at symptoms or simply surviving. This starts to add aspects from positive psychology to CBT, such as inviting clients to draw on their strengths.

This connection between CBT and positive psychology is debated. While positive psychology approaches are used in some approaches such as mindfulness, they are less common features in others, such as DBT, and therefore positive psychology is better positioned as 'beyond third wave CBT'.

An alternative view is to argue that third wave CBTs have a focus that is not purely symptom-based, but that encourages clients to consider their whole selves from behaviour, thoughts and emotion to values and identity.

Another way to differentiate third wave approaches from previous waves is by their focus on emotion and how clients are encouraged to engage with their emotional lives. A common feature is that third wave approaches typically place a greater focus on acceptance, non-judgement and compassion or enabling clients to more effectively manage unhelpful thoughts through separation or disassociation from them, while also placing a greater focus on overall wellbeing.

So, what is third wave CBT? There seems to be no clear conceptual bond that binds all the third wave approaches together. As such, in this book we have defined third wave CBT approaches as those that recognise:

- firstly, the relationship between cognition, emotion and behaviour
- second, the importance of values and identity
- third, the value in naming and being choiceful about which thoughts and emotions we choose to act upon
- Finally, that the approach has a strong evidence base, which demonstrates its efficacy.

While the evidence for third wave approaches is still growing, a number of studies have evaluated the evidence. For example, a study by Hunot *et al* (2013) examined the evidence for ACT and concluded that it achieved broadly similar outcomes to CBT for acute depression. Kahl *et al.* (2012) did a similar review and concluded there is 'little doubt that the presented third wave methods are principally efficacious'.

While the third wave approaches have generally developed since the 2000s, relatively little work has been done by coaches to translate these approaches for the client's presenting issues or contexts relevant to coaching. Some work has been done in the area of mindfulness, ACT and compassion-focused therapy. Our intent in this part of the book is to review this work and provide a more in-depth and comprehensive translation of these ideas relevant for advanced coaching practitioners interested in evidenced-based psychologically-informed practice.

References

Beck, A.T. (1976) *Cognitive Therapy and the Emotional Disorders*. New York: International Universities Press.

Ellis, A. (1962) *Reason and Emotion in Psychotherapy*. New York, NY: Citadel Press

Hunot, V., Moore T.H.M, Caldwell, D.M., Furukawa, T.A., Davies, P., Jones, H., Honyashiki, M., Chen, P., Lewis, G. and Churchill, R. (2013). 'Third wave' Cognitive and Behavioural Therapies versus other psychological therapies for depression (Review). *Cochrane Database of Systematic Reviews*, 10. DOI: 10.1002/14651858.CD008705.pub2.

Kahl, K.G., Winter, L. & Schweiger, U. (2012) The third wave of cognitive behavioural therapies. *Current Opinion in Psychiatry*, **25** (6) 522–528. Available online at: doi:10.1097/yco.0b013e328358e531 Accessed 10 July 2021.

Lazarus, A. (1976) *Multimodal Behavioral Therapy*. New York: Springer.

Chapter 4
Mindfulness and Coaching: Theory, research and practice

Jonathan Passmore, Katherine Finlay and Simon Barnes

Introduction

Mindfulness, an ancient Eastern practice, has become a modern and widely accepted workplace intervention over the last 40 years. Much of this successful transfer from religious observance to daily workplace routine is connected to the development of two highly successful programmes developed during the 1970s and 1990s – *mindfulness-based stress reduction* (MBSR), and *mindfulness-based cognitive therapy* (MBCT), as interventions to address stress, depression, and a range of other conditions.

In this chapter we will explore these foundational roots, and the wider theoretical underpinnings of mindfulness, before considering the developing evidence for its efficacy as a workplace tool and, lastly, practices which can be used by coaches to support themselves and their clients.

Theoretical foundations

The term mindfulness is derived from a translation of the Hindu term 'Sati'. The word combines aspects of 'awareness', 'attention' and 'remembering', these elements being conducted with non-judgment, acceptance, kindness and friendliness to oneself and to others.

The practice dates back over 2500 years, with origins in the Buddhist faith, although there are common parallel practices in the three Abrahamic faiths (Christianity, Judaism and Islam). Given this, it's likely the practice was a common pre-history practice used across cultures before written records emerged. Since the 1970s and an emergence of a literature describing, exploring and reviewing the nature of mindfulness, multiple writers have offered 'definitions' of the practice. Bhikkhu (1998) suggests that at its most simple mindfulness can be considered to be 'reflective awareness' (p47). Similarly, Chaskalson (2014) suggests it is:

> *'the quality of awareness that comes from paying attention to yourself, others and the world around you' (p6)*

Kabat-Zinn (1991), meanwhile, suggests:

> *'Mindfulness is simply a practical way to be more in touch with the fullness of your being through a systematic process of self-observation, self-inquiry and mindful action. There is nothing cold, analytical or unfeeling about it. The overall tenor of mindfulness practices gentle, appreciative, and nurturing.' (p13)*

However, there remains a lack of an agreed operational definition (Bishop *et al*, 2004), which has created difficulties in researching the concept (Lutz *et al*, 2015). This may be because there has been a shift in how mindfulness is used: it is no longer a purely religious practice, but has become increasingly secularised and decoupled from religion (Seema & Säre, 2019). Since globalisation made Buddhism accessible in the West, Cohen (2010) argued that this allowed the secularisation of mindfulness and it became possible to adopt mindful practices without making the complete life changes necessary to fully adopt Buddhism. Arat (2017) suggested that mindfulness has been 'hacked' by a post-secular culture which has adopted the language of mindfulness whilst isolating it from its religious foundations. This secularisation of mindfulness echoes changes in our culture, but as a result there is the risk of a weakened or diluted form of 'pop' mindfulness being disseminated. To avoid this, our objective in this section is to explore the underpinning theoretical foundations.

State and trait mindfulness

If mindfulness is understood at the most basic level as the ability to stay in the present moment, then it represents a fusion of *state* and *trait* processes. Typically, people will present as having a *trait-like* level of natural mindfulness that remains stable across their lifespan and is indicative of their intrinsic personality or disposition. Trait mindfulness can be assessed via questionnaires such as the Five Facet Mindfulness Questionnaire (Christopher *et al*, 2012). Higher levels of trait mindfulness positively predict many aspects of health, work and life satisfaction (Mesmer-Magnus *et al*, 2017).

By contrast, state mindfulness refers to fluctuating levels of mindfulness that may vary in response to stressors, health, situation and context (Brown & Ryan, 2003). For example, state mindfulness may drop after failing to meet a work deadline and negative thought processes may become problematic ('I'm clearly not able to deliver at this level') and lead to poor self-evaluations ('I am not worth employing'). State mindfulness is often measured using more rapid questionnaires such as the Toronto Mindfulness Scale (Lau *et al*, 2006). At work, higher levels of trait mindfulness lead to stronger job satisfaction, performance and interpersonal relationships (Mesmer-Magnus *et al*, 2017). Research does suggest, however, that it may be possible to improve trait mindfulness: Kiken *et al* (2015) asked 235 participants to undertake a brief mindfulness practice each week for eight weeks and tracked their state and trait mindfulness levels. Their data demonstrated that the trajectories of improvement in state mindfulness were linked to parallel changes in trait mindfulness. When participants had grown their state mindfulness through repeated practice, that contributed to a more mindful and positive disposition (trait mindfulness).

Monitor and acceptance theory (MAT)

The broader theoretical underpinnings of mindfulness have been relatively weakly outlined, but consistency emerges over the two components that are the most important: *Monitoring* and *acceptance* (Quaglia *et al*, 2014). *Monitoring* is the mechanism by which being mindful and remaining in the present moment allows us to notice our sensory and perceptual experiences (Lindsay & Creswell, 2017). *Acceptance* is a mental attitude of non-judgement, openness and receptivity (Brown & Ryan, 2003), which allows us to embrace experiences (positive and negative) and accept them as they are without need for change. These two components are the key skills targeted in most mindfulness-based interventions. Emerging from these components is one of the most promising theories attempting to explain mindfulness: monitor and acceptance theory (MAT).

MAT was first outlined by Lindsay and Creswell (2017). They argue that there are two active mechanisms which explain the impact of mindfulness:

1. By being more aware of present moment experiences, individuals' skills in attention monitoring are improved, as is their cognitive function. However, this can increase their levels of emotional reactivity, particularly in beginner meditators.
2. Heightened negative emotional reactivity, moods and stress can therefore be reduced by accepting present experiences and 'changing one's relationship' with the present.

Together, these two mechanisms explain how mindfulness training may improve monitoring and acceptance so that momentary emotional or situational stimuli may be processed more efficiently (Teper *et al*, 2013). This then allows for attention to be refocused on cognitive performance and self-compassion. If skills in monitoring (eg of increased heart rate or shallow breathing) are improved but acceptance does not increase, then emotional distress may be increased, which may be difficult to resolve (eg panic attacks may occur in situations of high workplace pressure). However, if acceptance grows alongside monitoring, then cognitive, emotional and physical experiences may be defused. MAT argues that mindfulness may initially trigger rises in emotional and physical agitation as individuals practice their monitoring skills. This increase then recalibrates when acceptance skills improve to the extent that the client can allow thoughts/emotions to exist and pass without avoiding, suppressing or fixating on them. MAT sees acceptance as a dynamic emotion regulation skill that requires practice and development, hence the need for the self-compassion practices that will be outlined later in this chapter. Currently, there has been little experimental literature which has tested the hypotheses outlined by MAT, but it is likely to be an area of research growth over forthcoming years.

Table 4.1: Cognitive and affective outcomes of mindfulness

Cognitive outcomes	Affective outcomes
Improved selective attention	Intensified positive and negative reactivity (initially)
Prolonged and sustained attention direction	Affect regulation
Enhanced ability to use task switching	Reductions in depressive and anxiety symptoms
Increased working memory	Lower perceived stress
Heightened capacity to have insight and 'aha' moments	Feelings of relaxation

(Adapted from Lindsay & Creswell, 2017)

Two further theories have been linked to mindfulness and they explain how mindfulness operates from different viewpoints: exposure theory and escape theory.

Exposure theory

Behavioural models of learning (such as those covered in Chapter 1) suggest that with repeated exposure to a stimulus, our responses can become habitual (Treanor, 2011). For example, with prolonged work-related stress, clients may experience reactive work avoidance and procrastination as a result of physical or emotional burnout. Supporting a client to break this response can therefore require repeatedly confronting the stressor/stimulus whilst simultaneously refusing to engage in the habitual behavioural pattern (Craske, 1999), allowing an inhibitory association to form – exposure therapy. Treanor (2011) argued that mindfulness can operate like a form of exposure therapy. By staying in the present moment, observing experiences, emotions and thoughts non-judgementally, mindfulness may heighten awareness of triggers (exposure) but decrease the individual's stress response and emotional reactivity to these triggers. Mindfulness interventions may therefore naturally increase awareness of these cues and interrupt the relationship between stimulus detection and affective response (Jha *et al*, 2007).

Escape theory

Heatherton and Baumeister (1991) were originally working in the field of binge eating, but their work has been widely adopted as a theory that extends beyond eating behaviour. Their seminal paper argued that people are motivated to escape from self-awareness as being self-reflective and highly self-aware is uncomfortable and even aversive. Certainly, when we focus on ourselves with high levels of introspection, we can encounter feelings of dissatisfaction with aspects of our current life such as in career progression or coping with failed expectations (Donnelly *et al*, 2016).

Escape theory argues that we engage in cognitive and behavioural responses to 'escape' from periods of heightened self-awareness (Wicklund, 1975). Most commonly, the chosen method of 'escape' is to narrow the focus of attention. Narrowing our attentional focus allows us to avoid thoughts about the implications of events and associated negative emotions. However, this is a form of cognitive blunting that limits our capacity for self-reflection, and could reduce personal growth and openness (Heatherton & Baumeister, 1991).

With repeated mindfulness practice it becomes possible to reflect on the self without the need to 'escape' from our minds or from heightened self-awareness (Baer, 2003). Escaping becomes less important as it becomes possible to observe and accept self-reflection and thoughts about life (dis) satisfaction without needing to hide from them (Finlay *et al*, 2021b). Segal *et al* (2004) consider this a process of 'meta-cognitive insight', where it is possible to notice and take a perspective on one's own thoughts without self-judgement and rumination. Mindfulness has an advantage in that it can be practised anywhere and at any time, therefore it can be used to respond to 'escape' thoughts and discomforting self-awareness whenever they occur (Teasdale *et al*, 2000).

Research evidence

As in many areas of coaching, the use of mindfulness as part of coaching practice while much discussed, is under researched. As a result, in this section we will draw on wider research from mindfulness studies over the last 40 years and in so doing consider their relevance for coaches and coaching clients.

There have been a large number of meta-analysis studies examining the evidence on mindfulness-based therapies (Bassam-Khoury et al, 2013) and specifically mindfulness in the workplace (Good et al, 2016; Passmore, 2019a)

Mindfulness in health

Mindfulness has been widely used in health research and clinical practice, principally with chronic health conditions (Cillessen et al, 2019). Giving patient populations some training in self-directed attention through mindfulness can result in increased tolerance of physical sensations, thoughts and emotions and allow them to improve their self-management of health and wellbeing (Finlay et al, 2021a). With practice, mindfulness is thought to allow people living with ill-health to separate their struggle with physical symptoms (primary suffering) from the psychological impact and distress brought on by those symptoms (secondary suffering) (Finlay et al, 2021b). For example, it is possible to observe pain sensations but mindfully choose to avoid catastrophising about that pain (Hearn & Finlay, 2018). By staying mindful in spite of pain, it is possible to engage in coping strategies and activities that minimise psychological distress and reduce the dominance of pain-related thoughts (Bawa et al, 2015).

The two dominant forms of mindfulness intervention programmes, mindfulness-based stress reduction (MBSR; Kabat-Zinn (2013); and mindfulness-based cognitive therapy (MBCT; Teasdale et al, 2000) have shown significant promise for managing physical and psychological health and secondary suffering. Mindfulness can be used in both clinical and non-clinical samples with comparable outcomes. In clinical samples, for example, mindfulness has been shown to improve recovery after cancer (Cillessen et al, 2019), reduces obesity and improves eating behaviours (Rogers et al, 2017), minimises stress during pregnancy (Dhillon et al, 2017) and reduces stress, anxiety and depression (Hofmann et al, 2010).

In the general population, a large-scale meta-analysis by Querstret et al (2020) with people who did not have chronic health conditions found that MBSR and MBCT both reduced symptoms of worry, stress, depression and anxiety and improved quality of life and wellbeing. Interestingly, MBCT outperformed MBSR and generated larger effect sizes in these non-clinical populations. This suggests that there is broad benefit of mindfulness-based programmes to health and wellbeing even in samples which do not have specific health conditions.

Part of the challenge of undertaking MBCT and MBSR relates to the number of weeks needed to complete the programme. Yet recent work on the number of mindfulness sessions needed to generate positive outcomes suggested that there was no difference between more sessions and fewer (Strohmaier, 2020). Instead, what mattered was the level of practice, the intensity of the learning and actually using the techniques. Consequently, there has been growth in the use of 'brief mindfulness practices' as an alternative to full mindfulness programmes.

Brief mindfulness refers to the use of short mindfulness techniques such as a body scan or breath awareness exercise in isolation, without completing a full MBCT or MBSR programme. Such brief interventions have been found to improve a huge range of physical and psychological factors, ranging from memory and learning (Alberts & Thewissen, 2011), pain tolerance and pain-related distress (Liu *et al*, 2013), to self-control and energy levels (Canby *et al*, 2015). Brief mindfulness practices can range from as little as ten minutes to multi-sessions across two weeks, all showing positive benefits, though with small effect sizes (Schumer *et al*, 2018). This flexibility to use mindfulness either as a full intervention programme or as a brief practice has particular application to the coaching psychology context.

Mindfulness in counselling

Given that mindfulness has proven beneficial for improving emotional wellbeing in clinical and non-clinical populations, its wider use in counselling settings will not come as a surprise. Mindfulness within counselling offers a way to encourage clients to experience events 'fully and without defence, as they are' (Hayes, 1994, p30). This may offer breathing space for clients to reflect on their thoughts, progress and therapy without feeling under pressure to demonstrate improvements to their therapist (Baer, 2003).

Mindfulness is used within a number of therapeutic modalities including:

- emotion regulation therapy (ERT)
- dialectical behaviour therapy (DBT)
- acceptance and commitment therapy (ACT)
- relapse prevention (RP).

Additionally, the foundations of MBCT are built on cognitive behavioural therapy and MBCT extends the core mindfulness approaches to include a greater focus on awareness of thoughts.

Mindfulness has been most impactfully incorporated within *acceptance and commitment therapy* (ACT) (Hayes *et al*, 1999), a third wave behavioural therapy. ACT is a model of psychotherapy that challenges many of the tenets of cognitive-behavioural therapy (as described in Chapter 6). Rather than putting the onus on clients to work harder to modify their dysfunctional thoughts and realign their thinking with reality, instead it focuses on helping clients recognise and observe their thoughts (Hayes *et al*, 2013). ACT encourages clients to recognise the futility of trying to control negative thoughts and mute the distress caused by that struggle (Hayes, 2016). It challenges the notion that we should be happy at all times and advocates for acceptance of negative emotions as part of the human experience (Pearson *et al*, 2010). Mindfulness meditations are often used within ACT to teach clients how to broaden their behavioural repertoire to respond to present-moment stimuli (Hayes *et al*, 2013). Mindfulness and ACT therefore have a close relationship and both prioritise defusion of thoughts and acceptance of our own experiences (Gaudiano, 2006).

Besides recognising the integration of mindfulness-based approaches within other counselling modalities, the most impactful aspect of mindfulness here may be less for coaching clients and more for coaches themselves. Building a personal mindfulness practice is a strong insulator against job-related burnout (Klein *et al*, 2020). Mindfulness meditation and heightened self-awareness are widely found to protect against emotional and physical fatigue (Luken & Sammons, 2016). Mindfulness also enables the coach to maintain increased levels of personal self-awareness and self-compassion, which then translates into greater empathy for their clients (Burton *et al*, 2017; Conversano *et al*, 2020). The benefits of engaging in mindfulness as a practitioner have been demonstrated in a huge variation of professional groups, from white collar workers (Pflügner *et al*, 2021) to healthcare professionals (Lomas *et al*, 2018) and sports coaches (Pawsey *et al*, 2021). As Kinser *et al* (2016) argued, 'awareness is the first step' to being a resilient practitioner and developing a personal mindfulness practice may be a wise decision as a coach.

Mindfulness at work

The introduction of mindfulness to organisation life can be largely attributed to Langer and colleagues' research (Weick & Roberts,1993), who presented mindfulness as cognitive flexibility and attention to novelty (Langer, 1989). We can divide the benefits from organisational mindfulness practice in to five aspects: attention, cognition, emotion, behaviour and physiology.

Mindfulness is theorized to affect human functioning primarily through attention, specifically it has been shown to improve three qualities of attention – *stability, control,* and *efficiency*. Stability refers to the ability of the mind to focus on a single task or event. Mindfulness training is associated with a reduction in mind wandering and greater focused attention (Brewer *et al*, 2011). These improved levels of attention relate to both visual (MacLean *et al*, 2010) and auditory tasks (Lutz *et al*, 2009). It is difficult to precisely identify why this occurs, and it may simply be related to the meta-attention of noticing the change in attention and returning the focus more quickly to the target experience.

There is considerable research linking mindfulness and attentional qualities to cognitive performance (eg, Smallwood & Schooler, 2015), specifically the two aspects of cognitive capacity and cognitive flexibility (see Chapter 6 for a discussion). In the former, research has shown working memory is effected through sustained mindfulness practice, with an increase in working memory capacity growing with experience (Roeser *et al*, 2013). Secondly, the evidence suggests regular mindfulness practice is also associated with the ability to process and respond to novel information by assessing patterns and relationships (Tang *et al*, 2007). Thirdly, mindfulness appears to influence emotions through the attentional processes. What is attended to, and the method of attention (non-judgmental), appears to alter how the observer evaluates and appraises the event, which in turn influences their emotional response. Evidence suggests that mindfulness may alter the lifecycle of emotional reactions as well as the overall strength of the emotional experience (Desbordes *et al*, 2014).

Emotional regulation also feeds through into behavioural control, with greater theoretical control over behavioural actions. This view is underpinned by a belief that monitoring of attention is associated with motivation (Deci & Ryan, 1985) and control (Carver & Scheier, 1982). Research on health-related behaviour change illustrates the role of mindfulness as a common feature in many changing behaviours, and is reflected in many of the chapters in this book, which draw on mindfulness-based approaches such as meta-cognitive therapy and dialectical behavioural therapy.

Finally, there is strong evidence of the impact of mindfulness on physiology, specifically the stress response. Mindfulness is related to dampened stress reactions and faster recovery to baseline levels (Brown *et al*, 2012). These effects have been linked both to stress related effects such as sleep patterns, where mindfulness training has been shown to improve sleep quality (Hülsheger *et al*, 2014).

What is clear from this review is the volume of research which has been conducted in multiple areas providing overwhelming evidence of the value of mindfulness practice and its associated long-term health and performance benefits. In Table 4.2 we summarise a selection of empirical studies.

Table 4.2: Summary of research

Study	Summary
Alexander et al (1989)	RCT study: 73 participants, elders, mean age 81. Control group and three interventions: transcendental meditation (TM) program, mindfulness training (MF) and relaxation /low mindfulness (LM) program. Measured cognitive flexibility, blood pressure and behavioural flexibility. Outcome: MF group improved most, followed by TM.
Anderson et al (2007)	RCT study: 72 health adult participants, 39 in mindfulness-based stress reduction (MBSR) and 33 in wait list control. Eight-week intervention. Outcome: MBSR greater improvement in emotional wellbeing and mindfulness, no improvement in attentional control compared with control group.
Astin (1997)	RCT study. 28 participants allocated to intervention or control group for an 8-week mindfulness meditation. Outcomes: significantly greater changes in terms of: (1) reductions in overall psychological symptomatology; (2) increases in overall domain-specific sense of control and utilization of an accepting or yielding mode of control in their lives, and (3) higher scores on a measure of spiritual experiences.
Brown et al (1984)	Experimental design Study> Three groups of monks. One group who regularly used meditation. Meditation practitioners were able to detect light flashes of shorter duration than the non-meditators.
Brown et al (2009)	Study of 221 UK students, average age 20. Outcome: Study revealed that mindfulness was associated with a smaller financial desire discrepancy in desire, past comparison, and social comparison.
Carson et al (2004)	RCT study. 44 Participants: 22 'relatively happy', 'non-distressed' couples and 22 couples in control group. Results suggested the intervention was efficacious in (a) favourably impacting couples' levels of relationship satisfaction, autonomy, relatedness, closeness, acceptance of one another, and relationship distress; (b) beneficially affecting individuals' optimism, spirituality, relaxation, and psychological distress; and (c) maintaining benefits at 3-month follow-up.
Chambers et al (2008)	Experimental design: 20 mindfulness novices. Results completing the mindfulness training demonstrated significant improvements in self-reported mindfulness, depressive symptoms, rumination, working-memory performance and sustained attention, relative to a comparison group

Table 4.2: Summary of research

Study	Summary
Chan & Woollacott (2007)	Experimental design: Participants 50 meditations and 10 non-meditators. Results showed that meditation experience was associated with reduced interference on the Stroop task, demonstrating enhanced task attention.
Chang et al (2004)	Within participant design. Intervention 8-week MBSR programme. Examined the effects on pain, positive states of mind, stress, and mindfulness self-efficacy. These measures were collected before and following an 8-week intervention. Post-intervention levels of stress were significantly lower than pre-intervention levels, while mindfulness self-efficacy and positive states of mind were at significantly higher levels.
Falkenström (2010)	Quasi-experimental design. 76 participants, regular meditators. 48 on an intensive meditation retreat. Mindfulness and wellbeing increased in the retreat group.
Grant & Rainville (2009)	RCT study. 26 participants, 13 meditation practitioners and 13 age and gender matched non-meditators. Participants given pain effect. Outcomes: Meditators needed higher levels of stimulus to report pain. In meditators, pain modulation correlated with slowing of the respiratory rate.
Heeren et al (2009)	Quasi-experimental design study. Participants 18 adults, on an 8-week mindfulness programme and a control. Measured pre and post: an autobiographical memory task, a cognitive inhibition task, a motor inhibition task, a cognitive flexibility task and a motor flexibility task. MBCT participants showed increased autobiographical memory specificity, decreased over generality, and improved cognitive flexibility capacity and capacity to inhibit cognitive prepotent responses.
Jain et al (2007)	RCT study. 83 participants in two groups, mindfulness and relaxation group. Measured psychological distress, positive states of mind, distractive and ruminative thoughts and behaviours, and spiritual experience. Results: meditation and relaxation groups both experienced significant decrease. No significant differences between meditation and relaxation on distress and positive mood states over time. Meditation group also demonstrated significant pre post decreases in both distractive and ruminative thoughts/behaviours compared with the control group.

Table 4.2: Summary of research

Study	Summary
Jha et al (2007)	Experimental between participant design. One group, inexperienced mindful practitioners, MBS 8-week programme. Second group, experienced practitioners, one-month intensive programme. Measured T1 and T2 in conflict monitoring. At T2, group 1 showed significant improvement. Results suggest that mindfulness training may improve attention-related behavioural responses.
Jha et al (2010)	Experimental between participant design. 31 armed forces participants in 2 groups. One group received mindfulness training, second control group. Test T1 (before) and T2 (after), of working memory (WM). Mindfulness group saw no decline in WM, while control group declined during stressful situation. Result: MT practice may protect against functional impairments associated with high-stress contexts.
MacKenzie et al (2006)	Experimental design. 30 participants nurses. Intervention group (16) received mindfulness intervention, wait list control groups (14). Results intervention group experienced significant improvements in burnout symptoms, relaxation, and life satisfaction. Concluded: mindfulness training is a promising method for helping manage stress.
Ortner et al (2007)	Study 1, MM practitioners (N = 28) categorized tones and measured Reaction times (RTs). Participants with more mindfulness experience showed less interference. Study 2 was a controlled, randomized experimental study in which participants (N = 82) received mindfulness training, relaxation meditation (RM) training, or no intervention (waiting-list control; WLC). Behavioural, self-report, and psychophysiological measures were administered T1 (before) and T2 (7-week after) intervention period. Although both MM and RM resulted in smaller skin conductance responses to unpleasant pictures and increased well-being, reductions in emotional interference from unpleasant pictures were specific to mindfulness group.
Shapiro et al (2008)	RCT Participants undergraduates in three interventions, Mindfulness Based Stress Reduction (15); Eight Point Mindfulness Program (14); and waitlist control (n=15). Pre-test, post-test, and 8-week follow-up data were gathered on self-report outcome measures. Compared to controls, participants in both treatment groups (n=29) demonstrated increases in mindfulness at 8-week follow-up. Further, increases in mindfulness mediated reductions in perceived stress and rumination.

Table 4.2: Summary of research	
Study	Summary
Valentine & Sweet (1999)	RCT Participants: 53 24–43 year olds in intervention (19) and control group (34), measured on an attention task. Meditators demonstrated superior performance on the test of sustained attention in comparison with controls, and long-term meditators were superior to short-term meditators.

Practice

In its simplest form, mindfulness trains the mind to focus on a single stimulus such as the breath or a sensation. Inevitably, attention will wander, but can be recaptured and returned to the focal stimulus again. It is important to take note of the internal and external causes of attentional distraction so that patterns can be noted and (potentially) interrupted (Baer, 2003). This attention training is something that can be widely used within coaching practice. There are two main schools of mindfulness that have emerged and both consider attention training as part of their core methodology.

Mindfulness-based stress reduction (MBSR)

MBSR is the most commonly used method of mindfulness training and has been manualised so that any variation between MBSR programme delivery is minimised (Kabat-Zinn, 2013). Typically, MBSR consists of an 8–10 week course which is undertaken in groups of up to 30 people, with participants meeting weekly for two or three hours to develop their mindfulness skills. The course begins with practices to 'ground the mind' and teaches body scanning and breath awareness. The programme then covers opening and understanding the mind by improving perception of stress and supporting participants in finding the mental space to make choices to reduce their stress. Finally, MBSR encourages self-compassion and supports you in taking this skillset out into the world by living fully and staying present and non-judgemental when interacting with others (Baer, 2003; Kabat-Zinn, 2013). Core techniques are shown in Table 4.3. Daily homework is expected, often of approximately 45 mins per day (six days per week) when body scans, guided relaxation audio recordings and quiet, seated meditation all may be used. Collectively, the aim of MBSR is to support participants in recognising that thoughts, emotions and sensations are transient and fluctuate, therefore can be observed without activating stress and negative emotional states (Creswell & Lindsay, 2014).

Table 4.3: Mindfulness practices

Mindfulness practices	Summary
Body scanning	Sequentially directing awareness to areas of the body, moving through the body to reduce muscular tension. Designed to heighten awareness of voluntary and involuntary patterns of postural stress and also check on physical sensations (eg pain) objectively.
Sitting meditation	Sitting in a relaxed but wakeful posture and directing attention towards the sensations of breathing. Eyes may be open or closed.
Mindful walking	Slowed and meditative walking, often in nature. Consciously pay attention to sensory information (eg sights, sounds, smells, walking surfaces) whilst moving. Designed to promote mental stillness.
Mindful eating	Focus direct attentional awareness on each aspect of the sensation of eating (often a raisin) and savour each moment of the experience.
Loving-kindness meditation	Repeating sentences or phrases which express caring and good wishes directed towards oneself. Phrases may be personalised to client.

Mindfulness-based cognitive therapy (MBCT)

MBCT is also a manualised eight-week programme of mindfulness training, pioneered in the early 2000s by Teasdale, Williams and Segal, who were working with patients experiencing severe episodes of major depressive disorder (Segal *et al*, 2004; Teasdale *et al*, 2000). Whilst MBCT is largely based on Kabat-Zinn's MBSR, it differs by emphasising to a greater extent the power of cognition and the difference between thoughts and facts.

In MBCT, mindfulness techniques are used to show individuals that they are not passive victims of negative thoughts but can observe them non-judgementally as mental events that will pass and which do not have to become or reflect reality (Baer, 2003). The purpose of this is to prevent negative thoughts escalating and to avoid ruminative patterns, where difficult thoughts loop repeatedly without interruption (van Ravesteijn *et al*, 2014). MBCT stops short of Cognitive-behavioural therapy as it focuses on observing thoughts without deliberately striving to rationalize, change or stop them.

We have suggested elsewhere (Passmore & Marianetti, 2007) that, as coaches start to consider how they might transfer these ideas to their practice they may consider four possible uses:

1. preparing for coaching
2. maintaining focus in a session
3. remaining emotionally detached from the client
4. teaching mindfulness to clients.

However, there is a step before this which is important to recognise.

Being not doing

Most coach practitioners move from understanding the core concept to thinking about how mindfulness may be applied through a specific tool and technique they can use with a client. Our view is that it may be more helpful to reframe this perspective and move from the question *'how can I teach mindfulness to clients'*? and towards *'How can I embody mindfulness in my own coaching practice?'* Mindfulness is more than a set of techniques to be learned, instead it's a way of being, which allows us to transcend fleeting emotions and experiences and simply to be with a client, in service of their agenda. Once this is mastered, or at least the journey is underway, the coach can think about the four potential uses described in the list above.

By focusing on developing a daily practice the coach can begin, over the weeks and months, to experience a gradual *state* change. This in turn will be beneficial to their coaching relationships and ultimately to the outcomes which their clients achieve.

Once the coach has moved their thinking from finding a specific tool to embodiment through regular practice, the coach can begin to focus on specific types of practice.

Attention

One challenge facing most coaches is distraction. These are 'interfering thoughts' from our continuous inner dialogue. They may be ruminations about past sessions: meetings or events, or anticipatory thinking: abstract ideas, hypotheses, mental problem solving, second-guessing, which involves thinking about where the client is going next in their thinking, or even mentally preparing the next question. Killingsworth & Gilbert estimated the humans mind spends up to 50% of its time during waking hours in this wandering state (2010).

Each thought brings with it associated emotional disturbance ranging from anxiety to excitement. These thoughts and feelings can interfere with the coach's presence, their engagement with the client, and their performance. By quietening this inner dialogue, the coach can focus their attention on the client.

In Passmore's model (Passmore & Marianetti, 2007), enhanced attention helps the coach in preparation before the session, engagement during the session and in managing emotional contagion.

Other benefits are present too. By managing their own emotions, the coach will be better placed to be in service of the client, being more aware of and responding more empathetically to the client's emotional content. Higher levels of empathy are likely to contribute to a stronger working alliance and in turn to more effective outcomes.

Finally, the higher levels of attention to the coaching level of attending will contribute to this meta-attention, as the self-monitoring muscle is developed, enabling the coach to be more aware of their own changing responses during the conversation, provoked in part by the client, the environment and their own interpretation of events.

Teaching mindfulness

Good practice guidelines suggest that mindfulness teachers should have in-depth personal experience of all the core meditation practices they teach, and completed an in-depth, rigorous mindfulness-based teacher training programme or supervised pathway over a minimum duration of 12 months. Unless a formal teaching qualification is in place, it is important for the coach to make explicit from the outset that they will 'share' mindfulness practices with a client, rather than teach them.

It is essential however, that the coach delivers mindfulness from a position of embodiment. The coach is creating a space for the client to be mindful and shares this space by doing the practice while guiding. Full experiential engagement with the practice is good for the client and the coach. For example, if the coach accesses moment-to-moment experience of the practice, rather than reciting a script, the guidance becomes imbued with an authenticity that makes it more engaging for the client. Not only is the client more likely to benefit from the practice, the coach will too.

Fundamentally, all mindfulness practices guide us to be aware of what's alive in the present moment, without judgment. However, the emphasis on how to work with this and to what end differs with each practice, as does the length of the practice. Certain practices may be more suitable than others at certain times, which underscores the importance of the coach practicing them daily and knowing them intimately. For example, it might be counterproductive for a coach to guide a 3-step breathing space practice when the client would benefit more from emotion regulation offered by the loving kindness practice. Or a simple sitting meditation may be the perfect way to start a coaching session.

Three practices

1. The 3 Step Breathing Space – time to pause

We often rush from one task to another, oblivious of the stress-energy we may carry into the next activity. Or we may be so focused on the next objective in our day that we are not present with what is in front of us. Either way, we benefit hugely when we take time to re-ground ourselves in the present moment.

The 3 Step Breathing Space is an informal mindfulness practice that can be done at any time during the day and for as long as feels comfortable or necessary. It affords an opportunity to pause for a few moments and check in with ourselves. Take our foot off the gas, so to speak, and unhook from unhelpful thoughts, feelings or emotions.

As with all mindfulness practices used in the coaching environment, it is important that the coach embodies each step, using the personal, moment-to-moment felt experience to guide the pace and energy of the practice, rather than reading from a page. For example, after making the invitation for the client to gently notice how the mind is, the coach will do the same and, when sufficient time has passed for this, the coach confidently moves to the next phase ie noticing how the body is.

The three steps are:

1. The coach gently invites the client to bring attention to the state of the mind and body. Offering suggestions such as *"How is the mind right now? Maybe noticing the mind is agitated, absorbed, calm or distracted"*. After a pause, turn attention to the body: *"How is the body in this moment? Maybe hungry, tense, heavy, or relaxed"*.

2. Having acknowledged the mind and body, the coach invites the awareness to drop down into the belly and notice the rise and fall as the body breathes, offering reassurance such as *"No need to manipulate the breathing in any way, just observing the direct felt sensations in the abdomen. However, there is no right way to feel."*

Also, *"If the mind wanders, simply inviting the awareness back to the belly, in a friendly and gentle way. The mind wandering is totally natural, it's not a mistake."*

3. Lastly, when the coach feels ready, invite the client to expand awareness to include a sense of the body as a whole.

Then, to finish, the coach invites the client to maintain a sense of expanded awareness as much as possible. Using a phrase such as *"As this practice comes to an end, holding on to this sense of expanded awareness, as best you can."*

The following link may be useful:

3 Step Breathing Space
https://beingmindful.me/2021/07/05/the-3-step-breathing-space-practice/

2. Sitting Meditation

Mindful sitting is a formal practice that is usually done in a more structured way than the informal practices like the 3-step breathing space, which can be done in any position at any time, even during a conversation.

The sitting meditation starts with an invitation to adopt a comfortable, upright posture, with the body balanced and relaxed. A sense of 'groundedness' is enhanced by bringing awareness to the points of contact with the chair and the floor.

Moment-to-moment awareness of the breath and body is used as an anchor point to keep the attention focused (we acknowledge whenever the mind switches to the narrative network and then switch back to the direct experience of the breath or body).

Traditionally, the length of a sitting practice varies from between five minutes to an hour or more but the essential elements are posture, feeling grounded, and attention of the body and breath.

In a coaching setting, a five to ten-minute practice may provide a calm and settled atmosphere to begin a session. When offering this practice for the first time it is important to check the client is happy to continue and it is helpful to let the client know that should they feel uncomfortable for any reason they can zone out of the guidance at any time.

The coach might use the following phrases to guide a short sitting meditation:

1. *"Let's start this practice by finding an upright and dignified posture that feels comfortable."*
2. *"And when you're ready, bringing awareness to the sensations of being supported by the floor and the chair. Just observing whatever sensations are here to be noticed."*

Short pause.

3. *"Now, if it feels comfortable for you, noticing the sensations of the body breathing in the abdomen. Following the gentle rise and fall of the belly as the breath comes into the body, and as it leaves the body".*

Long pause (the coach is guided by personal experience within the practice)

4. *"If you notice the mind has wandered off or is distracted at any time, just noticing where it went and gently bringing full awareness back to the breathing in the belly. This is just what minds do so it's not a problem, not a mistake."*

Long pause

5. *"Now, expanding the awareness to include a sense of the whole body sitting here, breathing... You may notice a sense of gravity bearing down, keeping you connected to the floor... You may also notice a sense of height coming up through the spine... Being curious and open to whatever arises in the field of awareness as you sit here."*

Pause (if the coach notices the mind wandering, this can be a cue to remind the client to bring the mind back to the anchor of the body or breath).

6. When the time feels right, or the allocated time is nearly over, the coach brings the practice to a close. *"And as this practice comes to an end, in your own time, opening the eyes and moving or stretching as the body wishes".*

The following link may be useful:

The Sitting Meditation
https://beingmindful.me/2021/07/06/awareness-of-breath-and-body/

3. Loving Kindness Meditation

Also known as self-compassion, this practice reminds us of the importance of nourishing ourselves with kindness in addition to offering it to others. It is easy to offer support and friendliness outwardly while forgetting our own needs. Self-compassion can help to restore balance to our sense of purpose, our sense of status and sense of fulfilment. It can also be a helpful antidote to the often-harsh voice of the inner critic which undermines these things.

During this meditation, phrases which express caring and good wishes are repeated and directed towards oneself and to others. The intention is to offer unconditional friendliness, but the phrases may feel distant or unreal to us at first. It is important to remind a client that they can change the phrases to suit them. For example, the first phrase might be *"May I be safe and protected"* whereas *"May I be peaceful and happy"* might be preferred. Finding comfortable alternatives will become easier once the practice is familiar.

After inviting the client to adopt a comfortable posture and sitting for a few moments, the coach might use the following phrases to guide a loving kindness meditation:

1. *"So, when you're ready, offering yourself unconditional friendliness by silently repeating these phrases: 'May I be free from suffering. May I be as happy and as healthy as it is possible for me to be. May I have ease of being'."*

    "Taking your time, and imagining that each phrase is a pebble dropped down into a deep well. You're dropping each one in turn, then listening

to any reaction in thoughts, feelings, bodily sensations or impulse to act. There is no need to judge what arises. This is just for you."

"If you find it difficult to bring forth any sense of friendship towards yourself, bring to mind a person (or even a pet) who, either in the past or present, has loved you unconditionally. Once you have a clear sense of their love for you, see if you can return to offering this love to yourself: 'May I be free from suffering. May I be as happy and as healthy as it is possible for me to be. May I have ease of being'."

Pause (remind client to be open to whatever arises)

2. *"And now bringing to mind a loved one, and wishing them well in the same way (using he, she, or they, as you prefer): 'May they be free from suffering. May they be as happy and as healthy as it is possible for them to be. May they have ease of being'."*

"Once again, see what arises in mind and body as you hold the person in mind and heart, wishing them well. Allowing responses to come. Take your time. Pause between phrases – listening attentively. 'May they be free from suffering. May they be as happy and as healthy as it is possible for them to be. May they have ease of being'."

3. *"Finally, extending loving kindness to all beings, including your loved ones and strangers and those whom you find difficult. The intention here is to extend love and friendship to all living beings on the planet – remembering that all living beings includes you! May all beings be free from suffering. May all beings be happy and healthy. May all of us have ease of being."*

"Allowing these well wishes to be present in this moment, however that is for you right now. Open-hearted. Non-striving. Non-judgemental."

Pause

4. *"As this practice comes to an end, maybe congratulating yourself for nourishing yourself in this way. And taking as much time as you wish to sit with the breath in the body, resting in clear awareness of how it is in this moment."*

Pause

"When you're ready, opening your eyes and gently emerging from the practice".

The following link may be useful:

Loving kindness
https://beingmindful.me/2021/07/06/loving-kindness-practice/

Mindfulness resources

There are a wealth of resources available on the internet. Coaches can access content on individual practitioner sites or on digital platforms such as YouTube. However, two useful sites which coaches can access for their own practice or refer clients to are: Search Inside Yourself and Insight Timer.

Insight Timer: https://insighttimer.com/about

Search Inside Yourself:
https://siyli.org/resources/category/guided-meditations/

Insight Timer offers a diverse range of programmes from multiple teachers, with some free content and some only available on subscription.

Search Inside Yourself was originally developed at Google and teaches practical mindfulness, emotional intelligence and leadership with a focus on workplace performance. In our own practice we make use of a number of these meditations, for example, to focus Loving Kindness, undertake body scans, enhance attention or build empathy (SIY 2021a, 2021b, 2021c, 2021d, 2021e). These can be easily downloaded to a phone and introduced as part of a regular daily routine.

Conclusion

While mindfulness offers a strong evidence-base developed over 40 years, mindfulness in coaching remains in its infancy. A number of theoretical papers and books have pointed a way forward, however more research is needed to help explore the benefits of mindfulness for coaches and for coaching clients. In this chapter we have sought to provide an insight into the science of mindfulness, and offered perspectives on how practitioners have been taking these ideas to apply in their own practice to both develop their own way of being, as well as sharing resources with clients.

Five questions for further reflection

1. **What will support you to develop a regular mindfulness practice?**

Adopting a new regime is not always about simply understanding what to do, but also finding a place in the day when there is time to practice. What might work for one, say early mornings, may be unsuitable for another, as they rush to get children ready for school. What is important is regular daily practice, in a space in time when there is calm.

2. **What ethical issues do coaches need to consider before bringing mindfulness into the coaching relationship?**

Most coaches believe coaching should be client led. If this is true, care needs to be given around introducing ideas which a client has not requested. When or how will these ideas be introduced and what effect might this have on the relationship?

3. **How might mindfulness help coaching practice?**

The scientific benefits have been set out in this chapter from a host of research studies. However, different people have different priorities and needs. Being clear about this can be helpful, and mindfulness can be used to complement other practice such as pilates, yoga etc.

4. **How might a Body scan or Loving Kindness Meditation help in a digital coaching relationship?**

Online coaching has become a significant part of most coach's work, and preparing for each session alongside building a relationship with clients in a digital environment is an important consideration. These practices, when engaged in regularly, may offer ways to minimise the challenges of online working practices.

5. **How can coaches enable mindfulness practice to transfer not just their practice but their very way of being?**

We have suggested in this chapter that mindfulness is not just a useful tool, but is about a state of being. To achieve this requires sustained practice over months and years, but the outcome may be a calmer, less stressed and more attentive human.

Suggested reading

Chaskalson, M. & McMordie, M. (2017) *Mindfulness for Coaches, Location.* London: Routledge.

Passmore, J. & Amit, S. (2017) *Mindfulness at Work: The practice and science of mindfulness for leaders, coaches and facilitators.* New York: Nova.

Passmore, J. (2019) Mindfulness at organisations: A critical literature review (Part 1). *Industrial and Commercial Training,* **51** (2) 104–113. Available online at: https://doi.org/10.1108/ICT-07-2018-0063. Accessed 10 July 2021.

Passmore, J. & Marianetti, O. (2007) The role of mindfulness in coaching. *The Coaching Psychologist,* **3** (3) 131–138.

Acknowledgement

With special thanks to Mark McMordie for his contributions.

References

Alberts, H.J.E.M. & Thewissen, R. (2011) The effect of a brief mindfulness intervention on memory for positively and negatively valenced stimuli. *Mindfulness,* **2** (2) 73–77.

Alexander, C.N., Langer, E.J., Newman, R.I., Chandler, H.M. & Davies, J.L. (1989) Transcendental meditation, mindfulness, and longevity: an experimental study with the elderly. *Journal of Personality and Social Psychology,* **57**, 950–964.

Anderson, N.D., Lau, M.A., Segal, Z.V. & Bishop, S.R. (2007) Mindfulness-based stress reduction and attentional control. *Clinical Psychology & Psychotherapy,* **14**, 449–463.

Anstiss, T., Passmore, J. & Gilbert, P. (2020) Compassion: The essential orientation. *The Psychologist*, May, pp38–42. Retrieved from https://thepsychologist.bps.org.uk/compassion-essential-orientation on 26 March 2020

Arat, A. (2017) 'What it means to be truly human': The postsecular hack of mindfulness. *Social Compass*, **64** (2) 167–179.

Astin, J. A. (1997) Stress reduction through mindfulness meditation: effects on psychological symptomatology, sense of control, and spiritual experiences. *Psychotherapy and Psychosomatics*, **66**, 97–106.

Baer, R. A. (2003) Mindfulness training as a clinical intervention: a conceptual and empirical review. *Clinical Psychology: Science and Practice*, **10** (2) 125–143.

Bawa, F.L.M., Mercer, S.W., Atherton, R.J., Clague, F., Keen, A., Scott, N.W. & Bond, C.M. (2015) Does mindfulness improve outcomes in patients with chronic pain? Systematic review and meta-analysis. *The British Journal Of General Practice: The Journal Of The Royal College Of General Practitioners*, **65** (635), e387–e400.

Bhikkhu, B. (1998), *Mindfulness with Breathing: A Manual for Serious Beginners*, Wisdom Press, Somerville, MA.

Bishop, S.R., Lau, M., Shapiro, S., Carlson, L., Anderson, N., Carmody, J., Segal, Z., Abbey, S., Speca, M., Velting, D. and Devins, G. (2004) Mindfulness: a proposed operational definition, *Clinical Psychology: Science & Practice*, **11** (3) 230–41.

Brewer, J. A., Worhunsky, P. D., Gray, J. R., Tang, Y.-Y., Weber, J. & Kober, H. (2011) Meditation experience is associated with differences in default mode network activity and connectivity. *Proceedings of the National Academy of Sciences*, **108**, 20254–20259.

Brown, K.W., Weinstein, N. & Creswell, J.D. (2012) Trait mindfulness modulates neuroendocrine and affective responses to social evaluative threat. *Psychoneuroendocrinology*, **37**, 2037–2041.

Brown, D., Forte, M. & Dysart, M. (1984) Differences in visual sensitivity among mindfulness meditators and non-meditators. *Perceptual and Motor Skills*, **58**, 727–733.

Brown, K.W., Kasser, T., Ryan, R.M., Alex Linley, P. & Orzech, K. (2009) When what one has is enough: mindfulness, financial desire discrepancy, and subjective well-being. *Journal of Research in Personality*, **43**, 727–736.

Brown, K.W. & Ryan, R. M. (2003) The benefits of being present: Mindfulness and its role in psychological well-being. *Journal of Personality and Social Psychology*, **84** (4) 822–848.

Burton, A., Burgess, C., Dean, S., Koutsopoulou, G.Z. & Hugh-Jones, S. (2017) How effective are mindfulness-based interventions for reducing stress among healthcare professionals? a systematic review and meta-analysis. *Stress and Health*, **33** (1) 3–13.

Canby, N.K., Cameron, I.M., Calhoun, A.T. & Buchanan, G.M. (2015) A brief mindfulness intervention for healthy college students and its effects on psychological distress, self-control, meta-mood, and subjective vitality. *Mindfulness*, **6** (5) 1071–1081.

Christopher, M.S., Neuser, N.J., Michael, P.G. & Baitmangalkar, A. (2012) Exploring the psychometric properties of the five facet mindfulness questionnaire. *Mindfulness*, **3** (2) 124–131.

Carson, J.W., Carson, K.M., Gil, K.M. & Baucom, D.H. (2004) Mindfulness-based relationship enhancement. *Behavior Therapy*, **35**, 471–494.

Carver, C.S. & Scheier, M.F. (1982) Control theory: A useful conceptual framework for personality – social, clinical, and health psychology. *Psychological Bulletin*, **92**, 111–135.

Chambers, R., Lo, B.C.Y. & Allen, N.B. (2008) The impact of intensive mindfulness training on attentional control, cognitive style, and affect. *Cognitive Therapy and Research*, **32**, 303–322.

Chan, D. &Woollacott, M. (2007) Effects of level of meditation experience on attentional focus: is the efficiency of executive or orientation networks improved? *Journal of Alternative and Complementary Medicine*, **13**, 651–657.

Chang, V.Y., Palesh, O., Caldwell, R., Glasgow, N., Abramson, M., Luskin, F. & Koopman, C. (2004) The effects of a mindfulness-based stress reduction program on stress, mindfulness self-efficacy, and positive states of mind. *Stress and Health: Journal of the International Society for the Investigation of Stress*, **20**, 141–147

Chaskalson, M. (2014), *Mindfulness in Eight Weeks: The Revolutionary 8 Week Plan to Clear Your Mind and Calm Your Life*. London: Harper Collins.

Cillessen, L., Johannsen, M., Speckens, A.E.M. & Zachariae, R. (2019) Mindfulness-based interventions for psychological and physical health outcomes in cancer patients and survivors: A systematic review and meta-analysis of randomized controlled trials. *Psycho-Oncology*, **28** (12), 2257–2269.

Cohen, E. (2010) From the Bodhi tree, to the analyst's couch, then into the MRI scanner: The psychologisation of Buddhism. *Annual Review of Critical Psychology*, **8**, 23.

Conversano, C., Ciacchini, R., Orrù, G., Di Giuseppe, M., Gemignani, A. & Poli, A. (2020) Mindfulness, Compassion, and Self-Compassion Among Health Care Professionals: What's new? A systematic Review. *Frontiers in Psychology*, 11.

Cowger, E.L. & Torrance, E.P. (1982) Further examination of the quality of changes in creative functioning resulting from meditation (Zazen) training. *Creative Child & Adult Quarterly*, **7**, 211–217.

Craske, M.G. (1999) *Anxiety disorders: Psychological approaches to theory and treatment*. Westview Press.

Creswell, J.D. & Lindsay, E.K. (2014) How does mindfulness training affect health? a mindfulness stress buffering account. *Current Directions in Psychological Science*, **23** (6), 401–407.

Deci, E.L. & Ryan, R.M. (1985) The general causality orientations scale: Self-determination in personality. *Journal of Research in Personality*, 19, 109–134.

De Grace, G. (1976) Effects of meditation on personality and values. *Journal of Clinical Psychology*, **32**, 809–813.

Desbordes, G., Gard, T., Hoge, E.A., Hölzel, B.K., Kerr, C., Lazar, S.W., Olendzki, A. & Vago, D.R. (2014) Moving beyond mindfulness: Defining equanimity as an outcome measure in meditation and contemplative research. *Mindfulness*, **6**, 356–372.

Dhillon, A., Sparkes, E. & Duarte, R.V. (2017) Mindfulness-based interventions during pregnancy: a systematic review and meta-analysis. *Mindfulness*, **8** (6) 1421–1437.

Donnelly, G.E., Ksendzova, M., Howell, R.T., Vohs, K.D. & Baumeister, R.F. (2016) Buying to blunt negative feelings: materialistic escape from the self. *Review of General Psychology*, **20** (3) 272–316.

Eberth, J. & Sedlmeier, P. (2012) The effects of mindfulness meditation: a meta-analysis. *Mindfulness*, **3**, 174–189.

Falkenström, F. (2010) Studying mindfulness in experienced meditators: a quasi-experimental approach. *Personality and Individual Differences*, **48**, 305–310.

Finlay, K.A., Hearn, J.H. & Chater, A. (2021a) The impact of neurological disability and sensory loss on mindfulness practice. Disability and Rehabilitation, 1–9.

Finlay, K.A., Hearn, J.H. & Chater, A. (2021b) Grieving a disrupted biography: an interpretative phenomenological analysis exploring barriers to the use of mindfulness after neurological injury or impairment. *BMC Psychology*. 24 9(1):124. doi: 10.1186/s40359-021-00628-0

Gaudiano, B.A. (2006) The "third wave" behavior therapies in context: review of Hayes *et al*'s (2004) mindfulness and acceptance: expanding the cognitive-behavioral tradition and Hayes and Strosahl's (2004) A practical guide to acceptance and commitment therapy. *Cognitive and Behavioral Practice*, **13** (1), 101–104.

Good, D., Lyddy, C., Glomb, T., Bono, J., Brown, K., Duffy, M., Baer, R., Brewer, J. & Lazer, D. (2016) Contemplating mindfulness at work: an integrative review, *Journal of Management*, **42** (1), 114–42.

Grant, J.A. & Rainville, P. (2009) Pain sensitivity and analgesic effects of mindful states in Zen meditators: a cross-sectional study. *Psychosomatic Medicine*, **71**, 106–114.

Hayes, S.C. (2016) Acceptance and commitment therapy, relational frame theory, and the third wave of behavioral and cognitive therapies – republished article. *Behavior Therapy*, **47** (6) 869–885.

Hayes, S.C. (1994) Content, context, and the types of psychological acceptance. In: S.C. Hayes, N.S. Jacobson, V.M. Follette and M.J. Dougher (Eds) *Acceptance and Change: Content and context in psychotherapy*. Reno, NV: Context Press, pp13–32.

Hayes, S.C., Levin, M.E., Plumb-Vilardaga, J., Villatte, J.L. & Pistorello, J. (2013) Acceptance and commitment therapy and contextual behavioral science: examining the progress of a distinctive model of behavioral and cognitive therapy. *Behavior Therapy*, **44** (2) 180–198.

Hayes, S.C., Strosahl, K.D. & Wilson, K. G. (1999) *Acceptance and Commitment Therapy: An experiential approach to behavior change. New York, NY, US: Guilford Press.* Guildford Press.

Hearn, J.H. & Finlay, K.A. (2018) Internet-delivered mindfulness for people with depression and chronic pain following spinal cord injury: A randomized, controlled feasibility trial. *Spinal Cord,* **56** (8) 750–761.

Heatherton, T. & Baumeister, R. (1991) Binge eating as escape from self-awareness. *Psychological Bulletin,* **110** (1), 86–108.

Heeren, A., Van Broeck, N. & Philippot, P. (2009) The effects of mindfulness on executive processes and autobiographical memory specificity. *Behaviour Research and Therapy*, *47*, 403–409.

Hofmann, S.G., Sawyer, A.T., Witt, A.A. & Oh, D. (2010) The effect of mindfulness-based therapy on anxiety and depression: a meta-analytic review. *Journal of Consulting and Clinical Psychology*, **78**, 169–183.

Hülsheger, U.R., Lang, J.W.B., Depenbrock, F., Fehrmann, C., Zijlstra, F.R.H. & Alberts, H.J.E.M. (2014) The power of presence: The role of mindfulness at work for daily levels and change trajectories of psychological detachment and sleep quality. *Journal of Applied Psychology*, **99**, 1113–1128.

Jain, S., Shapiro, S.L., Swanick, S., Roesch, S.C., Mills, P.J., Bell, I. & Schwartz, G.E.R. (2007) A randomized controlled trial of mindfulness meditation versus relaxation training: effects on distress, positive states of mind, rumination, and distraction. *Annals of Behavioral Medicine*, **33**, 11–21.

Jha, A.P., Stanley, E.A., Kiyonaga, A., Wong, L. & Gelfand, L. (2010) Examining the protective effects of mindfulness training on working memory capacity and affective experience. *Emotion*, **10**, 54–64.

Jha, A.P., Krompinger, J. & Baime, M.J. (2007) Mindfulness training modifies subsystems of attention. *Cognitive, Affective, & Behavioral Neuroscience*, **7** (2) 109–119.

Kabat-Zinn, J. (2013) *Full Catastrophe Living, Revised Edition: How to cope with stress, pain and illness using mindfulness meditation.* London: Hachette UK.

Klatt, M.D., Buckworth, J. & Malarkey, W.B. (2009) Effects of low-dose mindfulness-based stress reduction (MBSR-ld) on working adults. *Health Education & Behavior*, **36**, 601–614.

Khoury, B., Lecomte, T., Fortin, G., Masse, M., Bouchard, V., Chapleau, M-A., Paquin, K. & Hofman, S.G. (2013) Mindfulness-based therapy: A comprehensive meta-analysis. *Clinical Psychology Review*, **33** (6) 763–771.

Killingsworth, M.A. & Gilbert, D.T. (2010) A wandering mind is an unhappy mind. *Science*, 330, 932.

Kiken, L.G., Garland, E.L., Bluth, K., Palsson, O.S. & Gaylord, S.A. (2015) From a state to a trait: Trajectories of state mindfulness in meditation during intervention predict changes in trait mindfulness. *Personality and Individual Differences*, **81**, 41–46.

Kinser, P., Braun, S., Deeb, G., Carrico, C. & Dow, A. (2016) "Awareness is the first step": An interprofessional course on mindfulness & mindful-movement for healthcare professionals and students. *Complementary Therapies in Clinical Practice*, **25**, 18–25.

Klein, A., Taieb, O., Xavier, S., Baubet, T. & Reyre, A. (2020) The benefits of mindfulness-based interventions on burnout among health professionals: A systematic review. *EXPLORE*, **16** (1) 35–43.

Kozhevnikov, M., Louchakova, O., Josipovic, Z. & Motes, M.A. (2009) The enhancement of visuospatial processing efficiency through Buddhist Deity meditation. *Psychological Science*, **20**, 645–653.

Langer, E.J. (1989) *Mindfulness.* Reading, MA: Addison-Wesley.

Lau, M.A., Bishop, S.R., Segal, Z.V., Buis, T., Anderson, N.D., Carlson, L., Shapiro, S., Carmody, J., Abbey, S. & Devins, G. (2006) The Toronto mindfulness scale: Development and validation. *Journal of Clinical Psychology*, **62** (12) 1445–1467.

Lesh, T.V. (1970) Zen meditation and the development of empathy in counselors. *Journal of Humanistic Psychology*, **10**, 39–74.

Lindsay, E.K. & Creswell, J. D. (2017) Mechanisms of mindfulness training: monitor and acceptance theory (MAT) *Clinical Psychology Review*, **51**, 48–59.

Liu, X., Wang, S., Chang, S., Chen, W. & Si, M. (2013) Effect of brief mindfulness intervention on tolerance and distress of pain induced by cold-pressor task. *Stress and Health*, **29** (3) 199–204.

Lomas, T., Medina, J. C., Ivtzan, I., Rupprecht, S. & Eiroa-Orosa, F. J. (2018) A systematic review of the impact of mindfulness on the well-being of healthcare professionals. *Journal of Clinical Psychology*, **74** (3) 319–355.

Luken, M. & Sammons, A. (2016) Systematic Review of Mindfulness Practice for Reducing Job Burnout. *American Journal of Occupational Therapy*, **70** (2) 7002250020, p1–10.

Lutz, A., Slagter, H.A., Rawlings, N B., Francis, A D., Greischar, L L. & Davidson, R.J. (2009) Mental training enhances attentional stability: Neural and behavioral evidence. *The Journal of Neuroscience*, **29**, 13418–13427.

Lutz, A., Jha, A.P., Dunne, J.D. & Saron, C.D. (2015) Investigating the phenomenological matrix of mindfulness- related practice from a neurocognitive perspective. *American Psychologist*, **70** (7) 632–58.

MacKenzie, C.S., Poulin, P.A. & Seidman-Carlson, R. (2006) A brief mindfulness-based stress reduction intervention for nurses and nurse aides. *Applied Nursing Research*, **19**, 105–109.

MacLean, K.A., Ferrer, E., Aichele, S.R., Bridwell, D.A., Zanesco, A.P., Jacobs, T.L., King, B.G., Rosenberg, E.L., Sahdra, B.K., Shaver, P.R., Wallace, B.A., Magnun, G.R. & Saron, C.D. (2010) Intensive meditation training improves perceptual discrimination and sustained attention. *Psychological Science*, **21**, 829–839.

Marianetti, O. & Passmore, J. (2009) Mindfulness at work: paying attention to enhance well-being and performance. In: A. Lindley (Ed) *Oxford Handbook of Positive Psychology and Work*. Oxford, UK: Oxford University Press, pp189–200.

Mesmer-Magnus, J., Manapragada, A., Viswesvaran, C. & Allen, J.W. (2017) Trait mindfulness at work: A meta-analysis of the personal and professional correlates of trait mindfulness. *Human Performance*, **30** (2–3) 79–98.

Moore, A. & Malinowski, P. (2009) Meditation, mindfulness and cognitive flexibility. *Consciousness and Cognition: An International Journal*, **18**, 176–186.

Morone, N. E., Greco, C. M. & Weiner, D. K. (2008) Mindfulness meditation for the treatment of chronic low back pain in older adults: a randomized controlled pilot study. *Pain*, **134**, 310–319.

Nyklicek, I. & Kuipers, E. (2008) Effects of mindfulness-based stress reduction intervention on psychological well-being and quality of life: is increased mindfulness indeed the mechanism? *Annals of Behavioral Medicine*, **35**, 331–340.

Oman, D., Shapiro, S.L., Thoresen, C.E., Plante, T.G. & Flinders, T. (2008) Meditation lowers stress and supports forgiveness among college students: a randomized controlled trial. *Journal of American College Health*, **56**, 569–578.

Ortner, C.N.M., Kilner, S.J. & Zelazo, P.D. (2007) Mindfulness meditation and reduced emotional interference on a cognitive task. *Motivation and Emotion*, **31**, 271–283.

Orzech, K.M., Shapiro, S.L., Brown, K.W. & McKay, M. (2009) Intensive mindfulness training-related changes in cognitive and emotional experience. *Journal of Positive Psychology*, **4**, 212–222.

Pagnoni, G. & Cekic, M. (2007) Age effects on gray matter volume and attentional performance in Zen meditation. *Neurobiology of Aging*, **28**, 1623–1627.

Passmore, J. (2019a) Mindfulness at organisations: A critical literature review (Part 1). *Industrial & Commercial Training*, **51** (2) 104–113.

Passmore, J. (2019b) Mindfulness in organisations: Mindfulness as a tool to enhance leadership development, workplace wellbeing and coaching (Part 2). *Industrial & Commercial Training*, **51** (3) 165–173.

Passmore, J. (2018) Mindfulness coaching techniques: choosing our attitude. *The Coaching Psychologist*, **14** (1) 48–49.

Passmore, J. (2017) Mindfulness coaching techniques: STOP. *The Coaching Psychologist*, **13** (2) 86–87.

Passmore, J. (2017) Mindfulness in coaching. *The Coaching Psychologist,* **13** (1) 27–30.

Passmore, J. (2017) Mindfulness Coaching techniques: identifying mindfulness distractions. *The Coaching Psychologist,* **13** (1) 31–33.

Passmore, J. & Marianetti, O. (2007) The role of mindfulness in coaching. *The Coaching Psychologist,* **3** (3) 131–138.

Pawsey, F., Wong, J.H.K., Kenttä, G. & Näswall, K. (2021) Daily mindfulness is associated with recovery processes among coaches—a 4-week diary study. *International Sport Coaching Journal,* **1** (aop) 1–11.

Pearson, A., Macera, M.H. & Follette, V. (2010) Acceptance and Commitment Therapy for Body *Image Dissatisfaction: A practitioner's guide to using mindfulness, acceptance, and values-based behavior change strategies.* Oakland, USA: New Harbinger Publications.

Pflügner, K., Maier, C. & Weitzel, T. (2021) The direct and indirect influence of mindfulness on techno-stressors and job burnout: A quantitative study of white-collar workers. *Computers in Human Behavior,* **115**, 106566.

Quaglia, J.T., Brown, K.W., Lindsay, E.K., Creswell, J.D. & Goodman, R.J. (2014) From conceptualization to operationalization of mindfulness. In: K.W. Brown, J.D. Creswell and R.M. Ryan (Eds) *Handbook of mindfulness: Theory, research, and practice Guilford:* The Guilford Press, pp151–170.

Querstret, D., Morison, L., Dickinson, S., Cropley, M. & John, M. (2020) Mindfulness-based stress reduction and mindfulness-based cognitive therapy for psychological health and well-being in nonclinical samples: A systematic review and meta-analysis. *International Journal of Stress Management,* **27** (4) 394–411.

Roeser, R.W., Schonert-Reichl, K.A., Jha, A., Cullen, M., Wallace, L., Wilensky, R., Oberle, E., Thomson, K., Taylor, C. & Harrison, J. (2013) Mindfulness training and reductions in teacher stress and burnout: Results from two randomized, waitlist-control field trials. *Journal of Educational Psychology,* **105**, 787–804.

Rogers, C.R. (1957) The necessary and sufficient conditions of therapeutic personality change. *Journal of Consulting Psychology,* **21**, 95–103.

Rogers, J.M., Ferrari, M., Mosely, K., Lang, C. P. & Brennan, L. (2017) Mindfulness-based interventions for adults who are overweight or obese: A meta-analysis of physical and psychological health outcomes. *Obesity Reviews,* **18** (1) 51–67.

Schumer, M.C., Lindsay, E.K. & Creswell, J.D. (2018) Brief mindfulness training for negative affectivity: A systematic review and meta-analysis. *Journal of Consulting and Clinical Psychology,* **86** (7) 569–583.

Sears, S. & Kraus, S. (2009) I think therefore I am: cognitive distortions and coping style as mediators for the effects of mindfulness meditation on anxiety, positive and negative affect, and hope. *Journal of Clinical Psychology,* **65**, 561–573.

Seema, R. & Säre, E. (2019) There is no 'mindfulness' without a mindfulness theory – teachers' meditation practices in a secular country. *Cogent Education,* **6** (1), 1616365.

Segal, Z.V., Teasdale, J.D. & Mark, J. (2004) Mindfulness-Based Cognitive Therapy: Theoretical Rationale and Empirical Status. In: S.C. Hayes, V.M. Follette and M.M. Linehan (Eds) Mindfulness and *Acceptance: Expanding the cognitive-behavioral tradition.* New York, NY: Guilford Press, pp45–65.

Shapiro, S.L., Schwartz, G.E. & Bonner, G. (1998) Effects of mindfulness-based stress reduction on medical and premedical students. *Journal of Behavioral Medicine,* **21**, 581–599.

Shapiro, S.L., Brown, K.W. & Biegel, G.M. (2007) Teaching self-care to caregivers: effects of mindfulness-based stress reduction on the mental health of therapists in training. *Training and Education in Professional Psychology,* **1**, 105–115.

Shapiro, S.L., Oman, D., Thoresen, C.E., Plante, T.G. & Flinders, T. (2008) Cultivating mindfulness: effects on well-being. *Journal of Clinical Psychology,* **64**, 840–862.

SIY (2021a) 'Meditation to focus attention'. Retrieved on 23 June 2021 from https://siyli.org/a-meditation-to-focus-attention/. Accessed 10 July 2021.

SIY (2021b) 'Body scan.' Retrieved on 23 June 2021 from https://siyli.org/body-scan-with-marc-lesser/. Accessed 10 July 2021.

SIY (2021c) 'Just like me.' Retrieved on 23 June 2021 from https://siyli.org/just-like-me-with-meg-levie/. Accessed 10 July 2021.

SIY (2021d) 'Loving kindness.' Retrieved on 23 June 2021 from https://siyli.org/loving-kindness-with-meg-levie/. Accessed 10 July 2021.

SIY (2021e) 'Self compassion.' Retrieved on 23 June 2021 from https://siyli.org/guided-meditation-self-compassion/. Accessed 10 July 2021.

Smallwood, J. & Schooler, J.W. (2015) The science of mind wandering: Empirically navigating the stream of con- sciousness. *Annual Review of Psychology*, **66**, 487–518.

Strohmaier, S. (2020) The relationship between doses of mindfulness-based programs and depression, anxiety, stress, and mindfulness: a dose-response meta-regression of randomized controlled trials. *Mindfulness*, **11** (6) 1315–1335.

Tacon, A.M., McComb, J., Caldera, Y. & Randolph, P. (2003) Mindfulness meditation, anxiety reduction, and heart disease: a pilot study. *Family & Community Health: The Journal of Health Promotion & Maintenance*, **26**, 25–33.

Tang, Y.-Y., Ma, Y., Wang, J., Fan, Y., Feng, S., Lu, Q., Yu, Q., Sui, D., Rothbart, M.K., Fan, M. & Posner, M.I. (2007) *Short-term meditation training improves attention and self-regulation.* Proceedings of the National Academy of Sciences, **104**, 17152–17156.

Teasdale, J.D., Segal, Z.V., Williams, J.M., Ridgeway, V.A., Soulsby, J.M. & Lau, M.A. (2000) Prevention of relapse/recurrence in major depression by mindfulness-based cognitive therapy. Journal of *Consulting and Clinical Psychology*, **68** (4) 615–623.

Teper, R., Segal, Z.V. & Inzlicht, M. (2013) Inside the mindful mind: how mindfulness enhances emotion regulation through improvements in executive control. *Current Directions in Psychological Science*, **22** (6) 449–454.

Treanor, M. (2011) The potential impact of mindfulness on exposure and extinction learning in anxiety disorders. *Clinical Psychology Review*, **31** (4) 617–625.

Valentine, E.R. & Sweet, P.L.G. (1999) Meditation and attention: A comparison of the effects of concentrative and mindfulness meditation on sustained attention. *Mental Health, Religion & Culture*, **2**, 59–70.

van Ravesteijn, H.J., Suijkerbuijk, Y.B., Langbroek, J.A., Muskens, E., Lucassen, P.L.B.J., van Weel, C., Wester, F. & Speckens, A.E.M. (2014) Mindfulness-based cognitive therapy (MBCT) for patients with medically unexplained symptoms: Process of change. *Journal of Psychosomatic Research*, **77** (1), 27–33.

Walach, H., Nord, E., Zier, C., Dietz-Waschkowski, B., Kersig, S. & Schüpbach, H. (2007) Mindfulness-based stress reduction as a method for personnel development: a pilot evaluation. International *Journal of Stress Management*, **14**, 188–198.

Weick, K.E. & Roberts, K.H. (1993) Collective mind in organizations: Heedful interrelating on flight decks. *Administrative Science Quarterly*, **38**, 357–381.

Wicklund, R.A. (1975) Objective self-awareness, *Advances in Experimental Social Psychology*, **8**, 233–275.

Chapter 5
Compassionate Mind Coaching: Theory, research and practice

Tim Anstiss

Introduction

Compassionate Mind Coaching (CMC) is a coaching approach informed by compassion-focused therapy and compassionate mind training. It is a multi-modal approach with the potential to help clients with a range of challenges, goals and frustrations. Rather than directly target thinking patterns or behaviours, CMC focuses on helping clients tap into, activate, cultivate and apply the innate compassion pathways within the human mind, pathways which can sometimes be dormant, underdeveloped, blocked or resisted. In this way CMC can help clients relate differently to themselves and their different 'self-parts', such as their critical self, angry self, or anxious self. If the balance between a client's critical and compassionate self-part changes over time, then a client may come to spend less time as their criticised self and more as their reassured self, which is likely to be associated with improved health, wellbeing, performance and quality of life. In addition to helping clients, it is likely that coaches themselves may benefit from the insights, messages, exercises and activities associated with compassionate mind coaching (CMC).

Theoretical foundations

Compassionate mind coaching is informed by several psychological theories.

Evolutionary theory

Evolutionary theory (called a theory but should more accurately be labelled as a fact) describes how populations change over time as a result of variation, selection and reproduction. Relevant to CMC is:

- how mammals emerged from their non-mammalian ancestors, in no small measure due to the amount of care and attention they invested in their offspring (eg compared to reptiles and amphibians)

- how, in turn, modern humans emerged from pre-human ancestors, in part by building on and further extending the behavioural repertoire enabled by their caring neurological pathways and algorithms – extending care to non-kin, strangers and even different species.

This evolutionary understanding of the origins of compassion leads to the CMC/compassion focused terapy (CFT) definition of compassion as: *'sensitivity to suffering, in self and others, with a commitment to alleviate and prevent it'* (Gilbert & Choden, 2013, p94).

Attachment theory

Attachment theory (Bowlby, 1969; Bowlby & Ainsworth, 1966) suggests that how human beings relate to each other is strongly influenced by their earliest experiences with primary care givers. When distressed, primary care givers act as a *safe haven* to which the infant can return and be comforted, feel safe and protected. The primary care giver also acts as a *secure base* from which the infant can explore the world, learn and grow. How these early relations are experienced influences adult patterns of attachment and relating. Compassionate mind coaching seeks to activate and channel caregiving and care receiving pathways and flows in order that individuals can create, strengthen and experience their own internal safe haven and secure base – from which to feel calmed and soothed when distressed, and create a platform for learning, experimenting and growth.

Multiple-self theory

The view that the mind is not a single whole, but is made up from multiple self-parts (or 'selves') which interact and have relationships with another has a long history (Ellenberger, 1970). Several different psychotherapeutic approaches are informed by this idea (eg dynamic psychotherapy, voice dialogue, emotion focused therapy, internal family-systems therapy, etc). The different 'self-parts' or modules have different functions, pay attention to different things, have different motivations, and may be associated with different emotions and patterns of responding. Different self-parts take control in different situations or contexts (eg, threat, caring, paranoid, angry, etc), and each part is in a relationship with other self-parts, or can be in conflict with them. Different psychological approaches describe and emphasise different self-parts. The main parts talked about and explored in compassionate mind coaching and therapy are:

- the critical self and the criticised self
- the compassionate self and the reassured self
- the angry self
- the anxious self

- the sad self
- the guilty self
- the shamed self.

One aim of compassionate mind coaching it to help the client better understand the nature and function of their critical self-part (their inner critic), including the fear behind its behaviour and any positive intent it may have for the client (eg signalling threat, protection from loss, etc). Another aim is to help the client reframe some of their experiences from statements about the way they are (eg 'you're a loser') to the normal activity of a critical self-part, and one internal voice amongst many.

Systems theory

Systems theory (Cummings, 2015) suggests that systems are cohesive groups of interrelated, interdependent parts, contained within a boundary, with one or more goals, and which can interact with their environment. How well a system performs is influenced as much by the quality of the interaction between the parts as the parts themselves. Systems manifest *synergy* (being more than the sum of their parts), *emergent phenomena* (behaviour that is not in the parts themselves), and *non-linearity* (in which small changes can lead to unexpectedly large effects out of proportion to the size of the change made). Systems theory suggests that client wellbeing and performance may improve when some parts are strengthened (eg the compassionate self-part) and the relationship between parts are altered (eg between the compassionate self-part and the criticised, angry, anxious, shamed, or critical self-part).

Control theory

Control theory (Carver & Scheier, 1982) deals with the control of dynamic systems, in which one part of the system (the controller) monitors how well the system is performing, relevant to a target level of performance and uses the gap between desired and actual performance (the error signal) to generate a control action to try to bring about the desired level of performance. When some clients underperform or make mistakes, their harsh inner critic appears and engages in aggressive, condemning, shaming and undermining language and emotional tones which can result in worse performance over time. One aim of CMC is to help the client shift from hostile self-criticism when they make a mistake (detect an error signal), to compassionate self-correction, as this may be more likely to bring the dynamic system, which is their person, closer to the desired level of performance.

Self-efficacy theory

Self-efficacy theory (Bandura, 1977) states that self-efficacy (confidence in one's ability to do something) strongly influences the probability of commencing and persisting with behaviour change in the face of obstacles. Three important determinants of self-efficacy are vicarious learning (eg, watching someone else do the behaviour), previous mastery experiences, and persuasion from an authority. The compassionate mind coach builds client self-efficacy for cultivating their compassionate mind by modelling the desired behaviours and building on the client's previous experiences (eg of being kind and caring towards others, and of receiving caring from others). Once developed and strengthened, a client's own internal 'ideal compassionate other' or 'compassionate self' may further build their self-efficacy and confidence by acting as a wise, caring, inner coach which reassures them about their ability to change and grow in hoped for directions.

Cognitive theory

Cognitive theory (Leahy, 2015) suggests that it is not so much what happens to people which disturbs them, as the view they take of things. Many people blame themselves for their struggles, difficulties and poor life performance. The compassionate mind coach helps clients view and explain their problems and struggles differently – that they are the inevitable result of being a living organism trying to make progress alongside other living things, whilst in possession of a tricky brain, made for them (not by them), having had a set of early and recent life experiences they didn't ask for and may not have wanted. In this way the CM coach encourages the client to see that their difficulties are 'not their fault' – whilst accepting that it nevertheless remains their responsibility to make the best of what they have.

Hope theory

Hope theory (Snyder, 2002) states that hope is determined by both desired ends and pathways. CM coaching can strengthen client hope by helping them to realise that they are not the finished article, that there are multiple possible future selves which may come into being, and that developing their compassionate mind can help them to grow and evolve into their desired future self.

Broaden and build theory

Broaden and Build theory (Fredrickson, 2004) suggests that the evolved function of positive emotions is to broaden a person's behavioural repertoire and response set, whilst helping them to build resources for the future (skills, friendships, knowledge, etc). Compassionate mind coaching may help clients to experience several positive emotions (joy, forgiveness, warmth, acceptance, achievement, relief, etc), and in this way broaden their perspective and build resources to help with personal development and growth.

Humanistic (Rogerian) theory

Carl Rogers (1957) suggested that in order for a client to improve (and self-actualise) the therapist/counsellor should create the core conditions (aka facilitative conditions) of empathic understanding, congruence and unconditional positive regard. He stated:

> 'it is that the individual has within himself or herself vast resources for self-understanding, for altering his or her self-concept, attitudes and self-directed behaviour – and that these resources can be tapped if only a definable climate of facilitative psychological attitudes can be provided' (1980, p115–117)

Not only does the compassionate mind coach try to create the facilitative conditions in the coaching relationship, but by helping the client develop their compassionate mind they also help the client to develop these conditions internally, with one self-part (their compassionate self) acting with warmth, non-judgement and empathy toward other self-parts (the inner critic, the criticised self, the angry self, etc).

Research evidence

Context

Human brains are the result of millions of years of evolution (Buss, 2009; Panksepp, 2010). One function that has been selected for is the ability to enter and maintain relationships based on affection and caring, which is known to have many beneficial physiological and psychological effects, and can even influence genetic expression (Cozolino, 2007; 2008; 2013; Siegel, 2012). But humans don't just have relationships with others – they also enter into relationships with themselves, and these can be positive eg, self-care when wounded, learning to feed ourselves, positive self-talk when facing challenges, etc, or negative eg getting angry with ourselves, hating ourselves, etc.

The internal relationships we have with ourselves, especially those involving a sense of shame (Kim et al, 2011) and self-criticism (Kannan & Levitt, 2013), underpin a wide range of psychological health and wellbeing problems (Gilbert & Irons, 2005). Self-criticism is a powerful stimulator of threat processing in the brain (Longe et al, 2010). Two of the most pervasive problems in mental health are self-criticism and shame (Gilbert & Irons, 2005; Kannan & Levitt, 2013; Zuroff et al, 2005), and clinical levels of shame and self-criticism represent serious disruptions to the capacity for stimulating inner affiliative systems that are so important for emotion regulation and wellbeing. Self-criticism works through the threat system whereas compassion works with more affiliative brain systems (Longe et al, 2010; Weng et al, 2013).

There is also a growing body of evidence that self-compassion is linked to psychological health and wellbeing (Brach, 2003; Salzberg, 1997). Research suggests that individuals who are self-compassionate experience better psychological health than those lacking self-compassion, experiencing:

- lower levels of anxiety and depression (Neff, 2012)
- lower cortisol levels, increased heart-rate variability (Rockliff *et al*, 2008)
- less rumination, perfectionism, and fear of failure (Neff, 2003a; Neff *et al*, 2005)
- less suppression of unwanted thoughts and a greater willingness to accept negative emotions as valid and important (Leary *et al*, 2007; Neff, 2003).

Self-compassion also seems to be associated with such psychological strengths such as happiness, optimism, wisdom, curiosity and exploration, personal initiative, and emotional intelligence (Heffernan *et al*, 2010; Hollis-Walker & Colosimo, 2011; Neff *et al*, 2007), along with an improved ability to cope with such adversities as: academic failure (Neff *et al*, 2005); divorce (Sbarra *et al*, 2012); childhood maltreatment (Vettese *et al*, 2011); and chronic pain (Costa & Pinto-Gouveia, 2011).

Self-compassion may also be associated with improved health behaviours, such as:

- persistence with dietary changes (Adams & Leary, 2007)
- smoking reductions (Kelly *et al*, 2009)
- seeking appropriate medical care (Terry & Leary, 2011)
- physical activity (Magnus *et al*, 2010)
- improved relationship functioning (Neff & Beretvas, 2012; Yarnell & Neff, 2012)
- empathetic concern for others, altruism, perspective taking, and forgiveness (Neff & Pommier, 2012).

Evidence

As compassionate mind coaching is a comparatively recent development, little research has been undertaken to evaluate its efficacy in trials. Consequently, we will have to look elsewhere for evidence from similar practices. There are at least six current empirically supported interventions that focus on the cultivation of compassion: compassion-focused therapy (CFT; Gilbert, 2010); mindful self-compassion (Neff & Germer, 2013); compassion cultivation training (Jazaieri *et al*, 2013); cognitively based compassion training (Pace *et al*, 2009); cultivating emotional balance (Kemeny *et al*, 2012) and compassion and loving-kindness meditations (eg, Hoffmann *et al*, 2011).

A growing body of research indicates that training people in compassion is associated with a wide range of physiological benefits for both healthy people and for people with severe health problems (Desbordes *et al*, 2012; Jazaieri *et al*, 2012; Weng *et al*, 2013; Hoffmann *et al*, 2011; Braehler *et al*, 2013).

Pace and colleagues (2009) developed a 6-week Compassion Meditation program and found that in an undergraduate population, the amount of compassion-focused mediation practice was related to innate immune responses to a psychosocial stressor – eg decreases in interleukin 123(IL-6) and cortisol production. In a pilot study, participation in compassionate mind training yielded significant decreases in depression, self-attacking, shame, and feelings of inferiority (Gilbert & Procter, 2006).

Neff and Germer (2013) evaluated the effectiveness of an 8-week Mindful Self Compassion (MSC) program designed to train people to be more self-compassionate, in which only one of the sessions specifically focused on mindfulness. They found significant pre/post gains in self-compassion, mindfulness, and various wellbeing outcomes, with gains maintained at 6 and 12-month follow ups.

Jazaieri *et al* (2013) examined the effects of a 9-week Compassion Cultivation course in a randomized control trial using a community sample of 100 adults and found significant improvement in all three domains of compassion – compassion for others, receiving compassion and self-compassion. They concluded that specific domains of compassion can be intentionally cultivated in a training programme.

Mindful self-compassion (MSC) was developed by Kristin Neff and Christopher Germer specifically as a program to help cultivate self-compassion (Neff & Germer, 2013). MSC is an 8-week group program, with each session lasting between two and two and a half hours, with an optional half-day meditation retreat. In the foundation randomised controlled trial (RCT) of MSC, Neff and Germer (2013) assessed programme impact with 51 participants, randomized to either MSC or a wait-list control condition. Results found significant increases in self-compassion, mindfulness, and on wellbeing outcomes (eg, life satisfaction). A strength of the study was that the MSC condition was measured at four time points: pre-, post-, six-, and finally 12-month follow-up. However, only 15 of the 24 MSC participants completed 12-month follow-up, which may represent a bias of self-selection in measurement.

Galante *et al* (2014) conducted a systematic review and meta-analysis on loving kindness meditation (LKM). Eligibility criteria were that the study had to be an RCT, peer-reviewed, with an adult population, contain data on outcomes related to health and wellbeing, and include an intervention that was predominantly LKM. Twenty-two studies were included in the review and nine included in the quantitative meta-analysis. The results found that LKM was moderately effective at increasing compassion (Hedge's g = .61), self-compassion (Hedge's g = .45), mindfulness (Hedge's g = .63), and decreasing self-reported depression (Hedge's g = -.61). The majority of the studies involved multiple sessions of LKM across four to eight weeks, and five of the studies consisted of single sessions of seven to 15 min.

Compassion cultivation training (CCT) is a program developed by Thupten Jinpa and colleagues (contemplative scholars, clinical psychologists, and neuroscientists) at the Center for Compassion and Altruism Research and Education (CCARE) at Stanford University (Jazaieri *et al*, 2013). CCT has a structured protocol and spans nine weekly sessions, with each session lasting two hours and offering a mixture of activities including: pedagogical instruction with active group discussion; guided group meditation; interactive practical exercises and exercises designed to promote feelings of open-heartedness or connection to others. The sessions deliver both didactic and experiential training in compassion practices across six steps:

1. Settling the mind and developing mindfulness skills
2. Experiencing loving-kindness and compassion for a loved one
3. Practising loving kindness meditation (LKM) and compassion for oneself
4. Compassion towards others through embracing our shared common humanity
5. Compassion towards all beings
6. 'Active compassion' practice where one imagines taking away others' pain and sorrow and offering to them one's own joy and happiness.

Participants are assigned weekly meditative exercises and at the end of the course participants are introduced to an integrated practice where all six steps are included in a complete daily compassion-focused meditation (Jinpa, 2010). A randomised controlled trial of CCT with 100 psychopathology-free community sample participants was written up in three separate papers, indicating generally beneficial effects. One paper demonstrated the impact CCT had on participants' level of compassion (Jazaieri *et al*, 2013); another on improving participants' mindfulness, mental health and emotion regulation (Jazaieri *et al*, 2014); and a third demonstrated how CCT reduced mind wandering to unpleasant topics (Jazaieri *et al*, 2016). One nice aspect of the studies is that they examined compassion from three perspectives, for others, for self, and receiving from others (Jazaieri *et al*, 2013).

In a meta-analysis of data from 12 randomized controlled trials, Kirby *et al* (2015) explored the impact of compassionate mind interventions on several different outcome variables including: compassion, self-compassion, mindfulness, depression, anxiety, psychological distress, and life satisfaction and happiness. They reported significant short-term moderate effect sizes for compassion ($d = .559$), self-compassion ($d = .691$), and mindfulness ($d = .525$), with significant moderate effects for reducing suffering-based outcomes of depression ($d = .656$) and anxiety ($d = .547$), and small-to-moderate effects for psychological distress ($d = .374$). Significant moderate effects were also found for life satisfaction and happiness ($d = .540$). Recommendations for improving the methodological rigour of compassion-based intervention evaluation research included using self-report measures with normative data (eg, Beck Depression Inventory for depression), evaluating interventions with clinical populations, using active control comparison groups, and collecting follow-up data (eg, 6–12 months).

In a subsequent wide-ranging review article, Kirby (2016) provided an overview and synthesis of the currently available compassion-based interventions, including what the different programmes looked like, their aims, and the evidence base underpinning each. His review identified least eight different compassion-based interventions including compassion-focused therapy, mindful self-compassion, cultivating compassion training, and cognitively based compassion training. He found six of the compassionate mind-based interventions to have been evaluated in randomised controlled trials, and that a meta-analysis had shown that compassion-based interventions can produce moderate effect sizes for suffering and improved life satisfaction.

Kelly and Carter (2015) explored the benefits of a self-compassion intervention in binge-eating disorder. Thirty four participants were randomized to either food planning plus self-compassion strategies (n = 15, imagery and writing exercises), food planning plus behavioural strategies (n = 13; alternative activity exercises to binging) or a wait-list control condition (n = 13). The intervention took place over three weeks, and results indicated that the self-compassion intervention reduced global eating disorder pathology, eating and weight concerns, and increased self-compassion greater than the other two conditions, with participants low in fear of self-compassion deriving greater benefits. Although promising, the sample size was small, and there was a lack of follow-up data.

Arimitsu (2016) developed a group programme called the Enhancing Self-compassion Program (ESP). Based on CFT, and spanning seven weekly one-and-a-half-hour sessions, participants explore loving kindness meditation, mindfulness, imagery, letter writing, three-chair work, compassionate behaviours, and relating to self-critical thoughts. Forty-one participants (Mean age 23.25), with scores below 17.35 on the SCS, were randomized to either ESP or a wait-list control and a range of self-report measures were used at pre-, post-, and 3-month follow-up. Results found that ESP significantly improved self-compassion compared to the control group, and these results were maintained at follow-up.

In a study exploring the use of compassion focused therapy (CFT) as a self-help guide for enhancing public mental health, Sommers-Spijkerman *et al* (2018) randomised adults with low to moderate levels of wellbeing to either CFT (n = 120) or a waitlist control group (n = 122). Participants completed the Mental Health Continuum-Short Form, Hospital Anxiety and Depression Scale, Perceived Stress Scale, Self-Compassion Scale-Short Form, Forms of Self-Criticizing/Attacking and Reassurance Scale, Positive and Negative Affect Schedule, and Gratitude questionnaire (gratitude) at baseline, postintervention (3 months), 3- and 9-month follow-up. Compared with the waitlist control group, the CFT group showed better improvement on wellbeing at postintervention (d = .51, 95% CI [.25, .77], p < .001) and 3-month follow-up (d = .39, 95% CI [.13, .65], p < .001). On all secondary outcome measures but positive affect, the intervention group showed significantly greater improvements up to 3-month follow-up. At 9-month follow-up, improvements on all measures were retained or amplified among CFT participants. They concluded that CFT as guided self-help shows promise as a public mental health strategy for enhancing wellbeing and reducing psychological distress.

Cuppage *et al* (2018) examined the effectiveness of a compassion-focused therapy (CFT) intervention (n = 58) compared to treatment as usual (n = 29) with a population with different mental health problems. A secondary aim of the study was to explore potential processes of change within the treatment. Group CFT consisted of 14 sessions twice weekly for 5 weeks, and once weekly for 4 weeks. Participants completed measures of psychopathology, shame, self-criticism, fears of self-compassion, and social safeness, at pre-treatment, post-treatment, and two-month follow-up. Potential processes of change were examined using correlations and regression analysis. They found significantly greater improvements for levels of psychopathology, fears of self-compassion and social safeness for CFT, compared to TAU. Additionally, analyses showed improvements in shame and self-criticism within the CFT group but not the TAU group. All improvements were maintained at 2-month follow-up. Improvements in psychopathology were predicted by changes in self-criticism and fears of self-compassion. The authors concluded that compassion-focused therapy appears to be an effective group intervention for a range of mental health difficulties and felt that the positive impact of the CFT model with a transdiagnostic group reinforced the importance of addressing underlying psychological processes, rather than symptoms alone.

Thomason and Moghaddam (2021) conducted a systematic review and meta-analysis to try to identify whether compassion-focused therapy (CFT) or compassion-based interventions are effective in improving self-esteem. Ten eligible papers were identified. Within-group analysis of data from eight studies demonstrated a medium, significant overall effect size (g = 0.56, 95% CI [0.19-0.93], z = 3.54, p < .001), which increased slightly and remained significant (g = 0.61, 95% CI [0.05-1.17], z = 2.82, p = .005) when the lowest quality studies were removed. They concluded that compassion-focused therapy or compassion-based interventions may be effective in improving self-esteem, but noted a large clinical and methodological heterogeneity amongst studies, making further conclusions difficult.

Stroud and Griffiths (2021) examined the effectiveness of a compassion-focused therapy (CFT) group in improving patient outcomes compared to those receiving treatment as usual (TAU) within adult mental health inpatient settings. Those self-allocating to receive the intervention (n = 19) were compared to those who did not (n = 13). They found significant improvements to all CORE-OM measure subdomains for those receiving CFT, in particular the Wellbeing and Functioning subdomains, whilst those receiving TAU only noted a significant improvement in the area of Risk. They concluded that compassion-focused therapy appears to be an effective group intervention for a trans-diagnostic population within adult inpatient settings.

Wakelin *et al* (2021) conducted a review to estimate the overall effect of self-compassion-related interventions on self-criticism outcomes and investigate potential moderating variables. Nineteen randomized controlled trials (RCTs), involving 1350 participants in total were included in the meta-analysis. Findings indicated that self-compassion-related interventions produce a significant, medium reduction in self-criticism in comparison with control groups (Hedges' g = 0.51, 95% CI [0.33-0.69]) and moderator analysis found greater reductions in self-criticism when self-compassion-related interventions were longer and compared with passive rather than active controls. The authors felt the review provided promising evidence of the effectiveness of self-compassion-related interventions for reducing self-criticism, but that results were limited by moderate quality studies with high heterogeneity.

Practice

Compassionate mind coaching is a multi-modal approach in which the coach uses and shares a range of different strategies, tools and methods including psychoeducation; relationship building; socratic questioning; functional analysis; reframing; visualisation; guided imagery; chairwork; writing exercises; acting methods; homework assignments; self-disclosure, etc.

Psychoeducation

Most clients lack scientific understanding about how their minds works and are unlikely to be familiar with the key ideas and concepts associated with compassionate mind coaching. Exploring a client's current understanding of the origin of their difficulties and struggles before offering alternative (and hopefully more helpful) perspectives is a core task for compassionate mind coaches. Since delivering a lecture is typically not the best way to educate clients, compassionate mind coaches may wish to develop their skills in Socratic questioning, drawing diagrams, using metaphors, sharing video links and helpful books. Regardless of the approach used, here are some of the core concepts and messages to be shared during compassionate mind coaching – which importantly can help with reframing and motivation.

1. Old brain, new brain, tricky brain

Our brains evolved over millions of years. Unable to go back and start again, nature tinkers with and makes use of what it has, adapting what is already there. This has resulted in a multi-layered structure sometimes referred to as the triune brain (McLean, 1990). The oldest part of the brain is shared with our reptile ancestors and supports such functions and behaviours as breathing, eating, drinking, mating, fighting and protecting territory. About two million years ago, pre-humans started to evolve capacities for complex cognitive processes such as anticipation, imagination, perspective taking, mentalising, language, symbols and a new sense of self. Whilst these qualities gave rise to intelligence, science, culture, the arts and the modern world as we know it, they came with a downside. Other primates are not aware that they might die from a heart attack, nor do they ruminate about their appearance or how well they performed in some task. They probably don't stay up at night worrying about what other apes think about them, and most likely don't self-monitor as to whether they are doing well or badly in life. Humans do. This capacity for complex reflection, thinking, imagination and mentalising, along with having a sense of self and self-monitoring, can (and often does) spell serious trouble for humans.

The CM coach used this 'old brain, new brain' model to help clients understand that many of their problems stem from the way their brain has evolved, and that they (like all other humans) have 'tricky' brains containing different parts which are not well integrated and that can get them trapped in unhelpful loops and patterns. The coach can also use the old brain / new brain model to help underpin the 'it's not your fault' message (see later), as well as helping clients to understand why they can and do experience such a profound disconnect between their thoughts and feelings.

2. Your brain is made for you, not by you

Letting the client know that their brain was made for them – not by them – may help to reduce client feelings of confusion, guilt, shame and self-criticism about being the way they are and feeling the way they do. It can encourage the idea that it's not their fault for thinking, feeling and even behaving the way they do – even though it is their responsibility for doing something about it.

3. It's not your fault

Many clients experience unhelpful levels of self-blame, shame, regret, hurt, self-loathing and unhappiness about their current or past behaviours. They strongly feel that there is 'something the matter' with them. For such clients it can be helpful to provide an alternative explanation for their behaviour. That the reason they behaved the way they did, or behave the way they do, is not because they are 'bad' or because there is 'something is the matter with them', but rather that they have inherited this tricky brain with its unhelpful loops which get in the way of wise living, combined with their exposure to early social environments they did not choose. Of course, we don't want the client to use the 'it's not your fault' message as an excuse to persist in undesirable behaviour, such as abusing others or drinking too much. They still have responsibility to change. It is just that some of their problems may be better explained by the fact that they own a tricky brain, doing the best it can in an environment for which it did not evolve.

4. You are not the finished article

Just as different versions of the client could have come into being over the 20, 30, 40 years of their existence on the planet, depending on their earlier experiences (presence or otherwise of loving parents, part of the world they grew up in, experience of poverty or wealth, experience of violence, poor health, injury or abuse, exposure to sport and artistic role models, etc), so too there are multiple possible future versions of the client which may come into existence over the next 2, 5 or 10 years – including a desired version, their 'desired future self'. This true and essentially optimistic and hopeful message can help some clients be more open to change and personal growth, and links to the growth mindset of Carol Dweck (2006).

5. The three circles model (of emotional regulation)

Compassionate mind coaches Dweause the 'three circles model' to help clients understand how three evolved, basic functional emotional systems (or emotion regulation systems), interrelate and can become unbalanced (Depue & Morrone-Strupinsky, 2005; LeDoux, 1998; Panksepp, 1998). This three circles model is easily understood by clients who seem to readily identify with it. Coaches can use the model to help clients see in what way their emotional regulation system may have become unbalanced and to explore the benefits to them of spending less time in threat or drive mode and more time in safe, contented, recovery mode.

The threat and self-protection focused emotion system evolved to attract attention, tunes in to detect and respond to threats (LeDoux, 1998). There is a menu of threat-based emotions such as anger, anxiety and disgust and a menu of defensive behaviours such as fight, flight, submission, freeze etc. It is part of the 'fast brain' (Kahneman, 2011) and is one of the human brains dominant systems, running in the background, constantly monitoring for threats and ready to jump centre stage and grab the brain's attention at a moment's notice when serious actual or possible threats present themselves. This system is responsible for the 'negativity bias' (paying more attention to negative things that happen than positive things) and the 'smoke detector principle' (the tendency to overreact to ambiguous stimuli). It is much better for our survival to run away needlessly 99 times from a harmless rustle of leaves than miss the one time when it was a predator hiding in the bush (Baumeister *et al*, 2001). This system activates the sympathetic nervous system, and many forms of therapy tend to work directly with this threat system itself (Gilbert, 1993). In compassionate mind coaching, the coach tends to explore and help the client strengthen various 'positive' affect systems to help them counteract and better regulate their innate threat system.

The drive, seeking and acquisition focused system evolved to motivate and regulate our efforts at going and getting hold of resources, of desiring, seeking out, wanting and obtaining things which are to our advantage. It is involved in goal setting, striving and planning, exploring and capturing resources for ourselves and others, of being competent, achieving and experiences of mastery. This system is involved in competitive drives and mental states in which individuals seek dominance and social position and can involve striving to achieve, motivated by fear of rejection and social exclusion. This system (like the threat system) also activates the sympathetic nervous system. Consumer capitalism, with its tendency to market and sell to people more than they need, may be contributing to the overstimulation of 'wanting' 'craving' 'acquiring' 'me focused' competitive behaviours, and such an overreliance on acquisition and achievement may increase vulnerability to feelings of depression – especially when people feel defeated, unable to reach their goals, or feel they are doing poorly in comparison to other people (Taylor *et al*, 2011). Some clients spend a significant amount of time cycling between their threat and drive systems (or with both active or overactive), unable to relax and simply be. Which brings us to...

The Rest and Digest system (also known as the contentment, soothing and affiliative-focused system) is a positive affect system linked to calming, resting and contentment, a state of inner peace and slowing, where one does not feel threatened, is not seeking or striving and both the drive and threat systems are calmed (Depue & Morrone-Strupinsky, 2005). It evolved in mammals to enable states of peacefulness and quiescence when they are no longer threatened or focused on recovering and consuming resources. It is particularly linked to the parasympathetic system. Over evolutionary time this system of calming has been adapted for some of the functions of affiliative behaviour – so, for example, if a child is distressed, they can (re)turn to the parent who will hold, cuddle or reassure them and this has calming effect on their distress. This capacity to experience others as caring and helpful is often the way in which feelings of threat are reduced, and there are especially important brain systems that register the kindness of others and help tone down threat systems.

The compassionate mind coach uses the 'three circles model' to help clients understand that some of their problems or issues might be best explained by an overactivity of one of these three emotional regulation systems, or a lack of balance between them. Perhaps they are excessively worried, anxious, fearful or concerned about their reputation, status, social standing, or chances of loss, etc. Perhaps they are excessively competitive, or materialistic and consumed with thoughts about winning and losing, about getting hold of money, property, objects, etc. Or perhaps they experience excessive feelings of inferiority, of 'not being good enough', or of being a 'loser', or somehow inadequate, perhaps spending excessive amounts of time either trying to 'prove' themselves (in their own eyes or in the eyes of important others) or ruminating about how they came to be the way they are. The coach can use the model to help clients see that they may have an imbalance between their three main emotional regulation systems, and that one goal of a compassionate mind approach might be to 're-balance' their brain's basic emotional regulation systems.

6. The nature of compassion

One barrier to engaging in compassionate mind training can be unhelpful client beliefs about compassion. For instance, they may view compassion as a form of weakness not strength, or just the same as kindness or love, or just a feeling, or something self-indulgent that will undermine their motivation and drive. The compassionate mind coach might explore clients' beliefs about compassion before providing them with corrective information and experiences, perhaps via Socratic dialogue. For instance, if a client sees compassion as something weak, the coach might ask them to bring to mind people they see as very compassionate. And then ask them if they consider the person or people they identified as weak. Or perhaps ask their client to adopt the body posture of someone who is weak (they may curl up, depress their shoulders, look to the ground etc) and then say 'well, that doesn't look very compassionate to me'.

Sharing with the client the evolutionary-informed definition of compassion –

'sensitivity to suffering, in self and others, with a commitment to alleviate and prevent it'

(Gilbert & Choden, 2013, p94)

– may also help clients see that compassion is not just a feeling, but rather a motivation, mindset and set of skills.

7. The three flows of compassion

It is helpful for clients to understand that compassion flows, and in three ways. Just as you can be angry with someone, they can be angry towards you, and you can be angry towards yourself, so too compassion can flow from you to someone else, from someone else to you, and from yourself to yourself. This latter flow is called self-compassion, as is associated with range of health, performance and quality of life outcomes.

8. Self-parts

It is helpful for clients to understand that the self may perhaps best be viewed as made up of parts (eg the inner critic, the angry self, the anxious self, the compassionate self, etc) and that some parts can be strengthened with training (eg the compassionate self) and the relationship between different parts can be improved over time.

9. Who's in charge?

Related to the idea of the self being made up of parts, this question seeks to prompt the client to reflect on which self-part might be controlling their thinking, feeling and behaving at the moment, and whether or not things might work out better for them if a different self-part (eg their compassionate self) was more in charge.

10. The nature and power of imagery

Both a real snake and the thought of being attacked by a snake can powerfully stimulate the brain and the body, inducing changes in thinking, hormonal levels, heart rate, breathing rate, images of bad things happening, feelings of fear and urges/desire to escape. Similarly, being presented with real food when hungry and just imagining food can both stimulate the body's physiology and motivational systems. These examples can be used to help clients appreciate that receiving care, kindness and reassurance from another and imagining receiving care, kindness and reassurance can both help a person feel settled, less anxious, calmer and even more motivated and confident.

Soothing rhythm breathing

In compassionate mind coaching we help clients prepare the body to prepare the mind. One widely used method is to teach and encourage the client to engage in soothing rhythm breathing, having the client adopt a grounded and upright, open posture before settling their breathing into a natural, not strained or forced rhythm. And then encouraging them to slightly slow and deepen their breathing to around 5 to 6 breaths per minute, with a slight pause at the end of the inhalation, and another pause at the end of the exhalation – a pattern of breathing thought to be associated with activation of the parasympathetic nervous system.

Slight smile, friendly vocal tone

Whilst practising soothing rhythm breathing, clients are encouraged to bring a slight smile to their face and adopt a friendly vocal tone with themselves for any self-talk which may arise.

Body scan with compassionate focus

The client might be guided to focus their attention on different parts of their body, in sequence – helping them focus on the sensations of slowing down and noticing what that feels like in their mind and their body. The body postures are one of finding a sense of inner stillness and inner groundedness and rootedness.

Safe space

The safe space exercise involves guiding the client to imagining they are in a place where they feel safe. Have them imagine even that the place welcomes them and wants them to be there. Encourage them to form an emotional connection with the place and realise that this place is their creation and that it is always available to them – never more than a thought away. Encourage them to immerse themselves in their safe space imagery several times each week.

Mindfulness sitting practice and experiential acceptance

Help the client develop their mindfulness skills of focusing their attention and bringing it back to what is being attended to when the attention wanders, and doing this with gentleness, learning that wandering is one of the things that the mind does – it is not the being bad at mindfulness! Any thoughts about judging themselves or telling themselves 'I'm no good at this' are seen as the usual activities of the restless mind. Have them pay attention to various sensations which may come into awareness with a polite curiosity, as if noticing them for the first time. Encourage them to allow the sensation or urge to just be as it is, rather than what the mind says it is. Not necessarily wanting the sensation or feeling but being willing to have it, to make space for it, letting it come and go as it pleases.

Cultivating a compassionate image

Have the client think about and imagine a compassionate other being, one that cares deeply for them. This imaginary compassionate other may be old or young, male or female, from any ethnicity, or perhaps a species other than human. Have the client imagine the qualities they want their being to have – perhaps a complete acceptance of them as a person, a deep concern and care for them, a sense of belonging and kinship. Perhaps their compassionate other has experienced some of what the client has experienced. Then, whilst practising soothing breathing rhythm, have the client imagine their compassionate image saying the following words, in as warm a voice as can be imagined and with a full commitment to the person: 'May you be free of suffering [client says own name in their head]', 'May you be happy, [name]', 'May you flourish, [name]', 'May you find peace and wellbeing, [name]'. Have the client practise this exercise several times each week.

Cultivating the compassionate self

Whilst we are used to practising specific skills such as cooking, playing a sport, learning to paint, etc, most people are unaware that they can practise cultivating a particular self-identity and that this will have an effect on their mind (Jazaieri et al, 2012; Weng et al, 2013). One way of doing this and of helping clients develop their compassionate self is to use method acting techniques (Cannon, 2012). Good method actors use imagery to stimulate different neurological and physiological systems to help them perform a particular role. Compassionate mind coaches help their clients use these same method acting techniques to create a stronger experience of, and sense of, their compassionate self. Have them start by imagining and creating a compassionate facial expression – one of friendliness, perhaps with a gentle smile. Then have them focus on imagining what a compassionate voice sounds like, one that is friendly, supportive and understanding. Have them sit quietly, slow down their breathing, and notice the difference in feeling between saying hello to themselves (eg, 'Hello, Tim') using a neutral voice and saying the same phrase in a friendly voice. Reflect with the client on whether or not the deliberate creation of a friendly internal voice creates a different internal feeling. Then have the client imagine themselves having certain qualities, in particular wisdom, strength, sense of authority, and a commitment to be compassionate and helpful (Gilbert, 2010; Gilbert & Choden, 2013). Once this has been done, have the client imagine themselves being with others and undertaking activities from the perspective of their compassionate self. In addition to bringing about helpful psychological and physiological changes, these exercises can help create 'ideas' in the client's mind about the kind of person they might wish to become, over time.

Chairwork to help cultivate compassion for different self-parts

This exercise involves developing compassion and understanding towards these different parts of oneself using chairwork (Kellogg, 2004). Set out three chairs. Have the client sit in one chair and, being themselves, have them describe a particular issue which concerns or frustrates them, or which they beat themselves up about. Then have them sit in the 'critical self' chair, and have the critical self say things to the usual self. This is just 'externalising' what their inner critic is already saying to them inside their heads on a regular basis. Then have the client return to the normal self-chair and ask them what they would like to say to their critical self. Sometimes, you may notice a posture of defeat and submission as they agree with and give into the critical self. Then have the client sit in the third chair and, preparing themselves with breathing and postural exercises, adopt their compassionate self (previously practised and cultivated) and have this compassionate self talk with their critical self. What is it that the critical self wants for the client? What is it that the critical self is scared of, such that it says the nasty things it does to the normal self? (For more detailed descriptions of cultivating compassion for different aspects of the self, see Gilbert & Choden, 2013.)

Exploring self-compassion through writing

The compassionate mind coach can have the client undertake one or more writing exercises to help them develop their compassionate mind, including having them write about an aspect of themselves they do not like, and then having them write an imaginary letter to themselves from a wise and compassionate friend, and having them keep a self-compassion journal.

Functional analysis of inner critic and compassionate self

A functional analysis involves the client having a deeper look at and think about the appearance, behaviour and motivation of a particular self-part, and its effect on them. For a functional analysis of the inner critic, the exercise might start with asking the client how they feel about their inner critic, and any fears they may have of letting go of this self-part. It can then be helpful to have the client think about something for which they tend to be self-critical (but not overwhelmingly so) – for instance, their weight, relationships, financial behaviour, work performance etc. And then have them bring to mind their inner critic. A series of gentle questions then follows, for instance: what does the critic look like? What is its inner form? What does it actually say to the client? What does it feel about them? What does it want to do with them? Once the critical self-part has been met and explored, it can be useful to ask the client how they feel now that they have been in contact with the critic. Often, they realise that perhaps the critic is not as helpful or motivating as they may have originally thought.

For a functional analysis of the compassionate self, the exercise might start with asking the client what they feel their wise, compassionate self might want for them. Once again, ask a series of gentle, open-ended questions such as: what does your compassionate self look like? What is its inner form? What does it actually say to the you? What does it feel about you? What does it want to do with you? Once the compassionate self-part has been met and explored, it can be useful to ask the client how they feel now that they have been in contact with their compassionate self. Often, they may say they feel reassured, or calmer, or more confident about the future, which can then be followed by further questions about whether they think they might benefit from strengthening and spending more time in contact with their wise, compassionate self-part.

Conclusion

Compassionate mind coaching is the coaching version of compassion-focused therapy. It can be considered a fusion of coaching, mindfulness and compassion related practices and exercises, and is informed and underpinned by evolutionary psychology and neuroscience. It is both a way or style of doing coaching, as well as a discrete, holistic and multi-modal coaching methodology in its own right – helping clients to achieve a better balance between three important emotion regulation systems, toning down their 'threat' and 'acquisition' systems if these are interfering with their health, wellbeing and quality of life.

Compassionate mind coaching is a multi-modal coaching approach which can involve psychoeducation; relationship building; Socratic questioning; functional analysis; reframing; visualisation; guided imagery; chairwork; writing exercises; acting methods; and homework/practice assignments.

It can help clients to think about and grow into more of the person they want to be and provides them with a powerful and alternative framework for thinking about their problems, struggles, frustrations and path forwards.

Finally, engaging in some of the practices and activities outlined in the chapter may help coaches themselves to become both better coaches and happier, healthier, more fulfilled human beings.

Five questions for further reflection and exploration

1. **What proportion of your clients might benefit from an improved ability to regulate their emotional state, experience less self-criticism and more self-reassurance?**

2. **How strong is your own inner critic?**

3. **In what situations, circumstances and contexts does your inner critic become most vocal?**

4. **What are some of the main qualities and characteristics of your desired future self?**

5. **What might be your two or three best reasons for developing your skills in compassionate mind coaching?**

Suggested reading

Gilbert, P. (2010) *Compassion-focused Therapy: Distinctive Features.* Abingdon: Routledge.

Kolts, R (2016) *CFT Made Simple: A Clinicians Guide to Practicing Compassion-Focused Therapy.* Location: New Harbinger.

Irons, C. and Beaumont, E. (2017) *The Compassionate Mind Workbook. A step-by-step guide to developing your compassionate self.* London: Robinson.

Kirby, J.N. (2017) Compassion interventions: The programmes, the evidence, and implications for research and practice. *Psychological Psychotherapy,* **90** (3) 432–455.

Anstiss A., Passmore., J. & Gilbert, P. (2020) Compassion: the essential orientation. *The Psychologist,* **33**, 38–42.

References

Adams, C. E. & Leary, M. R. (2007) Promoting self-compassionate attitudes toward eating among restrictive and guilty eaters. *Journal of Social and Clinical Psychology,* **26**, 1120–1144.

Arimitsu, K. (2016) The effects of a program to enhance self- compassion in Japanese individuals: A randomized controlled pilot study. *The Journal of Positive Psychology.* Advance online publication. Available online at: doi:10.1080/17439760.2016.1152593. Accessed 10 July 2021.

Bandura, A. (1997) *Self-Efficacy: The exercise of control.* New York: W.H. Freeman.

Baumeister, R.F., Bratslavsky, E., Finkenauer, C. & Vohs, K.D. (2001) Bad is stronger than good. *Review of General Psychology,* **5**, 323–370.

Bowlby, J. (1969) *Attachment and Loss.* New York: Basic Books.

Bowlby, J. and Ainsworth, M. (1966) *Maternal Care and Mental Health.* New York: Schocken Books.

Brach, T. (2003) *Radical Acceptance: Embracing your life with the heart of a Buddha.* New York, NY: Bantam.

Braehler, C., Gumley, A., Harper, J., Wallace, S., Norrie, J. & Gilbert, P. (2013) Exploring change processes in compassion-focused therapy in psychosis: Results of a feasibility randomized controlled trial. *British Journal of Clinical Psychology,* **52**, 199–214.

Buss, D.A (2009) The great struggles of life: Darwin and the emergence of evolutionary psychology. *American Psychologist,* **64**, 140–148

Cannon, D. (2012) *In-Depth Acting.* London: Oberon.

Carver, C. & Scheier, M. (1982) Control theory: A useful conceptual framework for personality-social, clinical, and health psychology. *Psychological bulletin,* **92**, 111–35.

Costa, J. & Pinto-Gouveia, J. (2011) Acceptance of pain, self-compassion and psychopathology: Using the chronic pain acceptance questionnaire to identify patients' subgroups. *Clinical Psychology and Psychotherapy,* **18**, 292–302.

Cozolino, L. (2007) *The Neuroscience of Human Relationships: Attachment and the developing brain.* New York: Norton.

Cozolino, L. (2008) *The Healthy Aging Brain: Sustaining Attachment, Attaining Wisdom.* New York: Norton.

Cozolino, L. (2013) *The Social Neuroscience of Education.* New York; Norton.

Cummings. T.G. (2015) Systems Theory. Volume 11. *Organizational Behavior.* Wiley.

Cuppage J, Baird K, Gibson J, Booth R, Hevey D. (2018) Compassion-focused therapy: Exploring the effectiveness with a transdiagnostic group and potential processes of change. *British Journal Clinical Psychology,* **57**(2) 240–254.

Desbordes, G., Negi, L.T., Pace, T.W.W., Wallace, B.A., Raison, C.L. & Schwartz, E.L. (2012) Effects of mindful-attention and compassion mediation training on amygdala response to emotional stimuli in an ordinary, non-meditative state. *Frontiers in Human Neuroscience,* **6**, 1–15.

Depue, R.A. & Morrone-Strupinsky, J.V. (2005) A neurobehavioral model of affiliative bonding. *Behavioral and Brain Sciences,* **28**, 313–395.

Dweck, C.S. (2006) *Mindset: The new psychology of success.* New York: Random House

Ellenberger, Henri F. (1970) *The Discovery of the Unconscious: The history and evolution of dynamic psychiatry.* New York: Basic Books.

Fredrickson, B.L. (2004) The broaden-and-build theory of positive emotions. Philosophical transactions of the Royal Society of London. Series B, *Biological sciences*, **359** (1449) 1367–1378.

Galante, J., Galante, I., Bekkers, M.J. & Gallacher, J. (2014) Effect of kindness-based meditation on health and wellbeing: A systematic review and meta-analysis. *Journal of Consulting and Clinical Psychology*, **82**, 1101–1114.

Gilbert, P. (1993) Defence and safety: Their function in social behaviour and psychopathology. *British Journal of Clinical Psychology*, **32**, 131–153.

Gilbert, P. (2010) Compassion-focused *Therapy: The CBT Distinctive Features Series.* London: Routledge.

Gilbert, P. & Choden (2013) *Mindful Compassion.* London: Constable-Robinson.

Gilbert, P. & Irons, C. (2005) Focused therapies and compassionate mind training for shame and self-attacking. In: P. Gilbert (Ed) Compassion: Conceptualisations, Research and Use in Psychotherapy. London: Routledge, pp263–325.

Gilbert, P. & Procter, S. (2006) Compassionate mind training for people with high shame and self-criticism: overview and pilot study of a group therapy approach. *Clinical Psychology & Psychotherapy*, **13** (6) 353–379.

Heffernan, M., Griffin, M., McNulty, S. & Fitzpatrick, J. J. (2010) Self-compassion and emotional intelligence in nurses. *International Journal of Nursing Practice*, **16**, 366–373.

Hoffmann,S.G., Grossman, P. & Hinton, D.E. (2011) Loving-kindness and compassion meditation: potential for psychological intervention. *Clinical Psychology Review*, **13**, 1126–1132.

Hollis-Walker, L. & Colosimo, K. (2011) Mindfulness, self-compassion, and happiness in non-meditators: A theoretical and empirical examination. *Personality and Individual Differences*, **50**, 222–227.

Jazaieri, H., Jinpa, T., McGonigal, K., Rosenberg, E. L., Finkelstein, J., Simon-Thomas, E.,Goldin, P.R. (2013) Enhancing compassion: A randomized controlled trial of a compassion cultivation training program. *Journal of Happiness Studies*, **14**, 1113–1126.

Jazaieri, H., Lee, I.A., McGonigal, K., Jinpa, T., Doty, J.R., Gross, J.J. & Goldin, P.R. (2016) A wandering mind is a less caring mind: daily experience sampling during compassion meditation training. *The Journal of Positive Psychology*, **11**, 37–50.

Jazaieri, H., McGonigal, K., Jinpa, T., Doty, J.R., Gross, J.J. & Goldin, P.R. (2014) A randomized controlled trial of compassion cultivation training: effects on mindfulness, affect, and emotion regulation. *Motivation and Emotion*, **38**, 23–35.

Kannan, D. & Levitt, H.M. (2013) A review of client self-criticism in psychotherapy. *Journal of Psychotherapy Integration*, **23**, 166–178.

Kahneman, D. (2011) *Thinking, Fast and Slow.* London: Macmillan.

Kellogg, S.H. (2004) Dialogical encounters: Contemporary perspectives on "chairwork" in psychotherapy. *Psychotherapy: Research, Theory, Practice, Training*, **41**, 310–320.

Kelly, A.C., Zuroff, D.C., Foa, C L. & Gilbert, P. (2009) Who benefits from training in self-compassionate self-regulation? A study of smoking reduction. *Journal of Social and Clinical Psychology*, **29**, 727–755.

Kelly, A.C. & Carter, J.C. (2015) Self-compassion training for binge eating disorder: A pilot randomized controlled trial. *Psychology and Psychotherapy: Theory, Research, and Practice*, **88**, 285–303.

Kemeny, M.E., Foltz, C., Cavanagh, J.F., Cullen, M., Giese-Davis, J., Jennings, P., Rosenberg, E. L., Gillath, O., Saver, P., Wallace, B.A. & Ekman, P. (2012) Contemplative/emotion training reduces negative emotional behavior and promotes prosocial responses. *Emotion*, **12**, 338–350.

Kim, S., Thibodeau, R. & Jorgensen, R.S. (2011) Shame, guilt, and depressive symptoms: A Meta-analytic review. *Psychological Bulletin*, **137**, 68–96.

Kirby, J.N., Tellegen, C.L. & Steindl, S.R. (2015) Cultivating compassion: A systematic review and meta-analysis of compassion-based interventions. *PROSPERO: International Prospective Register of Systematic Reviews*, 2015, CRD42015024576. Retrieved from http:// www.crd.york.ac.uk/ PROSPERO/display_record.asp?ID = CRD42015024576. Accessed 15 July 2021.

Kirby, J.N.(2016) Compassion interventions: The programmes, the evidence, and implications for research and practice. *Psychological Psychotherapy*, **90** (3) 432–455.

Leahy, R. (2015) *Contemporary Cognitive Therapy: Theory, Research, and Practice*. New York, NY: Guilford Press.

LeDoux, J. (1998) *The Emotional Brain*. London: Weidenfeld and Nicolson.

Longe, O., Maratos, F.A., Gilbert, P., Evans, G., Volker, F., Rockliffe, H. & Rippon, G. (2010) Having a word with yourself: Neural correlates of self-criticism and self-reassurance. *NeuroImage*, **49**, 1849–1856.

Magnus, C., Kowalski, K. & McHugh, T. (2010) The role of self-compassion in women's self-determined motives to exercise and exercise-related outcomes. *Self & Identity*, **9**, 363–382.

Neff, K.D. (2003) The development and validation of a scale to measure self-compassion. *Self and Identity*, **2**, 223–250.

Neff, K.D. (2012) The science of self-compassion. In: C. Germer and R. Siegel (Eds) *Compassion and Wisdom in Psychotherapy*. New York, NY: Guilford Press, pp79–92.

Neff, K.D. & Beretvas, S.N. (2012) The role of self-compassion in romantic relationships. *Self and Identity*, **12** (1).

Neff, K.D., Hsieh, Y & Dejitterat, K. (2005) Self-compassion, achievement goals and coping with academic failure. *Self and Identity*, **4**, 263–287.

Neff, K.D. & Pommier, E. (2012) The relationship between self-compassion and other-focused concern among college undergraduates, community adults, and practicing meditators. *Self and Identity*, **12** (2) 160–176.

Neff, K.D. & Rude, S.S. & Kirkpatrick, K. (2007) An examination of self-compassion in relation to positive psychological functioning and personality traits. *Journal of Research in Personality*, **41**, 908–916.

Panksepp, J. (2010) Affective neuroscience of the emotional brainmind: evolutionary perspectives and implications for understanding depression. *Dialogues in Clinical Neuroscience*, **12**, 383–399.

Pace, T.W., Negi, L.T., Adame, D.D., Cole, S.P., Sivilli, T.I., Brown, T.D., Raison, C.L. (2009) Effect of compassion meditation on neuroendocrine, innate immune and behavioral responses to psychosocial stress. *Psychoneuroendocrinology*, **34**, 87–98.

Panksepp, J. (1998) *Affective Neuroscience. The Foundations of Human and Animal Emotions*. Oxford: Oxford University Press.

Rockliff, H., Gilbert, P., McEwan, K., Lightman, S. & Glover, D. (2008) A pilot exploration of heart rate variability and salivary cortisol responses to compassion-focused imagery. *Clinical Neuropsychiatry: Journal of Treatment Evaluation*, **5** (3) 132–139.

Rogers, C.R. (1957) The necessary and sufficient conditions of therapeutic personality change. *Journal of Consulting and Clinical Psychology*, **21**, 95–103.

Salzberg, S. (1997) *Loving Kindness: The revolutionary art of happiness*. Boston, MA: Shambala.

Sbarra, D.A., Smith, H.L. & Mehl, M.R. (2012) When leaving your Ex, love yourself: Observational ratings of self-compassion predict the course of emotional recovery following marital separation. *Psychological Science*, **23** (3) 261–269.

Siegel, D. (2012) *The Developing Mind*. 2nd Edition. New York, NY: Guilford Press.

Snyder, C.R. (2002) Hope theory: rainbows in the mind. *Psychological Inquiry*, **13** (4) 249–275.

Sommers-Spijkerman, M.P.J., Trompetter, H.R., Schreurs, K.M.G. & Bohlmeijer, E.T. (2018) Compassion-focused therapy as guided self-help for enhancing public mental health: A randomized controlled trial. *Journal of Consulting Clinical Psychology*, **86** (2) 101–115.

Stroud, J. & Griffiths, C. (2021) An evaluation of compassion-focused therapy within adult mental health inpatient settings. *Psychological Psychotherapy: Theory, Research and Practice*. Available online at: https://doi.org/10.1111/papt.12334. Accessed 15 July 2021.

Terry, M.L. & Leary, M.R. (2011) Self-compassion, self-regulation, and health. *Self and Identity*, **10**, 352–362.

Thomason, S. & Moghaddam, N. (2021) Compassion-focused therapies for self-esteem: A systematic review and meta-analysis. *Psychology and Psychotherapy: Theory, Research, and Practice*, a research paper. Available online at: https://doi.org/10.1111/papt.12319. Accessed 15 July 2021.

Vettese, L.C., Dyer, C.E., Li, W.L. & Wekerle, C. (2011) Does self-compassion mitigate the association between childhood maltreatment and later emotional regulation difficulties? *International Journal of Mental Health and Addiction*, **9**, 480–491.

Wakelin, K.E., Perman, G. & Simonds, L.M. (2021) Effectiveness of self-compassion-related interventions for reducing self-criticism: A systematic review and meta-analysis. *Clinical Psychology & Psychotherapy: Theory, Research and Practice*. Available online at: https://doi: 10.1002/cpp.2586. Accessed 15 July 2021.

Weng, H,Y., Fox A,S., Shackman, A, J., Stodola, D, E., Caldwell, J.Z.K., Olson, M.C., Rogers, G., M. & Davidson, R.J. (2013) Compassion training alters altruism and neural responses to suffering. *Psychological Science*, **24**, 1171–1180.

Zuroff, D.C., Santor, D. & Mongrain, M. (2005) Dependency, self-criticism, and maladjustment. In: J.S. Auerbach, K.N. Levy and C.E. Schaffer (Eds) *Relatedness, Self-Definition and Mental Representation. Essays in Honour of Sidney J. Blatt*. London: Routledge, pp75–90.

Chapter 6
Acceptance and Commitment Coaching: Theory, research and practice

Sarah Leach

Introduction

Acceptance and Commitment therapy (ACT), a third wave cognitive behavioural approach (Hayes, 2004), helps people to flourish by living a values-based life and developing psychological flexibility (Bohlmeijer *et al*, 2015). Acceptance and Commitment Coaching (ACC) applies the ACT principles, tools, and techniques to help people live their best possible lives by taking committed values-based action (Anstiss, 2021). The ACC philosophy often requires individuals to accept uncomfortable thoughts and feelings, but argues that if people are to live a fulfilling life they need to find ways to live with these thoughts (Hill & Oliver, 2019). ACT can help people to act in alignment with their values, by strengthening their motivation towards living their best life and honouring those things that really matter.

ACT is well suited to coaching due to its flexibility, adaptability, and practicality. It also has a strong evidence base in the world of work, sport, and therapy (Hill & Oliver, 2019). Its principles can be applied to a broad range of presenting client topics from procrastination to anxiety to sports performance to time management to stress to resilience to addiction and coping with disease. It does this by focusing on 6 core processes: values-based living, committed action, defusion, acceptance, present moment awareness and self as context (Harris, 2019), divided into 2 groups of acceptance and mindfulness processes, and commitment and behaviour change processes (Kennerly *et al*, 2017).

In this chapter we will review the theory and guiding principles of ACT, critically review the evidence of its efficacy in both therapeutic and coaching contexts, and lastly reflect on its applicability to coaching in practice, sharing some tools and techniques that you might find useful in your own coaching practice. The chapter concludes in recommending several key texts and some questions for you to reflect on as part of your own development.

Theoretical foundations

Acceptance and Commitment Therapy, known as 'ACT', is, at its core, a behavioural therapy evolved from the work of the behaviourists Pavlov, Skinner and Watson. Developed in the 1980s by Steven Hayes, this third wave cognitive behavioural therapy focuses on enabling individuals to take committed action guided by their core values and to develop psychological flexibility (Harris, 2019; Hayes, 2019). In addition to more traditional behavioural therapies, ACT places a strong emphasis on mindfulness, acceptance, and self-compassion (Harris, 2019; Kennerly *et al*, 2017; Cavanagh & Spence, 2013). However, unlike other cognitive behavioural therapies, ACT does not attempt to change the way clients think or feel about a situation but attempts to help individuals change the relationship they have with their thoughts and feelings. It encourages people to mindfully notice, allow and accept those thoughts, feelings, urges and sensations, and carry them lightly (Anstiss, 2021; Anstiss & Blonna, 2014). Thus, allowing people to consciously choose committed values-based action that move them towards a life fulfilled, rather than behaviours such as procrastination, avoidance, or distraction, which may reduce the discomfort in the short term, but prolong the disappointment or frustration in the long term. The core concept of psychological flexibility is described by Hayes (2019) as:

> *"the ability to feel and think with openness, to attend voluntarily to your experience of the present moment, and to move your life in directions that are important to you, building habits that allow you to live life in accordance with your values and aspirations".*

This is in contrast to psychological inflexibility where behaviour is rigidly guided by internal psychological reactions (Levin *et al*, 2014) on which people tend to become 'hooked' (Harris, 2019). This has been known to lead people towards depression, anxiety, substance abuse and eating disorders (Levin *et al*, 2014). Figure 6.1 summarises the difference between these two concepts.

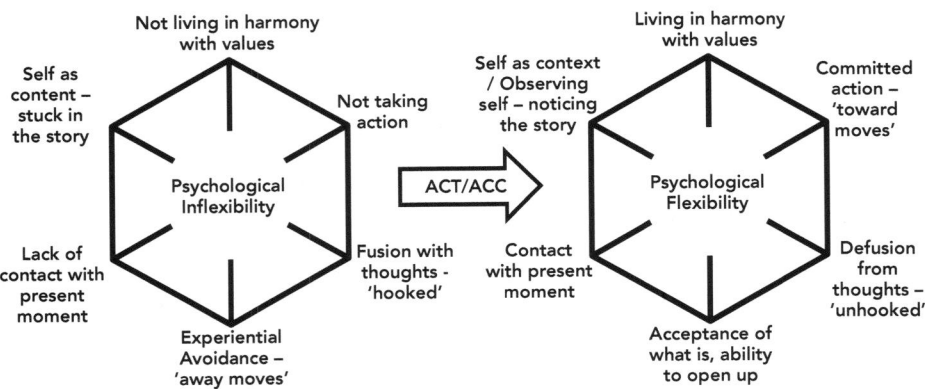

Figure 6.1: The ACT Hexaflex (adapted from Harris, 2019, p6)

ACT has two underlying principles, a theory of cognition called relational frame theory (RFT) and functional contextualism.

Relational Frame Theory

RFT considers humans' ability to relate ideas, objects, and concepts to each other using different 'frames', where things are either the same or different, are happening now or then (frame of time), and either here or there (frame of space) for example (Hill & Oliver, 2019; Hayes, 2004; Fletcher & Hayes, 2005). As people grow up and develop language skills and combine frames into cognitive networks, so the mind starts to use language to understand the complexity of the world around them. Humans derive meaning and relationships between things, relationships which may not be fact based, but more abstract and even imagined (Hayes, 2019). The language used in these comparisons, such as 'you are a much better person than me', begins to trap us. In so doing we start to feed our dictator or inner critic and increase its power and influence over the way in which we live our lives (Hayes, 2019). This provides an explanation as to why ACT practitioners believe experiential avoidance and cognitive fusion are at the heart of many problems (Hayes, 2004). Because of these relational frames that have been created, it is very likely that one person's thought will trigger a thought about something else entirely, which may or may not makes sense to anyone else! Hayes (2019) argues, therefore, that trying to unravel these complex cognitive connections, much like other CBC approaches, is pointless (Hayes, 2004). The group of acceptance and mindfulness processes within ACT set out to disrupt or undermine the power of the verbal networks we have created in our minds, particularly in relation to the frames of time and evaluation (Fletcher & Hayes, 2005), as opposed to trying to change them. Hayes (2004) also states that ACT is explicitly contextual. This brings us to the second underlying principal of ACT, functional contextualism.

Functional contextualism

Functional contextualism is about noticing what works or is functional within a given context. The focus here lies in the function or effect of the behaviour, rather than the behaviour itself. As coach there is no interest in evaluating or judging whether the behaviour is right or wrong, or good or bad, just whether the behaviour is 'workable' in the context of the client's life (Harris, 2019). In other words, is the behaviour enabling a life of the client's choosing. If not, it is considered 'unworkable'. For example, having an alcoholic drink at a wedding reception may be more 'workable' than drinking alcohol before driving children to school. Understanding the context, i.e. everything that is influencing behaviour in that moment, is extremely important in being able to determine whether behaviour is functional or not. Harris (2019) divides these influences into two groups. Antecedents are those thoughts, feelings and situations which trigger the behaviour, and consequences are those thoughts, feelings and situations which occur because of the behaviour. Some behaviours are said to have punishing or reinforcing consequences, much like described in Skinner's operant conditioning (Passmore, 2007). For example, cancelling an evening out with friends might make a client feel lonely and sad, or may provide a sense of relief from the associated anxiety leading them to cancel more often.

Core processes of psychological flexibility

In developing psychological flexibility and working with the core principles of RFT and functional contextualism, ACT enables clients to pragmatically focus attention on the idea of 'workability', 'the processes that move the person … towards a predefined set of values' (Hill & Oliver, 2019:20). There are six therapeutic processes of ACT which therapists and coaches alike can use to support their clients in moving towards psychological flexibility:

1. Values-based living

ACT focuses on enabling values-based living by helping clients to understand what matters most to them, what they stand for, and how they want to behave. Much like a compass, values give people direction (Harris, 2019). In clarifying their values, people start to see how a more meaningful and purposeful life, full of vitality and wellbeing, can be achieved by living in alignment with their values (Anstiss & Blonna, 2014). Values are personal to the individual, not imposed or chosen by others. They are not goals, but a helpful way of checking the individual is on course and heading in the right direction. Valued living is an ongoing process, not an outcome (Anstiss & Blonna, 2014). Harris (2019, p217) says 'pursue your values vigorously, but hold them lightly'. Values should not restrict our clients or become rules they feel they must obey, however the coach will notice that clients who are truly connected to their values will come alive and be fully engaged.

2. Committed action

Committed action or 'doing what it takes' (Harris, 2019, p7) is about enabling purposeful behaviour change, aligned to our core values. This is action, both physical and psychological action, an individual takes with a willingness to accept any thoughts, feeling or reactions that appear as a result (Anstiss, 2021). It means taking action even when your mind might be saying 'you will fail', 'everyone will laugh at you', or 'you can always do it later'. ACT encourages clients to commit to the action they know will serve them best in the long term, rather than taking steps that might feel easier in the short term and cause them to fall into the experiential avoidance trap.

3. Defusion

Defusion encourages clients to step back or detach from thoughts, images, and memories, seeing them for nothing more than they are, that of words or pictures (Harris, 2019). Defusion allows clients to observe and notice their thoughts, rather than get entangled with them. It helps to create a space between thoughts and actions, allowing other behavioural influences, such as values, to intervene (Hill & Oliver, 2019). Defusion begins with noticing a thought, then naming it and then neutralizing it by understanding how 'workable' it is in relation to the life your client wants to lead (Harris, 2019).

4. Acceptance

Acceptance is about welcoming, noticing and letting go of unwanted private experiences, rather than trying to control, fight or resist them (Hayes *et al*, 2006). The focus is not on removing or changing the thought but, as Hill and Oliver (2019) suggest, on changing the client's response to and relationship with their thoughts and feelings. Experiential avoidance is considered to be at the core of many people's issues (Hayes, 2004). The idea is that people struggle with, avoid, control, or supress unwanted thoughts to be able to cope with life, rather than acknowledge, accept, and accommodate (Harris, 2019) the thoughts to move on. Some psychoeducation may be useful to help clients understand that it is the things they are doing to avoid or control their experiences that are holding them back from the life they want to live (Anstiss & Blonna, 2014). The use of metaphors such as 'passengers on the bus' or 'leaves on a stream' (Passmore *et al*, 2021) might be helpful here (see Table 6.2)

5. Present moment awareness

ACT encourages clients to pay attention to what they are experiencing in the present moment, mindful that too much time spent looking forward may result in anxiety or hopelessness, whilst too much time spent looking backwards may result in guilt or shame, for example (Anstiss, 2021). The focus is on developing flexible attention to the world around us or the psychological world within us (Harris, 2019). When we become fused to a thought, our present moment awareness drops, and we become more rigid and inflexible. Consequently, experiential avoidance is more than likely to occur (Hill & Oliver, 2019).

6. Self as context

The observing self notices what we are thinking, feeling, or doing in any moment, without being engaged with it. Becoming overly attached to ourselves as content can greatly reduce flexibility (Hill & Oliver, 2019). Holding on to our own stories can provide a sense of security, safety and certainty which becomes very appealing when we're feeling particularly uncomfortable or challenged, however it can restrict us significantly from taking committed values-based action. Self as context also allows us to see things differently or, in ACT terminology, adapt a behaviour, known as flexible perspective taking (FPT). This means we have the mindfulness skills to notice and accept, and the thinking skills to understand alternative perspectives on a topic or situation (Harris, 2019). You may ask your client, for instance, 'If you were in his shoes, how would you feel?' to help them develop this way of thinking.

It is important to note that ACT places a large emphasis on compassion for self, as well as compassion for others. This encourages us to consciously acknowledge suffering but, instead of dismissing or ignoring it, to remain open and curious about it and respond with kindness rather than judgment (Harris, 2019). This is not something that comes easily to many of us and requires us to develop our capacity for compassion (Gilbert & Choden, 2015).

Research evidence

Thousands of studies have examined ACT across almost all areas of human functioning, although there is little research within coaching itself. Its transdiagnostic ability (Yildiz, 2020) means ACT works and can be applied across traditional mental health areas such as depression, anxiety, and substance abuse, as well as with topics such as coping with disease, managing relationships, minimising stress, playing competitive sports, and improving work performance (Hayes, 2019). In fact, Hayes *et al* (2012, p976) promote ACT as a 'unified model of behavior change and personal development'. The evidence base for ACT has grown rapidly. Gloster *et al* (2020) reviewed 20 meta-analyses of ACT finding that it was as effective as CBT for all conditions studied including anxiety, depression, and pain, and superior to inactive controls, normal treatment, and other active interventions. For instance, a study by Hunot *et al* (2013) suggested that the effect of ACT with CBT versus the effect of behavioural activation with CBT on people with acute depression was just as effective. However, both Hunot *et al* (2013) and Gloster *et al* (2020) recommend further research to be conducted and extended to other less common disorders where ACT is used, as well as examining a more diverse range of populations. The lack of cross-cultural diversity in the research appears to be one of the most common criticisms of ACT (Fischer *et al*, 2020).

One of the other criticisms of ACT, particularly in relation to psychological flexibility, is the basis on which it is measured. The Acceptance and Action Questionnaire (AAQ-I and II) is known to have serious limitations (Doorley *et al*, 2020). Doorley *et al* (2020) argue that we must use measures that examine a variety of flexible responses, considering the context of values and value-based goals. Francis *et al* (2016) also suggest the apparent positive signs of what ACT can do might be due to poor measurement of the process, similarly challenged by Wolgast (2014) who suggests AAQ-II measures items of distress rather than functional outcomes.

Regardless of these criticisms, most of the research in this field is overwhelmingly positive of ACT. Gloster *et al* (2020) found a positive correlation between using ACT and quality of life, psychological flexibility, and measures of wellbeing and functioning. This is supported by studies that support ACT as an effective psychological approach for enhancing college student wellbeing (Howell and Passmore, 2019), helping people with depressive symptoms to flourish (Bohlmeijer *et al*, 2015) and coping with cancer (Karekla, 2010), to name but a few. In fact, ACT has recently been approved by NICE, the National Institute for Health and Care Excellence in the UK, as a psychological therapy for chronic primary pain (NICE, 2021).

More recently, research has focused on the efficaciousness of ACT when used independently as a self-help tool, versus being guided in a professional one-to-one relationship or in group-based therapy. A study conducted during the Covid pandemic when people had to rely more heavily on self-guided interventions, did not mirror the same level of effectiveness as those using group therapies or seeking individual help (Fischer *et al*, 2020). Similarly, a web-based self-guided programme promoting values-based living in college students suggested that whilst the intervention had a positive effect on values-based living overall, there were no significant changes in psychological wellbeing (Firestone *et al*, 2019). Similarly, Thompson *et al* (2021) found that in a review of 25 studies, internet-based interventions were less effective than therapist interventions. Perhaps the more positive results from guided or group interventions suggests the need for psycho-educational training of the client for ACT to be most useful. Harris (2019) argues the case for explaining the approach at a bare minimum, perhaps becoming more directive with low-functioning clients, yet Hill and Oliver (2019) argue, in the coaching context, the learning is in experiencing it, rather than being told about it.

When looking at each of the six ACT processes in isolation, the evidence would also suggest very positive results. Whilst more research is required of the processes of change associated with psychological flexibility (Gloster *et al*, 2020; Doorley *et al*, 2020) and self as context (Godbee & Kangas, 2020), there has been encouraging signs in the efficaciousness of using values-based interventions in isolation (Rahal & Gon, 2020; Gloster *et al*, 2017; Moran, 2011; Katz *et al*, 2016) reinforced by more robust ways of measuring values (Reilly *et al*, 2019). Veage *et al* (2014) refer to a study of mental health practitioners where results showed using values clarification exercises and pursuing a role in line with your work values positively contributed to lower burnout rates and greater wellbeing. Rahal and Gon (2020, p369), having completed a review of values interventions in ACT, conclude, 'It's likely that values-based process, with its great focus on values-based action, is an important mediator of change', suggesting that this is how ACT distinguishes itself from other third wave approaches. Another example describes a randomized controlled trial (RCT) which looked at how patients with a panic disorder previously resistant to treatment responded to ACT, found that an increased focus on value-based behaviours reduced levels of suffering (Gloster *et al*, 2017). This view is supported by Hayes *et al* (2012) who suggest that in ACT we are always looking, as practitioners, for workable, pragmatic and committed actions, and as such values really matter and heavily influence behaviour. Another study, however, argues the importance of keeping all ACT processes together as part of the intervention, this time in relation to increasing and maintaining physical fitness (Manchón *et al*, 2020), raising a question as to whether the nature of the presenting issue dictates whether some or all the ACT processes need to be used.

A study by Skews (2018) looking at the outcomes and mechanisms of change of ACT informed coaching reveals similar benefits associated with general mental health, self-efficacy, the achievement of goals and psychological flexibility. For example, a teacher used ACT informed coaching with a music student to help him accept his music performance anxiety. This led to a successful audition for a lead role in a musical which he would have normally avoided (Shaw *et al*, 2020). Moran (2011, p66) talks of how ACT meets the challenge of creating 'an evidence-based framework for executive coaching', suggesting that the ACT model enables leaders to take committed action based on a clear values system unencumbered by faulty thinking or unhelpful feelings or emotions, and to carry out these actions in the present moment, when it really matters.

Some of the more recent systemic reviews and meta-analyses are summarised in Table 6.1.

Table 6.1: Summary of research

Study	Summary
ACT research in therapeutic contexts	
Bai *et al* (2020)	A systemic review and meta-analysis of 18 studies to examine effectiveness of ACT on the reduction, over time, of depression across different age groups. Concluded that ACT significantly reduced depression compared to the control group, especially with adults with mild depression after three-month follow up.
Bohlmeijer *et al* (2015)	Study evaluated the impact of ACT on flourishing. Conducted a post-analysis on a RCT of adults with symptoms of depression who participated in a guided self-help ACT intervention. Results showed a 5–28% increase of flourishing, maintained at the 3 month follow up. Increasing levels of psychological flexibility was a significant predictor of the ability to maintain flourishing.

Table 6.1: Summary of research

Study	Summary
ACT research in therapeutic contexts	
Brassington et al (2016)	Study examined an ACT group intervention with 43 adults suffering long term health conditions. Results showed an improvement in depression and anxiety, but limited changes in overall health condition and value-based living. Conclusions suggest ACT group interventions may be of more benefit for long term conditions and delivered trans-diagnostically.
Coto-Lesmes et al (2020)	Systemic review looked at ACT as an effective group treatment of anxiety and depression. Those receiving ACT treatment demonstrated better emotional state and psychological flexibility than those without treatment, but no better result than those receiving CBT.
Firestone et al (2019)	Pilot study of 133 undergraduate college students using a web-based self-guided 'Living Your Values' program. 98 students showed an increase in valued living overall and for leisure and community-based values. However, no significant changes in psychological wellbeing were observed.
Fischer et al (2020)	Rapid review and summary of 34 meta-analysis of self-guided interventions used during COVID social distancing to manage anxiety, depression, stress and wellbeing. Showed small to medium impact, particularly with mindfulness and acceptance interventions, positive psychology and activity-based interventions eg exercise. But not as effective as guided individual or group interventions.
Gloster et al (2017)	RCT testing ACT for treatment resistant patients with panic disorder. Results suggested values-based behaviour influenced subsequent suffering but decreases in struggle with symptoms and reduction of suffering itself didn't influence levels of value-based behaviour. Supports premise that psychological flexibility increases values-based action and precedes reductions in suffering.
Gloster et al (2020)	A review of 20 meta-analyses evaluating the efficacy of ACT. Results show it as efficacious for all conditions examined, including depression, substance abuse and transdiagnostic groups, and particularly psychological flexibility. It also found ACT to be as effective as CBT and more so than other active comparisons.

Table 6.1: Summary of research

Study	Summary
ACT research in therapeutic contexts	
Godbee & Kangas (2020)	Systematic review of the effects of 'self-as-context' (SAC) ACT process on improving emotional wellbeing. 20 studies were examined providing limited evidence that SAC can be taught and implemented as a separate process to manage emotional wellbeing.
Manchón et al (2020)	A systematic review of 21 studies showing effectiveness of ACT on increasing and maintaining physical activity. Emphasis placed on the need for all ACT processes to be included in a programme of 8–12 sessions.
Pears & Sutton (2021)	Looked at two studies in a systematic review to explore effectiveness of ACT on physical activity and identify the behavioural change techniques associated with ACT. Results suggest ACT shows promise for increasing physical activity but concluded that few of the 'active ingredients' of ACT interventions could be described as behavioural change techniques.
Rahal & Gon (2020)	Systematic review of 17 studies looking at effectiveness of working with values-based interventions. Results suggest that values interventions had the desired effect on outcome. 35% of studies reviewed found values having a significant effect on those suffering with chronic pain.
Stenhoff et al (2020)	Systematic review and meta-analyses of 11 RCTs examining ACT's impact on subjective wellbeing. Results showed subjective wellbeing scores were significantly higher for ACT intervention groups in all but one study, in both clinical and non-clinical populations.
Thompson et al (2021)	Transdiagnostic meta-analysis examining internet-based ACT effectiveness on anxiety, depression, quality of life and psychological flexibility. 25 studies reviewed finding that interventions with therapists were more effective than internet-based interventions. Impact greater for those dealing with depression and anxiety as opposed to non-clinical conditions. ACT found to be effective in improving mental health but limited evidence of significant effects.
Twohig & Levin (2017)	Study examined 36 RCTs and found ACT to be more efficacious than treatment as usual for anxiety and depression, due to increases in psychological flexibility as the process of change.

Table 6.1: Summary of research

Study	Summary
ACT research in therapeutic contexts	
Yildiz (2020)	Study, in reviewing 30 RCTs, examined the effects of ACT on lifestyle and behavioural change including weight management, managing addictive problems, eating and physical activity. Results suggest ACT, as a transdiagnostic approach, will help maintain long-term behavioural changes in many diseases and populations.
ACT research in non-therapeutic contexts	
Bond & Bunce (2000)	Study examined the use of ACT with 90 volunteers in a media company looking to enhance people's ability to cope with work related stresses. ACT compared to an alternative innovation promotion programme (IPP) and a control group, finding that improvements in mental health were found in both interventions. Improvements came with accepting uncomfortable thoughts and feelings with the ACT group and attempts to modify the stressors in the IPP group.
Bond & Bunce (2003)	Two-wave panel study to examine how acceptance can explain mental health, job satisfaction and work performance in a sample of customer service centre workers, finding that increased acceptance positively influenced mental health. Higher levels of acceptance also enhanced the benefits of increased job control.
Howell & Passmore (2019)	Study identifies 5 randomized experiments measuring improvement in student wellbeing as a result of using ACT as a positive psychological intervention.
Flaxman & Bond (2010)	Study looked at the effectiveness of ACT based stress management training in the workplace delivered to 311 local government employees. A significant reduction in employee distress was measured over a 6 month period. More meaningful effects were found on those who were already in a distressed state, 69% improving to a significant degree.
Gross et al (2018)	RCT examining the efficaciousness of mindfulness-acceptance-commitment (MAC) approach for improving the mental health and performance of 18 female athletes compared to traditional psychological skills training. Results showed reduced substance use and emotional dysregulation over time plus reduced levels of anxiety, fewer eating concerns, less psychological stress, and an increase in psychological flexibility as well as improved sport performance.

Table 6.1: Summary of research

Study	Summary
ACT research in non-therapeutic contexts	
Moran (2011)	Examines ACT being used as a leadership coaching model and suggests how ACT training can increase work performance (particularly in decision making), increase innovation, reduce workplace stress and reduction in errors. Concludes in suggesting psychological flexibility is key to crisis-resilient change leadership.
Noetel et al (2017)	A review of 66 studies looking at impact of mindfulness and experiential acceptance approaches in promoting athletic performance. Positive effects were found on flow, performance and competitive anxiety, however the evidence was graded as low quality and further research is required.
Reeve et al (2018)	A systematic review and meta-analyses of work-related stress in those in direct care roles in mental health settings. For those already at a higher stress baseline, ACT was effective in reducing psychological stress, but no statistically significant effect for the improvement of burnout or psychological flexibility. However, recommendations are made for the implementation of ACT for work-related stress.
Shaw et al (2020)	Study looks at how training a music teacher to use ACC with a student suffering from performance anxiety enabled an increase in ability to manage anxiety through acceptance and defusion processes.
Skews & Palmer (2016)	Makes the case that ACT offers an effective coaching approach to address psychological barriers whilst remaining goal focused; reduce emotional reactivity and increase acceptance, as well as being applicable to range of populations.

In reviewing the literature, the research is overwhelmingly positive for ACT as an efficacious intervention, comparable to any other CBT intervention, and more recent studies have shown how coaching using the ACT principles can be applied to a wide variety of presenting issues. It would be foolish to claim, however, that more research was not needed to examine the breadth of application in terms of both presenting topic and client population, as well as to address the degree of nervousness around how psychological flexibility can be measured accurately in the first place.

Practice

Acceptance and Commitment Coaching differentiates itself from other coaching interventions by addressing the other contextual barriers that can hinder behavioural change by developing psychological flexibility (Moran, 2011). This idea is supported in research by Skews and Palmer (2016) who identify 3 key benefits for coaching. Firstly, it addresses psychological barriers and remains goal focused. Secondly, it supports other mindfulness based coaching approaches to reduce the impact of emotional reactions and increase acceptance. Finally, it is highly adaptable to different populations.

ACC considers experiential avoidance to be at the core of many people's issues, the idea that people struggle with, avoid, control, or supress unwanted thoughts to be able to cope with life. Harris (2019) talks about helping people to understand the 'choice point' (see figure 6.1), to simply and efficiently map out their 'away moves' (experiential avoidance) and their potential 'towards moves' (values-based living), emphasising how we can consciously choose one direction over the other.

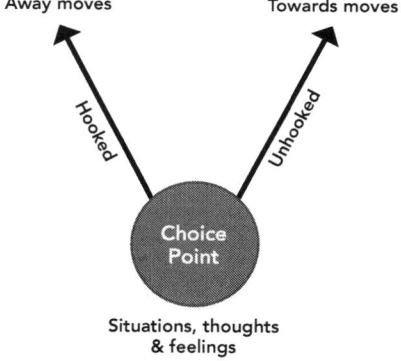

Figure 6.1: Choice point (Harris, 2019, p13)

The ACT Matrix (Figure 6.2) can be used to flesh out the choice point, bringing more focus to the importance of having clarity over values and what really matters to the client before understanding what committed based action might look like. It also helps to identify several clear areas to work on with clients by exploring the areas of cognitive fusion and experiential avoidance.

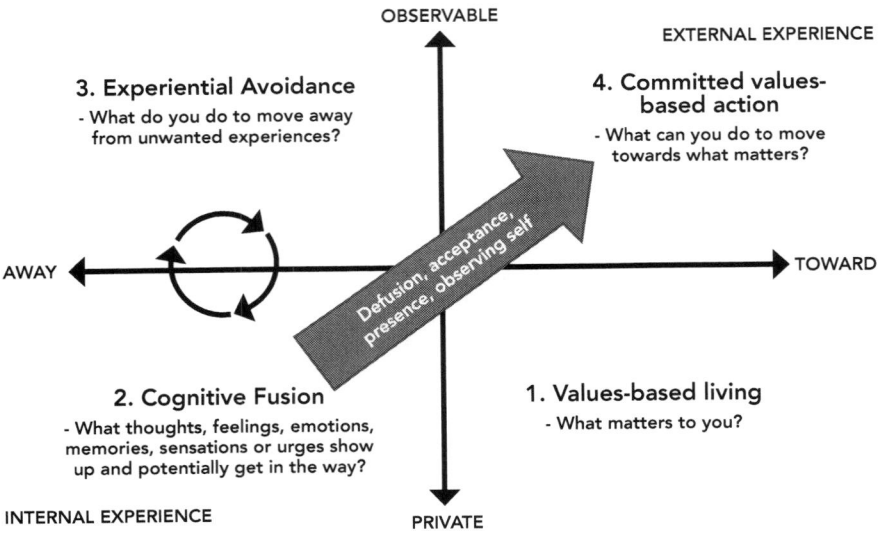

Figure 6.2: ACT Matrix (adapted from Anstiss, 2021, p309)

Having facilitated a conversation around the four quadrants of the matrix, the ACC coach then sets to work on using one or all the six core processes to enable forward momentum. There are many tools that can be used with each of the six processes, some of which are listed in table 6.2 (please see www.actmindfully.com.au/free-stuff/ for lots of useful tools and guidance), however for many the first place to start is in clarifying values.

As coach it is important to be mindful of the impact of cross-cultural differences and client diversity when using tools such as value interventions and metaphors, for values-based behavioural change, many of which are used in ACT. Depending on the client's specific context, the meaning derived from such interventions can be vastly different. The importance of 'workability' or functional contextualism (Hayes *et al*, 2006) is highlighted here and we are also reminded, as coach practitioners, to pay attention to these culturally sensitive boundaries as highlighted by the ICF code of ethics (2012). For example, East Asian cultures where values of family duty and responsibility are important, or even pre-determined, might cause conflicting feelings for a client when aspiring to live a life of their own choosing. Similarly, some may be concerned about whether ACT is compatible with all faiths. However, Hayes (2019) gives an example of how ACT was proactively chosen as one of 3 methods for US military chaplains to use because it was compatible with developing the flexibility skills as set out by different scriptural traditions. Similarly, Karekla and Constantinou (2010) talk of a devoted Christian Greek-Cypriot using ACT processes to help her cope with cancer.

ACT also works a lot with metaphors, helping clients to understand their feelings by relating them to abstract concepts. The use of metaphors stops clients getting lost in their own verbal processes (Stoddard & Afari, 2014). Yet at the same time we need to be mindful that symbols, symbolic interactions, and metaphors form the basis of many different cultures, differing widely in context and meaning. Similarly, people's attachment to and understanding of different words, the importance of which is highlighted by relational frame theory (Hayes, 2004), requires coaches to be mindful of cross-cultural dynamics. Whilst the impact of ACT does not seem to be restricted to use with a particular ethnicity or culture (Hayes *et al*, 2012), I would argue the coach or therapist needs to be mindful of the differences in values and traditions, and therefore cognisant of the importance of the value of the relationship between client and coach. A theme reiterated by Harris (2019) and Hayes *et al* (2012, p991) who said:

'the therapeutic relationship is important because it models, instigates and supports a more open, aware and engaged approach to life'.

Table 6.2: A selection of ACT tools and techniques, and how they might apply to coaching

ACT process	Tools and techniques	Applicability to coaching
Values-based living	1. Discovery questionnaire – using questions to uncover what matters most, role models, childhood dreams, words for obituary etc. 2. Life domains – exploring values in relation to different life domains and ranking current behaviour in accordance with values. 3. Value card sorting – identifying core values by identifying the ones that resonate the most.	Helps to clarify what is important to the client. Can be used to identify behaviours that move the client away from or towards their desired future state, by facilitating an understanding of what it means and how it feels to be living in alignment, or not, with values.
Committed action	1. 'Just because' – choose to do something just because, rather than because you have evaluated it as the 'right' course of action. 2. Making small adjustments – make small behavioural changes that do not feel like giant leaps; aim for quick, simple, and efficient. 3. Building new habits into established routines – anchor a desired change into an existing habit to make it easy.	Provides clarity on what the client wants to achieve and how to integrate new habits more easily in life/work.

Table 6.2: A selection of ACT tools and techniques, and how they might apply to coaching

ACT process	Tools and techniques	Applicability to coaching
Defusion	1. Naming the story – if all these thoughts and feelings were a story, what would it be called? Each time they show up, name it. 2. Quick repetition – say the word quickly over and over, reducing the significance of the word as it becomes just a series of sounds. 3. Leaves on a stream – visualise thoughts as leaves, floating down a stream and let them wash away.	Each technique helps the client to create space between their thought or feeling and the action they take as a result. It does not dismiss the thought but allows a degree of separation from it. The ability to unhook from our thoughts allows us to consciously choose 'towards' moves in line with values rather than 'away' moves caused by an impulse to respond to internal experiences.
Acceptance	1. Drop anchor – acknowledge the feeling and connect with your body to engage with the external world 2. Emotion surfing – surf feelings and urges as if they were a wave on the ocean 3. Normalising – acknowledging that we are human, with a heart who cares, and this is how we all feel when there is a gap between what we've got and what we want. Validate pain as natural and normal.	Human beings naturally find change difficult. These techniques allow clients to accept their thoughts, but not get stuck in them. In normalising the feeling, behavioural change becomes more workable and a pragmatic approach to change can be adopted.
Present moment awareness	1. Focusing on the breath – mindful breathing exercises 2. Listening to sounds and other attention training techniques 3. Body scan	Mindful breathing and attention training allows clients to focus the mind on the here and now, rather than what is to come or has been.
Self as context	1. The Stage Show metaphor – Looking at life as if it's a huge stage show, and sometimes you're watching all of the stage as a whole, and sometimes you notice a particular detail or pay attention to a particular actor. The show is changing all the time, but the part of you that watches doesn't change, just notices!	Allows client to step back from the details and to see a meta-perspective.

Table 6.2: A selection of ACT tools and techniques, and how they might apply to coaching

ACT process	Tools and techniques	Applicability to coaching
Self as context	2. Sky and weather metaphor – compares the observing self to the sky and thoughts and feeling as being like the weather. No matter how terrible the thunderstorm (our thoughts and feelings) it eventually passes and the weather changes. 3. Rewriting your story – write a brief story about yourself, then highlight all the words that describe a thought or feeling, and all the words that describe an external situation or fact. Now re-write the story so that the meaning is different, but the highlighted words are still included.	Allows client to step back from the details and to see a meta-perspective.

(Harris, 2019; Hayes, 2019; Hill & Oliver, 2019; Anstiss & Blonna, 2014)

Conclusion

This chapter has outlined the theory of ACT and reviewed the evidence to support the approach both in therapeutic and coaching contexts, both of which are resoundingly positive. More research is required on the breadth of presenting issues and type of populations to which ACT can most confidently be applied. However, its flexible and pragmatic approach to enabling behavioural change provides a solid basis for acceptance and commitment coaching. It is also complementary to other mindfulness and compassion-based coaching approaches which are gathering pace in the world of coaching today. Whilst the evidence to support using ACT as an independent self-help tool is limited (Bohlmeijer *et al*, 2015), I believe there is potential for this approach to enable greater resilience, self-reliance, and self-efficacy in our coaching clients, particularly as the evidence based around mindfulness and acceptance-based therapies grows.

Five questions for further reflection

1. **How useful might acceptance and commitment coaching be in this current world climate?**

Many of us not only struggle with our own internal experiences to things that happen in our everyday lives, but our behaviours are impacted and influenced by the world around us and the wider systems within which we operate. Environmental crises, economic downturns, global pandemics all take their toll, but if we are better able to recognise those impacts and our associated thoughts and feelings, yet still anchor our action in the things that matter, it may help us to continue to live a fulfilled life.

2. **With what type of clients and presenting issues could an acceptance and commitment-based approach to coaching be most helpful?**

The research presents a very positive outlook on the transdiagnostic possibilities of using ACT to address clinical issues, and more recently in enhancing sports performance and leadership capabilities. It seems that the principles of ACT are applicable to many of the common challenges most people face every day.

3. **How might you integrate some of the tools and techniques associated with ACT into your coaching practice?**

As we develop as coaches and become more confident with our own coaching styles, it is common practice for many to start de-constructing our coaching tools and techniques to adapt them to specific contexts and/ or clients, use them in conjunction with other tools, and get creative in the way in which we enable our clients' best thinking. Each of the six ACT processes have potential to add significant value to more traditional coaching approaches, particularly as the application of mindfulness-based approaches, for example, increases.

4. **Are there any cross-cultural considerations specific to ACT that we need to be mindful of as coaches?**

As coaching continues to grow internationally and we find ourselves coaching people from across the globe, cross-cultural considerations are becoming a part of everyday life for coaches. ACT presents some interesting considerations when we think of the implications associated with values-based living for example, including cultural values, traditions, legends, stories, and metaphors. Indeed, the practise of mindfulness is perhaps an approach more akin to Eastern, rather than Western, cultures. What does this mean for our coaching practices?

5. **How might applying some of the ACT principles help you in developing your own coaching practice?**

ACT presents a few opportunities for us, individually, as practising coaches. If we applied the six ACT processes to our own coaching practises, how might our approach and our ability to coach in service of our clients change? There appears to be some obvious benefits associated with the quality of attention paid to our clients, managing self in the moment, maintaining presence and building trusting non-judgmental relationships to name but a few… everything our code of ethics asks us to be and do.

Suggested reading

Anstiss, T. (2021) Acceptance and Commitment Coaching. In: J. Passmore (Ed) *The Coaches Handbook: The Complete Practitioner Guide for Professional Coaches, Routledge: Abingdon,* pp301–313.

Harris, R. (2019) *ACT Made Simple: An easy-to-read primer on Acceptance and Commitment Therapy,* 2nd edition. California: New Harbinger Publications.

Hayes, S. (2004) Acceptance and Commitment Therapy, Relational Frame Theory, and the third wave of behavioral and cognitive therapies. *Behavior Therapy,* **35,** 639–65.

Hayes, S.C. (2019) *A Liberated Mind: The essential guide to ACT. Transform your thinking and find freedom from stress, anxiety, depression and addiction.* London: Penguin Random House UK.

Hill, J. & Oliver, J. (2019) *Acceptance and Commitment Coaching: Distinctive Features.* Abingdon: Routledge.

References

Anstiss, T. (2021) Acceptance and Commitment Coaching. In: J. Passmore (Ed) *The Coaches Handbook: The complete practitioner guide for professional coaches,* Routledge: Abingdon, pp301–313.

Anstiss, T. & Blonna, R. (2014) Acceptance and Commitment Coaching. In: J. Passmore (Ed) *Mastery in Coaching: A complete psychological toolkit for advanced coaching,* London: Kogan Page Ltd, pp 253–281.

Bai, Z., Luo, S., Zhang, L., Wu, S. & Chi, I. (2020) Acceptance and commitment therapy (ACT) to reduce depression: A systematic review and meta-analysis. *Journal of Affective Disorders,* **260** (1) 728–737.

Bohlmeijer, E.T., Lamers, S.M.A. & Fledderus, M. (2015) Flourishing in people with depressive symptomatology increases with Acceptance and Commitment Therapy. Post-hoc analyses of a randomized controlled trial. *Behaviour Research and Therapy,* **65,** 101–106.

Bond, F.W. & Bunce, D. (2000) Mediators of change in emotion-focused and problem-focused worksite stress management interventions. *Journal of Occupational Health Psychology,* 5 (1) 156–163.

Bond, F.W. & Bunce, D. (2003) The role of acceptance and job control in mental health, job satisfaction, and work performance. *Journal of Applied Psychology,* **88** (6) 1057–1067.

Brassington, L., Ferreira, N.B., Yates, S., Fearn, J., Lanza, P., Kemp, K. & Gillanders, D. (2016) Better living with illness: A transdiagnostic acceptance and commitment therapy group intervention for chronic physical illness. *Journal of Contextual Behavioural Science,* 5, 208–214.

Cavanagh, M.J. & Spence, G.B. (2013). Mindfulness in Coaching: Philosophy, psychology or just a useful skill? In: J. Passmore, D. Peterson and T. Freire (Eds) *The Wiley Blackwell Handbook of the Psychology of Coaching and Mentoring.* Chichester: Wiley, pp112–134.

Coto-Lesmes, R., Fernández-Rodríguez, C. & González-Fernández, S. (2020) Acceptance and commitment therapy in group format for anxiety and depression. A systematic review. *Journal of Affective Disorders,* **263,** 107–120.

Doorley, J.D., Goodman, F.R., Kelso, K.C. & Kashdan, T.B. (2020) Psychological flexibility: What we know, what we do not know, and what we think we know. *Social and Personality Psychology Compass,* 14, 1–11 e12566.

Firestone, J., Cardaciotto, L., Levin, M.E., Goldbacher, E. Vernig, P. & Eubanks Gambrel, L. (2019) A web-based self-guided program to promote valued-living in college students: A pilot study. *Journal of Contextual Behavioral Science,* **12,** 29–38.

Fischer R., Bortolini T., Karl, J.A., Zilberberg, M., Robinson, K., Rabelo, A., Gemal, L., Wegerhoff, D., Nguyễn, T.B.T., Irving, B., Chrystal, M. & Mattos, P. (2020). Rapid review and meta-meta-analysis of self-guided interventions to address anxiety, depression, and stress during Covid-19 social distancing. *Frontiers in Psychology,* 11. Available online at: doi: https://doi.org/10.3389/fpsyg.2020.563876. Accessed 15 July 2021.

Flaxman, P.E. & Bond, F.W. (2010) Worksite stress management training: moderated effects and clinical significance. *Journal of Occupational Health Psychology*, **15** (4) 347–358. Available online at: https://doi.org/10.1037/a0020522. Accessed 15 July 2021.

Fletcher, L. & Hayes, S.C. (2005) Relational frame theory, acceptance and commitment therapy, and a functional analytic definition of mindfulness, *Journal of Rational-Emotive and Cognitive-Behavior Therapy*, **23** (4) 315–336.

Francis, A.W., Dawson, D. L. & Golijani-Moghaddam, N. (2016). The development and validation of the Comprehensive assessment of Acceptance and Commitment Therapy processes (CompACT), *Journal of Contextural Behavioral Science*, 5, 134–145.

Gilbert, P. & Choden (2015) *Mindful Compassion: How the science of compassion can help you understand your emotions, live in the present, and connect deeply with others.* London: Constable & Robinson Ltd.

Gloster, A.T., Klotsche, J., Ciarrochi, J., Eifert, G., Sonntag, R., Wittchen, H.U. & Hoyer, J.J.J. (2017) Increasing valued behaviors precedes reduction in suffering: Findings from a randomized controlled trial using ACT. *Behaviour Research and Therapy*, **91**, 64–71.

Gloster, A. T., Walder, N., Levin, M., Twohig, M. & Karekla, M. (2020) The empirical status of acceptance and commitment therapy: A review of meta-analyses. *Journal of Contextual Behavioral Science*, **18**, 181–192.

Godbee, M. & Kangas, M. (2020) The relationship between flexible perspective taking and emotional wellbeing: a systematic review of the "self-as-context" component of acceptance and commitment therapy. *Behavior Therapy*, **51** (6) 917–932.

Gross, M., Moore, Z. E., Gardner, F. L., Wolanin, A. T., Pess, R. & Marks, D. R. (2018) An empirical examination comparing the mindfulness-acceptance-commitment approach and psychological skills training for the mental health and sport performance of female student athletes. *International Journal of Sport and Exercise Psychology*, **16** (4) 431–451.

Harris, R. (2019) *ACT Made Simple: An easy-to-read primer on Acceptance and Commitment Therapy*, 2nd edition. California: New Harbinger Publications.

Hayes, S. (2004) Acceptance and commitment therapy, relational frame theory, and the third wave of behavioral and cognitive therapies. *Behavior Therapy*, **35**, 639–65.

Hayes, S.C. (2019) *A Liberated Mind: The essential guide to ACT. Transform your thinking and find freedom from stress, anxiety, depression and addiction.* London: Penguin Random House UK.

Hayes, S.C., Luoma, J.B., Bond, F.W., Masuda, A. & Lillis, J. (2006) acceptance and commitment therapy: model, processes and outcomes. *Behaviour Research and Therapy*, **44**, 1–25.

Hayes, S.C., Pistorello, J. & Levin, M. E. (2012) Acceptance and commitment therapy as a unified model of behavior change. *The Counseling Psychologist*, **40** (7) 976–1002.

Hill, J. & Oliver, J. (2019) *Acceptance and Commitment Coaching: Distinctive Features.* Abingdon: Routledge.

Howell, A.J. & Passmore, H. (2019) Acceptance and commitment training (ACT) as a positive psychological intervention: A systematic review and initial meta-analysis regarding ACT's role in wellbeing promotion among university students. *Journal of Happiness Studies*, **20**, 1995–2010.

Hunot, V., Moore T.H.M, Caldwell, D.M., Furukawa, T.A., Davies, P., Jones, H., Honyashiki, M., Chen, P., Lewis, G. & Churchill, R. (2013) 'Third wave' cognitive and behavioural therapies versus other psychological therapies for depression (review). *Cochrane Database of Systematic Reviews*, 10. Available online at: doi: 10.1002/14651858.CD008704.pub2. Accessed 15 July 2021.

ICF code of ethics (2012) *Available from* https://coachfederation.org/app/uploads/2020/01/ICF-Code-of-Ethics_final_Nov12.pdf. Accessed 15 July 2021.

Karekla, M. & Constantinou, M. (2010) Religious coping and cancer: proposing an acceptance and commitment therapy approach. *Cognitive and Behavioral Practice*, **17**, 371–381.

Katz, B. A., Catane, S. & Yovel, I. (2016) Pushed by symptons, pulled by values: promotion goals increase motivation in therapeutic tasks, *Behavior Therapy*, **47**, 239–247.

Kennerly, H., Kirk, J. & Westbrook, D. (2017) *An Introduction to Cognitive Behaviour Therapy: Skills and applications*, 3rd edition. London: Sage.

Kimsey-House, H., Kimsey-House, K., Sandahl, P. & Whitworth, L. (2011) *Co-Active Coaching: Changing business transforming lives.* Boston: Nicholas Brealey Publishing.

Levin, M.E., MacLane, C., Daflos, S., Seeley, J.R., Hayes, S.C., Biglan, A. & Pistorello, J. (2014) Examining psychological inflexibility as a transdiagnostic process across psychological disorder. Journal of *Contextural Behavioral Science,* **3**, 155–163.

Manchón, J., Quiles, M. J., León, E.M. & López-Roig, S. (2020) Acceptance and commitment therapy on physical activity: A systematic review. *Journal of Contextual Behavioral Science,* **17**, 135–143.

Moran, D. J. (2011) ACT for leadership: Using acceptance and commitment training to develop crisis-resilient change managers. *International Journal of Behavioral Consultation and Therapy,* **7** (1), 66–75.

NICE (2020) Chronic pain (primary and secondary) in over 16s: assessment of all chronic pain and management of chronic primary pain. *NICE guideline available online at:* www.nice.org.uk/guidance/ng193. Accessed 15 July 2021.

Noetel, M., Ciarrochi, J., Van Zanden, B. & Lonsdale, C. (2017) Mindfulness and acceptance approaches to sporting performance enhancement: A systematic review. *International Review of Sport and Exercise Psychology,* **12** (1) 139–175.

Passmore, J. (2007) Behavioural Coaching. In: S. Palmer and A. Whybrow (Eds) *The Handbook of Coaching Psychology.* London: Brunner-Routledge, pp99–107.

Passmore, J., Day, C., Flower, J., Grieve, M. & Moon, J.J. (2021) *WeCoach! The complete handbook of tools, techniques, experiments and frameworks for personal and team development.* London: Libre.

Pears S. & Sutton, S. (2021) Effectiveness of acceptance and commitment therapy (act) interventions for promoting physical activity: A systematic review and meta-analysis. *Health Psychology Review,* **15** (1) 159–184.

Rahal, G.M. & Gon, M.C.C. (2020) A systematic review of values interventions in Acceptance and Commitment Therapy. *International Journal of Psychology and Psychological Therapy,* **20** (3) 1577–7057.

Reeve, A., Tickle, A. & Moghaddam, N. (2018) Are acceptance and commitment therapy-based interventions effective for reducing burnout in direct-care staff? A systematic review and meta-analysis. *Mental Health Review Journal,* **23** (3) 131–155.

Reilly, E.D., Ritzert, T.R., Scoglio, A.A.J., Mote, J., Fukuda, S.D., Ahern, M.E. & Kelly, M.M. (2019) A systematic review of values measures in acceptance and commitment therapy research. *Journal of Contextual Behavioral Science,* **12**, 290–304.

Shaw, T. A., Juncos, D. G. & Winter, D. (2020) piloting a new model for training music performance anxiety: training a singing teacher to use acceptance and commitment coaching with a student. *Frontiers in Psychology.* Available online at: https://doi.org/10.3389/fpsyg.2020.00882. Accessed 15 July 2021.

Skews, R.A. (2018) *Acceptance and Commitment Therapy (ACT) Informed Coaching: Examining Outcomes and Mechanisms of Change.* (Unpublished doctoral dissertation). Goldsmiths, University of London, London, UK.

Skews, R. & Palmer, S. (2016) Acceptance and commitment coaching: Making the case for an ACT based approach to coaching. *Coaching Psychology International,* **9** (1) 24–28.

Stenhoff, A., Steadman, L., Nevitt, S., Benson, L. & White, R. (2020) Acceptance and commitment therapy and subjective wellbeing: A systematic review and meta-analyses of randomised controlled trials in adults. *Journal of Contextual Behavioral Science,* **18**, 256–272.

Stoddard, J. A. & Afari, N. (2014) *The Big Book of ACT Metaphors: A Practitioner's Guide to Experiential Exercises & Metaphors in Acceptance & Commitment Therapy.* Oakland,CA: New Harbinger Publications.

Thompson, E.M., Destree, L., Albertella, L. & Fontenelle, L.F. (2021) Internet-based acceptance and commitment therapy: A transdiagnostic systematic review and meta-analysis for mental health outcomes. *Behavior Therapy*, **52** (2) 492–507.

Twohig, M.P. & Levin, M.E. (2017) Acceptance and commitment therapy as a treatment for anxiety and depression: A review. *Psychiatric Clinics of North America*, **40**, 751–770.

Veage, S., Ciarrochi, J., Deane, F.P., Andresen, R., Oades, L.G. & Crowe, T.P. (2014) Value congruence, importance, and success in the workplace: Links with wellbeing and burnout amongst mental health practitioners. *Journal of Contextual Behavioral Science*, 3, 258–264.

Wolgast, M. (2014) What does the acceptance and action questionnaire (AAQ-II) really measure? *Behavior Therapy*, **45**, 831–839.

Yıldız, E. (2020) The effects of acceptance and commitment therapy on lifestyle and behavioral changes: A systematic review of randomized controlled trials. *Perspectives in Psychiatric Care*, **56**, 657–690.

Chapter 7
Dialectical Behavioural Coaching: Theory, research and practice

Jonathan Passmore

Introduction

Dialectical behaviour therapy has established itself as an intervention of choice for therapists working with specific types of presenting issue. More recently, the approach has been developing as therapists have recognised the value of the approach for a wider range of presenting issues, such as managing eating disorders and aggression behaviour. As yet, at the time of writing, DBT has not been applied to coaching. In this sense this chapter seeks to highlight DBT as an intervention which could be a useful addition to the coach's array of approaches, within a wider eclectic or integrated approach.

In this chapter we explore DBT as a model for behavioural change, review its efficacy from published research studies and start to consider what a DBC (dialectical behaviour coaching) approach might look like while considering its application through a select use of DBT techniques.

Theoretical foundations

Dialectical behaviour therapy (DBT) was developed by Marsha Linehan in early 1980s out of efforts to address the problems of clients with borderline personality disorder (BPD) engaging in suicidal behaviour (Lineham, 1993). Lineham tested out her theory, which contributed to further refinements. DBT appeared to have a positive effect, leading to a reduction in suicidal and self-harm behaviour for clients, particularly those presenting with BPD (Lineham *et al*, 1991). The result of this and subsequent studies have led to DBT becoming a widely used therapy with clients with BPD. While other BPD treatments have since been developed and tested, such as Schema-focused therapy, DBT remains a popular treatment by many clinicians as a result of its robust evidence base which we review below.

DBT is rooted in three philosophies which underpin the therapeutic intervention:

- behaviourism
- Zen Buddhism
- dialectics.

We will explore each in turn.

Behaviourism

DBT places its emphasis on behaviour, rather than cognition, within the CBT tradition. As a radical behaviourist treatment, the DBT therapist seeks to conceptualize everything the individual does – doing, feeling and thinking. The DBT therapist sees their clients' problems as behavioural, leading to the therapist targeting specific behaviours which need to change. This means that once the unhelpful behaviours are no longer observable, the disorder is considered to be resolved. In some senses, particularly when working with clinical populations, this philosophy provides hope that a stigmatising label, such as borderline personality disorder, can be removed by the application of behavioural interventions. Thus, it would be fair to say while DBT also considers emotions and cognitions which get in the way of the deployment of effective behaviours, it is at its heart a behaviouralist approach.

Zen Buddhism

The second strand is Zen, a practice which centres on complete engagement with, and acceptance of, the present moment. Linehan was fascinated by Zen, and contemplative practices. She wondered how such practices of full acceptance and living in the present moment could bring greater peace for clients who were experiencing distress as a result of rumination and anticipatory thoughts.

Dialectics

The third strand is dialectics. This provides a structural philosophical context to behavioural theory and Zen practice. Dialectics argues that we can only discover 'truth' through argument or thesis. Such argument elicits a counter-argument or antithesis that seeks to demonstrate the inaccuracy in some or all of the original argument. This process leads to a new proposition or synthesis, which, in its turn, forms a thesis eliciting a new antithesis. In the course of therapy, DBT therapists seek to engage their clients in such debates. The client, for example, wants to die; the therapist disputes that dying is a good idea. In so doing, the client argues for why they wish to die; perhaps they are overwhelmed with anxiety. The therapist validates the emotion, but counter argues that dying is not a solution to their problem. The client experiences the therapist's comments as indicating that the situation is understood. This helps to reduce their emotional distress, enabling them to start to explore the causes of their anxiety.

These three philosophical roots, behaviourism, Zen and dialectics, have informed the design of DBT, and its application in therapeutic settings for 1:1 client work, but also in group work. What is surprising is these ideas have yet to cross to other 1:1 relationships focusing on behavioural change, such as coaching.

Research evidence

There has been a multiplicity of meta-studies of DBT (DeCou et al, 2019; Cristea et al, 2017; Panos, Jackson & Hasan, 2013; Kliem et al, 2010; Ost, 2008), reviewing what is a substantial body of evidence on the efficacy of DBT. As with most other third wave CBT practices described in this book there is none, or virtually no research into the use of DBT in coaching, or in the workplace. As a result, at this stage, coaching practitioners must look solely to the research findings from therapy for evidence, but in doing so they must consider whether the findings might reasonably be repeated in coaching studies with non-clinical populations or in the workplace, where perhaps less extreme examples of these clinical behaviours might be displayed by individuals, such as through shouting, bullying and aggressive behaviours to colleagues.

Some meta-studies are in areas significantly outside the day-to-day experiences of most coaches, such as working with clients engaging in suicidal talk, repeated self-harming or eating disorders.

DeCou et al (2019) undertook a meta-analysis focusing on suicide treatments, in RCT studies comparing DBT with other interventions. The study included 18 RCT studies with a range of participants from young people to adults. They concluded the meta-analyses demonstrated that DBT reduced self-directed violence (d = -.324, 95% CI = -.471 to -.176), and reduced frequency of psychiatric crisis services (d = -.379, 95% CI = -.581 to -.176). While the evidence is strong, it is harder to argue the results are transferrable to workplace settings with unhelpful emotions or behaviours.

Cristea and colleagues systematic review and meta-analysis in 2017 focused on randomized clinical trials, and examined dialectical behaviour therapy and psychodynamic approaches. They included 33 trials in their study, involving 2256 participants. For borderline-relevant outcomes combined (symptoms, self-harm, and suicide) at post-test, they found DBT and other interventions were moderately more effective than control interventions.

Panos et al (2013) undertook a quantitative and qualitative review of the efficacy of DBT (eg, decreasing life-threatening suicidal and parasuicidal acts, attrition, and depression) explicitly with borderline personality disorder (BPD). The study only included five RCTs which sought to measure the efficacy of DBT on suicide attempts, parasuicidal behaviour, and symptoms of depression in adult patients diagnosed with BPD. The results indicated a net benefit in favour of DBT (pooled Hedges' g − 0.622). DBT was only marginally better than treatment as usual (TAU) in reducing attrition during treatment in five RCTs (pooled risk difference − 0.168). DBT was not significantly different from TAU in reducing depression symptoms in three RCTs (pooled Hedges' g − 0.896).

In 2010, Kliem *et al* undertook a meta-analysis to examine the efficacy and long-term effectiveness of DBT. Using a mixed-effect hierarchical modelling approach, based on 16 studies, they calculated global effect sizes for suicidal and self-injurious behaviours. There results revealed, from the sub-sample of 8 RCT studies, an effect size estimation of 0.39, classified by Hedges as a small to moderate effect size. However, the effect size rose when adding non RCT studies included in their trial, towards a moderate effect estimation of 0.44. The research team concluded:

> *'These findings support the assumption that DBT is effective in clinical practice.'*

(Kliem *et al*, 2010, p946)

Finally, Ost's study of 2008 sought to compare a range of third wave approaches, some of which we are examining in this book. Specifically, he examined acceptance and commitment therapy (ACT), dialectical behaviour therapy (DBT), cognitive behavioural analysis system of psychotherapy (CBASP), functional analytic psychotherapy (FAP), and integrative behavioural couple therapy (IBCT). He found 13 DBT studies, with 539 participants. Ost, having reviewed the data, noted the result of the overall meta-analysis with a mean effect size of 0.58 (z = 5.81, p < 0.0001) and 95 % confidence interval (.38, 0.77). This equates to a moderate effect size. What was interesting however, given the comparison of a similar number of DBT and ACT studies in the same paper was ACT demonstrated a higher overall effect size of 0.68, but given the relatively small sample in both Ost concluded there was no statistically significant difference between these two interventions.

Our experimentation with what we might call 'DBT lite', or dialectical behavioural coaching (DBC), suggests there is some value in applying these specifics with certain types of clients, specifically with those referred or self-referring to manage anger at work.

Table 7.1: Summary of research

Study	Summary
Linehan et al (1991)	RCT DBT v treatment as usual (TAU). Participants: 44 parasuicidal women, 12-month intervention. Outcome: DBT groups recorded fewer incidents of parasuicide behaviour and more likely to stay in therapy.
Linehan et al (1999)	RCT DBT v treatment as usual. Participants: 28 borderline personality disorder (BPD), suicidal behaviours and drug dependency. Outcome: DBT group significantly greater reduction in drug abuse, more likely to stay in therapy.
Linehan et al (2002)	RCT DBT v validation therapy with 12 steps. Participants: 23 heroin dependent BPD. Outcome: Both groups showed reduction in psychopathology and drug use.
Linehan et al (2006)	RCT DBT v community treatment by expert. Participants: 101 women with history of self-harm. Outcome: DVT participants were half as likely to make a suicide attempt and less likely to drop out of therapy.
Turner (2000)	CT DBT v client centred therapy. Participants: 24 patients with DBT, with 12mth treatment. Outcome: DB improved more than CCT group.
Koons et al (2001)	RCT DBT v TAU Participants: 20 women veterans with DBT. Outcome: Only DBT clients showed significant reduction in parasuicidal acts, anger experienced but not expressed, but not statistically significant.
Verheul et al (2003)	RCT DVT v TAU. Participants: 58 women, 12mths treatment. Outcome: BPD had better retention rates, greater reduction in self-harming.
Simpson et al (2004)	RCT 12-week trial DBT and drug treatment. Participants: 20 DBT clients. Outcome: DBT group showed improvement in all measures.
Soler et al (2005)	RCT 12-week trial DBT & drug treatment. Participants 60 DBT clients. Outcome: combined treatment showed overall improvement in most symptoms. Drug treatment also associated with reduced depression, anxiety and impulsive behaviour.

Table 7.1: Summary of research

Study	Summary
Safer et al (2001)	RCT v wait list on a 20-week trial. Participants: 31 women, experiencing at least one binge eating / purge episode per week. Outcome: Intent-to-treat analysis showed highly significant decreases in binge/purge behaviour with dialectical behaviour therapy compared to the waiting-list condition.
Telch et al (2001)	RCT DBT v wait list Participants: 44 women with binge eating disorder. Outcome: DBT evidenced significant improvement in measures of binge eating, 89% of group had stopped binge eating by end of treatment.
Lynch et al (2003)	Randomised pilot: DBT+Med v Meds. Participants: 34 depressed individuals, aged 60+ yrs, 28-week treatment plan. Outcome: Only DBT+Med showed significant decrease in self-rated depression. 71% of DBT+Med in remission compared with 47% of meds-only group.
Evershed et al (2003)	Pre, mid and post study. Participants: 8 men in high security hospital. Outcome: Reduction in self-report measures of hostility, cognitive anger and outward expressions of anger.
Shelton et al (2011)	Pre and post measures. Participants: 38 male prisoners. Outcome: Significant reduction in physical aggression and using distancing as a coping strategy.
Shelton et al (2009)	RCT 6 and 12-month assessment. Participants: 45 male and 18 female prisoners, with history of violence. Outcome: 6mth reduction in violent behaviour, sustained at 12mth.

The evidence from these studies confirms DBT is a highly effective treatment for BPD. This has led researchers to conclude:

'DBT is a superior treatment to usual treatments in reducing the high-risk behaviours of patients with BPD.'

(Verheul et al, 2003, p135)

The evidence appears to be echoed in the treatment of binge eating disorder and self-harm. But what is more interesting for those working in coaching is the evidence for DBT with respect to anger management and aggression (Frazier & Vela, 2014). Frazier and Vela reviewed nine DBT studies with clients displaying anger or aggression. The two researchers concluded from their review:

> *'Research has shown that there are potentially clinically significant results when using DBT to treat anger and aggression in various samples.'*

(Frazier & Vela, 2014, p156)

It is this body of evidence which arguably has the greatest relevance for coaches working with non-clinical populations, and which the author has experimented with in a number of assignments with clients. At this stage this is preliminary work, and it is too early to provide evidence of its effectiveness as a coaching tool, but individual case studies provide some evidence that in these specific cases clients have found the DBC approach helpful.

Practice

As an approach rooted in behavioural therapy, DBC offers the coach a wide range of practical tools to share with clients who display challenges in managing their anger or previously 'uncontrolled' behavioural displays. The tools in this section have been adapted from therapy where they were originally developed to support clients diagnosed with BPD and have been trialled with coaching clients.

We should highlight that, at the time of writing, this is frontier work in coaching practice, in that DBC is not a 'thing'. But we should also point out that the author pioneered the application of mindfulness into coaching practice during 2002–7 (Passmore & Marianetti, 2007) and the application of motivational interviewing in coaching during the same period (Passmore & Whybrow, 2007). Over the past two decades, both have become widely-used approaches complementing more popular approaches, such as CBC and solution-focused coaching, in their use in coaching conversations.

RESISTT

The first tool to consider is RESISTT. RESISTT is really a set of seven tools that can help clients manage overwhelming emotions (Van Dijk, 2020). Like many of these tools it works best by explaining the framework to the client in the context of their behavioural trigger and inviting them to consider which of the seven techniques best fits them and the context in which they are working. By using the word 'experiment' in the introduction of the framework, the expectation of a magical outcome is downplayed. Secondly, the client is given the freedom to 'play' with the intervention as they engage in an adult-adult relationship with the coach.

1. **Reframing the situation**: Invite your client to step away from black-and-white thinking and adopt grey thinking or reframing with a more evidenced-based, logical and helpful thinking style.

2. **Engaging in a distracting activity**: Remind your client that telling themself 'Stop thinking about so-and-so' will just make them think more about that thing. Invite them to focus on something else: cooking a meal, preferably one they have not cooked before and thus requires careful planning; talk to a friend about their friend's problem; watch a TV show or film; play an instrument or go for a run. The more the task requires sustained mental concentration, the better this activity acts as a distraction.

3. **Someone else**: Refocus your attention on somebody else. This is a great way to shift your attention to something other than the overwhelming emotions that you're feeling or the situation that triggers your urges. For example, talk to a friend about a problem they have, this could be a DIY challenge or thoughts about changing their job.

4. **Intense sensations**: Experiencing intense sensations that are not harmful for you can serve as a useful distraction. For example, take a cold shower, visit a sauna or stream room, or go for a wild swim in open water, lake or mountain tarn.

5. **Shut it out**: In a situation where the client starts feeling angry or anxious, a useful strategy is to leave the situation and go somewhere to relax or calm down. Encourage your client to visualize putting their problem in a box and putting the box aside for the time being.

6. **Neutral thoughts**: Invite your client to focus on neutral thoughts by, for example, focusing on their breath or observing the environment around them and noticing the colours of the objects around them.

7. **Take a break**: Taking a break will look different for everybody. Invite your client to pause and take some time off.

Through a collaborative conversation the client can be invited to reflect on the different approaches and consider which might be most helpful for them in the different situations which trigger their behaviour.

By inviting the client to monitor their application of the different approaches and reviewing their use at the next coaching session, greater awareness can be generated by the client about themselves, the content which triggers their behaviour and their preferred interventions. What is helpful is supporting the client with repeated use of the tools, as rarely, if ever, does a single use lead to behavioural change. Instead, the aim is to enhance awareness and strengthen the habituated nature of the new response.

ACCEPTS

ACCEPTS is a second framework, with multiple dimensions, that can be offered to coaching clients to consider and explore their preferred strategies. ACCEPTS aims to help clients by distracting them from focusing on the trigger event and the associated emotions, and encouraging them to focus on more positive aspects. By focusing on more positive situations as a distraction, clients may elicit feelings of joy and happiness and, in so doing, strengthen the pathways in their brain associated with the experience of pleasure, and reduce their experience both in the short and longer term of the negative emotions which cause them distress.

ACCEPTS stands for:

- **A**ctivities – engage in activities you enjoy
- **C**ontribution – to others and the community
- **C**omparisons – to others less fortunate, or comparison to worse situations you have been in
- **E**motions – engage in positive feelings and humour
- **P**ush away – put the situation to the side for a while
- **T**houghts – think about something else
- **S**ensations – experience a different intense feeling (eg, take a cold shower, eat a spicy food)

Using this approach, the coach would typically start by describing the ACCEPTS model, offer the seven steps as a menu from which the client can select. Like a buffet, the client can sample each before they choose what to have on their plate for the main course.

The coach may invite the client to describe and capture in a table an item for each of the seven elements of the framework (see Table 7.2).

Table 7.2: ACCEPTS client table

ACCEPTS	My actions
Activities	
Contribution	
Comparisons	
Emotions	
Push away	
Thoughts	
Sensations	

Having used Table 7.2, the coach encourages the client to describe the option in more detail. The aim here is for the coach to create a visceral or emotional response associated with the item.

Finally, in the session, the coach would invite the client to plan a homework assignment where they would experiment with the use of each of the items, in response to challenges that create the emotional presenting issue or trigger the behaviour they are trying to address.

Some clients experience out-of-control behaviours infrequently, others more frequently, and thus the experiment may need to last a week, or two months, before the person has had an opportunity to experiment with all or several of the interventions. After each trial of an intervention, in the next session, the coach and client can review the usefulness for the client and lessons learned. What typically emerges is that clients prefer 2 or 3 of the 7 interventions over 4 or 5 of the others. It is these that then become the focus for continued practice and refinement.

Radical acceptance

Radical acceptance is a technique focused on helping the client look after themself in a situation, seeing it for what it really is, without judgment or criticism, and focusing the client's attention on what can be done 'now' as opposed to ruminating about the past and fantasying or imagining possible future consequences and outcomes. The approach, like much of DBT, has similarities with other cognitive behavioural approaches in helping clients identify faulty or unhelpful thinking, and to focus on the now.

The coach starts by inviting the client to describe a typical situation which caused them intense emotions: anxiety, anger, sadness. The coach explores with the client what the trigger for this event was and invites the client to explore the physiological sensations in their body, when the event was happening. These may include 'sweaty palms', 'raised heart rate', 'blood boiling' or 'tears'. As in a cognitive behavioural approach, the coach explores what emotions may sit behind these bodily sensations and encourages the client to avoid judging themself or the emotions as 'good' or 'bad', but to accept these emotions as natural human emotions, felt by everyone, and to accept the emotion for what they are – a sign of being human. Nothing more, nothing less. The next step in the process is for the coach to invite the client to reflect on how they have behaved and what they were thinking about the others in the situation and themselves. The coach might encourage the client to capture their thoughts in a journal. The final step is for the coach to support the client to develop a proactive plan to move forward which would help them to accept themselves, accept others, and to prevent themselves moving to judgement – either about themselves or others. Simply accepting who they are, who others are, and that being so is simply being human.

DBT techniques

There are a wide range of DBT techniques that coaches can draw upon and that may prove helpful for clients in bringing strong emotional surges and the associated behaviours into awareness, with the increased chance of these behavioural displays being managed. Given, at the time of writing, this approach is untested in coaching beyond experimentation by the author, coaches are encouraged to experiment with these approaches, working with client consent to trial a new approach and to monitor the impact on the target emotions and behaviours.

Conclusion

The evidence for DBT as an effective treatment for BPD has been demonstrated through multiple trials. The intervention shows that for some types of behaviour it's more effective in reducing self-harming than traditional forms of treatment for BPD. The approach has also demonstrated efficacy in helping clients manage previously uncontrolled behaviours. This aspect of managing such behavioural displays may have value for helping coaching clients become more aware of, and to more effectively manage, unhelpful emotions in non-clinical populations. For example, it may be useful for managing anger in the workplace where such behaviours can lead to claims of harassment, bullying and dismissal. Using techniques such as radical acceptance or ACCEPTS may help coaching clients. However, research is needed to compare the effectiveness of such interventions with more traditional coaching approaches.

Five questions for further reflection

1. **How should coaches adapt dialectical behaviour therapy to a coaching approach?**

DBT approaches can work well for anxiety issues at work, from presentations to managing returns to work after prolonged absence. Adopting a more client-centred, facilitative approach, enables meta-cognitive approaches to be offered as an option to add to other CBT interventions.

2. **With what types of clients and presenting issues could dialectical behavioural coaching (DBC) be most helpful?**

Given the background of DBT in helping BPD clients and uncontrolled emotions, how might DBT be useful in managing extreme emotions in the workplace? While these may not be psychotic episodes, the evidence from multiple workplace reports and studies suggests high levels of emotions can be generated.

3. **What techniques from DBC could you see working with coaching clients?**

DBT has a wide array of techniques, some of which may be highly suited to use in the workplace with non-clinical populations.

4. **What ethical considerations should coaches give to the application of DBC with coaching client?**

Coaching clients differ from clinical clients. As has been noted elsewhere, there is no compulsion to engage in coaching. However, many clients with extreme emotional issues may be referred by their workplace employer with the expectation that unless the unhelpful behaviours stop, dismissal may be the only option.

5. **When applying DBC, what cross cultural factors should coaches consider?**

Most coaches work with diverse populations and the growth of digital coaching means that most coaches now work across geographical boundaries. How might cultural differences play out in DBC?

Suggested reading

Frazier, S.N. & Vela, J. (2014) Dialectical behavior therapy for the treatment of anger and aggressive behavior: A review. *Aggression and Violent Behavior*, **19** (2) 156–163.

Lineham, M. (1993) *Cognitive Behavioural Treatment for Borderline Personality Disorder*. New York, NY: Guilford Press.

Mckay, M., Wood, J.C. & Brabley, J. (2019) *The Dialectical Behavior Therapy Skills Workbook* (2nd edition). Oaklands, CA: New Harbinger.

Van Dijk, S. (2013) *DBT Made Simple*. Oaklands, CA: New Harbinger.

References

Cristea I.A., Gentili C., Cotet C.D., Palomba D., Barbui C. & Cuijpers P. (2017) Efficacy of psychotherapies for borderline personality disorder: a systematic review and meta-analysis. *JAMA Psychiatry*, **74** (4) 319–328.

DeCou, C. R., Comtois, A. & Landes, S. J. (2019) Dialectical behavior therapy is effective for the treatment of suicidal behavior: a meta-analysis, *Behavioural Therapy*, **50** (1) 60–72.

Evershed, S., Tennant, A., Boomer, D., Ress, A., Barkham, M. & Watson, A. (2003) Practice-based outcomes of dialectical behavior therapy (DBT) targeting anger and violence, with male forensic patients: A pragmatic and non-contemporaneous comparison. *Criminal Behaviour and Mental Health*, **13** (3) 198–213.

Frazier, S.N. & Vela, J. (2014) Dialectical behavior therapy for the treatment of anger and aggressive behavior: A review. *Aggression and Violent Behavior*, **19** (2) 156–163.

Kliem, S., Kröger, C. & Kosfelder, J. (2010) Dialectical behavior therapy for borderline personality disorder: a meta-analysis using mixed-effects modeling. *Journal of Consulting and Clinical Psychology*, **78** (6) 936–951.

Koons, C. R., Robins, C. J., Tweed, J. L., Lynch, T. R., Gonzalez, A. M. Morse, J. Q., Bishop, K., Butterfield, M. I., & Bastian, L.A. (2001) Efficacy of dialectical behavior therapy in women veterans with borderline personality disorder. *Behavior Therapy*, **32**, 371–390.

Lineham, M. (1993) *Cognitive behavioural treatment for borderline personality disorder*. New York, NY: Guilford Press.

Lineham, M.M., Armstrong, H.E.E., Suarez, A., Allmon, D. & Heard, H.L. (1991) Cognitive-behavioral treatment of chronically parasuicidal borderline patients, *Arch Gen Psychiatry*, **48** (12) 1060–4.

Linehan, M.M., Schmidt, H., Dimeff, L.A., Craft, C., Kanter, J. & Comtois, K. A. (1999) Dialectical behavior therapy for patients with borderline personality disorder and drug-dependence. *The American Journal on Addictions*, **8**, 279–292.

Linehan, M.M., Dimeff, L.A., Reynolds, S.K., Comtois, K.A. Welch, S.S., Heagerty, P., & Kivlahan, D. R. (2002) Dialectical behavior therapy versus comprehensive validation therapy plus 12-step for the treatment of opioid dependent women meeting criteria for borderline personality disorder. *Drug and Alcohol Dependence*, **67**, 13–26.

Linehan, M.M., Comtois, K.A., Murray, A.M., Brown, M.Z. Gallop, R.J., Heard, H. L., Korslund, K. E., Tutek, D., Reynolds, S. K., & Lindenboim, N. (2006) Two-year randomized controlled trial and follow-up of dialectical behavior therapy vs therapy by experts for suicidal behaviors and borderline personality disorder. *Archives of General Psychiatry*, **63**, 757–766.

Lynch, T.R., Morse, J.Q., Mendelson, T. & Robins, C.J. (2003) Dialectical behavior therapy for depressed older adults. *American Journal of Geriatric Psychiatry*, **11**, 33–45.

Lynch, T. R., Cheavens, J. S., Cukrowicz, K.C., Thorp, S.R., Bronner, L. & Beyer, J. (2007) Treatment of older adults with co-morbid personality disorder and depression: A dialectical behavior therapy approach. *International Journal of Geriatric Psychiatry*, **22**, 131–143.

Ost, L-G. (2008) Efficacy of the third wave of behavioral therapies: A systematic review and meta-analysis, *Behaviour Research and Therapy*, **46** (3) 296–321.

Passmore, J. & Marianetti, O. (2007) The role of mindfulness in coaching. *The Coaching Psychologist*. 3 (3) 131–138.

Passmore, J. & Whybrow, A. (2007) Motivational interviewing: A specific approach for coaching psychologists. In: S. Palmer and A. Whybrow (Eds) *The Handbook of Coaching Psychology*. London: Brunner-Routledge, pp160–173.

Panos, P.T., Jackson, J.W. & Hasan, O. (2013) Meta-analysis and systematic review assessing the efficacy of dialectical behavior therapy (DBT). *Research on Social Work Practice*, **24** (2) 213–223.

Safer, D.L., Telch, C.F. & Agras, W.S. (2001) Dialectical behavior therapy for bulimia nervosa. *American Journal of Psychiatry*, **158**, 632–634.

Shelton, D., Kesten, K., Zhang, W. & Trestman, R. (2011) Impact of a dialectic behavior therapy—Corrections modified (DBT-CM) upon behaviorally challenged incarcerated male adolescents. *Journal of Child Adolescent Psychiatric Nursing*, **24** (2) 105–113.

Shelton, D., Sampl, S., Kesten, K.L., Zhang, W. & Trestman, R.L. (2009) Treatment of impulsive aggression in correctional settings. *Behavioral Sciences and the Law*, **27** (5) 787–800.

Simpson, E. B., Yen, S., Costello, E., Rosen, K., Begin, A. Pistorello, J., & Pearlstein, T. (2004) Combined dialectical behavior therapy and fluoxetine in the treatment of borderline personality disorder. *Journal of Clinical Psychiatry*, **65**, 379–385.

Soler, J., Pasqual, J. C., Campins, J., Barrachina, J., Puigdemont, D. Alvarez, E., & Perez, V. (2005) Double-blind, placebo-controlled study of dialectical behavior therapy plus olanzapine for borderline personality disorder. *American Journal of Psychiatry*, **162**, 1221–1224.

Telch, C. F., Agras, W. S. & Linehan, M.M. (2001) Dialectical behavior therapy for binge eating disorder. *Journal of Consulting and Clinical Psychology*, **69**, 1061–1065.

Turner, R.M. (2000) Naturalistic evaluation of dialectical behavior therapy-oriented treatment for borderline personality disorder. *Cognitive and Behavioral Practice*, 7, 413–419.

Van Dijk, S. (2013) *DBT Made Simple*. Oaklands, CA: New Harbinger.

Chapter 8
Schema Coaching: Theory, research and practice

Iain McCormick

Introduction

Coaching helps individuals identify and work towards their goals using evidence-based psychological methods (Grant & Cavanagh, 2007). Coaching has grown as a business, with The International Coaching Federation 2020 study report indicating a 33% increase in the number of coach practitioners globally (over the 2015 estimate) and a total global estimated revenue from coaching in 2019 of USD 2.849 billion (ICF, 2020). Conversations and questions are at the centre of coaching (Whitmore, 2017) yet it has been argued that traditional coaches can often be engaged in inactive analytic discussions about client's concerns rather than actively addressing issues (Pugh & Broome, 2020). In contrast, schema coaching involves applying the active experiential methods of schema therapy when coaching executives (McCormick, 2016). It is a new approach where, as yet, there are few presentations or publications (Handrock *et al*, 2015; McCormick, 2016).

This chapter firstly explores the theory and the research behind schema therapy, which was developed for assisting clinically disturbed individuals, often in forensic settings. Secondly, it shows how this approach can be adapted for use in the coaching context with high functioning but troubled individuals in organisational settings.

Theoretical foundations

Schema therapy was developed by Jeffrey Young and colleagues in the early 2000s and integrates a range of techniques from existing therapies and theories, including cognitive behavioural therapy, psychodynamic therapy, attachment theory and gestalt therapy (Young *et al*, 2003).

In schema therapy, a schema is an organised persistent pattern of thought and behaviour that is self-defeating or dysfunctional. The schema develops during childhood or adolescence and can impact an individual throughout his or her life (Young *et al*, 2003). For example, clients suffering from the *unrelenting standards schema* have a very strong belief that they must constantly strive to meet very high internalised performance standards in order to avoid criticism. This schema frequently results in feelings of being pressured and unable to slow down, combined with exaggerated criticism of themself and others (Young *et al*, 2003).

The goal of both schema therapy and coaching is to help clients get their core needs met in an adaptive manner through changing their maladaptive schemas (McCormick, 2016).

Schema therapy has three levels of analysis:

- The schemas themselves, that is the organised persistent patterns of dysfunctional thoughts and behaviours
- Coping mechanisms which clients use in the mistaken belief that these will eliminate or reduce their pain caused by the schema
- Modes or the 'moment-to-moment' emotional states seen in therapy sessions.

One way to understand the difference between schema/coping mechanisms and modes is to draw a parallel with the concept of anxiety which can be both a long-term trait (generally feeling anxious) and a short term state (feeling more or less anxious in any particular situation) (Vera-Villarroel *et al*, 2007). For example, a client with an *instability schema* may generally believe that others around them cannot be counted on, but in a therapeutic session flip between the *vulnerable child* mode when feeling sad about their situation and the *maladaptive attack* mode when feeling angry at others' unreliability. Schema therapy may work on either the schema/coping mechanisms or the modes level or both.

Types of schema

Young and colleagues (2003, p14–17) outline five broad categories of unmet needs that lead to 18 early maladaptive schemas which they describe in client-centred language rather than in terms of psychiatric labels. These are summarised below:

- **First domain**: *Disconnection/rejection*, which includes five schema: abandonment/instability, mistrust/abuse, emotional deprivation, defectiveness/shame and social isolation/alienation.
- **Second domain**: *Impaired autonomy and/or performance* which includes four schema: dependence/incompetence, vulnerability to harm or illness, enmeshment/undeveloped self and failure.
- **Third domain**: *Impaired limits* includes two schemas: entitlement/ grandiosity, insufficient self-control and/or self-discipline.

- **Fourth domain**: *Other directedness* includes three schemas: subjugation, self-sacrifice, approval-seeking/recognition-seeking.
- **Fifth domain**: *Over-vigilance/inhibition* includes four schemas: negativity/pessimism, emotional inhibition, unrelenting standards/hyper-criticalness, punitiveness.

Coping styles

Due to the pain and suffering generated by the 18 schema, Young and colleagues (2003, p33) suggest that there are three coping styles which clients use in the mistaken belief that these will eliminate or reduce their pain in the long term. These coping styles are:

Schema surrender: The client gives in to the schema and acts it out without trying to change it. For example, the client with the *self-sacrifice* schema will typically fail to meet his or her own needs, regularly make sacrifices for others and in the long term feel deeply resentful towards those they have made sacrifices for.

Schema avoidance: The client reacts by trying to escape the schema. For example, a client with *defensiveness/shame* schema may become a proud competitive bodybuilder in an attempt to avoid the feelings of his or her underlying inadequacy. This strategy may work well for a few years while the client is participating in high profile competitions but in the long term may lead to greater shame when their physical prowess decreases.

Schema compensation: The client reacts in exactly the opposite way to which the schema may suggest. For example, a client with a *negativity/ pessimism* schema may develop an unrealistic positivity that is defended in an exaggerated manner, however, in the long term, this may lead to the person taking risks that are life-threatening in the mistaken belief that nothing can go wrong.

Schema modes

Roediger *et al* (2018, p39) suggest that when Jeffrey Young (Young *et al*, 2003) was treating disturbed clients he:

> '*found that the schema model was too complicated and that some clients "flipped" (rapidly) between different schema, coping styles and mood states (during the therapy session).*'

This led to the classification of these schema modes or the emotional state changes (Young *et al*, 2003, p37).

Roediger *et al* (2018, p40) summarises the types of schema modes as follows:

- **Child modes**, which involve the client expressing basic and often primitive emotions when attachment or self-assertiveness needs are not met. The child modes include: vulnerable, angry, enraged, impulsive, undisciplined and happy.

- **Inner critic modes** are the client's pervasive internalised core negative messages, beliefs and judgements that he or she has developed over a lifetime. Inner critic modes include both the punitive and demeaning critic.
- **Maladaptive coping modes** are the behaviours aimed at trying to deal with the dysfunctional child and inner critic modes. These coping modes would have been temporarily effective in childhood but are maladaptive in the long term. They include: compliant surrender, detached protector, detached self-soother, self-aggrandiser and bully/attack.
- **Healthy adult mode** is the client's executive function that displays effective coping behaviour.

The conceptual model of schema assessment and change

Young and colleagues (2003) presents an overview of this process which is summarised below.

Assessment and education phase

In this first phase the therapist helps educate the client about the schemas, assists him or her to identify their own schemas and to understand their origin in childhood and adolescence. Clients also learn to identify their own maladaptive coping styles (surrender, avoidance or compensation) and to understand how these coping styles perpetuate the schema. For example, a client may learn about the subjugation schema and how allowing domination by their boss, wife and friends represents a surrender to this schema.

Change phase

Throughout this phase the therapist uses a mix of cognitive, experiential, behavioural and interpersonal strategies depending on the needs of the client. There are no rigid protocols to follow in schema therapy.

Cognitive techniques

As long as the client believes that their schemas are necessary, they will not change, so the therapist helps them to identify and challenge their schema. The client and therapist work together to build up a rational case against the schema. During this process the client also begins to understand that they are not inherently defective, incompetent or a failure but rather they learned as a child to behave in a certain way that is now ineffective.

Experiential techniques

These involve the client fighting the schema on an emotional level. Using imagery techniques, they learn to express anger and sadness about what happened to them as children. With the help of the therapist, they learn to stand up to parents and other authority figures in order to protect and comfort the vulnerable child. For example, forcefully telling the feared bully to stop and leave them alone!

Behavioural pattern breaking

The therapist and client work together to develop homework assignments that replace the ineffective coping behaviour. These involve rehearsal of new behaviours in imagination and in safe circumstances combined with the use of cognitive techniques to confront the inner critic and fear of failure. For example, a client with unrelenting standards may practise doing work assignments to an acceptable but not perfect level while telling themselves that this will not lead to catastrophic consequences.

Research

Jacob & Arntz (2013) reviewed studies that used schema therapy to treat patients with borderline personality disorder, which is a condition characterised by impulsiveness, a long-term pattern of unstable relationships, a distorted sense of self and unusually intense emotional reactions. After conducting a meta-analysis of the first five studies in Table 8.1, Jacob & Arntz (2013) concluded that schema therapy demonstrated preliminary effectiveness in the treatment of borderline personality disorder patients in both inpatient and outpatient settings and using individual, group and combined therapy. Schema therapy was also rated positively by both patients and therapists (Reiss *et al*, 2013).

Table 8.1: Sample of schema therapy efficacy research studies

Study	Summary
Nordahl & Nysaeter (2005)	Analysed results from six single cases of schema therapy with borderline personality disorder patients.
Giesen-Bloo *et al* (2006)	Conducted a random controlled trial comparing schema therapy to transference-focused psychotherapy in 86 patients over a period of three years and a one-year follow-up.
Farrell *et al* (2009)	Compared the effects of group schema therapy with 32 borderline personality disorder outpatients where this therapy was given in addition to treatment as usual, with a control group of 16 patients that received only treatment as usual.

Table 8.1: Sample of schema therapy efficacy research studies

Study	Summary
Nadort et al (2009)	Used a random controlled design and compared individualised schema therapy with telephone crisis support provided by the therapist.
Dickhaut & Arrant (2013)	Conducted a pilot study over a two-year period assessing a combination of individual and group schema therapy.
Carter et al (2013)	Used a random controlled design and compared schema therapy to cognitive behavioural therapy in the treatment of depression.
Malogiannis et al (2014)	Conducted a single case series without a control condition to investigate the effectiveness of schema therapy in treating chronic depression patients.
Bamelis et al (2014)	Used a multicentre randomised controlled trial (RCT) of the clinical effectiveness of schema therapy for personality disorders.
Dickhaut & Arntz (2014)	Conducted a pilot study that used the combination of group and individual schema therapy for borderline personality disorder.
Renner et al (2013)	Used a one group pre/post design to investigate short-term group schema cognitive-behavioural therapy for young adults with personality disorder features.
Bernstein et al (2012)	Used a multicentre randomised controlled trial of schema therapy for forensic patients with personality disorders.
Reiss et al (2014)	Reported on the results of three pilot studies of inpatient schema therapy with patients with severe borderline personality disorder.
Van Vresswijk et al (2014)	Used a one group pre/post design to investigate changes in symptom severity, schemas and modes in heterogeneous psychiatric patient groups following the use of short-term schema cognitive-behavioural group therapy.
Videler et al (2014)	Used a one group pre/post design to investigate the effects of schema group therapy in older outpatients.

In 2015 Bakos *et al* published a more extensive systematic review of the effectiveness of schema therapy. They identified 3,200 published research abstracts and then excluded:

i. studies with participants younger than 18 years old

ii. research involving treatment in fewer than 10 sessions, and

iii. case studies with three participants or fewer.

That left only nine studies which were used in the systematic review. They concluded that the effectiveness of schema therapy was preliminary but that favourable treatment results were reported for personality disordered patients. They noted that empirical support for schema therapy was growing but there was a need for more randomised controlled trials to increase generalisation of findings.

Avramchuk & Hlyvanska (2018) evaluated the literature using dialectic behavioural therapy, mentalisation-based therapy and schema therapy methods to overcome borderline personality disorders. They found 309 articles in total and selected those with:

i. subjects having a mean age of 18 years or older

ii. a diagnoses of borderline personality disorder

iii. randomised controlled trials (RCTs)

iv. publication in English.

Thirty-three studies were examined and they concluded that all three therapeutic methods could be usefully used for patients with borderline personality disorder. However, schema therapy produced one of the longest periods without recurrence of co-morbid states and lowest dropout rates. They also concluded that schema therapy could provide these patients with greater benefit in terms of improved quality of life compared to other psychotherapies (Avramchuk & Hlyvanska, 2018).

Körük & Özabacı (2018) undertook a meta-analysis of 35 studies with schema therapy and depression in their titles. These studies all included an experimental group (a control group was not used as a criterion, but improvements between post-test and pre-test scores were analysed) and they specified the number of sessions, session duration and session process (number of weeks of therapy). Using these criteria, seven studies were analysed (Hashemi & Darvishzadeh, 2016; Heilemann *et al*, 2011; Malogiannis *et al*, 2014; Renner *et al*, 2016; Wegener *et al*, 2013; Gheisari, 2016; Rashidi & Rasooli, 2015). Körük & Özabacı (2018) concluded that schema therapy had a high level of efficacy in the treatment of depressive disorders and this effect was not significantly impacted by the country or culture the work was undertaken in, the type of depressive disorder, the number of participants, the number of sessions, the type of session (individual or group), the duration of the session (minutes), or the number of sessions per week.

Nick *et al* (2019) conducted a systematic review of psychological interventions for individuals with borderline personality disorders in forensic settings. Their nine selected studies used a range of therapies including schema therapy and six of these studies reported improvements in overall symptoms for all therapy types. They concluded that in the forensic setting, it is challenging to draw any firm conclusions about the effectiveness of any one form of intervention over another, nor about which intervention may best suit a particular setting.

In later research, Koppers *et al* (2020) examined the effectiveness of group schema cognitive behavioural therapy on patients with both personality disorders and depressive symptoms. This type of schema therapy proved to be effective for a broad group of these patients. However, the majority of patients did not achieve full symptom remission.

Peeters *et al* (2020) found that the combination of schema therapy and exposure to the source of fear with response prevention is a viable treatment for patients with chronic anxiety and co-morbid personality disorder.

Schema therapy has more recently been used outside the clinical and forensic setting. Shahsavani *et al* (2020) concluded that schema therapy was effective in reducing migraine severity at post-test and follow up.

Eckhard *et al* (2020) used a random controlled trial with 12 couples and found that couple imagery re-scripting based on schema therapy had strong positive effects on the felt closeness and mood of both partners.

When considered in total, the research support for the efficacy of schema therapy to treat a wide range of psychological disorders is growing but there is a need for more large scale random controlled trials to demonstrate broader utility. As the use of schema techniques in coaching is in its infancy there is a need to build empirical support in this area.

Practice

Much of what has been discussed so far in this chapter relates to the application of schema therapy and its impact on clinical populations. In this section I will explore how the schema approach can be adapted to coaching clients. Schema coaching involves using the conceptual model and approach with executives who are generally functioning well in many areas of their lives, but who have a small number of critical personal flaws which they want to change (McCormick, 2016). I will start by comparing and contrasting schema therapy and schema coaching, and move to consider the practices used within schema coaching.

Comparing and contrasting schema therapy and schema coaching

Schema therapy and schema coaching both aim to help clients get their core needs met in an adaptive manner through challenging their maladaptive schemas and by learning more functional ways of coping. However, table 8.2 describes how they differ:

Table 8.2: Differences between schema therapy and schema coaching

Schema therapy	Schema coaching
A widely practised approach with a range of promising research demonstrating its effectiveness.	A new approach that has, as yet, no research demonstrating its effectiveness.
Used with clinical and forensic clients who typically have moderate to severe dysfunctions.	Used with executives and other business leaders who are typically high functioning but have a small number of core dysfunctions.
Uses a wide range of schema definitions to address the broad variety of dysfunctions seen in forensic and other clinical settings.	This coaching typically involves a limited number of schema such as *unrelenting standards, subjugation, self-sacrifice, approval-seeking/ recognition-seeking*.
Clients often use a range of coping mechanisms to try to reduce the impact of schema (surrender, avoidance or compensation).	Clients typically only use the surrender coping.
Clients are more likely to switch between schema modes in a therapeutic session.	While analysing modes is still very useful, clients are less likely to switch rapidly in any session between schema modes.

Practice of schema coaching

Schema coaching draws on the following five phases and methods from schema therapy.

1. Assessment and education phase

The opening phase of schema coaching aims to help the client to:

- understand their dysfunctional life patterns
- identify the early maladaptive schema, coping styles and predominate modes
- learn about the origins of the schema (Rafaeli *et al*, 2011, p81).

The process usually starts by taking a life history, using this to understand the client and form a case conceptualisation. This builds an understanding of:

- the client's major problems or life patterns
- the origins of these
- the core childhood memories or images
- the client's unmet needs
- the most relevant schema and their triggers
- how the client copes
- the most relevant schema modes seen in the therapeutic sessions (Roediger *et al*, 2018, p62).

The coach may use a range of questionnaires such as: the Young Schema Questionnaire, the Young Parenting Inventory, the Young Compensation Inventory or the Young-Rygh Avoidance Inventory (Roediger *et al*, 2018, p66). These can help to better understand the schema and the relevance of them.

The coach and client jointly draw up a summary of the maladaptive behaviour and its origins which provides an agreed reference point for the ongoing work (Roediger *et al*, 2018, p58).

Using this case conceptualisation method, the coach helps the client understand that he or she is not alone in suffering from the maladaptive schema, that such schema are not uncommon in the population and how together they can treat the problem using the schema tools and methods.

This phase may also include mode monitoring or helping the client understand how he or she switches between emotional states in the session, sometimes feeling vulnerable, at other times angry. Roediger *et al* (2018, p70) sets out a process for developing descriptive mode diagrams, which are charts to show the relevant modes displayed by the client and the movement between these. The process involves the coach:

- introducing the need for drawing a chart to show the various modes
- summarising what has been learned from the client's history
- communicating to the client how this has left him or her with unmet needs
- describing the modes and their functions
- educating the client about the healthy adult mode
- gaining informed consent to use experiential schema exercises.

An example of a case conceptualisation is set out below:

> ### Case study – an example of case conceptualisation
>
> Alice was a successful, 43-year-old project manager. She was regarded as highly intelligent and very capable at both analysing problems and inspiring her team to address these. She had successfully managed a range of projects, yet in her biggest and most challenging project, the head of the organisation funding the project complained to Alice's manager that she seemed to lack the necessary confidence to lead the project. After much discussion it was agreed that Alice would remain as project manager but that she would receive coaching to address the issue of a perceived lack of confidence. In the first session she disclosed that her enduring childhood memory was of her father taking her to netball games every week but never showing any enthusiasm for Alice's playing or the outcome of the game. Based on the case conceptualisation the coaching sessions focused on addressing the emotional deprivation, as well as helping Alice change her hesitant language and passive body language. This highly focused analysis of the situation provided a clear framework for the coaching to move beyond a discussion about the quality of the funder's judgement and Alice's relationship with her manager.

2. Experiential techniques

The purpose of experiential techniques is to allow the client to get in touch with the emotions connected to their maladaptive schema and to enable the coach to begin to reparent the client so he or she can start to heal these painful memories. Reparenting involves the coach actively assuming the role of a parental figure to assist the client to resolve problems and trauma caused by defective, even abusive, parenting (Young *et al*, 2003).

Imagery is the primary experiential technique used in schema coaching. Young *et al* (2003) suggests devoting a whole hour to the first imagery session with a client and include the following steps: presenting the rationale for the experiential approach and answering any questions, undertaking the imagery exercise and then spending time to process what happened in the session.

It can be very helpful to start and finish an imagery session with an imaginary safe place. This is very important for clients who are fragile or traumatised as it gives them a simple and non-threatening way to start and end the exercise (Young *et al*, 2003). For example, a safe place may involve the client imagining he or she is lying on a favourite beach sunbathing on a warm day with a cooling sea breeze.

Once a safe place has been established, the coach can encourage the client to explore an upsetting childhood image that has been identified in the case conceptualisation phase. After exploring the childhood image, the coach may ask the client to explore a current or adult situation that feels the same. In this way the coach helps the client to see the link between the childhood memory and their present adult life. After returning to an imaginary safe place the coach can help the client interpret the experience in schema terms (Young *et al*, 2003). For example, exploring a childhood scene of being ignored by a parent after a significant achievement and then exploring an adult scene of being ignored by a boss after completing a challenging assignment, may help the client understand the link between these events and to the emotional deprivation schema.

Imagery work for reparenting is particularly helpful for almost all clients, especially those with disconnection and rejection schema. The process involves three steps:

1. After the client is fully engaged in an imagery experience the coach asks permission to enter the imaginary situation and speak directly to the client's vulnerable child.
2. The coach helps to validate the client's feelings and find out what the client needs at that time. It may be the client wants to be told he or she is a good child or that they deserve a hug or they have permission to play.
3. The coach encourages the client to access the nurturing part of themselves and to strengthen their healthy adult (Young *et al*, 2003).

Imagery exercises can also be used to help clients break unhelpful patterns, especially when the client suffers from the *failure* schema. For example, an imagery exercise may involve suggesting to the client that he or she do something that they would normally avoid such as asking for recognition from a boss or spouse. The exercise can involve the client using his or her healthy adult to stay and master the situation thereby breaking through their typical avoidance patterns (Young *et al*, 2003).

The section above illustrates the rich range of powerful experiential techniques that the schema coach can draw upon.

3. Transformational chairwork

Chairwork refers to a collection of techniques that use chairs to help clients better gain perspective on themselves in the here-and-now (Kellogg, 2015). It was first used in psychodrama (Moreno, 1946) and popularised through Gestalt therapy (Perls, 1969). It is one of the main schema therapy techniques used in mode work (Roediger *et al*, 2018).

There are a range of different ways in which chairwork can be used in schema coaching. It is very helpful in exploring and better understanding troubling historical events. For example, it may be used to help a client explore the circumstances surrounding the trauma generated by their mother picking them up late from kindergarten. The coach may ask the client to close their eyes and explore being four years old and waiting for her mother to arrive. Then the coach may ask the client to sit in a separate chair, play the role of her mother and talk about what happened that day. Finally, the coach may ask the client to sit in a third chair and explore the issue from the perspective of the healthy adult. Using this mode, the client may talk to her vulnerable child about why her mother was late and provide a rational explanation and reassurance (Roediger *et al*, 2018).

A second approach is to work with two chairs to strengthen the client's healthy adult. For example, the coach and client may sit side by side and explore the client's demanding critic mode. The client would then move to a second chair and with the coach's assistance address the critic. When the client becomes more comfortable at talking back to their critic the coach can move away from guiding him or her to simply asking questions such as, 'How does it feel when you tell your demanding critic to be quiet and get lost?' (Roediger *et al*, 2018, p182).

Chairwork can also be used to help the client explore the mode map that was developed in the case conceptualisation phase. For example, the coach can put the client's inner critic mode voice in one chair, then sit side by side with the client to support the vulnerable child mode and interact with the inner critic. If the client becomes angry, he or she can sit in a third chair and act out the angry child mode. Finally, a healthy adult mode chair can be added and the client can provide reassurance and guidance to the various child mode chairs (Roediger *et al*, 2018).

4. Emotional regulation techniques

These help the client to engage in more functional and self-caring behaviours. There are three groups of emotional regulation techniques: cognitive, perception-focused and physical techniques (Roediger *et al*, 2018).

Cognitive techniques

These help the client to think differently about their difficulties and include:

- counting down numbers – eg, counting down from 100 by 7s
- expressive writing – spending 15 minutes writing down whatever comes to mind
- mindfulness of the breath – a simple meditation technique focusing on breathing.

Perception-focused techniques

These help the client to focus on other areas not just focus on their struggles:

- 5-4-3 grounding exercise – the client starts by noticing five things he or she can see, four things he or she can hear and three things he or she can feel on their skin.
- focused attention – encouraging clients to describe exactly what they see – eg, the sun shining on the lawn outside and the two birds flying by
- listening to music – using headphones to flood the mind.

Physical activities

These help distract the client from their challenges and include:

- using physical activity eg, intense exercise to distract from unwanted emotions

- light physical pain – using a rubber band to snap on the wrist as a means of distraction
- 4–8 breathing – breathing in to the count of four and out to the count of eight.

5. Schema homework

These are activities the client undertakes between coaching sessions to strengthen their healthy adult and to better manage dysfunctional thoughts, feelings and behaviour. They include:

- the *schema flash card* on which the client writes down: the triggering situation and the resulting emotion, the link between the emotion and the schema, the dysfunctional thoughts that arise to maintain this link, the challenging of these unhelpful thoughts, the coping actions undertaken and the outcome
- the *talking back diary* – this involves drawing two columns on a piece of paper and labelling one inner critic and the other healthy adult. The client can then practise writing out the dialogue between the two modes and so strengthen their use of the healthy adult
- another technique involves writing a *never-to-be-sent letter* to a parent or other individual who caused the schema. The letter can help the client express their anger, sadness etc as well as reinforce their own coping through building up their Healthy Adult (Young *et al*, 2003, p135).

Case study – working with schema

Brian is a 38-year-old, well built, immaculately dressed partner in a major law firm. He had been a very successful student at law school and after serving as a summer clerk he was recruited by a leading firm immediately after graduation and so began his stellar career. He was one of the youngest members of the firm to be made partner, built himself an enviable reputation in the marketplace as a top litigator and was rewarded in the top remuneration range by the firm. Despite all his obvious success he had started to become deeply troubled over the last two years. This had been triggered by two very able senior associates who worked for him resigning at the same time and complaining to the People and Culture Department in their exit interviews about being unable to work with Brian who they described as hypercritical and completely unsupportive. About a year later it was compounded by an important client complaining to the firm's CEO that Brian was very difficult to work with and that his relentless attention to detail was unhelpful and unwanted. The final straw that drove Brian to seek executive coaching was when he had an argument with his wife about his over-critical and unsupportive interaction with his eldest son. Brian was horrified to come to the conclusion that he was perpetuating the perfectionist style that he had learned from his own father and was now inflicting on his son.

In the first few sessions of coaching, it became clear that this pattern of perfectionism was both long standing and deeply engrained for Brian. At this point the coach introduced the concept of schema coaching and specifically the *unrelenting standards* schema. It was a turning point for Brian who could relate to the concept and was immediately impatient to make progress. The coach discussed a range of options with Brian and it was decided that they would hold an extended all day one-on-one coaching session together and see how much progress they could make.

Case study – working with schema

The day began with a discussion about schemas and how they develop. A detailed family history was made and the case conceptualisation was undertaken with a central focus on the unrelenting standards schema. After a morning tea break, Brian and the coach began on a period of experiential work. Brian was able to vividly recall his father's angry impatience when he was a child and described how, after a period of feeling deeply intimidated, he found that gaining top grades at school, doing all his household chores before being asked and being very tidy in his appearance, seemed to keep his father's criticism at bay, at least in the short term. Brian was able to recall and recount in the first person present tense an important incident of paternal criticism. This incident was used in a limited reparenting phase in which the coach modelled the healthy adult and sternly talked back to Brian's father and told him to 'lay off and just let Brian grow up'. This had a powerful effect on Brian who was close to tears at the end of this work. After a lunch break the coach assisted Brian to once again recall the same emotional event, but this time, talk back to his father himself. Despite Brian's initial reluctance to do so, he overcame his concerns and found the experience very helpful. Towards the end of the session, the coach introduced the schema flash cards and Brian was rapidly able to use these to challenge the schema and foster more healthy coping strategies. The session ended with Brian developing a clear action plan to talk over the coaching day with his wife, gain her support for his efforts to change, have regular one-on-one catch ups with each of his staff and to focus on listening to them and being supportive – rather than being critical. He would regularly use the schema flash cards when he found himself exasperated by his son, his team or his clients.

Brian and the coach met on a regular fortnightly basis for the next two months and despite a number of times when he reverted back to his old style, he made steady progress. His relationship with his wife and son improved a great deal and he had no further staff resignations. He recognised that he would need to continue to work at change and that vigilance was essential if he was to maintain the improvements.

Case study - working with modes

Emma was a 32-year-old, successful pharmaceutical sales representative who had one young son and a supportive marriage. The Young Schema Questionnaire indicated unrelenting standards, self-sacrifice and pessimism. A detailed family history revealed a father who was an entrepreneur and salesman who had a career that ranged from great success to complete business failure. In times of crisis, he deserted his family for months at a time. Emma's mother was superficially calm, self-sacrificing and sharply compartmentalised her life to protect her children from her deep underlying anxiety generated by the marital turbulence. Emma was diagnosed with life-threatening Type 1 Diabetes from an early age, and this resulted in the need to continuously monitor and adjust her blood sugar and food intake.

When undertaking the case conceptualisation, it became clear that Emma was unable to identify many clear childhood memories that related directly to the unrelenting standards, self-sacrifice or pessimism schemas. She knew a range of traumatic childhood stories that had been told to her by her siblings, including one about being chased around and held down by her sister so her mother could inject her with insulin. It became clear that working to counter the schema directly would not be useful. However, the coach noted that during the session Emma moved between mood states, at times being vulnerable and crying, at others being very critical and later being highly demanding of herself. So, the coach decided to focus on mode work and together they identified and drew up a mode map of vulnerable child, compliant surrender, demanding parent and healthy adult. The client talked through a recent challenging customer meeting and how she had felt inadequate

Case study – working with modes

and very exposed. Discussing this experience enabled the exploration of the vulnerable child mode, the associated pain and the need for self-care and compassion. The coach then used chairwork to explore the relationship between the vulnerable child and the demanding parent. This was then used to strengthen the healthy adult and reduce the unhelpful impact of the demanding parent. This process was painful but powerful for the client. After an hour debriefing, Emma and coach explored possible ways that she could implement change within her extremely demanding lifestyle. She also expressed gratitude for being heard and for the steps towards being the healthy adult. The session lasted five hours. A three-week follow-up indicated that progress was being made, with the client being more caring and compassionate towards her vulnerable child as well as using her healthy adult mode to reduce the impact of the demanding parent.

Extended schema coaching sessions

As a coach working with senior executives, I have often found that the typical coaching hour is not enough time to address critical issues. Some clients will vent for an hour, finding this very cathartic but making little real progress. Others need more time than an hour to process complex issues. Many executives who enter schema coaching have been struggling with their inner issues for many years and so want to progress rapidly on these. For these reasons I have started to use extended coaching sessions, sometimes 3 or 4 hours but often a whole day. The client comes to my office at 9am and leaves at 5pm giving us time to work systematically and thoroughly on their challenges.

Before any extended schema session starts, there is a need for a series of preliminary one-hour sessions. Schema coaching begins with a sound understanding of the challenges the client is bringing to coaching and what they hope to achieve. These insights can be used to determine the usefulness of the schema approach for any individual case. Early sessions should include providing the client with an understanding of what schema coaching is, how it works and what it can achieve. It can often be useful to give the client reading on the schema approach, such as 'Reinventing Your Life: The Breakthrough Program to End Negative Thinking and Feel Great Again.' (Young & Klosko, 1993). Undertaking a psychological risk assessment before beginning schema coaching is also important.

An example of a whole day one-on-one schema coaching session is set out below.

Start 9am

- Welcome the client, explain the purpose of the day, talk over the results of the initial sessions and the conclusions reached. Discuss the reading the client has done and their understanding of the schema model. Allow time for questions from the client.
- Undertake the appropriate psychometric testing such as the Young Schema Questionnaire, The Multidimensional Perfectionism Scale or similar. Score the tests and discuss the results.
- Talk over the difference between intellectual understanding and experiential understanding and how schema aims to deal with both these areas.
- Allow the client 15 or so minutes to reflect and make notes in their journal of the day.
- Have a morning coffee break.

10.30am

- Agree an imaginary 'safe place' and help the client picture the scene.
- Explore the schema, its origins, its value and implications for the future.
- Explain the nature of the limited re-parenting experiential exercise to challenge the emotional basis of the schema. Undertake the exercise with the coach confronting the imagined individual at the centre of the schema or related exercise.
- Debrief the client.
- Allow the client 15 or so minutes to reflect and make notes in their journal.

12.30pm

- Repeat the limited re-parenting exercise but have the client play the role of his or her own healthy adult and confront the imagined individual at the centre of the schema.
- Debrief the client.
- Allow the client time to make notes in their journal.

1pm   *Lunch*

2pm

- Discuss the importance of cognitive distortions in maintaining the schema. Jointly work with the client on a Schema Flash Card and debrief. Have the client work on a second Schema Flash Card by themselves with support as needed.
- Debrief the client.
- Allow the client 15 or so minutes to make notes in journal.

3pm   *Afternoon break*

3.15pm

- Identify the modes that are relevant to the client. Undertake chairwork to challenge the inner critic and to strengthen the healthy adult. Have the client develop and work on a second chairwork exercise with support as needed by the coach.
- Allow the client 15 or so minutes to make notes in journal.

4.30 pm

- Prepare the homework exercises – eg, more self-directed emotional challenging of the schema, the use of Schema Flash Cards, repeated chairwork, as needed.
- Review the day and the lessons learned.
- Agree a follow-up session.

5pm   *Finish*

Conclusion

Schema therapy is an evidence-based approach developed by Jeffrey Young and colleagues (2003) to deal with long-standing and deep-seated clinical issues, especially borderline personality disorder. The concepts and tools of schema therapy can be usefully integrated into coaching and used with troubled but functioning executives. One clear advantage of the schema approach is the wide range of therapeutic methods and tools that it uses to address maladaptive patterns. While there is very little written on schema coaching and even less research on its effectiveness, this new area appears to have promise.

Five questions for further reflection

1. What are the limitations of the schema model?

For anyone starting out in this area the model can seem overwhelmingly complex with the 18 schema, three coping styles and numerous modes. Fortunately, when applied in schema coaching, many of the schema such as abuse are rarely seen, the main coping style is schema surrender, and the most common modes are vulnerable child, inner critic and healthy adult. This represents a much simpler and easier to understand sub-model.

2. Who should undertake schema coaching?

Coaches formally trained in clinical psychology who have undertaken a schema therapy training programme and who have a supervisor with extensive schema therapy experience are best placed to undertake schema coaching.

3. What types of client is schema coaching most suitable for?

Traditional coaching approaches are suitable for most coaching clients, however, if the presenting issue is deeply embedded and has a long history, then schema coaching may be suitable.

4. What are the most important elements in the schema model?

The case conceptualisation is central to the model. Gaining a clear case history and understanding the types, origins and consequences of any schema are vital to understanding the client and shaping the coaching approach. Experientially-based, limited, re-parenting exercises are also central to breaking the hold the schema has on the client and giving the individual a way of dealing with trauma from the past.

5. What is the future for schema coaching?

Although schema therapy has been well documented and there is a useful level of research about its effectiveness, this is not the case for schema coaching. There is a need for schema coaching to be explored and the approach written about. Research on the effectiveness of schema coaching needs to be started. In addition, the schema model focuses on maladaptive schema and modes yet much of the focus on coaching is positive, such as building on strengths and finding purpose in life. There is a need for schema coaching to expand into these areas for example to explore modes such as the values-guided adult, the astute adult or the compassionate parent. Given the richness of the underlying model, schema coaching has a promising future.

References

Avramchuk, O. & Hlyvanska, O. (2018) comparative analysis of modern methods of psychotherapy for patients with borderline personality disorder. *European Journal of Interdisciplinary Studies,* **10** (1) 50–61.

Bakos, D.S., Gallo, A.E. & Wainer, R. (2015) Systematic review of the clinical effectiveness of schema therapy. *Contemporary Behavioral Health Care,* 1. Available online at: doi: 10.15761/ CBHC.1000104 Accessed 15 July 2021.

Bamelis, L.L., Evers, S.M., Spinhoven, P. & Arntz, A. (2014) Results of a multicenter randomized controlled trial of the clinical effectiveness of schema therapy for personality disorders. *American Journal of Psychiatry* **171**, 305–322.

Bernstein D.P., Nijman H.L.I., Karos, K., Kuelen de Vos, M., Vogel, V. & Lucker, T.P. (2012) Schema Therapy for forensic patients with personality disorders: design and preliminary findings of a multicenter randomized clinical trial in the Netherlands. *International Journal of Forensic Mental Health,* **11**, 312–324.

Carter, J. D., McIntosh, V.V., Jordan, J., Porter, R.J., Frampton, C.M. & Porter, P. R. (2013) Psychotherapy for depression: a randomized clinical trial comparing schema therapy and cognitive behavior therapy. *Journal of Affective Disorders,* **151**, 500–505.

Dickhaut, V. & Arntz, A. (2013) Outpatient group schema therapy for borderline personality disorder: A pilot study. in preparation. Cited in: G.A. Jacob and A. Arntz (2013) *Schema Therapy for* personality disorders – a review. *International Journal of Cognitive Therapy,* **6** (2) 171–185.

Dickhaut, V. & Arntz, A. (2014) Combined group and individual schema therapy for borderline personality disorder: a pilot study. *Journal of Behavioral Therapy and Experimental Psychiatry,* **45**, 242–251.

Farrell, J., Shaw, I. & Webber, M. (2009) A schema-focused approach to group psychotherapy for outpatients with borderline personality disorder: A randomized controlled trial. *Journal of Behavior Therapy and Experimental Psychiatry,* **40**, 317–328.

Gheisari, M. (2016) The effectiveness of schema therapy integrated with neurological rehabilitation methods to improve executive functions in patients with chronic depression. *Health Science Journal,* 10, 14.

Giesen-Bloo, J., van Dyck, R., Spinhoven, P., van Tilburg, W., Dirksen, C. & van Asselt, T. Kremers, I., Nadort, M. & Arntz, A. (2006) Outpatient psychotherapy for borderline personality disorder: Randomized trial of schema-focused therapy vs. transference-focused psychotherapy. *Archives of General Psychiatry,* **63**, 649–658.

Grant, A.M. & Cavanagh, M.J. (2007) Evidence-based coaching: Flourishing or languishing? *Australian Psychologist,* **42**, 239–254.

Handrock, A., Schwantes, U. & Baumann, M. (2015) Schema coaching as a resource-oriented method for behavioral change. *Verhaltenstherapie und Verhaltensmedizin,* **36**, 78–89. (Abstract only cited with full paper in German only.)

Hashemi R. & Darvishzadeh K. (2016) Effectiveness of group schema therapy in reducing the symptoms of major depression in a sample of women. *Asian Social Science,* **12**, 232–238.

Heilemann, M.V., Pieters, H.C., Kehoe, P. & Yang, Q. (2011) Schema therapy, motivational interviewing, and collaborative-mapping as treatment for depression among low income, second generation Latinas. *Journal of Behavioral Therapy and Experimental Psychiatry,* **42**, 473–480.

ICF, International Coaching Federation, (2020). https://coachingfederation.org/app/uploads/2020/09/FINAL_ICF_GCS2020_ExecutiveSummary.pdf Website viewed 29 July 2021.

Jacob, G.A. & Arntz, A. (2013). Schema therapy for personality disorders—a review. *International Journal of Cognitive Therapy*, **6** (2) 171–185.

Kellogg, S. (2015) *Transformational Chairwork: Using psychotherapeutic dialogues in clinical practice.* London: Rowman & Littlefield.

Koppers, D., Van, H., Peen. J, Alberts, J. & Dekker J. (2020) The influence of depressive symptoms on the effectiveness of a short-term group form of schema cognitive behavioural therapy for personality disorders: a naturalistic study. *BMC Psychiatry*, **20**, 271. Available online at: https://doi.org/10.1186/s12888-020-02676-z. Accessed 17 July 2021.

Körük, S. & Özabacı, N. (2018) effectiveness of schema therapy on the treatment of depressive disorders: a meta-analysis. *Current Approaches in Psychiatry*, **10** (4) 460–470.

Malogiannis, I.A., Arntz, A., Spyropoulou, A., Tsartsara, E., Aggeli, A., Karveli, S., Vlavianou, M., Pehlivanidis, A., Papadimitriou, G. N. & Zervas I. (2014) Schema therapy for patients with chronic depression: a single case series study. *Journal of Behavioral Therapy and Experimental Psychiatry*, **45**, 319–329.

McCormick, I.A. (2016) *Using Schema Therapy in Executive Coaching.* Paper presented to the Industrial and Organisational Special Interest Group of the New Zealand Psychological Society. Available online at: https://www.organisationalpsychology.nz/_content/Schema_therapy_in_executive_coaching.pdf Accessed 17 July 2021.

Moreno, J.L. (1946) *Psychodrama* (Vol. 1). Beacon, New York: Beacon House.

Nadort, M., Arntz, A., Smit, J. H., Giesen-Bloo, J., Eikelenboom, M., Spinhoven, P., van Asselt, T., Wensing, M., & van Dyck, M. (2009) Implementation of out- patient schema therapy for borderline personality disorder with versus without crisis support by the therapist outside office hours: A randomized trial. *Behaviour Research and Therapy*, **47**, 961–773.

Roediger, E. Zarbock, G., Frank-Noyon, E., Hinrichs, J. & Arntz, A. (2020) The effectiveness of imagery work in schema therapy with couples: a clinical experiment comparing the effects of imagery rescripting and cognitive interventions in brief schema couples therapy. *Sexual and Relationship Therapy*, **35** (3) 320–337.

Nordahl, H.M. & Nysaeter, T.E. (2005) Schema therapy for patients with borderline personality disorder: A single case series. *Journal of Behavior Therapy and Experimental Psychiatry*, **36**, 254–264.

Perls, F.S. (1969) *Gestalt Therapy Verbatim.* Reprinted by Gestalt Journal Press, (1992).

Pugh, M. & Broome, N. (2020) Dialogical coaching: An experiential approach to personal and professional development. *Consulting Psychology Journal*, **72**, 223–241.

Rafaeli, E., Bernstein, D.P. & Young, J. (2011) *Schema Therapy: Distinctive features.* Sussex: Routledge.

Rashidi, Z. & Rasooli, A. (2015) Effectiveness of therapeutic schema on reducing the anxiety and depression in patients with major depressive disorder. *Journal of Applied Environmental and Biological Sciences*, **5**, 279–285.

Reiss, N., Lieb, K., Arntz, A., Shaw, I.A. & Farrell, J.M. (2014) Responding to the treatment challenge of patients with severe BPD: Results of three pilot studies of inpatient schema therapy. *Behavioural and Cognitive Psychotherapy*, 1–13.

Renner, F., Arntz, A., Peeters, F.P., Lobbestael, J. & Huibers, M.J. (2016) Schema therapy for chronic depression: results of a multiple single case series. *Journal of Behavioral Therapy and Experimental Psychiatry*, **51**, 66–73.

Renner, F., van Goor, M., Huibers, M., Arntz, A., Butz, B. & Bernstein, D. (2013) Short-term group schema cognitive-behavioral therapy for young adults with personality disorder features: associations with change in symptomatic distress, schemas, schema modes and coping styles. *Behaviour Research and Therapy*, **51**, 487–492.

Roediger, E., Stevens, B. A. & Brockman, R. (2018) *Contextual Schema Therapy: An integrative approach to personality disorders, emotional dysregulation, and interpersonal functioning.* New Harbinger Publications, Inc.

Shahsavani, S., Mashhadi, A. & Bigdeli, I. The Effect of Group Emotional Schema Therapy on Cognitive Emotion Strategies in Women with Migraine Headaches: a Pilot Study. *Journal of Cognitive Therapy*, **13**, 328–340 (2020). https://doi.org/10.1007/s41811-020-00073-8

Stewart, N.A.J., Wilkinson-Tough, M. & Chambers, G.N. (2019 Psychological interventions for individuals with a diagnosis of borderline personality disorder in forensic settings: A systematic review. *Journal of Forensic Psychiatry & Psychology*, **30** (5) 744–793.

van Vresswijk, M.F, Spinhoven, P., Eurelings-Bontekoe. E.H.M. & Broersen, J. (2014) Changes in symptom severity, schemas and modes in heterogeneous psychiatric patient groups following short-term schema cognitive-behavioral group therapy: a naturalistic pre-treatment and post-treatment design in an outpatient clinic. *Clinical Psychology and Psychotherapy*, **21**, 29–38.

Vera-Villarroel, P., Celis-Atenas, K., Cordova-Rubio, N., Buela-Casal, G. & Spielberger, C.D. (2007) Preliminary analysis and normative data of the state-trait anxiety inventory (stai) in adolescent and adults of Santiago, Chile. *Terapia Psicológica*, **25** (2) 155–16.

Videler, A.C., Rossi, G., Schoevaars, M., van der Feltz-Cornelis C.M. & van Alphen S.P. (2014) Effects of schema group therapy in older outpatients: a proof of concept study. *International Psychogeriatrics*, **26**, 1709–1717.

Wegener, I., Alfter, S., Geiser, F., Liedtke, R. & Conrad, R. (2013) Schema change without schema therapy: The role of early maladaptive schemata for a successful treatment of major depression. *Psychiatry*, **76**, 1–17.

Whitmore, J. (2017) *Coaching for Performance: The principles and practice of coaching and leadership* (5th edition). London, UK: Nicholas Brealey Publishing.

Yip, V. & Eddie W. (2020) Self-compassion and attention: self-compassion facilitates disengagement from negative stimuli. *Journal of Positive Psychology*, 1–17. Available online at: doi: 10.1080/17439760.2020.1778060. Accessed 17 July 2021.

Young, J.E. & Klosko, J.S. (1993) *Reinventing Your Life: The breakthrough program to end negative thinking and feel great again.* New York: A Plume Book.

Young, J.E., Klosko, J.S. & Weishaar, M.E. (2003) *Schema Therapy: A practitioner's guide.* New York, NY: Guilford Press.

Chapter 9
Metacognitive Approaches: Theory, research and practice

Jonathan Passmore

Introduction

Metacognitive therapy (MCT) continues to gain ground as a treatment for psychological complaints, specifically anxiety and depression. Since its development by Adrian Wells in the early 2000s (Wells, 2009), its use has spread with other researchers, writers and practitioners researching its efficacy or adopting the approach into their practice with service users. However, no work has been undertaken to review the potential value of metacognitive approaches to coaching, and specifically applying these ideas to work-based issues and problems. In this chapter we will review the theoretical basis of metacognitive therapy, critically review the evidence for its efficacy with clinical populations, and finally reflect on its potential as a tool for application in coaching conversations.

Theoretical foundations

The *cognitive behavioural approach* is predicated on a chain of causation often referred to as ABC. The client experiences an activating event (A) which triggers the response. This response is observed by others; consequences (C), however, are mediated by beliefs (B). In the behavioural model the activating event (A) of a bell ringing is observed to result in the animal salivating. The behaviouralist argues that all we can observe is the behaviour and are unable to step into the black box of the mind. In contrast, cognitive behaviouralist argue we can infer there is a cognitive process occurring when we observe. The dog 'thinks': 'that's a bell it must be lunchtime'. Clearly, a dog may not be able to articulate their thoughts, while a therapist working with a human client can help the client to identify their initial thoughts and to identify the belief behind these thoughts, ultimatley chaining down to the core belief. This chain of causation or flow is highlighted in Figure 9.1. The activating event occurred which creates a belief (possibly based on past experience) and thus belief results in consequences, behaviours (salivation), emotions (excitement) and thoughts ('will it be pizza or fish and chips today?')

Figure 9. 1: Traditional CBT process

Metacognitive therapy adds a step in this chain that, at least for mammals with the ability to reflect or engage in thoughts about their thoughts, starts a metacognitive process. The client, again using our food example, hears the bell and thinks 'lunchtime', but they also may think 'oh no here you go again, all you want is chips, but you'll never get a partner if you're fat'. This addition of the metacognitive stage which links to the beliefs is shown in Figure 9.2.

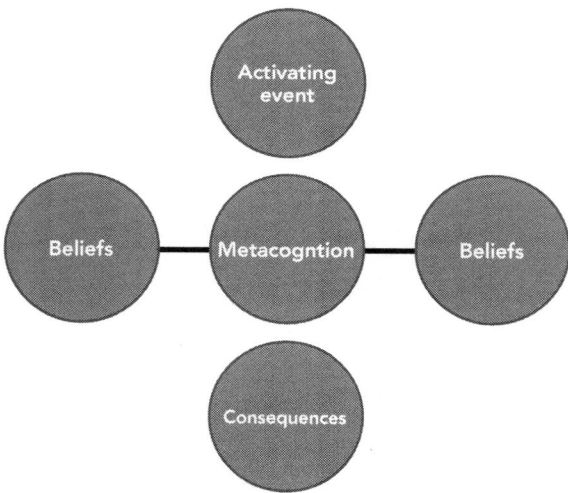

Figure 9. 2: Metacognitive process

Metacognitive therapy is theoretically grounded in the self-regulatory executive function model (Wells & Matthews, 1994). The model suggests that psychopathology arises as a result of a perseverative thinking style called the cognitive attentional syndrome (CAS). The CAS consists of dysfunctional coping strategies that individuals employ in their attempts to manage distressing thoughts and emotions. These emotions include worry and fear, and thoughts such as rumination and threat-monitoring, leading to behavioural responses, such as avoidance and reassurance-seeking. The model proposes that negative thoughts and feelings are usually temporary in nature, however when an individual responds to these with a dysfunctional coping strategy, the result is that the distress is extended and potentially exacerbated. The model further suggests that these dysfunctional coping strategies arise from a person's positive and negative metacognitive beliefs, that is their reflections on or their beliefs about their own cognitions. 'Positive metacognitions' are beliefs about the need to engage in specific cognitive processes, for example, the client thinks: 'Worry helps me stay prepared'. In contrast, 'negative metacognitions' are beliefs held by the client about the uncontrollability or dangerous nature of their thoughts, for example the client may think 'I have no control over my anxiety' or 'these thoughts mean I am losing my mind'.

The aim of metacognitive therapy is to help the client to identify and modify their dysfunctional coping strategies (cognitive attentional syndrome) using a systemized process set out by Wells (2009). The process can be varied depending on the client and their presenting issue. Wells suggests the first step is to create a unique case formulation in collaboration with the client. Secondly, the therapist aims to explore with the client the impact of their rumination, how these are maintained and how effective their current coping strategies have been. The third step is to explore and challenge through Socratic questions and experiments the client's metacognitive beliefs. The main emphasis is placed on challenging the negative metacognitive beliefs – such as 'if I think like this, I must be going mad' – before moving to challenge the positive metacognitive beliefs, such as 'if I worry it will help me to perform better'. The patient is invited to postpone their rumination processes by engaging in other tasks such as attention techniques or mindfulness. The client is firstly advised about the techniques, invited in the session to practise these and then to deploy them when anxiety triggers are present. By using the techniques, the client begins to recognise that their previous positive metacognitive beliefs are no longer required and that alternative strategies can be useful.

Research evidence

Several clinical trials have examined the efficacy of metacognitive therapy, although as previously noted the approach has not yet made the transition into coaching research with populations with less extreme (non-clinical) presenting problems. A study by Normann *et al* (2014) summarized a number of randomised control trials (RCTs) conducted to evaluate metacognitive therapy. Norman and colleagues concluded that MCT is very effective in the specific populations assessed. A more detailed review of Normann *et al*'s analysis reveals that only nine of the trials in the meta-analysis were controlled trials with the majority of trials based on small samples, a common problem also experienced in many coaching studies.

In a second meta-analysis, Rochat *et al* (2018) reviewed the efficacy of single-case studies on metacognitive therapy. They reported that these studies support treatment efficacy of metacognitive therapy for anxiety, depression, and a number of other psychopathological symptoms.

A third meta-analysis by Normann and Morina (2018) examined MCT's impact on primary and secondary outcome variables. The study included a total of 25 uncontrolled as well as controlled trials, in total 15 RCTs were included. With regard to the secondary outcomes, they aimed at assessing whether treatment has an impact on comorbid anxiety or depression as well as metacognitions. As Normann and Morina (2018) noted:

> '*The comparison with waitlist control conditions... resulted in a large effect (Hedges' g = 2.06). The comparison of MCT to cognitive and behavioral interventions at post-treatment and at follow-up showed pooled effect sizes (Hedges' g) of 0.69 and 0.37 at post-treatment (k = 8) and follow-up (k = 7), respectively'.*

These results provide further evidence for metacognitive therapy being a highly effective intervention for supporting clients to manage and overcome anxiety.

Finally, in 2015, a systemic literature review and meta-analysis (Sadeghi *et al*, 2018) explored the contribution of MCT on anxiety disorders. The researchers identified 15 studies within their criteria and concluded MCT showed better results when compared with control groups, and specifically they concluded: 'meta-analysis also showed that MCT had statistically significant better results compared to the control group in GAC (both immediately post-treatment and 12 months post-therapy results), OCD, and PTSD (p-values ranged < 0.0001-0.025)' (Sadeghi *et al*, 2018, p901).

I have previously argued that the lower effect sizes shown in the generic meta-analysis studies, such as Theeboom *et al* (2013) and Jones *et al* (2015), may result from the higher starting point for coaching clients, thus lower effect sizes are revealed in comparison to therapy. While no data exists for metacognitive coaching I would hypothesise that using metacognitive approaches with coaching clients would also see lower effect sizes, but that the approach will produce positive results for coaching clients experiencing anxiety and excessive rumination.

Table 9.1: Summary of research

Study	Summary
Capobianco *et al* (2018)	Study compared MCT and MBSR in treating anxiety and depression with 40 participants. Outcome: MCT was found to be more effective in treating anxiety and depression in comparison to MBSR.
Dammen *et al* (2015)	Study with 11 clinically depressed Norwegian participants. Outcome: Clinically significant improvements across all measures post-treatment and 6-month follow up outcomes maintained.
Dammen *et al* (2016)	Follow up study to Dammen *et al* (2015) paper. Follow up 12 and 24 months. Outcome: 70% of the patients were classified as recovered at 1 year and 80% at two-year follow up.
Fisher *et al* (2015)	Study examined the potential of MCT for alleviating emotional distress in adolescent and young adult cancer (AYAC) survivors (18–23). Twelve participants each received 8–14 interventions of MCT. Outcome: Statistically significant reductions in anxiety, depression, trauma symptoms.
Hagen *et al* (2017)	RCT examined the efficacy of MCT for depression, with 39 participants comparing MCT and wait list condition. Outcome: Large controlled effect sizes for depressive (d = 2.51) and anxious symptoms (d = 1.92). Approximately 70-80% could be classified as recovered at post-treatment.
Hjemdal *et al* (2017)	Follow up study to Hagen *et al* (2017) at one year with same sample. Outcome: For those who completed the programme 73% reported recovery, 12% improved, and 15% were unchanged.
Johnson *et al* (2017)	RCT compared MCT and CBT for 90 participants with anxiety disorders (such as PTSD, social phobia and panic disorder). Outcome: Significant difference in the level of anxiety favouring MCT at post-treatment (d=0.7), but there were no differences at one-year follow-up, mainly due to a further improvement in the CBT group during the follow-up period.
Jordan *et al* (2014)	RCT pilot study compared MCT with CBT in 48 participants with depression. Received 12 weeks of either MCT or CBT. Outcome: Both therapies were effective in producing clinically significant change, with moderate-to-large effect sizes. No differences were detected between MC and CBT.

Table 9.1: Summary of research

Study	Summary
Morrison et al (2014)	Study to examine efficacy of MCT in treating schizophrenia spectrum diagnosis based on a sample of 10 participants. Outcome: Effect sizes were moderate to large, with participants metacognitive beliefs significantly changed over treatment and follow-up periods.
Nordahl (2009)	RCT study comparing treatment as usual and MCT, with a sample of 13 participants from mental health outpatients. Outcomes showed MCT participants showed greater levels of reduction in anxiety and worry than treatment as normal.
Nordahl et al (2018)	RCT study of 246 participants with general anxiety disorder, three conditions: wait list, CBT and MCT. Both CBT and MCT effective, but MCT more effective, with higher recovery rate than CBT, at 65% compared to 38%. Differences maintained at two-year interval.
Papageorgiou & Wells (2015)	Study evaluated group MCT for participants who had not responded to CBT or antidepressant treatments. Outcome: MCI intervention results in reduced depression, anxiety, rumination, and positive and negative metacognitive beliefs, with gains maintained at follow-up. Analyses of rates of recovery revealed that 70 % of participants were classified as 'recovered' and a further 20 % as 'improved' at both post-treatment and 6-month follow-up.
Rabiei (2012)	RCT study exploring MCT and body dysmorphic disorder (BDD) with 20 participants in Iran. MCT significantly reduced the symptoms of BDD and of thought-fusion, compared to the wait-list, with effects on both outcome measures maintained at 6-month follow-up.
Ramezani et al (2017)	RCT study comparing MCT with Masters-Johnson sex therapy (MJST) for clients suffering with hypoactive sexual desire disorder (HSDD) in Iran. Participants received ten sessions. Outcome: MCT showed increase in desire compared with MJST, but this was not maintained at 6-month follow-up.
van der Heiden et al (2013)	Within participant study of 33 participants suffering with general anxiety disorder (GAD), with pre, post and 6-month follow up. Outcome: Study found reductions in worry, trait-anxiety, and general psychopathology. The magnitude of change and the degree of clinical significance were smaller than those reported in individually delivered MCT for GAD, and attrition rate (27 %) was higher than in individual sessions.

Table 9.1: Summary of research

Study	Summary
van der Heiden et al (2012)	RCT compared MCT with intolerance-of-uncertainty therapy (IUT) for General Anxiety Disorder (GAD) and waitlist / delayed treatment with 126 participants in in patent service based on up to 14 sessions of treatments. Measures at pre, post and 6-month follow-up. Outcomes: Both MCT and IUT, but not DT, produced significant reductions in GAD-specific symptoms with large effect sizes (ranging between 0.94 and 2.39) and high proportions of clinically significant change (ranging between 77% and 95%). MCT outperformed IUT and wait list conditions.
van der Heiden et al (2016)	Open trial study of 25 participants with obsessive compulsive Disorder (OCD). Exposure and response prevention (ERP), has been shown to lead to statistically significant improvements in 75% of OCD patients. However, only about 60% of treatment completers achieve recovery. Outcome: At post-treatment and follow-up, MCT produced significant and large reductions across all outcome variables, with high proportions of clinically significant change (patients recovered at post-treatment, 74%; at follow-up, 80%). In addition, the majority of patients (63% and 80% respectively) no longer fulfilled the diagnostic criteria for OCD.
Wells & Colbear (2012)	Study of wait list compared to MCT for stress disorder with 20 participants, who received up to 8 sessions of MCT. Outcomes: Statistically significant reductions in PTSD symptoms, depression, and anxiety at post-treatment were observed in the MCT group but not in the control group. Changes were maintained over follow-up.
Wells & King (2006)	Study of MCT in 10 participants experiencing general anxiety disorder (GAD). Assessment pre and post, plus 6 and 12-month follow up. Patients were significantly improved at post-treatment, with large improvements in worry, anxiety, and depression (ESs ranging from 1.04–2.78). In all but one case these were lasting changes.
Wells et al (2012)	Study to examine MCT on attentional control, rumination, worry and metacognitive beliefs. Each participant received eight sessions with pre, and post assessment, with follow up at 6 and 12 months. Outcome: Large and statistically significant improvements occurred in all presenting symptoms at post treatment and were maintained at follow up.

Table 9.1: Summary of research

Study	Summary
Wells *et al* (2015)	RCT study comparing MCT with prolonged exposure (PE), and a control waitlist group, involving 32 participants. Each participant received 8 sessions. Outcome: At post-treatment MCT was superior to PE on self-report symptoms of PTSD and superior to WL on objective measures of hyper-arousal (heart-rate). Both treatments were effective with MVT judged superior.
Wells *et al* (2010)	RCT comparing MCT with applied relaxation involving twenty participants suffering with general anxiety disorder. Outcome: At post-treatment and at both follow-up points MCT was superior to AR. At 6-month follow-up, recovery rates for MCT were 70% on both measures compared with 10% and 20% for AR.
Wenn (2017)	Study exploring use of MCT for participants suffering with prolonged grief. Outcome: The findings supported the utility of metacognitive grief therapy for reducing psychological distress and improving quality of life for people experiencing prolonged grief symptomatology.
Zahedian *et al* (2021)	RCT study for 24 participants in experimental and control groups. Experimental group received 8 weekly sessions of MCT, control treatment as usual. Pre and post Beck Depression Inventory and cognitive emotional regulation metacognitive questionnaire. Outcome: Lower depression, no change in cognitive scores and improved metacognitive score in MCCT compared with control group. MCT out-performed treatment as usual for this study.
Zemestani *et al* (2016)	Study comparing MCT and behavioural activation (BA) for depression, anxiety, and emotion regulation in university students, involving 41 participants randomly assigned to MVT, BA or wait list condition. Outcome: Both MVT and BA were equally effective for depressive and anxiety symptoms, in some specific categories, such as emotional regulation, MCI was judged superior.

In reviewing the literature, we can conclude from the number of meta-analysis and systematic reviews which explore the data on MCT that the intervention is more effective than waitlist and treatment as normal, and in many studies outperforms other comparable interventions, most specifically in the long term, 6- and 12-month post intervention period. This suggests that MCT through addressing the meta cognitions of clients provides them with more sustainable resources than traditional CBT or other interventions which simply address the core beliefs through disputation.

Caution however needs to be exercised in reviewing the data. Firstly, the number of studies is comparatively small when compared with the hundreds of MI or CBT studies. Secondly, the sample sizes used in these studies are comparatively small, with participants often numbering 30 rather than 300. Thirdly, many cases studies used a control or wait-list. Evidence suggest that gains are often shown simply with a placebo and thus a better research design using a comparable intervention would have been preferred.

As is often the case with these third wave approaches, almost no research has been undertaken applying the approach with a non-clinical population in the workplace. The approach can be adapted to use with coaching clients and research is needed to provide the evidence that it is at least as effective as CBT, and our hypothesis is that it will be more effective for clients with extreme anxiety which presents itself in the workplace.

Practice

The starting point for effective practice of metacognitive coaching is the use of a range of fundamental skills. Wells (2009) identifies four *foundation skills*:

1. The first skill relates to the ability of the coach to understand the different levels of cognition, specifically the difference between metacognition and what is ordinary cognition.
2. The second skill is the ability to identify maladaptive cognitions which constitutes the negative and positive CAS.
3. The third skill is using Socratic dialogue to help clients explore their cognitive processes.
4. The final skill is learning to implement metacognitive interventions, specifically attention training and mindfulness diffusion.

Coaches trained in traditional CBC are experienced in helping clients explore their thoughts, the relationship between their thoughts, feelings and behaviours, and in using tools such as chaining to uncover core beliefs, and Socratic questioning or chairwork to explore illogical or irrational thoughts, while helping clients to develop a more evidenced based outlook. This approach encourages the client to engage in reality testing by testing their cognitive distortions through adopting alternative perspectives and by challenging their thinking through a rational exploration of the evidence. In contrast, in MCC the coach suspends their own rational mind to join the client in assuming the client's thoughts may be correct. They then move to explore with the client their thoughts though a metacognitive process: that is helping the client to think about their thinking. This is done by testing out whether the client's assumptions about the helpfulness of their positive and negative beliefs are borne out by reality. The belief being within MCC is that through enabling clients to become aware of their maladaptive thinking and, through this understanding, the client is better equipped to change their mental model.

This exploration is achieved largely through two meta-tools: attention training and detached mindfulness. Let's look at each in turn and explore two or three techniques from each.

As we discussed above, some clients are locked into unhelpful thinking patterns that they find difficult to break. The traditional behavioural approach results in a wrestling match between their old style of thinking (distorted) and the new challenger (disputation). The result for clients is not a new effective outlook but a back and forward as the two ideas grapple for control.

Attention training technique (ATT)

Wells (2009) suggests attention training technique (ATT) as an intention to reduce this wrestling match. ATT consist of three components: selective attention, rapid attention switching and diverted divided attention. Wells has developed a procedure which lasts approximately 12 minutes and can be divided as follows: 5 minutes for selective attention, 5 minutes for attention switching and 2 minutes for divided attention.

Selective attention guides the client attention to individual sounds among a variety of competing sounds in different special locations in their environment. The instruction is to give attention to specific individual sounds while resisting distraction from other sounds.

Rapid attention switching consists of instructions to shift attention between 10 individual sounds and specific location with increasing frequency as the phase progresses. At the beginning of the phase approximately 10 seconds is devoted to different individual sounds. This is followed by an increase in the speed of switch between different sounds.

The ATT technique ends with a brief two-minute divided attention task, during which the patient is asked to expand their breadth and depth of attention and process multiple sounds and locations spontaneously.

The technique can be taught within the session, possibly practised during the next session and set as a homework task, with clients invited to repeat the process regularly for review at a future session. For the practice, the coach may need to ensure sounds can be heard from different locations. These might be a ticking clock, a radio and a mobile phone, or involve opening a window to allow birdsong or traffic and external noises to enter. The coach thus needs to plan in advance of a session, if they anticipate using ATT to ensure everything is in place for the client.

Progress can be monitored over time using the self-attention scale displayed in Figure 9.3. The coach might invite the client to answer the scaling question prior to the first use of an ATT, then after a period of home use, and finally at the end of the coaching intervention.

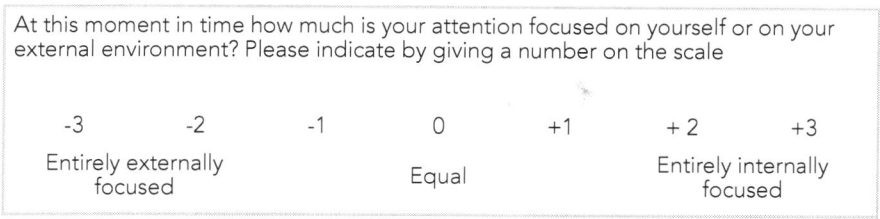

Figure 9.3: Scaling assessment

Detached mindfulness techniques

The second recommended practice by Wells (2009) within MCT are *detached mindfulness techniques* (DM). Detached mindfulness has two features, firstly mindfulness and secondary detachment. We have explored mindfulness already in this book (see Chapter 4). The benefits are well known, and chapter 4 describes ways to incorporate this into coaching practice.

Detachment has two aims:

- The first is to help the client to refrain from appraising the situation, and in so doing reduce worry, rumination and threat monitoring
- The second is to encourage the client to experience an inner event as an occurrence that is independent of general consciousness of themselves.

It is as if the person is aware of their perspective of their self, as an observer of the thought or belief. One way to illustrate this is *the tiger technique.*

The tiger technique

The coach invites the client to engage in an experiment, by bringing to mind a tiger and observing its behaviour. The coach asks the client not to influence or change the image of the tiger in any way but simply to watch the tiger in their mind and observe its behaviour. The tiger may move or stand still. It may blink or look straight ahead. It may shake its tail or keep it still. The client is invited to note how the tiger has its own behaviour while being reminded to do nothing but simply watch the tiger. At the end of the task the client is invited to reflect on the exercise: 'Did you make the tiger move, or did it happen spontaneously?' Through discussion the client recognises that the tiger moved without direction and was separate from the direct thoughts or cognitive instruction of the client's mind.

Clouds metaphor

As with ACT, the clouds metaphor in metacognitive therapy is a useful tool to help clients observe their thoughts. The coach might invite the client to engage in a thought experiment. As part of introducing the visualisation the coach may describe to the client that clouds are part of the Earth's weather system and we have no influence or control over it. Instead, the client is invited to bring to mind a cloudy day, observe the passing clouds and allow them to occupy their own space and time, whilst also recognising the clouds will pass overhead in their own time. In some cases, this will be quickly as they scud across the sky, and other times they may last a day a week or a month. The coach can then engage in a discussion about how the metaphor is like the client's thinking, helping the client to recognise they may be unable to fully control the thoughts which come to mind but, like the clouds, the client can let these clouds have their own space, until they pass.

Passengers at the station metaphor

An alternative to the clouds metaphor is the passenger and a station metaphor. The client is invited to bring to mind standing on a busy railway station. As they stand on the platform trains may pass by on the track. There is no point in the passenger trying to stop the train or climb aboard a non-stopping train. Instead, the client is invited to be a bystander and watch the trains pass by. The coach can then explore the metaphor and how this relates to the client's thinking. Which trains does the client need to allow to pass by? What happens if the client tries to climb aboard a speeding train?

The observing self

This technique involves inviting clients to observe themselves, and in particular their thought processes, after engagement in one of the metaphor techniques or stories from metacognitive coaching. The coach may ask: 'Are you the thought, or the person observing the thought?' This leads to a discussion about metacognition and can help clients to be more aware of their thinking process. By becoming more of an observer, the client is less drawn into identifying with the unhelpful thoughts and is more able to simply view their thought stream as separate to themselves. A stream which they can observe from the bank and which they do not need to enter.

Review

As can be seen through these tools, there is much similarity between MCT approaches and mindfulness and acceptance and commitment coaching. The real value of metacognitive therapy and its adaptation for coaching is the ability to work with clients who bring an anxiety-based issue to coaching, and particularly for those clients who have previously tried other cognitive behavioural approaches but have found these unsuccessful.

Conclusion

This chapter explores the emergence of a comparatively new third wave approach – metacognitive therapy. The evidence from a relatively small number of studies, primarily in clinical settings mostly with small sample sizes, suggests MCT is an effective intervention for anxiety-based conditions. No research has yet been conducted on non-clinical populations using metacognitive coaching, but anecdotal experience from practice suggests MCT can be successfully transferred to MCC for clients with anxiety-related issues. The application of MCC is based on similar techniques to MCT, such as mindfulness and attention training, but is approached in a collaborative style with clients. Research is needed to explore coaching client perceptions and measurement of the impact of the approach, and its comparability with second wave CBT and comparable third wave approaches, such as mindfulness stress-based coaching or ACT.

Five questions for further reflection

1. **How should coaches adapt metacognitive therapy to a coaching approach?**

Metacognitive approaches can work well for anxiety issues at work, from presentations to managing returns to work after prolonged absence. Adopting a more client-centred, facilitative approach enables metacognitive approaches to be offered as an option to add to other CBT interventions.

2. **With what types of client and presenting issues could metacognitive coaching be most helpful?**

Given the high levels of efficacy for MCT, the approach can be applied to presenting problems involving anxiety and clients with unhelpful reinforcing behaviours, such as vomiting before public presentations or compulsion to use the last carriage on a train when travelling to work, based on the fear of an accident while travelling on public transport.

3. **What techniques from metacognitive therapy could you see working with your clients?**

As with many third wave approaches, techniques such as mindfulness to aid diffusion and attention training can be useful additions to the coach's armoury.

4. **What ethical considerations should coaches give to the application of metacognitive therapy in coaching?**

Coaching clients differ from clinical clients. There is no compulsion to be present and, I would argue, coaching is more collaborative and future-focused in its approach than therapeutic approaches in general. Respecting the client, providing full information and allowing clients to make choices can ensure the approach is a joint collaborative effort, rather than one imposed on the client.

5. **When applying metacognitive coaching what cross cultural factors should coaches consider?**

There is little evidence about the use of these approaches with diverse populations outside of the Americas and European settings. More research is needed to explore if or how these approaches can be suitably adapted to become a useful tool in different contexts.

References

Capobianco, L., Reeves, D., Morrison, A.P. & Wells, A. (2018) Group metacognitive therapy vs. mindfulness meditation therapy in a transdiagnostic patient sample: a randomised feasibility trial. *Psychiatry Res.* **259**, 554–561.

Dammen, T., Papageorgiou, C. & Wells, A. (2015) An open trial of group metacognitive therapy for depression in Norway. *Nord. J. Psychiatry* **69**, 126–131.

Dammen, T., Papageorgiou, C. & Wells, A. (2016) A two year follow up study of group metacognitive therapy for depression in Norway. *Journal of Depression and Anxiety*, **5**, 227.

Fisher, P.L., McNicol, K., Young, B., Smith, E. & Salmon, P. (2015) Alleviating emotional distress in adolescent and young adult cancer survivors: an open trial of metacognitive therapy. *Journal of Adolescent and Young Adult Oncology*, **4**, 64–69.

Hagen, R., Hjemdal, O., Solem, S., Kennair, L.E.O., Nordahl, H.M. & Fisher, P. (2017) Metacognitive therapy for depression in adults: a waiting list randomized controlled trial with six months follow-up. *Frontier Psychology*,. **8**, 31.

Hjemdal, O., Hagen, R., Solem, S., Nordahl, H., Kennair, L.E.O., Ryum, T., Nordahl, H.M. & Wells, A. (2017) Metacognitive therapy in major depression: an open trial of comorbid cases. *Cognitive Behaviour in Practice*, **24**, 312–318.

Johnson, S.U., Hoffart, A., Nordahl, H.M. & Wampold, B. (2017) Metacognitive therapy versus disorder-specific CBT for comorbid anxiety disorders: a randomized controlled trial. *Journal of Anxiety Disorders*, **50**, 103–112.

Jones, R.J., Woods, S.A. & Guillaume, Y.R.F. (2015) The effectiveness of workplace coaching: a meta-analysis of learning and performance outcomes from coaching. *Journal of Occupational and Organizational Psychology*, **89** (2) 249–277.

Jordan, J., Carter, J.D., McIntosh, V.V., Fernando, K., Frampton, C.M., Porter, R.J. & Joyce, P.R. (2014) Metacognitive therapy versus cognitive behavioural therapy for depression: a randomized pilot study. *Australia and New Zealand Journal of Psychiatry* **48**, 932–943.

Morrison, A.P., Pyle, M., Chapman, N., French, P., Parker, S.K. & Wells, A. (2014) Metacognitive therapy in people with a schizophrenia spectrum diagnosis and medication resistant symptoms: a feasibility study. *Journal of Behaviour Therapy and Experimental Psychology*, **45**, 280–284.

Nordahl, H.M. (2009) Effectiveness of brief metacognitive therapy versus cognitive-behavioral therapy in a general outpatient setting. *Journal of Cognitive Therapies*, **2**, 152–159.

Nordahl, H.M., Borkovec, T.D., Hagen, R., Kennair, L.E., Hjemdal, O. & Solem, S. (2018) Metacognitive therapy versus cognitive-behavioural therapy in adults with generalised anxiety disorder. *BJPsych Open*, **4**, 393–400.

Normann, N., Emmerik, A.A. & Morina, N. (2014) The efficacy of metacognitive therapy for anxiety and depression: a meta-analytic review. *Depression and Anxiety*, **31**, 402–411.

Normann, N. & Morina, N. (2018) The efficacy of metacognitive therapy: a systematic review and meta-analysis. *Frontiers in Psychology*, **9**, 2211.

Papageorgiou, C. & Wells, A. (2015) Group metacognitive therapy for severe antidepressant and CBT resistant depression: a baseline-controlled trial. *Cognitive Therapy and Research*, **39**, 14–22.

Rabiei, M., Mulkens, S., Kalantari, M., Molavi, H. & Bahrami, F. (2012) Metacognitive therapy for body dysmorphic disorder patients in Iran: acceptability and proof of concept. *Journal of Behavior Therapy and Experimental Psychiatry*, **43**, 724–729.

Ramezani, M. A., Ahmadi, K., Besharat, M., Noohi, S. & Ghaemmaghami, A. (2017) Efficacy of metacognitive therapy for hypoactive sexual desire disorder among Iranian couples. *Psychotherapy Research*, **28**, 902–908.

Rochat, L., Manolov, R. & Billieux, J. (2018) Efficacy of metacognitive therapy in improving mental health: a meta-analysis of single-case studies. *Journal of Clinical Psychology*, **74**, 896–915.

Sadeghi, R., Mokhber, N., Mahmoudi, L.Z., Asgharipour, N. & Seyfi, H. (2015) A systematic literature review and meta analysis on controlled treatment trials of metacognitive therapy for anxiety disorders. *Journal of Research in Medical Sciences*, **29**(9), 901–909.

Shareh, H. & Dolatshahi, B. (2012) Effectiveness of Group Metacognitive Therapy in Major Depressive Disorder. Unpublished Manuscript.

Theeboom, T. Beersma, B. & van Vianen, A.E.M (2013) Does coaching work? A meta-analysis on the effects of coaching on individual level outcomes in an organizational context. *Journal of Positive Psychology*, **9** (1) 1–18.

van der Heiden, C., Melchior, K. & de Stigter, E. (2013) The effectiveness of group metacognitive therapy for generalised anxiety disorder: a pilot study. *Journal of Contemporary Psychothery*, 1–7. Available online at: doi:10.1007/s10879-013-9235-y. Accessed 17 July 2021.

van der Heiden, C., Muris, P. & van der Molen, H. (2012) Randomized controlled trial on the effectiveness of metacognitive therapy and intolerance-of-uncertainty therapy for generalized anxiety disorder. *Behaviour Research and Therapy*, **50**, 100–109.

van der Heiden, C., van Rossen, K., Dekker, A., Damstra, M. & Deen, M. (2016) Metacognitive therapy for obsessive-compulsive disorder: a pilot study. *Journal of Obsessive Compulsive Related Disorders*, **9**, 24–29.

Wells, A. (2009) Metacognitive Therapy for Anxiety and Depression. New York, NY: Guilford Press.

Wells, A. & Matthews, G. (1994) Attention and Emotion: A Clinical Perspective. Hove: Psychology Press.

Wells, A. & Colbear, J. (2012) Treating posttraumatic stress disorder with metacognitive therapy: a preliminary controlled trial. *Journal of Clinical Psychology*, **68**, 373–381.

Wells, A. & King, P. (2006) Metacognitive therapy for generalized anxiety disorder: an open trial. *Journal of Behavior Therapy and Experimental Psychiatry*, **37**, 206–212.

Wells, A., Fisher, P., Myers, S., Wheatley, J., Patel, T. & Brewin, C. (2012) Metacognitive therapy in treatment-resistant depression: a platform trial. *Behavior Research Therapies*, **50**, 367–373.

Wells, A., Walton, D., Lovell, K. & Proctor, D. (2015) Metacognitive therapy versus prolonged exposure in adults with chronic post-traumatic stress disorder: a parallel randomized controlled trial. *Cognitive Therapies Research*, **39**, 70–80.

Wells, A., Welford, M., King, P., Papageorgiou, C., Wisely, J. & Mendel, E. (2010) A pilot randomized trial of metacognitive therapy vs applied relaxation in the treatment of adults with generalized anxiety disorder. *Behavior Research and Therapy*, **48**, 429–434.

Wenn, J.A. (2017) Development and Testing of Metacognitive Therapy for Prolonged Grief Disorder: A Randomised Controlled Trial. Doctoral thesis, Curtin University. Available online at: https:// espace.curtin.edu.au/handle/20.500.11937/59668. Accessed 17 July 2021.

Zahedian, E., Bahreini, M., Ghasemi, Z. & Mirzaei, K. (2021) Group metacognitive therapy and depression in women with breast cancer: a randomized controlled trial. *BMC Women's Health*, **21**, 111.

Zemestani, M., Davoodi, I., Honarmand, M.M., Zargar, Y. & Ottaviani, C. (2016) Comparative effects of group metacognitive therapy versus behavioural activation in moderately depressed students. *Journal of Mental Health*, **25**, 479–485.

PART FOUR:
Beyond

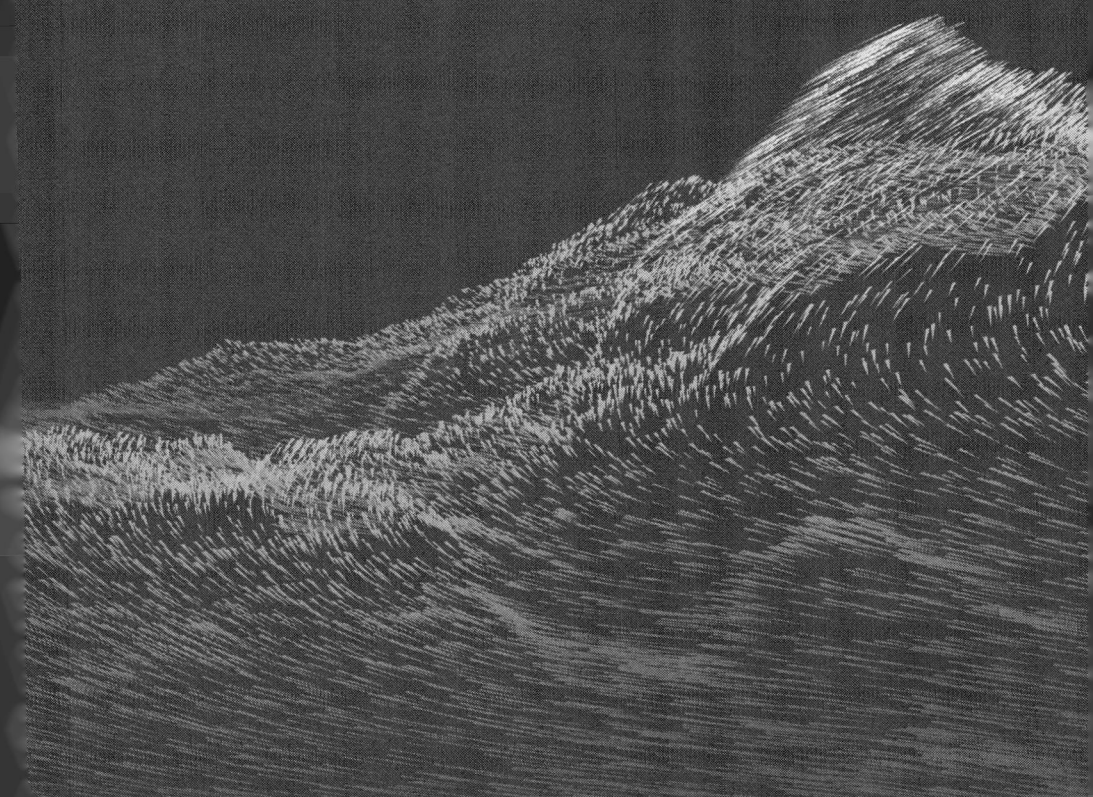

Introduction: Beyond Third Wave Approaches

Jonathan Passmore & Sarah Leach

If defining third wave approaches was difficult, the complexity increases for interventions which we have categorised here as beyond third wave CBT approaches. Certainly, each of the approaches included in this section draws upon a theory and evidence base. They also commonly help clients explore emotions and cognitions, and how these influence or drive their behaviour. Finally, they place an importance on identity and values. In spite of this, they come with differences which prevent their inclusion as a third wave approach. In some cases there is a greater emphasis on the relationship so their originators may thus categorise their approach as more person centred.

In this sense, the fourth wave may be a collection of diverse and eclectic approaches that are useful for more experienced coaches, but which lack a single over-arching principle that ties them to together or unites them in the mind of the originators and practitioners.

Some writers such as Peteet (2018) have argued for a fourth wave of psychotherapy in general, being more focused towards positive psychology, combining the humanistic and cognitive traditions, with a focus on the client, their story, their values, and faith, and encouraging clients to focus on thriving not just surviving.

One example of this may be Motivational Interviewing, although categorising approaches in this way is often controversial and suggests some form of hierarchy, where 3rd wave is better than 2nd wave and 4th wave is better than 3rd wave. In reality, the boundaries between these waves is arbitrary, and each wave offers value to clients.

In some senses it may be better to see fourth wave approaches as process coaching. In process coaching the coach draws on the evidence of practice from diverse sources. This would include cognitive behavioural approaches, with its recognition that human experience is at four levels, behaviour, physiology, cognition, and emotion. It draws from person-centred approaches, placing the client at the centre of the story, focusing on building the relationship but not at the expense of doing the work. In some ways the development of motivational interviewing fits here.

It draws on positive psychology, with a belief that all individuals can find ways and times in their lives they can flourish, and the idea that focusing on what people can do is more powerful than focusing on what they cannot do. Finally, it draws on our growing understanding of neuroscience, of the structure, processes, and natural biases of the brain, and how an understanding of the motor can help the 'driver' make best use of the system as it has been 'designed'.

The fourth wave is just emerging with developments continuing to happen in the areas of practice from ACT to DBT. The next twenty years will see further developments, and as always happens in any field, practitioners will learn from each other moving us further from schools of coaching and closer towards a single way of coaching, a single process of coaching: evidenced based and client centred, which takes account of the presenting problem, the unique individual (client), and the cultural context (system) in which they operate.

References

Peteet, J. R. (2018) A fourth wave of psychotherapies: Moving beyond recovery toward well-being. *Harvard Review of Psychiatry*, **26** (2) 90-95.

Chapter 10
Neuroscience of Coaching: Theory, research and practice

Patricia Riddell

Introduction

The process of coaching involves an exploration of the way in which individuals make sense of their world and an ability to help individuals to notice ways in which this sense-making might be changed to improve their outcomes. In order to do this, coaches are required to make hypotheses about how another person might be thinking and how this might relate to subsequent behaviour. In psychology, this process is known as developing a theory of mind (Frith & Frith, 2012). We use information from other people's spoken language, body language and behaviour to make predictions about the thinking behind behaviour and test these predictions through questions that help individuals to become more aware of the relation between their thinking and their actions.

Understanding how the brain works can help to tune the theories of mind we create since this can help to elucidate the, sometimes not wholly rational, ways that humans make sense of their world. This chapter aims to provide a basic understanding of how the brain perceives, learns and acts on the world with reference to ways in which an increase in understanding is useful to coaches. We will explore the processes that allow us to change behaviour, both in terms of the way in which change occurs in the brain and with respect to the processes that are used in coaching to help elicit change. We will then consider the effect of stress on behaviour and how coaches can help individuals to be better able to cope with stress and increase resilience. We will also consider decision-making, especially in relation to leadership, in order to show how this understanding might be particularly useful in executive coaching. (Further information on the neuroscientific basis of coaching can be found in Bossons et al, 2016; Riddell, 2019; and Riddell, 2021.)

Theoretical foundations

Coaching provides opportunities for individuals to reflect on their goals and to make changes to these in order to improve outcomes. This often requires the ability to change behaviour. Since every thought, emotional response, and behaviour starts in the brain, making behavioural changes requires that something changes in the brain. Awareness of the capacity for the brain to change is, therefore, an important first step in understanding the human capacity for change. This can help to answer questions like whether it is true that we can't teach an old dog new tricks, or that some people have more capacity for change than others. Being able to help coachees to understand the degree of change that is possible can be important in addressing beliefs that can constrain willingness to try new ways of thinking and doing.

Change in the brain

Epigenetics

We can begin to understand the brain's potential for change by considering how the brain has evolved to learn. This starts with a consideration of how the components of the nervous system are constructed through genetics and then altered during the lifespan through a process known as epigenetics.

It is now well known that the information required to create a human being is stored in the genes (Ilies *et al*, 2006). Germ cells (sperm and eggs) contain half of the DNA of other cells in the body. When sperm and egg come together at conception, therefore, the resulting foetus will receive half of its DNA from the mother and half from the father thus providing a full genome. During development, some genes from the maternal line and some from the paternal line are 'turned on' (or transcribed) and so some aspects of our personality, intelligence and looks will be similar to our mother, and some similar to our father.

To begin to understand how genetics provides the information to create a human body, imagine the difference between a cell that becomes part of the muscle of the heart and a cell that becomes a neurone in the brain. Every cell in your body contains the full set of 23 genes and therefore, early in development, each cell has the capacity to become any other cell. Specific signals are required to activate different parts of the DNA for the cells that become heart muscle compared to cells that become neurones in the brain. Thus, genetics is the process by which we inherit the genetic information to make the human body and interpret this so that the right genes are turned on in the right places at the right time (Ilies *et al*, 2006). However, it is clear that, while genes provide a starting point for our intelligence, personality and abilities, they do not provide a complete explanation for how these develop. Research has demonstrated that there are few complex behaviours for which genetics explains more than half of the variance in ability (Plomin

& Daniels, 1987). This suggests that there are other ways in which we can adapt to our individual environment (Sherman *et al*, 1997).

More recently, it has become evident that, while the structure of DNA is relatively fixed at birth, the way that we activate DNA can be changed during the lifespan. Some parts of our genetic material are being used over and over again, while other parts lie dormant only to spring to life in response to some signal (Carey, 2012). For example, we continually replace our skin cells and so this piece of genetic code is being used again and again. In comparison, there are large changes in the structure of our bodies at puberty. This involves particular parts of the genetic code becoming active in response to some (partially unknown) signal. The point here is that the genetic code is not all or nothing – it is flexible and different parts can be activated at different times. This understanding has led to the introduction of a new field of study – epigenetics (Carey, 2012; Sweatt, 2009).

Epigenetics can be defined as the study of (heritable) changes in gene activity within an individual's lifetime that are not caused by changes in the structure of the genes. Instead, epigenetic changes refer to activation of new parts of DNA within a particular gene.

DNA is formed in long strands that take the shape of a double helix. In the nucleus of the cell, these strands are partially wound around protein blocks called histones. Between each block, a part of the DNA is left unwound. This part of the DNA is therefore available to be activated. The parts of the DNA that are bound or unbound will be different for different types of cell providing a mechanism for controlling which DNA is activated in different parts of the body. In addition to this, it is possible for the parts of DNA that are wound or unwound to be changed during the lifespan. Adding molecules (eg, acetyl, methyl or ubiquityl) to the DNA or histone blocks causes the DNA either to be wound tighter (decreasing the availability of the DNA for activation) or to become looser (increasing the availability of parts of the DNA for activation). In this way, the parts of DNA that are available for activation can be changed. For instance, if you were to start an exercise regime at the gym which worked a particular muscle, this would result in changes to the activation of the DNA in that muscle in order to build more muscle fibres.

To show how this would apply in the brain, think about a time when you learnt a new skill or some new facts. This required the creation of new connections between neurones. In order to create these new connections, a part of the genome that was previously inactive in some of the cells in your brain became active. So, every new experience that is remembered or that creates new learning involves new activation within your genome – or epigenetic change (Keverne *et al*, 2015).

Neuroplasticity

Since epigenetics has demonstrated that we can change aspects of our neural connectivity within our lifespan, it is worth asking what can be changed in the brain and how does this happen. Neuroplasticity is the term used to describe changes (-*plasticity*) in components of the nervous system (*neuro-*). We need mechanisms that allow us to learn quickly and efficiently in order to adapt to changes in our environment. Consider, for instance, starting a job in a new organisation: there will be new people to remember, new tasks to learn, a new culture to absorb. And there might be some expectation from our new boss that this will happen quite quickly. We have to be able to learn fast.

This ability to learn primarily relies on changes that occur in the synapses (or connections) between our neurones. Neurones can connect with thousands of other neurones, creating networks that can contain all the information associated with learning a new role. By creating new synapses, new information can be connected into an already existing network of relevant, stored information from our previous experience (Sultan & Day, 2011). This allows us to learn what is new in our role and connect this to our existing expertise in this area.

It might be tempting to think that once a synapse is created, and if it continues to be used, it becomes permanent ('use it or lose it'). However, this is not quite the case. Synapses are more like skin cells – they are lost and replaced. The strength of a connection between two neurones remains relatively constant over time (same number of synapses), however, the actual synapses creating this connection change regularly. Indeed, it has been estimated that, in one part of the mouse brain, 20% of synapses change in a 24-hour period (Purves *et al*, 1987; Umeda & Okabe, 2001). Humans have lower metabolic rates than mice and so the turnover of synapses in the human brain might be slower. But this might still lead to replacement of all the synapses in a given part of the brain over the space of about one week to ten days.

Creating and destroying synapses is an energy consuming process and so this has to provide a substantial benefit to survival. The importance of this process is that it gives the brain its huge capacity for change – or 'plasticity' – and, therefore, learning and memory. If the brain made synapses but did not unmake them, we would have no means to unlearn facts that were no longer useful. Consider something that you might have learned as a young child, for instance, the idea that mothers are there to provide all your needs. This information might be less useful, or no longer relevant, as an adult, and so we need a mechanism to both learn and unlearn quickly. The strength of the connection between two neurones is retained if the information represented is repeated or is marked as important. This allows us to learn and retain information that is useful. But information that is no longer useful can be replaced by destroying synapses that are no longer in use and creating new synapses that represent new information or behaviour.

There is also research that suggests that new neurones can be created in some parts of the brain, particularly in areas associated with memory (eg, the hippocampus: Fuchs, 2000). This confers a fundamental evolutionary benefit since it provides us with an additional means of learning in new environments.

A great example of new learning is when London taxi drivers learn 'the knowledge'. Good taxi drivers are able to plot a route between any two destinations since they have such an excellent knowledge of the map of London, including which streets are one way, where traffic hold ups are likely to occur, when during the day these are most likely and so on. It has been shown that learning the knowledge results in the expansion of the part of the brain that holds the addresses of our memories – the hippocampus (Maguire *et al*, 1997). The size of the hippocampus in London taxi drivers increases in relation to the depth of their knowledge.

Since learning 'the knowledge' is a clear example of learning that has taken place in adulthood, it suggests that our ability to learn does not decline substantially with age. This was further supported by Boldrini and colleagues who used samples of post-mortem, heathy human brains to determine the number of new neurones created in individuals at different ages (Boldrini *et al*, 2018). They studied the brains of healthy adults from 14 to 79 years with no signs of cognitive impairment and found that the number of new neurons showed little decline with age. On the basis of this evidence, we can conclude that old dogs *can* learn new tricks.

Research has demonstrated that we create more new neurones and synapses when we have rich lives with many new experiences (van Praag *et al*, 2000) and when we exercise aerobically (Hillman *et al*, 2008). However, there is also evidence that there is a reduction in neuroplasticity in individuals who are stressed, depressed and/or anxious (Lucassen *et al*, 2010). This is worth bearing in mind if you are coaching someone with mental health challenges.

Neurostability

If it is not our brains that prevent us from learning, then there might be other reasons that some people find it harder to learn and change. While it is important for learning and memory that the brain continues to be neuroplastic throughout adulthood, having the same degree of neuroplasticity at all points in development would not be ideal. During infancy, there are many things to learn. Once this learning is established, it is preferable that much of it becomes relatively fixed. Imagine that each time you learned the meaning of a new word, it was forgotten again quickly. This would make it quite difficult to learn a language. It is therefore necessary for the brain to retain learning over time, and this requires a balance between neuro*stability* (stability of networks so that information is retained) and neuro*plasticity* (ability to change networks to replace learning that is no longer required) in the adult brain.

Recent research is beginning to determine how the brain accomplishes this balance, and how it changes during development (Bavelier *et al*, 2010). There are two ways in which the brain reduces plasticity:

1. There are two types of connections (or synapses) that link neurones together. *Excitatory synapses* release a neurotransmitter that results in an increase in activity in the next neurones in the chain. By contrast, *inhibitory synapses* release neurotransmitters that decrease the activity in connected neurones. The balance between excitatory and inhibitory connections in neural networks changes across the lifespan (Takesian & Hensch, 2013). Initially, neural networks have more excitatory than inhibitory connections and are therefore neural networks are easily changed. This is because activation is required to increase the strength of connections between neurones. During the course of development, more inhibitory connections are established, which reduces the activity in neighbouring neurones and therefore stabilises networks.

2. Additional structural brakes on plasticity are activated later in the development of the brain. These include epigenetic changes that decrease the number of new synapses that can be created in individual networks thus ensuring network stability.

The result of this is that adult brains retain information that has been learned across the lifespan but at the expense of ease of learning. There is some evidence to suggest that we can reinstate some plasticity for learning in adults by increasing motivation to learn, making learning more fun, adding humour, or creating flow states (Bavelier *et al*, 2010). Exploring where, when, and how they learn best can help a coachee to recreate the conditions they need to reinstate plasticity to create more efficient learning.

Fixed and growth mindset

While neurostability makes learning in adults less efficient than learning in children, we still have the capacity to learn throughout the lifespan. Research into neuroplasticity provides evidence to suggest that any adult with a typical brain has the potential to learn new knowledge and skills if they are prepared to put in sufficient practice. Practice is the first step in creating the necessary neural networks for expertise in any skill. Since all adults can learn with sufficient practice, there must be additional reasons that explain why we sometimes find learning difficult.

When we try something new, we use feedback to determine how good we are at this. This feedback will be derived both from assessment of our performance in relation to our own expectations and through comparisons between our performance and how others perform. This allows us to assess our current ability.

Since assessment of performance in the moment is only a measure of ability at a fixed point in time, it provides no information about potential. It would be more useful to know what we might be capable of achieving with the right belief in ourselves, encouragement, and training. Measuring potential, however, is at least partly dependent on our current beliefs.

Imagine the behaviour of individuals who believe that intelligence, personality, or any ability is fixed and that a current measure of our ability predicts how we will always be (fixed mindset: Dweck, 2006). This group might believe that they are too old to learn, too young to learn, not clever enough to learn etc.

Compare this to people who believe that we do not yet know our own potential but that it is always possible to improve (growth mindset: Dweck, 2006). These people might be looking for the right training, seeking a suitable mentor or role model, or wondering what new strategy they can learn to get better at a particular skill.

It is easy to see how a belief can become a self-fulfilling prophecy. If you believe that ability is fixed, there is no point in seeking out new experiences from which to learn. While this belief will not stop you from becoming highly skilled in an area in which you believe in your own ability, it will stop you from trying to learn new things at which you do not believe you can succeed. Lack of confidence in our ability can negatively impact our willingness to try and therefore the possibility of learning.

If you believe that growth is possible, then there is a reason to try new things, and this very process will help you to sculpt your brain to take better advantage of your new experiences. Practising new skills creates the connections within the neural networks required to get better at this new skill.

It is important to recognise that everyone will have growth mindset in some areas of their lives and fixed mindset in others. Noticing during coaching where a fixed mindset might be stopping someone from trying to learn a new skill is therefore important. By explaining that practice, effort, and perseverance is required to create appropriate neural connections to improve in any area, we can help coachees to commit to trying something new even when they lack confidence in their abilities. Reflecting back after some practice on the change this has created can draw attention to any improvement that has occurred and can increase confidence in the ability to change.

Just like any other ability, with the right strategies and commitment to practise, it is possible to change mindset. Here are some strategies that you might try:

1. Notice when you want to prove your ability in a situation and when any criticism feels harsh. What would change if you just wanted to improve your ability and therefore listened openly to the feedback?

2. What do you do when a task becomes hard? Do you find an excuse to stop? If so, catch yourself and think what you would do if you were really in a growth mindset in which the hardest tasks represent the best opportunity to grow and learn.

3. Notice when you want to be with people who agree with you. What might you learn from people who are more willing to criticise you?

4. Reflect on any events in your past where you feel your ability was judged and found wanting (an exam mark, a parent or teacher's comment on your ability, a job review). What could you learn from this if you were to take a truly growth mindset? And what would you have to believe about yourself to remain in a fixed mindset?

5. Reflect on times when you gave up on learning because it seemed too difficult, or your progress was not as fast as you wanted. What goals were you setting yourself? What would happen if you set more realistic goals? What additional strategies might you put in place?

6. Finally, who do you know that might feel that their behaviour is being (or has been) judged harshly? This is particularly true of people for whom society has negative stereotypes (gender, race, religion, sexuality). How might you help them to achieve a growth mindset? What steps might you take to help them to challenge societal beliefs in their abilities and therefore to help them learn?

GROW model

Coaching is the process of holding a space in which a coachee can systematically explore an area in which they would like to make a change. The most popular model for this process is the GROW model that was developed by Whitmore in the 1980s (Whitmore, 2009) and is still widely used today. It is therefore worth considering what we know about the neuroscience of this model.

Goals

The GROW process starts by defining an overall goal, and a goal that is achievable within the session. Creating goals allows us to consciously process our aspirations making it more likely that we will reach these. While Whitmore (2009) focuses on the end goal (or final objective) and performance goals (the level at which you would have to perform to reach your end goal), more recent literature differentiates between performance goals (a level you that would demonstrate your skill level) and mastery goals (a desire to increase learning or skill acquisition to continuously improve overall competence). These two goal types have been linked to fixed and growth mindset respectively (Dweck & Leggett, 1988).

Individuals who aim for performance goals tend to have a fixed mindset and therefore believe that their ability in this area is fixed. This results in setting performance goals that allow them to demonstrate their ability with the consequent aim of avoiding failure (Spielberger *et al*, 2011). Goals which avoid potential failure are driven by activation of the right dorsolateral prefrontal cortex, an area of the brain which focusses on prevention of harm (Davidson & Irwin, 1999). The potential for failure if the goal is not attained can result in increased stress (Elliot *et al*, 2011). However, it is important for coaches to understand that individuals whose brains work in this way will not necessarily benefit from attempts to persuade them to set different goals. It is sometimes necessary to work with the brain of the coachee. More effective questions for this type of coachee might be:

- What would happen if you fail to take action?
- What is the worst possible outcome for you?
- What do you most not want to happen?

Individuals who aim for mastery goals, on the other hand, have a growth mindset in this area and therefore believe that ability can be improved through persistent effort and the right strategy. They therefore set goals that approach the challenge and help them develop (Spielberger *et al*, 2011). When approach goals are set, the left prefrontal cortex is activated (Davidson & Irwin, 1999). This area of the brain focuses on potential rewards. Failure to improve fast enough or to a high enough level is therefore regarded as the result of either a lack of effort or the need for a new strategy. This demonstrates a growth mindset in which the belief might be that the goal has not been achieved *yet* (Dweck, 2006). Effective questions for this type of coachee might be:

- Who do you know that already does this well and what strategy do they use?
- What is a realistic goal for the time you have available for this challenge?
- How might you create more opportunities to practise this skill?

Reality

The next phase in the GROW model asks coachees to focus on the reality of the current situation. Again, the way in which a coachee frames their goals will influence the way in which they construct their reality. A coachee with a growth mindset who approaches situations in which there is the potential for reward tends to consider ways in which their plan will be successful. They are often optimistic, believe that their plans have a good chance of success (hope) and are willing to take risks (Dardick & Tuckwiller, 2019). Their blind spots are more likely to be failure to notice potential threats or obstacles to their plans.

A coachee who sets goals that avoid failure is more likely to notice the obstacles and threats to their plans. They tend to be more pessimistic, less hopeful and risk averse (Dardick & Tuckwiller, 2019). Their blind spots are more likely to be the potential rewards their plan might bring if it were to succeed, ways in which they have succeeded in plans like this before and resources that they have available to increase the potential success of their plan.

Options

What happens in the brain when we start to think of options? Where do more innovative responses come from?

In order to be creative about finding solutions to challenges we need to use divergent thinking (Beaty *et al*, 2015). This is the ability to generate novel new solutions for problems that do not have a right or wrong answer. It involves fluency, flexibility, and novelty of ideas.

There are three processes involved in divergent thinking. To think divergently, we need to:

1. Make associations across different domains of knowledge and concepts which results in the generation of possibilities. This is known as 'conceptual expansion'. A concept can be thought of as the set of features or parameters that define how objects or events in the world are classified. Thus, in order for an object to be a bird, we know that typically it should have wings, a beak and be able to fly. Conceptual expansion is the ability to create larger concepts. In order for a penguin to be classified as a bird, we need to expand our category to include flightless birds in addition to birds that fly. Coaches can aid the process of conceptual expansion by asking coachees to think of unusual ways to solve a challenge or by putting constraints on how the challenge might be solved.

2. Creativity can be limited by the inability to conceive of an object in a manner different from its customary or habitual use (functional fixedness), therefore we need to be able to inhibit these habitual responses. This requires activation of the dorsolateral prefrontal cortex.

3. We are more likely to become fixed on an idea or a process if we use the same strategy in more than one context. So, if we always use wheels to make it possible to move objects, or always use salt to make our food taste better, then it is more difficult to think about other ways to do the same thing. This creates a bias towards this single strategy making it more difficult to inhibit it. By using more than one strategy for problem solving, we can decrease the likelihood of functional fixedness.

Coaches can aid divergent thinking by asking for several alternative strategies that might be used to solve a challenge. You can then explore different possibilities with your coachee to determine how well each of these provides a solution to the challenge. Testing out possible ideas involves imagining each of the new ideas. The more vivid a coachee's imagination, the easier it will be for them to select the best options from their new ideas.

This research points to an important and learnable skill in encouraging creativity: the process of inhibiting previous learned responses. It suggests that if we want to encourage creativity in others, it might be necessary to teach them ways of capturing and eliminating all the typical learned responses in order to encourage new thinking. As new ideas emerge, it will then be possible to imagine these solutions to decide which options should be pursued.

Will

When options have been created, the next stage is to create an action plan that the coachee is motivated to follow. From the options created, the coachee can choose which they will do and to encourage this, the coach can ask the coachee 'What are you going to do?'. Here there is an assumption that the coachee will do something so remember that as a coach your role is to allow the coachee choice, and this can include choosing to do nothing.

Just as some coachees will set avoid goals while others set approach goals, some coachees will be intrinsically motivated to complete their goals while others are extrinsically motivated.

Intrinsic goals are easy to reach since they usually fulfil psychological needs directly. These include a sense of autonomy, good relationships with others, and competence and personal growth (Deci & Ryan, 2000). Completing intrinsically motivated tasks is associated with increased wellbeing (Sheldon, *et al*, 2004). Intrinsic goals increase wellbeing because:

i. They are chosen by the coachee from a desire to develop and therefore increase the feeling of autonomy and identity.

ii. When others are involved in the goal, they can increase feelings of belonging.

iii. They are often associated with a sense of fun or playfulness.

iv. When these are framed as stretch goals, they provide an opportunity for growth and personal development.

Extrinsic goals are harder to fulfil since they only fulfil psychological needs instrumentally (more money means...). A coachee can believe that they have to complete a particular goal because they need money to live, they will feel guilty if they don't, or because it will make them look good to others (McGregor & Doshi, 2015). As a result, these types of tasks are associated with decreased wellbeing (Sheldon *et al*, 2004). Specifically, extrinsic goals decrease wellbeing because:

1. They result in increased social comparison.
2. As a result of this, they can lead to more competitive and less loving relationships (keeping up with the Joneses, being part of a particular gang).
3. They create contingencies between self-worth and goals (I am only worthy if....).
4. Time and effort are limited resources so that the greater the investment in extrinsic goals the lower the investment in intrinsic goals.

Coaches can help to increase the motivation to try a particular option by focusing on the intrinsic motivation for this. Direct the coachee's thinking to their choice in how to address their challenge (autonomy), the people they might be able to help them with this (relatedness and belonging) and how they might develop personally through completing the challenge (personal growth).

Another concept which is important in increasing the will to complete a goal is the coachee's belief in their own self-efficacy. This is the degree to which the coachee believes that they will be able to cope effectively with the challenge. Self-efficacy has been demonstrated to have three components: capability, opportunity, and motivation (Michie *et al*, 2011). Capability is a measure of our own internal resource that can be brought to the challenge. This might include ways in which we have successfully addressed similar challenges in the past, new knowledge, or skills that we did not have previously, and psychological factors including self-belief and confidence. Coaches can increase capability by focusing on previous successes and recent personal development. Opportunity refers to the physical requirements for success including any training required, resources including technology, space, and time, and also the opportunity to practise any new skills required for the challenge. Failure to put all the necessary physical resources in place can lead to a loss of self-efficacy. To help with this, coaches can explore the physical resource and the potential to practise any skills required. Motivation partly results from knowing that the capability and opportunity for the task are in place. Coaches might also choose to focus on ensuring that chosen options are intrinsically motivating.

Stress and resilience

The stress response

Another common topic in coaching conversations is stress caused by work-related factors, personal life experiences or the combination of both. Having an understanding of what stress is and how it influences function in the brain can provide coaches with tools to help address stress in their coachees.

The first thing to realise is that stress does not always have a negative impact. An influential model of stress suggests that moderate, short-term stress improves cognitive processing in the brain and is therefore a highly adaptive functional response (McEwen, 2013; 2008). According to this model, perceived stress results in increased activity in the amygdala which then causes a cascade of changes in hormonal and neural systems.

First, the increased activity in the amygdala causes increased activity in the hypothalamus, the area of the brain which co-ordinates hormonal responses. This results in the release of corticotrophin releasing factor (CRF). This chemical causes release of adrenocorticotropic hormone (ACTH) from the pituitary gland. Receptors for this hormone are found in the adrenal glands which release adrenaline causing increases in blood pressure and heart rate and diverting blood to the muscles in preparation for action. Receptors for ACTH are also found in the prefrontal cortex (decision-making) and the hippocampus (memory). Activation of these receptors result in improved function and better ability to make decisions quickly and to use experience and expertise appropriately. Low to moderate increases in ACTH have also been shown to protect the brain from anxiety.

Stress is one of many homeostatic mechanisms in the brain. Homeostasis is the process of maintaining a constant level. An example of this is hunger which is used to keep our blood sugar level relatively constant. Similarly, stress is used to improve brain function temporarily but then has to be reset to bring the system back to baseline. In order to achieve this, the effect of ACTH has to be counter-regulated to maintain levels of neurochemicals in the brain and prevent these from being over-produced. This is accomplished through the release of cortisol from the adrenal glands in response to increasing blood levels of ACTH. Cortisol decreases the response in the prefrontal cortex and hippocampus bringing this system back into balance. This balance between responses in the hippocampus and cortex is important in maintaining resilience.

How do we respond to stress?

Research suggests that our response to stress depends on the intensity and frequency of perceived stressful events (McEwen, 2016a). Thus, a short, sharp stressful event for which we have the resources to cope has a positive effect on our brains, increasing the function of our synapses in the hippocampus and readying us neurologically to be at our best.

However, when the level of stress increases in either frequency or intensity to a point where we can no longer cope, then we move into distress. At this point, we lose both synapses and neurones in the hippocampus (memory) and medial prefrontal cortex (cognitive function) but increase the number of synapses in the amygdala (emotional response: McEwen, 2016b). As a result, stress produces a reduction in memory and a decrease in the flexibility and creativity of planning. This can be accompanied by an increase in vigilance and a loss of value in life ultimately leading to anxiety and depression. The cumulative result of this is to decrease our resilience to future stress. If the stress does not go on for too long then these effects are reversible, but if the stress is prolonged, then there can be permanent effects.

The degree to which a particular event activates the amygdala, and therefore the strength of the stress response, will depend on the individual assessment of the degree of threat involved – the allostatic load. The higher the perceived stress (high allostatic load), the harder the body has to work to return to equilibrium (McEwen & Gianaros, 2011). What this suggests is that high levels of acute stress are not functional. When ACTH levels are increased too high and/or for too long, this can result in emotional and cognitive instability through overactivity in the prefrontal cortex and hippocampus.

It is important to notice, however, that in this model, the stress is not actual but perceived. There will be examples of stressors that produce similar responses in most individuals, but many stressors are the result of experiences that we have had during childhood and are therefore individual to us. In these cases, the stress response is not being driven directly by external stimulation but by our interpretation of particular situations. It is therefore possible to decrease or eliminate a stress response by changing the interpretation of the 'stressful' stimulus. Coaches can ask coachees to reflect on the story that they have either created about past events or are creating about future events. This can help determine whether coachees are using all relevant evidence when constructing their story or whether they have focused, for instance, mostly on the negative evidence. Expanding the awareness of the evidence that is available can help a coachee to construct a more helpful narrative.

Individual response to stress

Each individual responds to stress in their own way and how we react to stress can result from negative childhood events that increase reactivity to future stress. A simplified description of the effects of differences in stress reactivity divides the response to stress into three categories (McEwen, 2016a):

Good stress (or Eustress) involves the stress associated with successfully rising to a stretch challenge or taking a risk which is therefore ultimately rewarding. This success increases self-esteem, and the ability to self-regulate (choose the difficult option over the easy one). The consequences of experience with good stress are that there is an increase in the likelihood that an individual will be willing to take on challenges in the future. For stress to be considered good stress, not all challenges need to be met successfully however, since treating failures as an opportunity to grow can maintain self-esteem.

Tolerable stress can be seen when the challenge of a particular situation is greater than we can cope with alone but is still able to be overcome with the help of support networks including family, friends, colleagues etc. This can lead to distress depending on the degree to which the individual feels in control of the situation. The lower the feeling of control, the greater the distress.

Toxic stress is the response to challenges that are felt to be beyond an individual's current resources even with social networks activated. This is found more often in individuals who might have had an adverse early life event, and therefore are more highly reactive to stress. It might also be found in people that have never overcome challenges (either because they failed or because they have never had the opportunity) or in people who have limited or no support network. These conditions are likely to limit the opportunities for developing self-esteem and self-control. As a consequence, individuals experience significant distress.

Stress awareness

While being under stress at some point in our lives is inevitable, our response to this is not. Both our own past experience with stress, and the support we receive from family, friends, colleagues and even our organisation can influence our degree of stress.

One way that coaches can help their coachees is to help them to become aware of their own response to stress. Sometimes we are so busy that we are not aware of how stressed we are. It is only when it stops that we notice. Being able to notice when stress is beginning, therefore, is vital to prevent this. For instance, if you notice that a coachee is aware that they are becoming tolerably stressed, they can activate their support networks to make best use of their personal resources. Or, if they notice that their stress is becoming toxic, they can arrange to discuss this with their line manager in order to take immediate steps to prevent this.

Each individual will have their own early warning signs. Coaches can help their coaches to use their memory of past stressful experiences to begin to notice the early warning signs that might indicate that they are becoming more stressed. Moving from good to tolerable and tolerable to toxic stress, will result in changes to emotional responses, bodily feelings, and behaviour changes. For instance, one sign of moving to tolerable stress might be a tightening of the muscles in the upper back and neck, with accompanying neck or headache. When moving into toxic stress, an individual might eat less healthily, or become less tolerant of interruptions, or people in general.

Ask a coachee to remember a time when they moved from good stress into tolerable stress. What were the early warning signals that they might have used to notice this change? You might ask them to consider changes in their emotional responses, changes in their body including muscle tightness and other physical signs, and changes in their behaviour including how they reacted to others. Encourage your coachee to write down some early signs that they might use to notice this change in future.

When they have completed this, you can ask them to remember a time when they moved from tolerable to toxic stress. Again, reflect on the early warning signs that they could use to notice this change in their level of stress and write down some signs for future reference. You might suggest that they include the ways that their behaviour affects others which will allow them to consider whether there is someone close to them that might be better at noticing the changes in their level of stress than they are.

We have a right not to be placed under too much stress, but with this comes a responsibility to notice our own levels of stress so that we can take appropriate action at the right time. Practising an awareness of our own stress levels is the first step that we can take in meeting this responsibility.

It is apparent that part of our response to stress derives from individual interpretations of events. A person who thinks of challenges as opportunities to grow and who believes that failures are ways in which we can learn is likely to have a different response to a challenging event than a person who treats challenge as threatening and failure as a devastating indication that they are no good as a person. Thus, stress is a response to our interpretation of events rather than to the events themselves.

It should also be clear from these definitions that an individual's response to stress is a function of their individual experience (Wood *et al*, 2010) and therefore that no judgement should attach to this. The environment in which we developed and the experiences to which we have been exposed have a substantial impact on our response to stress, and therefore those of us who do not experience events as toxic have a lot to be thankful for.

When people experience long periods of tolerable stress or short periods of toxic stress, this has a direct effect on their motivation (Maier, *et al*, 2015). As cognitive abilities decrease, self-esteem and self-control also decrease. This might lead to disrupted sleep, increased food and alcohol intake, reliance on legal or illegal drugs – all ways in which we can find relief from stress. However, these solutions do not work well with the brain's own ability to regulate stress and to improve function. Therefore, it is possible to refresh an individual by removing the sources of stress (even if only temporarily) and providing the best conditions for the brain to act in its own defence. Coaches who are dealing with coachees with high levels of stress can encourage the coachee to consider ways in which they might (even temporarily) remove the stress to give their brain time to recover fully.

Resilience

Resilience is a trait that many organisations would like to encourage in their employees. The definition of resilience in this context is:

> *'the ability of an organization to anticipate, prepare for, respond and adapt to incremental change and sudden disruptions in order to survive and prosper'*

BSI https://www.bsigroup.com/en-GB/our-services/Organizational-Resilience/

On the basis of this definition, resilience is clearly important in order for organisations to adapt to a changing landscape. However, this definition is quite different from that used by psychologists to define individual resilience:

> *'the process of adapting well in the face of adversity, trauma, tragedy, threats, or significant sources of stress – such as … serious health problems, or workplace and financial stressors.'*

American Psychological Association https://www.apa.org/topics/resilience

This definition suggests that resilience is an individual response to significant stress or trauma. Using this definition of stress, it might be concluded that organisations want to be able to put their employees under stress but provide them with the tools to bounce back effectively. As previously discussed, toxic stress causes damage to the brain, cardiovascular system and gut and so should be prevented as much as possible. It is therefore important to differentiate between naturally occurring situations that result in stress for which individual resilience is a good adaptive strategy, and imposed stress for which individual resilience should not be expected. Helping coachees to become aware of their sources of stress, and whether these are appropriate or not, can be an important role for a coach.

In order to improve resilience for situations where this is an appropriate response, it would be useful to understand what resilience is and whether it can be developed. One influential model of how resilience can be increased is based on the tripartite model of depression and anxiety (Clark & Watson, 1991). They suggest that there is an increase in negative emotional responses (or affect) in both depression and anxiety. This is thought to result from increased activity in amygdala. Individuals with depression, however, are also more likely to show a decrease in positive emotional responses that are not found in those with anxiety. An example of this might be a failure to correctly anticipate whether future events will be rewarding. This is a result of decreased activation of the dopamine reward system including the nucleus accumbens and ventral tegmental area. By contrast, individuals with anxiety are more likely to show states of hyperarousal that are not found in those with depression. An example of this might be increased attention to any social interaction that might be considered threatening. This is thought to be related to increased activation of the default mode network which is responsible for considering our relationships with others.

Tabibnia (2020) used this to create a model for building resilience which has three components:

1. Increase positive affect by increasing activation of the dopamine reward system. Studies have shown that resilience is related to positivity (Fredrickson *et al*, 2003). People that are more positive about their experiences after the 9/11 attacks were found to be less stressed and more resilient (Fredrickson *et al*, 2003). Compassion, gratitude, optimism, humour and positive memories are also ways in which greater activation of the reward system can be achieved.

2. Decrease negative affect by decreasing the activation of the amygdala. Inoculating against stress by mild exposure to a stressful event is one way that has been shown to reduce the activity in the amygdala (Lyons *et al*, 2010). Other ways to reduce negative affect include reframing events, increasing self-efficacy by learning new skills, and naming the emotion.

3. Decrease hyperarousal by decreasing activation of the default mode network. Research by Zeidan *et al* (2014) has demonstrated that mindfulness meditation can reduce anxiety through reduction of activity in components of the default mode network (eg, anterior cingulate cortex). Increased sense of purpose, nature and a sense of awe have also been associated with reducing in hyperarousal in anxiety.

Our response to stress will depend on a number of additional factors including our genetics, development and experiences in life. For instance, women have been shown to react more emotionally to stressful events (Pilar Matud, 2004). However, men have been shown to become more cognitively impaired than women when stressed (Pilar Matud, 2004). It is important to remember that gender differences are found between populations not individuals – while, on average, women are more emotional but have better cognitive processing when stressed, there will be some women who do not respond emotionally to stress and some men who will show little cognitive impairment when stressed.

Early life events also affect our stress response. People who have suffered childhood trauma, including abuse, are more easily stressed than those who have not (Bremner, 2003). It appears that our response to stress is set in childhood partly as a result of the security of our environment. Children who are securely attached and who grow up in supportive environments are less reactive to stressful events than children who are insecurely attached and grow up in environments in which they have to guard against threat (Bender & Ingram, 2018). The level of stress that creates the same allostatic load is therefore higher for insecurely attached children than for securely attached children. There is hope, however, because the way that people react to stress can be altered in adulthood.

Decision-making

The goal of a coaching session often revolves around a decision that has to be made. Knowing how we make decisions and the systems involved in this can help coaches to improve decision-making in their coachees.

Fast and slow thinking

Fast thinking (System 1) and slow thinking (System 2) were terms developed by Nobel Prize winner Daniel Kahneman to describe the two types of decision-making processes that are available in the brain (Kahneman, 2012). Slow thinking, or system 2, is used to describe conscious decision-making processes which are slow, subject to reasoning or cost-benefit analysis and more deliberative. In comparison, fast thinking, or System 1, decisions are subconscious, holistic and based on pattern matching the current situation to previous situations in order to activate stored reactions or habits. Neither type of processing is ultimately superior; they are both useful in particular situations.

Table 10.1 summarises many of the properties that have been associated with each type of thinking. However, we can demonstrate that decisions made with System 1 will not necessarily meet all of these criteria simultaneously. For instance, we sometimes have to wait until our other-than-conscious mind develops a new solution, perhaps the next day in the shower or when out running, in which case System 1 can be slow. Alternatively, we can sometimes know exactly the right solution for a problem, and why this is the right solution, immediately from past expertise making slow thinking fast. These criteria should therefore be taken as indicative of System 1 and 2 thinking rather than being rigid and immutable.

Table 10.1: Fast and slow thinking

Fast thinking (System 1)	Slow thinking (System 2)
Unconscious	Conscious
Implicit	Explicit
Automatic	Controlled
Low effort	High effort
Rapid	Slow
High capacity	Low capacity
Holistic, perceptual	Analytic, reflective
Associative	Rule based
Context specific	Abstract
Pragmatic	Logical
Parallel	Sequential
Stereotypical	Egalitarian
Independent of intelligence	Linked to intelligence

When deciding what to do in a new situation, System 1 is used to determine whether previously generated behaviours might be used again. To do this, the sensory input from the current situation is compared with stored sensory patterns from past situations (comparing current perception with memory for previous similar situations). If a similar situation has been encountered in the past, the sensory patterns of the current situation will (partially) match a stored pattern, which will activate the behaviour that was previously successful (Hutton & Klein, 1999).

However, in some situations, there might not be a previous experience that matches, or we might choose consciously to think about what we will do. This will require paying attention to our perception of the current situation and the actions that might be appropriate for this. This involves mental simulation of possible actions to allow us to choose which might be most effective (Hutton & Klein, 1999). This requires System 2 thinking.

Coaching decision-making

It can be useful for coaches to become familiar with the preferred decision-making style of their coachee. Some coachees will decide quickly, choosing options that are good enough. These are System 1 thinkers or gut feelers. Other coachees will want to consider all options fully and consciously before making a decision. These are System 2 thinkers or maximisers. Knowing this preference can both help coaches to work with the preferred system and to expand the frame by asking questions that direct attention to the non-preferred decision-making system.

Before describing ways that coaches might help their coachees to expand their decision-making to their less preferred system, it is worth pointing out that the processes involved in conscious (System 2) and unconscious (System 1) decision-making are very similar (Kruglanski & Gigerenzer, 2011). When making a decision, the brain assigns the expected value of a successful outcome for each option; the benefit or value of each option can thereby be calculated (O'Doherty, 2004; Tobler *et al*, 2007). By assigning a value to each option, the options can be compared to determine which provides the greatest benefit. Neurones responsible for this coding have been found in the ventral striatum and prefrontal cortex.

Many decisions, however, come with some risk. In this case, there has to be some neural calculation of the approximate expected likelihood of the outcome of each choice based on past experience (Christopolous *et al*, 2009). It might be that one option has a potentially high value but is also highly risky. In comparison, another option might provide a lower value but a higher likelihood of success. Neurones that code the uncertainty of value calculations have been found in the lateral orbitofrontal cortex. Deciding between a high value risky option and a lower value safe option will depend on the degree of risk that is acceptable for an individual.

Some individuals are risk seeking while others are more risk averse. Individuals that are risk averse show greater activity in the amygdala, anterior insula and anterior cingulate than individuals who are more risk seeking. This suggests that risk-averse people have a high negative emotional response to risk. This might imply that when a person who is risk averse assesses that an option is riskier, this stops the person from choosing this option. However, studies suggest that simply measuring the strength of the neural response to different risks does not differentiate between high and low risk situations (the amygdala is activated for both high and low risk, Christopolous *et al*, 2009). This suggests that people who are risk averse over estimate the potential risk in many situations – the amygdala is activated by any risk, and all risk over a certain value is deemed too much. This is often associated with System 2 decision-making since knowing the basis for any decision provides a sense of control and certainty.

Similarly, individuals who are risk seeking show higher activation in the ventral striatum and cingulate cortex when faced with risky choices and so potentially over estimate the potential reward from these choices. This is often associated with system 1 decision making.

Since individual differences in risk seeking and risk aversion will affect the outcome of any decision-making process, it is useful to be aware of whether individuals are more risk averse or risk seeking, so that the bias in their reaction to risk can be taken into account.

For gut feelers who are more risk seeking, here are three things that coaches might consider:

Risk

- Is your coachee underestimating the risk in the situation?
- To what are they comparing this risk?

The starting point for their risk comparison acts as an anchor. If your coachee wants to take no risk, then a 10% chance they might fail will seem too high. If they are happy with a high risk, then a 50% chance of failure might seem acceptable. To determine whether an anchor is in play, ask your coachee:

- Would you make the same decision if there was nothing to lose?

Emotion

- Has your coachee been involved in decisions leading up to the current situation?
- Is there a reason that they are particularly attached to an outcome at some unconscious level?

For instance, if your coachee recruited people that might be adversely affected by their decision, this might be colouring their judgement. Ask your coachee:

- What emotions are driving this decision? Would you make the same decision if you ignored these?

Detail

- Is your coachee failing to detect a detail in this problem that might make it different from previous situations they have dealt with successfully?

Humans are exceptional at pattern recognition to the extent that we will try to make circumstances fit a pattern even when details don't match. This can have serious consequences if this detail is the one thing that changes the decision that should be made. To add to this, humans have a tendency to look for information that confirms their opinions rather than facts that contradict them. This is known as conformation bias. As a result of this, your coachee might be failing to see a detail that argues against the decision they want to make. Ask your coachee:

- What detail might someone with a different perspective to you notice that you are currently ignoring?

For rationalisers, who can be risk-averse, here are three things that coaches might consider:

Risk

- Is your coachee over-assessing the risk in the situation?

- With what are they comparing this risk?

To determine whether your coachee is being influenced by an inappropriate risk anchor, ask:

- Would you make the same decision if there was nothing to gain or lose?

Emotion

- Is your coachee underestimating the emotional impact their decision might have on themselves or others involved in the outcome of the decision?

Maximisers can hold a belief that decisions should be rational and therefore can attempt to remove any emotional content from their decision-making. This can leave them prone to treating people as cogs rather than with empathy. To help a coachee who does not want to consider the emotional implications of their actions on themselves or others you might ask:

- How might someone more emotional than you view this situation?
- What decision might this lead them to make?

Detail

- Is your coachee considering the problem in too much detail?

Maximisers can be data fiends who want to know as much as possible about every situation in an attempt to create certainty about the decision they are about to make. In leadership, there are often situations in which decisions have to be made with only partial information. This can be more difficult for a maximiser. Coaches can help coachees with this by asking:

- Are some of the details less important and could they be ignored in this instance, in order to make the decision-making process simpler?
- If you had to focus on three factors for this decision, what would they be and what decision would you therefore make?

Cognitive biases or shortcuts

While individuals might have preferences for one or other system when making decisions, it is important to understand that both systems are always working, and therefore that most decisions use System 1 to some extent. Indeed, a little reflection on the average day might indicate that most of our decisions are not conscious and therefore that System 1 thinking has a large part to play in decision-making. This is particularly the case when we are tired or under stress. For this reason, it is worth understanding both how this system works in more detail and the impact it has on decision-making.

System 1 thinking is responsible for the cognitive biases in our decision-making (Kahneman, 2012). The term cognitive bias implies that these types of decision are not fully rational and therefore should not be relied upon. However, there is a major benefit in having quick decision-making processes

(Ariely, 2011; Gigerenzer, 2008). If we were to try to make conscious decisions about every detail of our lives, our brains would very soon become overwhelmed. System 2 does not have the capacity to make every decision.

Another, more positive, way of explaining cognitive biases is that they are the result of the evolution of useful decision-making shortcuts that work most of the time and provide us with quick decisions based on much more information than our conscious system can take on board (Gigerenzer, 2008). System 1 learns quickly through experience and notices when the same outcome is rewarded on more than one occasion. While our cognitive shortcuts, therefore, can sometimes let us down, they are also the source of expertise both in our professional lives and in general daily living.

There are four main situations in which we are more likely to use cognitive biases or short cuts:

1. When memory is limited and we have too much to remember, we reduce the load on our memories by extracting the main points or gist rather than trying to remember the detail. Here are some ways that we do this:

   We act on strong, immediate emotions since these are likely to be important.

An example of this is the *current moment bias*, or 'a bird in the hand is worth two in the bush'. We do not weigh reward in the future as highly as reward now! Because we are better able to feel the emotional response to immediate reward but find it more difficult to imagine how we will feel in the future, we discount our future reward in comparison to immediate reward. This can be a really useful bias to understand as a coach who is helping coachees to set goals which require change in their behaviour. The reward in the future should be perceived to be greater than the current reward in order for a coachee to be motivated to put effort in to changing their behaviour. We will discuss this in more detail when we explore temporal discounting.

   We reconstruct our memory each time with different details depending on our goals.

An example of this is the false memory effect. Professor Elizabeth Loftus has spent her career demonstrating how we are prone to creating false memories (Loftus, 2003). Our memory does not operate like a video camera recording all the facts but instead remembers the typical things that happen in a particular context, and then differentiates our memories of, for instance, a particular day at work by adding relevant detail (Hassibis & Maguire, 2009).

Our memory is a combination of real and typical so is both correct and partly wrong. We are able therefore to create false memories by adding details that are likely but that didn't actually happen. For instance, we might remember that there was a discussion at a meeting and that someone came up with a brilliant idea. We might wrongly remember the person that came up with the idea as the one who is usually the most innovative because there were too many people at the meeting for us to be sure of who the actual person was.

2. When we have too much information to process, we simplify the decision by focussing on the most salient information and ignoring information that is more difficult to notice. For instance:

We notice evidence that confirms our previous beliefs (and ignore evidence that does not).

An example of this is the *confirmation bias*. Our brains are biased to seek out information that confirms our sense of self – so we are more likely to attend to opinions that agree with ours than those with which we disagree. We find *cognitive dissonance* (when there is a conflict between our understanding and information in the world) uncomfortable, and the confirmation bias reduces the likelihood of cognitive dissonance.

The unfortunate aspect of this bias is that it prevents us from challenging our own viewpoint even when there is plentiful evidence against it since we ignore information that does not confirm our bias. So, while it can help us to feel good about ourselves, it can also lead to poor decisions and failure to take others' perspectives into account.

We notice other people's flaws but not our own.

An example of this is the *fundamental attribution error*. We are social animals since we are able to accomplish more, and are safer, in groups. We have therefore evolved mechanisms that help us to work with others. This includes an ability to theorise about what other people are thinking and therefore how they might choose to behave. This is important since we need to be able to choose to work with people who are fair and choose not to work with those that only look after their own interests.

In order to protect ourselves, it is better to be biased towards choosing carefully to trust, and therefore it is important to pay attention to behaviours that indicate that trust has been breached. If we focus only on outcomes, we might wrongly believe that someone has breached our trust even if the act was unintended. This is a fundamental error in our attribution of the event – we have failed to account for the intention of the action. To prevent this, it is important to consider what other explanations there are for the same outcome without it having been consciously planned to affect us.

3. When we have too little information to make meaning, we need to use the information that we do have to make decisions. We do this by adding information from the environment and our memory which is not always directly relevant to the situation. For instance:

We form patterns from sparse data.

The *turkey fallacy* is a belief that past events have an influence on future outcomes. Each day of the turkey's life is an individual event that is not dependent in any way on previous days – there is no memory of what has gone before. And so, each day might be the day that the turkey is needed as the main dish for a celebratory meal. This belief has consequences in organisations because you might notice trends in economic performance and assume that these are going to continue. This might prevent you from managing risk appropriately.

We use stereotypes and generalisations.

An example of this is the *in-group bias*. This bias is activated when we are asked to decide, for instance, who should be trusted, allocation of resource, or who we want to work with. Since in each case there is a decision to be made about who we are best able to trust, we will tend to choose the people with whom we are most familiar. This results in an unconscious belief that our own social group are more trustworthy, more deserving or smarter – without any good evidence. As a result, we treat people from our own group better than we treat those from other, equivalent groups.

We use our own thinking as a proxy for what others are thinking.

An example of this is the *projection bias*. This bias is another way that we can reduce the need to use slow thinking. Rather than working out what every person we meet might think, feel, prefer – we make the assumption that people are like us and therefore that their likes and dislikes, their emotions and their decisions will be much like our own. In order to reduce this bias, we have to consciously honour the uniqueness of the individual over our own opinions thus substantially reducing the projection bias.

4. When we need to act fast, we do not have time to look at all the evidence available and so we require mechanisms that will allow us to decide on incomplete information. In such situations:

We use group decisions to avoid mistakes and to preserve autonomy and status.

An example of this is the *bandwagon effect*. This refers to the idea that, as social animals, we have a tendency to agree with the crowd. It is very easy to fall in to 'groupthink' since this enables us to avoid being held accountable for mistakes. When mistakes happen, and we are thought to be responsible for these, we can lose credibility and might be more carefully monitored in future in order to prevent further mistakes. Agreeing with the crowd is therefore a means to maintain our status and autonomy since it will not be our fault if things go wrong. Having the courage to speak up when you disagree with the majority and creating cultures in which everyone has a voice and is heard fairly can help prevent the main downfalls of groupthink.

We choose to complete things that we have invested energy and time in whether they are important or not.

An example of this is the *sunk-cost fallacy*. This occurs when we continue a behaviour or invest more time or resource in an endeavour on the basis of the amount of previously invested resource (time, energy or money). We do not want to feel that we have spent resource without gaining some return from this (loss aversion) and therefore continue to commit resource even when we would be better to cut our losses. In coaching, this can be seen when a coachee wants to continue to put time and effort into completing a goal, even when it is clear that this effort is no longer effective.

There are two particular cognitive biases that are worth exploring in more detail because of the impact that these can have on decision-making process. These are temporal discounting and the Dunning-Kruger effect which are described in more detail below.

Temporal discounting

Temporal discounting is another way in which our decision-making is not rational. This describes the fact that the value of objects decreases over time. Research has clearly demonstrated that rewards in the present are valued more than those in the future – or a bird in the hand is worth two in the bush.

To take a concrete example, if you were asked if you would prefer £10 now or next week, you would be slightly mad to take £10 in the future since you would have no idea whether you would be around to accept the money.

Which would you choose, however, if you were offered £10 now versus £12 next week? You still might not think it worth waiting. What if you are offered £10 in four weeks' time versus £12 in 5 weeks' time or even £10 in 52 weeks' time versus £12 in 53 weeks' time. As we look further into the future, waiting one week for the larger sum of money seems less difficult. This is known as *temporal discounting* – the value of time seems to shrink in the future and therefore a slightly larger reward seems worth the wait. This has been shown to involve the reward system (ventral striatum) and the prefrontal cortex (inhibition: Christakou *et al*, 2011; 2013). People who are reward-focused find it harder to inhibit the desire for immediate reward in order to wait for a future reward.

Another example of this is when we believe in the morning that we will use our evening to go to the gym, complete a work-based project, or learn a new skill. When evening comes, we find ourselves sitting down to, for instance, watch junk on TV when we had believed that we could so easily resist this to make progress on our project. In this case, the reward of the immediate option to relax in front of the television was easy to resist when it was distant in time but is much harder to resist when it can be accessed immediately. We discounted the reward from television when we thought about it from a distance in time.

Temporal discounting can help to explain some typical human behaviours including, for instance, procrastination. When we procrastinate, we choose the immediate reward of not doing the work for our current self and leave the more difficult task of completing the work to our future self. Similarly, it explains impulsive behaviour. Imagine that you have arranged with your line manager that you will complete a project by the end of the week. Thursday comes and the project is not complete, but you are given the opportunity to work on a really important bid for new work. The new project is exciting and novel and, if it comes off, there is a real chance you might get promoted. What do you do? Do you complete the work that you promised you would have finished, or do you work on the new project? The more impulsive you are, the more you will be attracted by the new project since there is immediate reward in this.

There are individual differences in temporal discounting (Christakou *et al*, 2011; 2013). For a person who is able to delay gratification, there is only a gradual decrease in the value of time into the future such that immediate rewards are not valued significantly more than rewards in the future. By contrast, someone who finds delaying gratification difficult, or is impulsive, values the immediate reward much more highly than the future reward and so finds it much harder to resist this in return for a reward in the future. For this person, there is a steep decrease in the value of time in the future. This makes it harder to resist a large immediate reward with a discounted future reward.

When coaching a coachee with a steep temporal discounting curve, coaches can focus on making the future reward as large as possible so that it is more likely to be preferred to the current reward. This can be achieved by having your coachee think of all the potential benefits of a proposed action and then find a means to make these easy to remember (a photograph, a strong memory, an action). The coachee can then be encouraged to use this memory aid if they find their willpower is slipping.

The Dunning-Kruger effect

This is a cognitive bias through which people with low ability overestimate their confidence in their own ability (Dunning, 2011). This effect is universal – we are all ignorant, and we are all ignorant of our own ignorance, in at least some areas of our lives. This can be described as a relationship between competence and confidence. Sometimes, the least competent people can appear the most confident.

The Dunning-Kruger effect was demonstrated by testing people in a particular skill and then asking them how confident they were about achieving good results on this test (Dunning, 2011). People who scored lowest on the test were unjustifiably more confident of their ability than those scored in the middle range. People who scored high on the test were justifiably confident in their ability.

Why are we overconfident in areas of low competence? There are several possible reasons:

- *Unknown unknowns*: Consider a complex project to which you are contributing. There are three categories of information that can be differentiated: First, there is the information that is available and that you know you have (the known knowns); next, there is information that is not available, and you know that you do not have (then known unknowns); and finally, there are pieces of information that are not available and that you do not know that you don't have (the unknown unknowns). People who are unskilled in a particular area are likely to underestimate the unknown unknowns and therefore underestimate the size of the problem. As competence grows, the understanding of the extent of the unknown unknowns will increase causing confidence to first fall and then increase as expertise grows.

- When we do not know much about a particular area, we are likely to reflect on our competence in a similar area and over-generalise this to solve the problem – even when this competence is not relevant. For instance, people are more confident that they know how everyday items like toilets or mirrors work but when they are asked to explain this, they often fail. We believe that we have this expertise because of our familiarity with the items rather than our understanding of how they work.

- People will claim to know about areas that they do not in order to maintain status. When asked if you have read a popular book, you might falsely agree that you have in order that your intellectual abilities are not challenged. We maintain status by claiming more knowledge than we actually have.

It is interesting to reflect on the meaning of uncertainty or under-confidence in a particular area. This is not a show of weakness, but instead demonstrates a realistic understanding of our own competence in an area where we have some skill but are not yet expert. When someone is willing to admit that they don't know how to solve a problem, this suggests that they have a good understanding of their own ability. They are potentially more reliable than someone who is confident that they have the answer. When coaching someone who has high confidence in an area, it is worth checking whether this is the result of expertise, or whether this is false confidence resulting from lack of knowledge in the area. It is then possible to help a coachee to understand that their confidence is understandable but unwarranted. It is also useful for coaches to understand that lack of confidence in an area might be the result of increasing awareness of how much there is to learn and therefore indicates improving ability. This might be useful to reflect back to a coachee who is doubting their own competence.

Coaching cognitive biases

Imagine you are coaching someone who is dealing with a sudden global outbreak of a highly contagious virus. They *need to act fast* to take the decisions that will both keep their employees safe and protect the organisation against economic catastrophe. There is information coming in from a variety of sources including international and national medical institutes, scientists, economists, government, and the extended leadership of their own organisation, which makes processing and integrating this information very difficult – they have *too much information*. Not only that, but some of the information about how the virus is transmitted is very sparse so that they do no*t have enough information to make clear sense of this – thus, they have too little information.* Finally, they are trying to remember to consider the needs of employees as a whole, particular employees that might be more adversely affected, employees with particular skills that might be useful, the direction they have received from leadership, instructions from government and all of the useful experience they might have from other situations that they can bring to this – this is just *too much to remember* all at once.

As a result, your coachee will have to simplify information for some aspects of the decision while making meaning from sparse information for other aspects. All this needs to happen while working fast at the limits of their memory. The natural response of the brain in this situation will be to invoke cognitive short cuts (System 1 thinking) since their processing capacity will otherwise be overloaded. Coaching can help individuals to become more aware of the short-cuts they are taking and whether these are appropriate. Understanding some of the more common cognitive biases can help coaches to be more aware of when these might be impacting their coachee's decisions. It is then possible to bring this to the attention of the coachee so that they are able to decide whether their decision-making strategy is appropriate.

Ego depletion

Coaching requires the ability to help coachees make decisions, small and large, easy and hard, trivial and important. It is therefore useful to know under what circumstances we make our best decisions.

Imagine that you are working with a coachee who has had a busy day at the office. It is nearing the end of the financial year and they have had to make a million small decisions about how to spend remaining resources. As they leave a meeting, they are immediately faced by an employee who wants them to attend to another set of decisions about hiring and firing for the year; and then they have to decide whether to exercise or not. One of the coaching objectives for this coachee has been to increase the time they spend exercising. But it is a strong person that would not begin to feel that enough is enough and that, in these circumstances, exercise can wait for another day!

This situation describes a case of ego depletion. Research has suggested that decision-making capacity is like a battery which is successively drained a little by each decision taken that requires some self-restraint. Eventually, over the course of a day, the battery will flatten, and the ability to make difficult decisions (like whether or not to go the gym) will be depleted. This is referred to as ego depletion because it is the decision-making part of yourself (or your ego – in the Greek sense not in the Freudian sense) that is being depleted (Baumeister & Vohs, 2016).

It is important to note that different people will have different sizes of decision-making battery – ranging from something like a watch battery, through the battery for a modern laptop, to a car battery. However, the battery size can be increased through practice. It is also possible to top up the battery using a number of different tips and tricks including:

1. Sleep – even short naps work.
2. Since the decision-making battery is depleted by lack of glucose, add energy through food.
3. Feeling more energetic will increase battery life.
4. Feeling motivated and believing that there is no limit to capacity for will power increases battery life.
5. Being given great feedback (constructive or positive) will increase battery life.

While this is one important view of self-control, it is not the only view. An alternative to this is that self-control is a result of balancing the desire for external rewards that come from labour and internal rewards that come from doing the things we want to do. In other words, we struggle to motivate ourselves when tasks require us to switch from 'I want-to', to 'I have-to' goals (Inzlicht *et al*, 2014).

In this model, decreases in will power arise because we require greater motivation to sustain our attention when we have to work on tasks that we find less rewarding (have-to tasks) than when we are doing tasks that we find rewarding (want-to tasks). The sustained mental effort of staying on tasks that we do not enjoy creates an increasing desire to do something less taxing and more rewarding. The feelings of fatigue after sustained work may therefore serve the purpose of preventing fixation on current tasks and switching our behaviour to tasks that might ultimately be more rewarding. Again, there will be individual differences in the length of time that an individual is able to maintain attention on a task in which they find little reward. Coaches can help to build greater will power by encouraging their coachees to swap tasks before their will power fades. A little break to do something more rewarding can increase the total time paying attention to a less rewarding task.

Followership and leadership

There is a vast quantity of literature introducing different leadership styles and considering which are most effective in terms of organisational needs. One important aspect of leadership is the ability to lead so that others are willing to follow. It is therefore important to consider the effect of different leadership styles on the activity in the brains of followers in order to determine how best to create positive motivational states. In addition, different leadership styles are likely to activate different neural networks. Knowing which network is required for different types of task can help leaders to learn to activate the appropriate network for different leadership situations.

The follower's brain

Recent work considering different leadership styles has drawn a distinction between resonant and dissonant leaders (Boyatzis, 2012). Resonant leaders have been described as having a socially shared vision that is communicated across the organisation. They are empathetic and interested in the employee's response to a situation rather than projecting their own response onto the employee. Resonant leaders have high quality and positive interactions with employees, even when these are fleeting. This sort of interaction is thought to activate positive emotional states, leading to a reduction in employee stress responses. This is an example of emotional contagion in which the emotional response of a leader, for instance, can infect the emotional response of their team. Positive emotional contagion can increase team morale.

By contrast, dissonant leaders are described as having a more personalised vision, designed more to meet the goals of the leader than those of the team. They are more likely to disagree with their employees and to impose decisions on groups. Interactions with dissonant leaders are thought to be more likely to be discordant as a result of this, and therefore invoke negative emotional states and sympathetic nervous system activation in their employees. Activation of the sympathetic nervous system can result in unhealthy increases in the stress response. This can result in a negative emotional contagion leading to reduced motivation, and therefore decreased productivity in the workforce. It should be noted that research has demonstrated that employees remember hassles with their leader more than uplifts and so negative emotions appear to be more contagious than positive emotions (Boyatzis *et al*, 2012).

The leader's brain

Being a great leader involves a multitude of different skills and abilities. A number of leadership styles that combine these skills in different combinations have been identified. For instance, as early as the 1950s, a distinction was drawn between task-oriented leaders and socio-emotional leaders (Bales, 1950). This division has been verified behaviourally in subsequent studies. It also is a useful model with which to consider the neural networks that are activated in the brain for different leadership tasks.

One of the important functions of the brain is to scan the environment for opportunities for reward, potential threats, and uncompleted goals. Whenever rewards, threats or uncompleted goals are detected, there is the potential to choose to act on this and this is described as task-positive (a task is present) or task-oriented behaviour. When leaders spend much of their time completing tasks, this can be described as task-oriented leadership.

The brain areas that are involved in task-oriented leadership are activated during focused attention, language, logical reasoning, mathematical reasoning, and causal reasoning. These abilities allow leaders to direct their attention to specific goals, make decisions often based on their past experience and expertise, and act on their goals. The network of brain areas that are required to be active for these abilities is known as the cognitive control network (Menon, 2011).

When no tasks are detected in the environment, a task-negative (no task is present) situation, different areas of the brain are activated. This neural network is less focussed, is more able to consider future possibilities and is more creative than the cognitive control network. It is the network that is active during socio-emotional leadership.

Specifically, socio-emotional leadership activates areas of the brain involved in emotional self-awareness, social cognition and ethical decision-making. This type of leadership is linked to consideration of self in relation to others or emotional intelligence but also creativity and insightful problem solving. This involves a network of brain areas that are collectively referred to as the default mode network (Menon, 2011).

Interestingly, activation of the network of brain areas involved in task-oriented leadership causes suppression in the socio-emotional networks, and vice versa (Jack *et al*, 2013). Thus, leaders can only access one or other mode of thinking at any point in time. Additionally, some people will have a preference for one mode of activation and will therefore suppress the other network most of the time. Since the brain operates on strengthening the connections that we use and weakening those that we don't use, this suggests that some leaders will have become more adept at one type of leadership at the expense of the other.

But that does not have to be the case. We know that our brains are able to change as adults. Evidence for neuroplasticity demonstrates that, if we are motivated to change, our brains will change in response to new experiences. We can therefore explore ways in which we can become more adept at choosing when to use different systems in our brain by creating experiences that allow us to practise both types of leadership. Practising the type of leadership that a leader is less good at can help to build stronger connections in their less familiar network. Coaches can help with this by asking questions that will direct their coachee to the areas of leadership that are currently less often considered. For instance, to increase activation in the task-oriented domain, a coach might ask questions like:

- What is your ultimate goal?
- What resources do you need to accomplish this?
- When have you succeeded in a challenge like this before?
- What is the first step, and the second step?
- What is your Plan B if Plan A does not succeed?

In contrast, to activate the socio-emotional domain of leadership, a coach might ask questions like:

- What is the impact of your current plans on your team or employees?
- What can you do to help colleagues who might struggle with this?
- Who might be best placed to help you to implement your plans?
- How might you approach colleagues who think differently to you?

One other important implication of the networks that are activated during leadership is that, while the task-oriented network and the socio-emotional network do not work together at the same time, research suggests that, given enough time and space to think, the brain will naturally cycle between activation of each of these networks, passing information from one to the other. Therefore, any leadership task that requires both decision-making and consideration of others (for instance, strategy) is best conducted with sufficient time and space to allow full activation of both networks.

Recent research suggests that these three networks function together when we are being creative (Beaty *et al*, 2015). The default mode network is thought to generate new ideas. The salience network identifies the new ideas which are generated within the default mode network and sends these to the cognitive control network for evaluation.

One way to maximise this process is to spend some time outlining the aims and objectives of a particular strategy using the task-oriented network. Creating novel solutions is more likely to happen when leaders are not focused on the challenge and therefore the default mode network becomes active. Making time to spend away from tasks and not thinking about the challenge is required in order for a more creative solution to emerge. Task free time is therefore important for leadership, especially when developing strategy, since this allows more creative solutions to emerge.

Conclusion

In this chapter, we have explored a number of ways in which knowing more about the way the brain works can help coaches to better understand their coachees. This included:

- increasing our belief in the potential for change through a better understanding of neuroplasticity
- noticing different goal-setting styles and their impact on responses to the GROW model
- understanding the stress response and considering ways that we can take more responsibility for our own levels of stress
- tools for increasing the level of resilience in our coachees
- consideration of the different decision-making processes and individual differences in decision-making styles. Use of this to consider how coaches might help their coachees to improve their decision-making
- exploring cognitive biases, what they are and when we use them to increase the chances of spotting cognitive biases in decision-making so that coachees have more choice in whether they use the results of this unconscious processing
- understanding what might cause ego depletion and therefore how coaches can help coachees to make better decisions
- understanding the neuroscience of followership and leadership in order to help leaders to consciously choose the neural networks that are activated for different leadership tasks.

These provide a number of ways in which understanding the brain can provide coaches with more insight into the processing of their coachees. The list is far from comprehensive and further information on the neuroscientific basis of coaching can be found elsewhere (eg, Bossons *et al*, 2016; Riddell, 2019, 2021).

Five questions for further reflection

1. **Why is neuroscience relevant to coaching?**

While there is no need to understand what changes in the brain during coaching, this understanding can be helpful in refining the way that coaching techniques are designed and used so that they work best with the ways that our brains work. The working of the brain is not always intuitive and sometimes a better understanding of the processing that is occurring can help to create more effective techniques.

2. **Do I have to have a neuroscience qualification to use neuroscience in my coaching?**

No. It is sufficient to understand the basics of how the brain is operating and most often there is no need to share this knowledge with your coachee. Just being able to say that a particular behaviour is to be expected because of the way the brain works is often sufficient to increase the motivation to try a particular technique.

3. **When is neuroscience most useful in coaching?**

Coachees who have an engineering or science background are often reassured that there is neuroscientific evidence supporting the way that their brain is working for a particular coaching technique.

4. **What one piece of neuroscience knowledge is most important for coaching?**

Understanding the capacity of the human brain for change is fundamental to coaching. Without this understanding, it is possible to underestimate our amazing capacity for change and therefore to limit the potential for change in our coachees.

5. **What is the future of neuroscience in coaching?**

While we currently understand why some techniques work, we have yet to demonstrate that particular techniques result in particular changes in the brain. As techniques for measuring brain activity in the workplace emerge, it will become possible to measure real-time brain changes and to evidence the impact of particular coaching techniques.

Suggested reading

Bossons, P., Riddell, P. & Sartain, D. (2015) Chapter 3: Introduction to Neuroscience. In: *The Neuroscience of Leadership Coaching*. London: Bloomsbury Press, Pp 21-41.

Brown, P. & Brown, V. (2012) *Neuroscience for Coaching: Understanding the basics*. Oxford: Oxford University Press.

Dweck, C. (2006) *Mindset: The New Psychology of Success*. New York: Random House.

Kahneman, D. (2012) *Thinking: Fast and Slow*. London: Penguin Books

Riddell, P.M. (2021) Chapter 23: Neuroscience coaching. In: J. Passsmore (Ed) *The Coaches' Handbook: The complete practitioner guide for professional coaches*. London: Routledge.

References

Ariely, D. (2011) *The Upside of Irrationality: The unexpected benefits of defying logic at work and at home*. Harper Collins: NY

Bales, R.F. (1950) A set of categories for the analysis of small group interaction. *American Sociological Review*, **15**, 257-263.

Baumeister, R. & Vohs, D. (2016) Strength model of self-regulation as limited resource: assessment, controversies, update. *Advances in Experimental Social Psychology*, **54**, 67-127.

Bavelier, D., Levi, D., Li, R., Yang, D. & Hensch, T. (2010) Removing the brakes on adult brain plasticity. *Journal of Neuroscience*, **10**, 14964-71

Beaty, R., Benedek, M., Kaufman, S. & Silvia, P. (2015) Default and executive network coupling supports creative idea production. *Scientific Reports*, **5**, 10964.

Bender, A. & Ingram, R. (2018) Connecting attachment style to resilience: contributions of self-care and self-efficacy. *Personality and Individual Differences*, **130**, 18-20.

Boldrini, M., Fulmore, C., Tartt, A., Simeon, L., Pavlova, I., Poposka, V., Rosoklija, G.B., Stankov, A., Arango, V., Deork, A.J., Hen, R. & Mann, J.J. (2018) Human hippocampal neurogenesis persists throughout aging. *Cell Stem Cell*, **22**, 589-599.

Bossons, P., Riddell, P. & Sartain, D. (2015) Chapter 3: Introduction to Neuroscience. In: *The Neuroscience of Leadership Coaching*. London: Bloomsbury Press, Pp21-41.

Boyatzis, R. (2012) Neuroscience and the link between inspirational leadership and resonant relationships. *Ivey Business Journal*, https://iveybusinessjournal.com/publication/neuroscience-and-the-link-between-inspirational-leadership-and-resonant-relationships-2/

Boyatzis, R.E., Rochford, K. & Jack, A.I. (2014) Antagonistic neural networks underlying differentiated leadership roles. *Frontiers in Human Neuroscience*, **8**, 114.

Boyatzis, R.E., Passarelli, A., Koenig, K., Lowe, M., Mathew, B., Stoller, J. & Phillips, M. (2012) Examination of the neural substrates activated in memories of experiences with resonant and dissonant leaders. *The Leadership Quarterly*, **23** (2), 259-72.

Bremner, J.D. (2003) Long-term effects of childhood abuse on brain and neurobiology. *Child and Adolescent Psychiatric Clinics*, **12** (2) 271-292.

Carey, N. (2012) *The Epigenetics Revolution: How modern biology is rewriting our understanding of genetics, disease and inheritance*. St Ives: Icon Books.

Christakou, A., Brammer, M. & Rubia, K. (2011) Maturation of limbic corticostriatal activation and connectivity associated with developmental changes in temporal discounting. *NeuroImage*, **54**, 1344-1354.

Christakou, A., Gershman, S., Niv, Y., Simmons, A., Brammer, M. & Rubia, K. (2013) Neural and psychological maturation of decision-making in adolescence and young adulthood. *Journal of Cognitive Neuroscience*, **25** (11) 1807-1823.

Christopoulos, G.I., Tobler, P.N., Bossaerts, P., Dolan, R.J. & Schultz, W. (2009) Neural correlates of value, risk, and risk aversion contributing to decision-making under risk. *Journal of Neuroscience*, **7**, 12574-12583.

Clark, L.A. & Watson, D. (1991) Tripartite model of anxiety and depression: psychometric evidence and taxonomic implications. *Journal of Abnormal Psychology*, **100**, 316–336.

Dardick, W. & Tuckwiller, E. (2019) Optimism shapes mindset: understanding the association of optimism and pessimism. *Journal of Interdisciplinary Studies in Education*, **8** (2) 21–56.

Davidson, R.J. & Irwin, W. (1999) The functional neuroanatomy of emotion and affective style. *Trends in Cognitive Science*, **3**, 11–21.

Deci, E.L. & Ryan, R.M. (2000) The 'what' and 'why' of goal pursuits: Human needs and the self-determination of behaviour. *Psychological Inquiry*, **11**, 227–268.

Dunning, D. (2011) The Dunning-Kruger effect: on being ignorant of one's own ignorance. In *Advances in Experimental Social Psychology*, **44**, 247–296.

Dweck, C. (2006) *Mindset: The New Psychology of Success*. New York: Random House.

Dweck, C. & Leggett, E.L. (1988) A social-cognitive approach to motivation and personality. *Psychological Review*, **95**, 256–273.

Elliot, A., Thrash, T. & Murayama, K. (2011) A longitudinal analysis of self-regulation and wellbeing: avoidance personal goals, avoidance coping, stress generation, and subjective wellbeing. *Journal of Personality*, **79** (3) 643–674.

Fredrickson, B., Tugade, M., Waugh, C. & Larkin, G. (2003) What good are positive emotions in crises? A prospective study of resilience and emotions following terrorist attacks on the United States on September 11th, 2001. *Personality Processes and Individual Differences*, **84** (2) 365–376.

Frith, C.D. & Frith, U. (2012) Mechanisms of social cognition. *Annual Reviews of Psychology*, **63**, 287–313.

Fuchs, E. (2000) In vivo neurogenesis in the adult brain: regulation and functional implications. *European Journal of Neuroscience*, **12**, 2211–2214.

Gigerenzer, G. (2007) *Gut Feelings: Short cuts to better decision-making*. London: Penguin Books.

Hassabis, D. & Macguire, E.A. (2009) The construction system of the brain. *Philosophical Transactions of the Royal Society of London B Biological Sciences*, **364**, 1263–1271.

Hillman, C.H., Erickson, K.I. & Kramer, A.F. (2008) Be smart, exercise your heart: exercise effects on brain and cognition. *Nature Review: Neuroscience*, **9**, 58–65.

Hutton, R. J. B. & Klein, G. (1999) Expert decision making. *Systems Engineering*, **2** (1) 32–45.

Ilies, R., Arvey, R. & Bouchard, T. (2006) Darwinism, behavioral genetics, and organizational behavior: a review and agenda for future research. *Journal of Organizational Behavior*, **27**, 121–141.

Inzlicht, M., Schmeichel, B. & Macrae, C.N. (2014) Why self-control seems (but may not be) limited. *Trends in Cognitive Sciences*, **18** (3) 127–133.

Jack, A.I., Dawson, A., Begany, K., Leckie, R.L., Barry, K., Ciccia, A. & Snyder, A.Z. (2013) fMRI reveals reciprocal inhibition between social and physical cognitive domains. *NeuroImage*, **66** (Supp. C), 385–40.

Kahneman, D. (2012) *Thinking: Fast and Slow*. London: Penguin Books

Kempermann, G. & Gage, F. (1999) Experience-dependent regulation of adult hippocampal neurogenesis: Effects of long-term stimulation and stimulus withdrawal. *Hippocampus*, **9**, 321–332.

Keverne, E., Pfaff, D. & Tabansky, I. (2015) Epigenetic changes in the developing brain: effects on behaviour. *Proceedings of the National Academy of Sciences*, **112**, 6789–6795.

Kruglanski, A. & Gigerenzer, G. (2011) Intuitive and deliberate judgements are based on common principles. *Psychological Review*, **118**, 97–109.

Loftus, E. (2003). Make-believe memories. *American Psychologist*, **58** (11) 867–73.

Lucassen, P.J., Meerlo, P., Naylor, A. S., van Dam, A.M., Dayer, A. G., Fuchs, E., Oomen, C.A., & Czeh, B. (2009) Regulation of adult neurogenesis by stress, sleep disruption, exercise and inflammation: Implications for depression and antidepressant action. *European Journal of Neuropsychopharmacology*, **20**, 1–17.

Lyons, D.M., Parker, K.J. & Schatzberg, A.F. (2010) Animal models of early life stress: implications for understanding resilience. *Developmental Psychobiology*, **52**, 616–624.

Maguire, E., Frackkowiak, R. & Frith, C. (1997) Recalling routes around London: activation of the right hippocampus in taxi drivers. *Journal of Neuroscience*, **17**, 103–110.

Maier, S., Makwana, A. & Hare, T. (2015) Acute stress impairs self-control in goal directed choice by altering multiple functional connections within the brain's decision-making circuits. *Neuron*, **87**, 621–631.

McEwen, B. (2016a) Stress effects on neuronal structure: hippocampus, amygdala, and prefrontal cortex. *Neuropsychopharmacology Reviews*, **41**, 2–23.

McEwen, B. (2016b) In pursuit of resilience: stress, epigenetics, and brain plasticity. *Annals of the New York Academy of Sciences*, **1373**, 56–64.

McEwen, B.S. (2008) Central effects of stress hormones in health and disease: understanding the protective and damaging effects of stress and stress mediators. *European Journal of Pharmacology*, **583**, 174–185.

McEwen, B.S. (2013) Brain on stress: How the social environment gets under the skin. *Proceedings of the National Academies of Science*, **109**, 17180–17185.

McEwen, B.S. & Gianaros, P.J. (2011) Stress- and allostasis-induced brain plasticity. *Annual Reviews of Medicine*, **62**, 4431–445.

McGregor, L. & Doshi, N. (2015) How company culture shapes employee motivation. *Harvard Business Review, November 25th, 2015*. Available online at: https://hbr.org/2015/11/how-company-culture-shapes-employee-motivation. Accessed 17 July 2021.

Menon, V. (2011) Large-scale brain networks and psychopathology: a unifying triple network model. *Trends in Cognitive Sciences*, **15**, 483–506.

Michie, S., van Stralen, M. & West, R. (2011) The behaviour change wheel: a new method for characterising and designing behaviour change interventions. *Implementation Science*, **6**, 42.

O'Doherty, J.P. (2004) Reward representations and reward-related learning in the human brain: insights from neuroimaging. *Current Opinions in Neurobiology*, **14** (6) 769–776.

Pilar Matud, M. (2004) Gender differences in stress and coping styles. *Personality and Individual Differences*, **37** (7) 1401–1415.

Plomin, R., Fulker, D.W., Corley, R. & DeFries, J.C. (1997) Nature, nurture and cognitive development from 1 to 16 years: a parent-offspring adoption study. *Psychological Science*, **8**, 442–447.

Purves, D., Voyvodic, J., Magrassi, L. & Yawo, H. (1987) Nerve terminal remodelling visualized in living mice by repeated examination of the same neuron. *Science*, **20**, 1122–1126.

Riddell, P.M. (2021) Chapter 23: Neuroscience coaching. In: J. Passsmore (Ed) *The Coaches' Handbook: The complete practitioner guide for professional coaches*. London: Routledge.

Riddell, P.M. (2019) Chapter 2: Coaching and Neuroscience. In: S. Palmer & A. Whybrow (Eds) *Handbook of Coaching Psychology: A guide for practitioners*, 2nd Edition. London: Routledge.

Sheldon, K.M., Ryan, R.M., Deci, E.L. & Kasser, T. (2004) The independence effects of goal contents and motives on wellbeing: it's both what you pursue and why you pursue it. *Personality and Social Psychology Bulletin*, **30**, 475–486.

Sherman, S.L., DeFries, J.C., Gottesman, I.I., Loehlin, J.C., Meyer, J.M., Pelias, M.Z., Rice, J. & Waldman, I. (1997). Recent developments in human behavioral genetics: past accomplishments and future directions. *American Journal of Human Genetics*, **60**, 1265–1275.

Spielberger, J., Miller, G., Engels, A., Herrington, J., Sutton, B., Banich, M. & Heller, W. (2011) Trait approach and avoid motivation: lateralized neural activity associated with executive function. *NeuroImage*, **54**, 661–670.

Sultan, F.A. & Day, J.J. (2011) Epigenetic mechanisms in memory and synaptic function. *Epigenomics*, **3**, 157–181.

Sweatt, J.D. (2009) Experience-dependent epigenetic modifications in the central nervous system. *Biological Psychiatry*, **65** (3) 191–7.

Tabibnia, G. (2020) An affective neuroscience model of boosting resilience in adults. *Neuroscience and Biobehavioral Reviews*, **115**, 321–350.

Takesian, A.E. & Hensch, T.K. (2013) Balancing plasticity/stability across brain development. *Progress in Brain Research*, **207**, 3–34.

Tobler, P.N., O'Doherty, J.P., Dolan, R.J. & Schultz, W. (2007) Reward value coding distinct from risk attitude-related uncertainty coding in human reward systems. *Journal of Neurophysiology*, **97**, 1621–1632.

Umeda, T. & Okabe, S. (2001) Visualizing synapse formation and remodelling: recent advances in real-time imaging of CNS synapses. *Neuroscience Research*, **40**, 291–300.

Van Praag, H., Kempermann, G. & Gage, F. (2000) Neural consequences of environmental enrichment. *Nature Reviews: Neuroscience*, **1** (3) 191–8.

Whitmore, J. (2009) *Coaching for Performance: GROWing Human Potential and Purpose.* 4th Edition. London: Nicholas Brealey Publishing.

Wood, S., Walker, H., Valentino, R. & Bhatnagar, S. (2010) Individual differences in reactivity to social stress predict susceptibility and resilience to a depressive phenotype: role of corticotropin-releasing factor. *Endocrinology*, **151** (4) 1795–1805.

Zeidan, F., Martucci, K.T., Kraft, R.A., McHaffie, J.G. & Coghill, R.C. (2014) Neural correlates of mindfulness meditation-related anxiety relief. *Social, Cognitive and Affective Neuroscience*, **9** (6), 751-759.

Chapter 11
Motivational Interviewing Coaching: Theory, research and practice

Katherine A. Finlay

Introduction

Motivational Interviewing (MI) was developed by William (Bill) Miller and Stephen Rollnick in the 1980s. When working with people with addictions, they noticed that there was unusual power in how warmly they interacted with their clients. The more they created a collaborative atmosphere within their sessions, the more the client started to think aloud about making changes to their own behaviour. When Rollnick and Miller actively listened as much as possible and asked broad, open questions without giving advice or acting as the authority figure, the client was much more likely to talk through their own reasons for and against change. This meant that Rollnick and Miller were able to avoid tutoring or convincing their clients to change and instead their clients became more self-motivated. These strategies became formalised as Motivational Interviewing techniques and they have been widely used across a huge range of work and clinical settings.

Motivational Interviewing is considered a key strategy for supporting clients to explore their own thoughts and motivations around changing behaviour (Miller & Rose, 2009). It has been used to improve motivation in people struggling with issues as diverse as living with chronic disease, developing their career, and returning to work after medical leave. MI is often part of health coaching, career coaching and life coaching and is now increasingly common in the business arena (Anstiss & Passmore, 2013). In business coaching, MI has proven particularly helpful as it provides coaches with a strong set of practical guidelines for building active, empathetic and productive coaching conversations (Passmore, 2011a, 2011b, 2012a, 2012b, 2013).

This chapter will first explore the theory behind MI and then will present some of the research evidence for the use of MI in different types of coaching, ranging from employment coaching through to health coaching. Despite acknowledging that there is a need for much more research on how MI can best be used in business, this research will give a preliminary insight into the impact that MI can have on a client's likelihood of changing behaviour. Finally, this chapter will offer some practical strategies for developing your MI skills in your own coaching practice.

Theoretical foundations

Rollnick and Miller are highly skilled practitioners and, interestingly, did not specifically set out to generate a theoretical basis to explain MI (Miller & Rollnick, 2009). However, research has shown that the unusual success of MI could be because it naturally falls in line with several theoretical models. The key theoretical standpoints that will be covered in this chapter are: (1) the Transtheoretical Model (DiClemente & Velasquez, 1985; Prochaska & DiClemente, 1983); (2) Self-determination Theory (Deci & Ryan, 1985; Ryan & Deci, 2000b); and (3) the 'three hypotheses' (Arkowitz et al, 2008). We will look at these in greater detail to explore how they link with MI and help inform our coaching practise.

The transtheoretical model

The transtheoretical model (TTM) of change (DiClemente & Velasquez, 1985; Prochaska & DiClemente, 1983) has often been linked to MI. The TTM is a way of explaining how people can display different stages of 'readiness' for change. People who are 'ready' for change are more likely to enact it, whereas people who are not yet 'ready' may be resistant and avoidant, rejecting any steps towards change. The TTM has been closely aligned with MI, but it should be viewed as a separate theory which is helpful for better understanding the process of moving clients towards change (Miller & Rollnick, 2009).

The TTM argues that there are five stages which people pass through when deciding to make a change (Prochaska & Velicer, 1997; see Table 11.1. The model begins with a stage in which people have no intention of changing (*precontemplation*), then moves through the thought processes (*contemplation*) and planning (*preparation*) which might come before beginning to make a change. If a client then decides to take action, testing out their planned change, in an ideal world they would be able to *maintain* this change indefinitely. If so, then they will reach *termination*, which is when the behaviour change becomes established and no longer takes any effort to maintain.

In real life though, getting to the termination stage is rare (Brogan et al, 1999). Instead, many people remain at the maintenance stage, continuing to work for some time on their desired change. The TTM is therefore best viewed more as a cyclical model than a linear model (Nigg et al, 2019; see Figure 11.1): clients may cycle through the stages and relapse several times, failing to maintain the change they had hoped to achieve before they eventually manage to make a change that lasts longer-term. Certainly, changing behaviour is rarely as simple as passing straight through each stage once and having immediate success. Changing behaviour is difficult and often uncomfortable, so relapse should be expected rather than unexpected. The TTM helps coaches to recognise that relapse does not mean failure (Miller & Rollnick, 2012). Relapse is just part of the very common and challenging process of moving towards change.

The TTM framework is a strong fit with MI because motivation is the primary reason why people change (Harakas, 2013). Without (self-) motivation, true change does not happen. It is highly likely that clients may be 'stuck' in a single stage of change and may need additional support from their coach to help them move forwards. Examples of these clients may be 'chronic contemplators' (DiClemente et al, 1991), people who spend large amounts of time thinking about making a change, but never reach the later stages of planning or taking action. Prochaska and Velicer (1997) reviewed twelve different behaviour changes and argue that there is a rule of thumb where, at any given moment, approximately 40% of people tend to be in precontemplation, 40% in contemplation and 20% in the preparation stage. Given that so many people may be 'stuck' in an early stage, MI can help clients think through a proposed behaviour change and work with them to make that change happen.

Table 11.1: The stages of change in the transtheoretical model

Stages of change	Description
Precontemplation	No intention to change behaviour
Contemplation	Intending to take action and considering the implications of this
Preparation	Intending to make a change imminently and preliminary steps have been taken to prepare for this change
Action	Change has been actioned but has not yet become embedded or stabilised
Maintenance	Changed behaviour is maintained over time
Termination	Temptation to relapse is no longer present and behavioural change is embedded

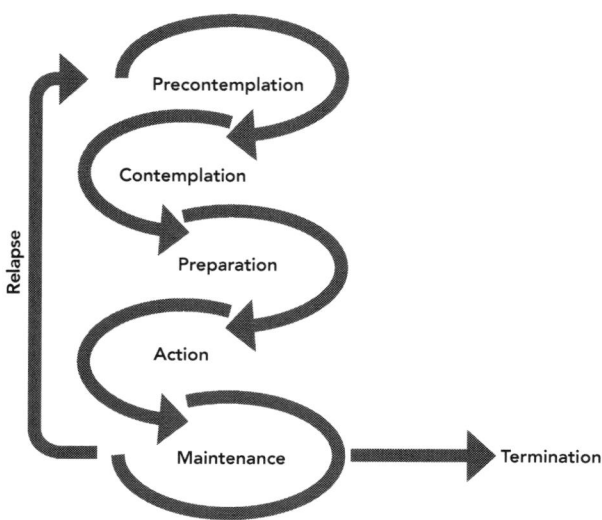

Figure 11.1: Cyclical progression through the stages of the transtheoretical model

Self-determination theory

Self-determination theory (SDT; Deci & Ryan, 1985; Ryan & Deci, 2000b) is a theoretical approach which came from work on motivation and social psychology in the 1970s and 1980s. It argues that we have an innate psychological need to see our own personal and professional growth as self-motivated (Deci & Ryan, 2012). When we feel in control of our own work and home lives, then our motivation and life satisfaction are high. However, if we see our professional and personal lives as entirely determined by other people or pressurising situations/factors, then we can feel demotivated and devalued. Ryan and Deci (2000b) found that work-related factors, such as a person's working environment or their interpersonal working relationships, had a powerful impact on their intrinsic (self-) motivation. If employees felt their work was self-determined then they delivered persistent and effective performance, whereas if they had little control over their jobs then their output was reduced and they had poor psychosocial wellbeing (Ryan & Deci, 2000a).

According to SDT, to function at our best in a professional or personal context, we have three basic psychological needs which must be satisfied: (1) *competence*, (2) *autonomy*, and (3) *relatedness* to others (see Figure 11.2). *Competence* explains our need to feel that we are effective in what we do, both in terms of our job-related activities and our leisure time. *Autonomy* describes how individuals need their work and personal situations to provide conditions that respect, support, and value their integrity and volition. In this way, people can 'be themselves' fully at home and at work. Finally, *relatedness* argues that individuals are more fulfilled when they are connected with others and appreciated as an integral part of a team or group. Without these three conditions, people will fail to thrive and achieve growth at work or at home (Deci & Ryan, 2012). Within a coaching context, the coach should therefore maintain an awareness of these three basic psychological needs. For example, coaches may use open questions and MI to support clients in identifying their own priorities in the three domains of competence, autonomy and relatedness.

Ryan and Deci progressed the idea of basic psychological needs by linking them directly with motivation. We often think of motivation being split into intrinsic (internal) and extrinsic (external) motivation. But Ryan and Deci (2008) add detail to this division. They argue that intrinsic (self-) motivation is not simply the opposite of extrinsic (external) motivation, but that there are six sub-types of motivation:

1. **Amotivation**: the client is completely unmotivated and has no autonomy or drive and rarely has their three basic psychological needs met.

2. **Intrinsic motivation**: Behaviour is intrinsically (self-)motivated in full, and the client feels they are working in harmony with their values, hopes and desires, gaining high levels of enjoyment and satisfaction from their activities.

3. **Extrinsic motivation** (4 sub-types):

    a. **External behavioural regulation**: a client's behaviour is entirely motivated by compliance, external rewards and punishments.

    b. **Introjected behavioural regulation**: external motivation remains important, particularly when it relates to protecting your self-image or ego, but the client also employs some form of self-control which pushes them towards their own internalised rewards and punishments.

    c. **Identified behavioural regulation**: motivation is largely internal, and clients may review their own behaviours by evaluating their activities in terms of how much personal importance and value they represent.

    d. **Integrated behavioural regulation**: clients show heightened self-awareness and a strong match between their job role activities/behaviours and their personal values.

Collectively, these sub-types show how motivation can be controlled or autonomous. Controlled motivation functions like an external regulator of your behaviour, forcing you to behave in particular ways because of threat of punishment or your own desire to strive to gain (external) rewards. By contrast, autonomous motivation can be both internally or externally motivated and refers to when you have made a choice to engage in an activity which aligns with your own values and sense of self (Harakas, 2013).

This complex view of motivation informs the core work and strengths of MI; to seek out and grow intrinsic motivation. Having this level of detail in the understanding of motivation is highly beneficial. It helps us to understand that with external motivation comes the risk of loss of enjoyment and engagement at work and home because our tasks are no longer experienced as self-initiated or engaging (Vansteenkiste & Sheldon, 2006). Both SDT and MI believe that individuals have a powerful capacity for change and a natural tendency to seek personal development and growth (Vansteenkiste & Sheldon, 2006), something that can be well supported within a coaching relationship.

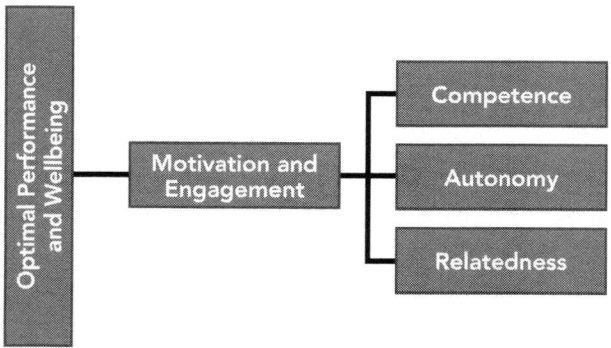

Figure 11.2. Basic psychological needs according to self-determination theory

The three hypotheses

The TTM and SDT can explain *what* may be happening but are less helpful for understanding *how* MI brings about behaviour change. In fact, very little research has attempted to find out what the *process* of change activated by MI is; the *'how'*. *How* does MI support client action? How does the listening style mean people become willing to verbalise their unspoken thoughts and opinions about change? *How* does MI support people who do not appear at all interested in changing?

Arkowitz *et al* (2008) proposed three theoretical pathways in an attempt to answer the *'how'* question, explaining how MI brings about change. There is definitely a need for further validation of these pathways, but preliminary research suggests that the mechanisms outlined in the following hypotheses can be proven with many different MI client bases (Magill *et al*, 2014, 2018; Magill & Hallgren, 2019). It is likely that these three hypotheses work together, with the first (technical) hypothesis taking priority over the other two pathways.

The technical hypothesis

The technical hypothesis has received the greatest research attention as its focus on the technical proficiency and delivery of MI allows it to be easily assessed. The hypothesis argues that technical proficiency in the core MI skillset (e.g. Open Questions, Affirmations, Reflections and Summaries)

enhances the coach's likelihood of moving clients towards behaviour change. By reflecting back what a client voices during a session, a coach's words act like a mirror, showing clients their own desire for change more clearly. The Technical Hypothesis can be measured by the Motivational Interviewing Treatment Integrity code (MITI; Moyers et al, 2016). This is a scoring tool which assesses whether an MI professional maintains fidelity in their delivery of MI, or goes off-track, using non-MI techniques. The MITI allows a coach's MI sessions to be audited for MI-consistent or MI-inconsistent technical proficiency, checking how much they really did deliver 'true' MI, rather than just using their broader coaching skills. A meta-analysis which explored the technical hypothesis suggested that MI-consistent delivery in a 62–83% increased likelihood that the client will then voice their own reasons for change (Magill & Hallgren, 2019). Therefore, helping a client explain *why* they want to change is the first step towards actually making that change.

The relational hypothesis

The relational hypothesis predicts that successful MI is down to the quality and warmth of the relationship between coach and client. MI practitioners are encouraged to provide 'accurate empathy'. Accurate empathy is when the MI coach does not condone behaviour but reflects back the challenges that the client describes in a skilled, supportive and non-judgemental way. This means that the coach and client can collaborate effectively to work through the ups and downs of behaviour change. Though this hypothesis does require further investigation, empathy is clearly powerful in a work context. Leaders who are more empathic in their communication style, are rated as more likeable by employees and the employee is more likely to want to improve their work performance (Meinecke & Kauffeld, 2019). Empathy is not enough by itself, however. Research suggests that the relational hypothesis must be combined with technical skill if it is going to successfully encourage change (Villarosa-Hurlocker et al, 2019).

The conflict resolution hypothesis

The final hypothesis is the most under-researched of the three theoretical pathways. It argues that change initiated by MI is specifically the result of working through *ambivalence* to a potential change (Magill & Hallgren, 2019). Ambivalence is when a client holds both positive and negative attitudes towards change and expresses them both. This gives us an insight into their struggle to decide whether one side of their argument outweighs the other. MI sees ambivalence as evidence of internal conflict about behaviour change. This ambivalence must be resolved, with the coach using MI techniques to support the client through their internal 'conflict resolution' (Arkowitz et al, 2008). This conflict resolution may represent a standout moment in the experience of the client, a sort of 'aha moment' when they finally work out what is important to them and their pathway to change becomes clear. Whilst this hypothesis has common-sense appeal, the lack of research in this area may reflect the fact that pinpointing the exact moment when ambivalence and internal conflict is resolved is difficult. Typically, it occurs late in an MI session or after a series of sessions moving towards behaviour change (Miller & Rose, 2009). Alternatively, it may be triggered by the coaching, but happen when a client is thinking things through after the session has been concluded. Proving this hypothesis is therefore difficult, though it seems a viable answer to the 'how' does MI function question.

Research evidence

There has been a gradual increase in motivational interviewing research since the method was first introduced in 1983. An increasing number of trials have used robust research designs such as randomized controlled trials (RCTs), but these are largely in a healthcare context and are not specific to organisational psychology or coaching. This makes it difficult to determine whether MI has the same influence in coaching and organisational settings as it does in a clinic, but overall the evidence for the success of MI seems positive, though the effect sizes are usually small-to-moderate (Zomahoun *et al*, 2017). The risk of bias and quality of MI trials typically remains weak or moderate, though stronger RCTs have emerged, particularly where MI techniques have been applied in health coaching contexts (Zomahoun *et al*, 2017). Passmore and Whybrow (2019) have argued that, despite the clear lack of business coaching research, there is a strong case for using MI in organisational psychology and coaching.

Early indications suggest that MI could be used to support people in returning to work after prolonged periods of sick leave or injury. A systematic review by Aanesen *et al* (2021) mapped the sparse evidence, finding only two RCTs with very mixed outcomes. The first RCT found no effect of MI in improving return to work likelihood for disability claimants with back pain (Magnussen et al, 2007). Whereas the second RCT showed that MI reduced benefit claims by 4.6% and supported people in returning to part-time work (Gross *et al*, 2017; Park *et al*, 2018).

Gross *et al* (2017) was the second study in Aanesen *et al*'s review and used a cluster RCT design to compare MI against standard rehabilitation for people returning to work after being diagnosed with chronic musculoskeletal disorders such as back pain. Their results suggested that MI increased clients' participation in a job search programme by more than two-fold and reduced the likelihood of people seeking further unemployment benefits. More research is definitely needed to show conclusively whether MI is helpful for returning to work, but Park *et al* (2018) argued that the best way of using MI could be to view it as part of a 'return to work toolkit'. For example, you could combine MI with other business management and human resource strategies to re-engage struggling employees.

MI is showing promise in encouraging employment in people who do not have long histories of maintaining job security. Britt *et al* (2018) asked more than 900 unemployed people to take part in a series of three MI workshops and three one-to-one MI interviews. They compared this group against people who had no MI. They also did a further large-scale replication study to test whether their original results were sound and found that again the same results emerged. The MI group did show increased employment likelihood and employment retention. These results lasted and were shown when participants were tested again six months and then over a year later. MI coaching therefore has strength in encouraging employment in people who are unemployed.

Building on these findings, Rochat (2019) explored whether or not you could use MI as a technique in career development coaching. Their study did not look at the outcomes for the people who had been coached, but focused instead on how the career coaches experienced using MI. The career counsellors felt that MI as a methodology was both positive and feasible for use in their day-to-day work.

MI has most often been employed in a business setting to help support employee wellbeing. There are currently no systematic reviews or meta-analyses looking at employee health and MI. However, there have been some strong RCT trials. Kouwenhoven-Pasmooij *et al* (2018) did a multicentre cluster RCT for 491 employees in the Dutch police, military and health service. They were trying to reduce the cardiovascular disease risk in these professions as these employees often have high stress jobs and do shift work, both risk factors for early death and chronic illness. Kouwenhofen-Pasmooij *et al* (2018) audiotaped the MI sessions and checked their quality using the MITI. They found that MI increased engagement with a healthy diet and exercise in employees. What was really impactful, though, is that the quality of the MI delivery was key. Having more and better-quality MI sessions meant that employees were able to maintain their commitment to a healthy diet and exercise for longer. The positive results were still more than twice as evident at 12 months when compared against participants who had not had MI. Other studies have agreed with these findings, for example a number of studies have shown that MI coach expertise and MI-fidelity combine together to provide the greatest benefits to clients (Madson *et al*, 2012; Pace *et al*, 2017).

Pedersen *et al* (2019) did a cluster RCT with 202 transport employees, targeting their physical activity levels. Employees who attended exercise support group meetings and who took part in MI workshops run in line with self-determination theory became more motivated to exercise and were more physically active. This evidence leads us to the conclusion that MI may help with improving self-management of health in employees.

Looking more widely at physical health and MI, Ghizzardi *et al* (2021)'s systematic review investigated recovery from after chronic heart failure in nine RCTs. MI did not help the physical health of the patients in the studies they reviewed, but those people who had MI improved their self-care and their confidence to look after themselves rose. They concluded from this that MI has an ability to increase self-regulation and self-management, even if the physical health effects of heart failure could not be reversed.

In studies which have used MI as method to help people stop smoking, Lindson *et al* (2019) evaluated 37 studies in a large-scale systematic review. Their results found that there was a lot of variability between studies in the way in which they used MI and the risk of bias within studies was high as a result of small sample sizes. Despite the methodological limitations, the results still showed that MI was better than not having any support to quit smoking. MI was also more successful than all other (non-MI) forms of stop smoking support. It was particularly beneficial if smokers completed more MI coaching sessions. This is known as 'high intensity MI' and is more successful than fewer sessions, which is the format for 'lower intensity MI'.

Finally, the effects of MI on medication adherence have been widely assessed in many high quality systematic reviews (Palacio *et al*, 2016). Zomahoun *et al*'s review (2017) identified seventeen RCTs which measured medication use. There was a small but positive impact of MI on medication adherence and this was increased if the coaches maintained their skillset and kept their MI integrity high. If the intervention was delivered face-to-face rather than remotely (via phone or online) then the effect sizes were greater and the intervention was more successful. Other systematic reviews in MI have also shown that face-to-face interventions have a slight advantage over remote delivery (Bus *et al*, 2018).

Table 11.2: Summary of recent research

Study	Summary
Britt *et al* (2018)	MI workshops were compared against controls for preparation for employment. After the MI, more participants were employed (63% vs. 47.1%) and retained at 6 months (62.9% vs. 53.4%) than controls. Retention was 5.3% higher after MI at 15 months post-intervention.
Ellingson *et al* (2019)	RCT targeting physical activity and sedentary time using a Fitbit combined with MI and habit education (FB+), or (control) Fitbit-only. FB+ increased steps/day and moderate physical activity but with small effect sizes.
Foldal *et al* (2021)	Mixed methods evaluation of an RCT using MI for sick-listed workers undertaking a Return to Work (RTW) support programme. 99% of workers were satisfied/very satisfied with MI sessions.

Table 11.2: Summary of recent research

Study	Summary
Grimolizzi-Jensen (2018)	RCT assessing the impact of MI or no intervention on readiness for job change in 56 employees of a company undergoing restructure. MI increased readiness to change ($\eta\_(p^2)$ = .072) and MI group participants were higher in readiness after 3 weeks than controls ($\eta\_(p^2)$ = .773).
Gross et al (2017)	Cluster RCT comparing MI against standard rehabilitation for 729 people with chronic musculoskeletal disorders who were returning to work. MI participants had a reduced likelihood of claiming unemployment benefits and returned to modified work duties (Odds Ratio (OR) = 2.09).
Kouwenhoven-Pasmooij et al (2018)	Cluster RCT supporting 491 employees (8 clusters) across three organizations who were at increased risk of cardiovascular diseases. Longer duration MI sessions increased diet and exercise participation (OR = 1.01). MI quality also improved participation at 1 year (ORrange = 1.48-2.34).
Michaelis et al (2021)	Feasibility study assessing MI counselling against hypertension counselling in 34 manufacturing workers in Germany. No impact of MI, but underpowered and small sample.
Park et al (2018)	Cluster RCT assessing successful return-to-work (RTW) for 728 employees who had musculoskeletal injury. RTW was 12.1% higher for unemployed claimants after MI. Therapist MI adherence enhanced outcomes by 33.3%.
Pedersen et al (2019)	12-month follow up of an RCT evaluating group MI against control for physical activity levels in 202 employees. Motivation increased for all employees and they either maintained stable physical activity or increased physical activity.
Rochat (2019)	30 career counsellors were trained in MI over 2-days. Gender differences were shown in MI fidelity by coaches and junior counsellors were most effective (β = -.45).
Sayegh et al (2017)	RCT for employment counselling in 202 18–24-year-olds. MI increased change talk frequency (β = .86). MI group participants with a high motivation to appear consistent were 2.05 times (OR) more likely to complete their school diploma.
Van Dongen et al (2017)	RCT to reduce work-related burnout. A four-group design was used: (1) Group MI-based social environment intervention, (2) a physical environment intervention, (3) their combination, or (4) usual practice. Combined social and physical interventions reduced need for rest/recovery. Cost-effectiveness was weak but a high ROI was present for the combined intervention.

Practice

The spirit and processes of MI

The 'spirit of MI' is the phrase that is used by Rollnick and Miller to talk about atmosphere they aim to create during client conversations (see Figure 11.3; Miller & Rollnick, 2012). They argue convincingly that a good coaching relationship should prioritise partnership between the coach and client. For Rollnick and Miller, a strong MI session should be collaborative, accepting and respectful of the views, actions and values of the client, and must help the client generate their own reasons for change. By building an empathetic, warm, collaborative atmosphere within the coaching sessions, clients can explore their own ambivalence and perceived barriers to change without fear of being judged by the coach.

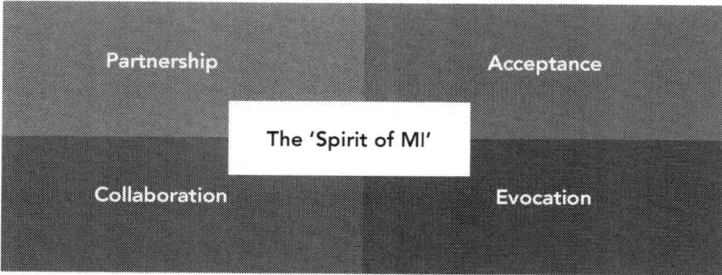

Figure 11.3: The 'spirit of MI'

1. Using MI in coaching starts by the coach working within the framework of MI's four foundational processes (Miller & Rollnick, 2012):
2. Engaging: Using empathic and active listening to create an atmosphere in line with the 'spirit of MI'.
3. Focusing: Identifying the 'what', reviewing the core areas that the client wants to work through.
4. Evoking: Exploring the 'why', establishing the client's motivation for and against change – their ambivalence.
5. Planning: Working on the 'how', supporting the client in stepping towards a change.

The first two stages are relatively simple and common to other coaching styles, but the evoking stage offers an opportunity for a skilled MI-coach to showcase their skillset. MI uses some key catchphrases that can help coaches understand their role in this phase. We can aim to help our clients by *developing discrepancy*. This describes what happens when we support our clients in exploring any mismatch between their current actions (behaviours) and their hopes or values.

The second catchphrase is known as *'rolling with resistance'*. This is helpful for the coach who encounters some opposition to change in their clients, something that can often be verbalised quite strongly. Resistance should be expected by the coach, and they should respond sensitively, 'rolling' with it. When clients push back against their own reasons for change, then coaching them through this resistance is an integral part of supporting them in moving towards change and resolving their own ambivalence (Miller & Rollnick, 2012).

If we can maintain the four foundations of MI during our coaching conversations, then the likelihood of developing a strong coaching relationship and supporting our clients in moving towards behaviour change becomes more likely. We have to remember when *evoking* that extrinsic motivation generated by the coach is not the aim of MI. Our goal in MI is to grow the intrinsic motivation within our clients. As coaches, we recognise that when people make their own decision for change, that choice is often more powerful (Miller & Rollnick, 2009).

Change talk and sustain talk

As coaching sessions progress, it is likely that clients may begin to generate *change talk* (Miller & Rollnick, 2012). Change talk is the active language people use when they are considering making a behaviour change. This change talk language can strengthen in commitment and intention-likelihood over time. For example, consider the difference between needs-based change talk, 'I need to search for a new job', when compared with commitment-based change talk, 'this week I am going to apply for the junior partner role that just came up'.

The opposite of change talk is *sustain talk*, where clients give their reasons for resisting change. This may be by providing counterarguments to change talk, or simply stating the reason for not making a change in the first place: 'I am just not feeling ready or qualified enough to go for that position'. A skilled coach will be able to explore this ambivalence through the use of targeted open questions that can soften sustain talk and respond with gentle curiosity to change talk. We can be mindful in our coaching to pick up on or reflect back change talk and gently downplay sustain talk, all the while respecting and engaging with the ambivalence that the client is expressing.

In coaching, we should avoid 'jumping' at change talk or responding to change talk with a notable uptick in our verbal and non-verbal responses. There is a risk that we might desire-based change talk ('I would love to be able to balance my workload better so that I don't feel so overwhelmed') as intention-based change talk ('I am going to change my schedule for this week so that I have some space for me'). Commitment to behaviour change can vary hugely within language (see Table 11.3), and we need to be sensitive to what we *really* hear. Change talk acts as an indicator of likelihood of change (Pace *et al*, 2017).

To help us spot change talk in our coaching, within MI, the acronym DARN CATS is used (see table 11.3). The DARN part of the acronym relates to *preparatory change talk*, and the CATS refers to *mobilizing change talk*, where change is more likely to happen.

The MITI argues that coaches should show a 'marked and consistent effort to increase the depth, strength, or momentum of the client's language in favour of change' (Moyers *et al*, 2014; p.6). When coaching we try to balance this against the opposite, a marked and consistent effort to soften sustain talk. Being able to soften sustain talk is a challenging but rewarding indicator of excellent coaching. It helps move our clients towards change without the need for any extrinsic persuasion or pressure. It is possible, however, that some coaching clients may display signs of 'stuckness' (Arkowitz *et al*, 2008), in which case the coach could consider employing some of the strategies outlined below.

Table 11.3: Preparatory and mobilization change talk using DARN CATS

Change talk category	Type of change talk	Examples	Coaching strategies
Preparatory change talk	Desire	I want to… I wish…	■ Ask evocative open questions ■ Seek clarification by asking open questions to elicit more detail ■ Explore goals and values ■ Use an imagined future task ■ Query best- and worst-case scenarios ■ Decisional balance task
	Ability	I could… I can…	
	Reasons	I would like to have more energy I need to feel less stressed	
	Need	I ought to… I have to…	
Mobilizing change talk	Commitment	I intend to… I will…	■ Action planning ■ Elicit and reflect on major reasons for change ■ Affirmations
	Activation	I am ready to… I am willing to…	
	Taking Steps	Yesterday I went out and… This week I started to…	

Foundational skills

The core skills within motivational interviewing are widely used in other coaching styles. These are known as 'OARS' and we will look at each of them in more detail in the next section:

- Open questions
- Affirmations
- Reflections
- Summaries

Open questions

Simply put, open questions encourage the client to speak. Strong open questions may include simple requests for clients to explain more about their thoughts and feelings, such as 'how do you feel your workload impacts you?', 'what makes you think it's time for a change?', or 'where do you want to be in five years?'. They may be preliminary questions, which set up the focus and context of a coaching session ('what were you hoping to focus on in today's discussion?'), or they may be fact-finding or evocative. It is often beneficial to avoid 'why' questions, as these can feel more confrontational for the client. Coaches should also aim to avoid stacking questions together, where one question is closely followed by another as this can reduce the feeling of collaboration in the coaching session.

Affirmations

Affirmations are widely used in coaching (Anstiss & Passmore, 2021) and in MI they help to communicate the 'spirit of MI'. Affirmations are a way of verbally acknowledging and accentuating something positive about your client's strengths, efforts, intentions or worth (Moyers *et al*, 2014). They help to build up a client's feelings of self-efficacy and control and show them that they have the strength to make progress (Anstiss, 2020). Affirmations are experienced most positively by clients if they are closely linked to their behaviours or characteristics. The best examples of affirmations are 'affirming reflections', such as 'you are the kind of person who takes their work responsibilities seriously and goes the extra mile to support your colleagues when they've got deadlines'. Note that this example is specific to an incident or situation or value, rather than generic ('great work').

When coaching, we aim to affirm what is important to our client from our *client's perspective* ('it's really important to you that you're a great parent and also a productive employee'), rather than judging from our perspective as the coach ('I think you did a brilliant job today'), something which is not encouraged in MI. When MI coaching delivery is audited for MI-consistent technical skills using the MITI code (Moyers *et al*, 2016), specific scoring is given to affirmations and they are equally as important as open questions and reflections. Coaches should, however, take care not to overuse affirmations by repeating similar affirmations within a session – this can devalue their impact and could be experienced as patronising.

Reflections

Reflections come in many formats, as you can see in Table 11.4. As MI-based coaches, we should be aiming for a ratio of reflective listening which is weighted towards reflections rather than towards questioning (minimum 2:1 reflections-to-questions; Moyers *et al*, 2014)). When we achieve this ratio, it has the benefit of improving our client's feelings of collaboration with us and typically enhances the quality of our coaching conversations. Reflections should avoid our tone of inflection rising at the end as this can turn what should be a neutral reflection into a closed question. For example, notice the difference between the reflection 'you're feeling overwhelmed' delivered in a neutral tone, versus 'you're feeling overwhelmed?' with a rise in the voice at the end. The first feels empathetic, whereas the second could cause the client to feel as if their capacity to cope is being judged.

Simple reflections are used to show that the coach understands the meaning in what their client is saying, reflecting this back (Passmore, 2011a). Whereas complex reflections do more than just paraphrasing a client's comments. Instead, they may reflect the implicit meaning, feeling, intention or experience behind what the client says. They may extend the client's comments, reflecting the unspoken emotion behind their words and lift or lower the intensity in the language that the client uses.

'Advanced' complex reflections such as amplified and double-sided reflections should be used with caution and only when the coaching relationship is strongly established (Passmore, 2011a). Amplified reflections could be received by your client either as humorous or inflammatory, depending on the tone of your conversation. An amplified reflection or 'overstatement' can work really well to lighten the tone of discussion and prompt the client to soften their opposition to change but must be wisely used, with restraint. When coaches choose to use double-sided reflections, it helps to present the positive reasons for change *after* reflecting back the client's resistance to change. This harnesses the recency effect, where the most recent parts of a discussion are recalled more easily, becoming more salient. For example, a coach could reflect:

> *'Prepping for that deadline further in advance feels impossible at the moment and you also wonder if your team would perform better if they had more time'.*

Here, the coach has primed the importance of time and performance through the recency effect and used the mid-anchor 'and' instead of 'but'. This use of 'and' in the middle of the reflection means that the coach is softening the ambivalence and reducing any intrinsic conflict that may be battling within a client who is holding these two perspectives. A slight pause in verbal delivery may be necessary at the mid-anchor so that the client has time to hear their own ambivalence in full.

Table 11.4: Types of reflective listening

Category of reflection	Subtype of reflection	Content
Simple reflection		Reflection captures the words, phrases and meaning of client's conversation and uses simple synonyms or direct repetition of client's language.
Complex reflection		Reflection is more progressive, and may reflect the coach's observations of unspoken meaning, intention, emotions or experiences.
	Continued reflection	Coach extends the reflection to offer information that was unsaid (implicit) or to offer an interpretation of the client's communication.
	Double-sided reflection	Coach reflects the client's ambivalence by reflecting first the arguments against change followed by the reasons for change (last), with 'and' as a mid-point anchor.
	Amplified reflection	Coach may amplify (sensitively exaggerate) the emotional content of the client's discussion point
	Muted reflection	Coach may lower the intensity of the client's emotional language (e.g. reducing *anger* to *frustration*)
	Metaphorical reflection	Coach reflects via imagery or pictorial language, providing a model for improved understanding

Summaries

Summaries are, in their simplest form, collections of reflections which the coach may offer at points of transition to new topics/questions, or when a client appears to become stuck or lost during the conversation. Summaries help clients to regain clarity on their viewpoints to (re-)enable their ability to move forwards or to redirect the discussion. By analogy, if reflections are 'sentences', then summaries are effectively 'paragraphs' which can help conclude or draw together topics of discussion. Summaries may also allow the experienced coach to offer reflective interpretations of what the client is expressing, potentially prompting the client to engage in deeper self-reflection to really identify what may be limiting their behaviour change.

Best practices

Agenda mapping

Agenda mapping is a motivational interviewing technique that is typically used early in a coaching conversation to set the priorities for that session. This may take the format of an open question such as 'what do you think should be the focus of our conversation today?', with follow-up questions building upon this, so that a clear 'map' or plan is developed collaboratively. Some clients respond well to agenda mapping by bringing a specific concern or target for discussion which the coach can then explore further to help their client plan the session and identify key issues for discussion (Passmore, 2013). However, other clients may not have a clear agenda. If this is the case, coaches should consider this an opportunity to spend further time engaging with their client through asking open questions and offering reflections, supporting the client in identifying some specific goals for coaching. Coaches may need to support the client in moderating their goals in line with short- or longer-term targets which are achievable within the timelines of the scheduled coaching sessions.

Typical day technique

The typical day technique is a beneficial tool which can support clients in identifying patterns of behaviour/habits which have unconscious or implicit influences on their personal or working life. The coach will ask a series of questions which move the client from the beginning of a 'typical day', starting from the time when they wake up, through to the time when they retire to bed. Responding to the typical day technique can feel uncomfortable for the client as it requires a certain level of willingness to be vulnerable and gives the coach a window into their daily life. It is important, therefore, to explore the client's willingness to engage with this technique:

> 'Would it be ok if we took some time now to think through a typical day together, to see if we can identify anything that might help us to know more about the challenges you're facing?'

If agreement is granted, the coach may explain the concept behind the technique:

> 'It would be really helpful for me to get a complete understanding of your average day, starting from when you get up in the morning until you go to bed. How does your day typically get started?'

By setting the beginning (waking) and end (bedtime) of the typical day, the coach is allowing the client to provide a detailed overview of the ways in which they balance their work and home life. Some clients may rush or gloss over the detail, needing their coach to encourage them to slow down and provide a fuller description. Other clients may instead use this technique as an opportunity to review the minutiae of their day in great detail. We need to seek a balance so that the technique moves consistently through the client's day and does not overly fixate on any particular time periods (e.g. the commute). Short reflections on items in the client's day by the coach can help clients keep up their momentum. In the background, the coach should make a specific effort to (mentally) note any sustain talk and change talk that occurs, so that this can be explored further when the technique is concluded.

Readiness ruler

The readiness ruler emerged from work by Miller and Rollnick (2012), who identified that by scaling a client's desire for change on a verbal numerical scale, you can tip the balance towards action and behaviour change. This tool should be used sparingly, as over-assessment can feel formulaic and awkward and reduce the collaborative 'spirit of MI'. Carefully used, however, the ruler can enable a client to identify that they may have more motivation for change than they originally thought.

The technique asks a client to complete the following assessment:

> 'Using a scale from 0–10, if 0 is not at all important and 10 is extremely important, how important do you feel this change is to you?'

The client responds by giving a rating, and the coach asks a follow-up question:

> 'Why do you think you are at [use number that the client provides] and not at 0'?

This follow-up question encourages the client to verbalise why they feel change is important. By using zero rather than ten, the coach is encouraging the client to recognise that they likely possess (at least) a small amount of motivation (perhaps a 3 or 4) and that can be encouraging for the client to verbalise. The original question can be varied so that 'important' is swapped for 'how ready do you feel you are to make this change' or comparable questions which lend themselves towards measuring behaviour change readiness.

Decisional balance task

The decisional balance task is not considered a core MI technique, but is a compatible task which can be used in conjunction with MI (Miller & Rollnick, 2009). Miller and Rollnick highlight that it is really important not to use this too late in a coaching conversation. If the technique is employed too late, it can reactivate sustain talk and halt progress towards change as it forces the client to review the costs (sustain talk) of their actions.

This task asks clients to think through their ambivalence by identifying their reasons for and against change on a worksheet/whiteboard/screen (see Figure 11.5). It works like this:

1. The coach begins by exploring the behaviour that is being considered, encouraging the client to reflect first on the benefits of their current behaviour, for example, 'how do you think [current behaviour] is benefitting you at the moment?'.

2. The coach can then explore the costs of that behaviour, for example, 'what do you think your [current behaviour] might be costing you?'. By drawing out the benefits of the existing behaviour before the costs, the coach is minimising the client's initial resistance to opening up a discussion about a behaviour that they wish to change and highlighting the negative aspects of those costs.

3. We then use reflective listening to respond to the issues raised by the client and support them in moving through the different columns sequentially, ideally without jumping between topics. For example, the coach might ask: 'what challenges do you think you might face if you made this change' or 'what do you think you might gain if you did make the change?'.

4. When the decisional balance sheet is complete, coaches should encourage a reflective review of the proposed behaviour change as a whole, directing attention towards change by softening sustain talk and eliciting change talk if the client is evidencing readiness.

	Present (no change)	Future (with change)
Benefits/gain		
Costs/pain		

Figure 11.5: Sample decisional balance sheet (adapted from Passmore, 2011b)

Two possible futures

The two possible futures techniques can build on the decisional balance task by personalising it further. It encourages the client to envisage themselves in the future in two possible scenarios. As is standard in MI, coaches should first engage their clients in this task by asking for permission to trial the technique: 'I wonder whether you might be interested in thinking through some possible futures, where you imagine yourself in different scenarios?'. If the client is willing to continue, the coach first identifies a timeline that would be important for the client: 'what is the next most important life milestone or age for you, do you think?'. The coach then uses this timeline to present two different scenarios through open questions, such as:

Scenario 1: 'if you were to imagine yourself aged 40 [adjust timeline/ milestone as appropriate], what would it be like for you if you didn't make this change?'

Scenario 2: 'So now, thinking of yourself aged 40 [insert timeline/milestone], you've decided to go for this promotion, and you've been in that role for a few years [replace with desired behaviour change], what do you think it would be like from your point of view?'.

The coach can respond to these scenarios using a combination of OARS, EARS (elaborate, affirmation, reflect and summarise) and an awareness of DARN-CATS change talk.

Elicit-provide-elicit

The final technique in the MI toolkit, elicit-provide-elicit, is particularly useful in contexts (such as health coaching) where there may be information that the coach needs to communicate with the client. Rollnick *et al* (1992) argue that information delivery should be circular, where the coach *elicits* the client's existing knowledge about an issue, then seeks permission to *provide* them with information, then asks about their response to that information (*elicit*). This may follow the format of the conversation represented in Box 11.1.

Key to the success of the EPE approach is that the coach's information is *never* given unsolicited. When the coach elicits and seeks permission before information is given, clients are more likely to be invested in receiving that information and the coach is more likely to give targeted information which is not a repeat of the client's existing knowledge. It is important that the coach delivers any information neutrally and in a non-personalising way. This allows their client to pick from the coach's information delivery what is most interesting and relevant to their concerns. Finishing the interaction with a further eliciting question values the autonomy of the client and re-engages them with conversation and provides another opportunity for change talk.

Box 11.1: Sample elicit-provide-elicit conversation in coaching

Coach: You've been off work for a while and are feeling apprehensive about coming back and about the workload that you might be facing as soon as you return. Have you ever investigated which return to work strategies might be available to you? (*confirmatory closed question, eliciting the client's knowledge base and activity*)

Client: To be honest, no. I've not really had the opportunity to talk to anyone who knows much about going back to work after time off, other than perhaps my friends. I know for myself that it might be best to take it gradually and not try to do it all straight away, but I'm just worried that I won't be able to do that as I'll want to jump straight back in at full speed.

Coach: You've been thinking about how a gradual return to work might play out and you're also recognising that you might find it a challenge if you went back full-time. You really are someone who wants to contribute totally to your team (*complex double-sided reflection, affirmation*). Would it be ok if I talked with you a bit about what other clients have found useful when they're coming back to the office after some time off? (*Elicit the client's permission to exchange information*)

Client: Sure. I'm interested to hear how they managed it without feeling like they were sort of a spare part if they weren't back to full-time straight away.

Coach: Quite a few people who've been off work have decided that taking a 'phased return' was something that would be useful for them. You've mentioned this idea already – it's when you come back part-time at first and then gradually build up to full-time over a course of a few weeks or months. People tend to feel like this gives them a bit of a roadmap for coming back to work because they know what they are building up to. They can work out a way of doing it gradually so that it works for them and for their team too. For example, you might start back one day a week and then each week or so add an extra day in the office. This helps you to get used to re-joining the team and you can catch up with what's happened over the past few months without being overloaded (*provide information*). What do you think about a phased return as an option? (*Elicit client's thoughts on the information*)

Client: I like the idea, but I'm really worried that people will judge me for it and that they won't see it as a positive thing.

Coach: It's like the phased return idea appeals to you and yet you're also thinking you might feel judged by your colleagues (*double-sided reflection*). Can you tell me a little more about what you think might worry your colleagues if you came back more gradually? (*Open question*)

Conclusion

In this chapter we explored the weight of evidence for the use of motivational interviewing in coaching contexts as varied as return-to-work interventions and health coaching. There is an increasingly large body of evidence suggesting that MI is a strong technique which should form a core part of your coaching practice. Yet it has also become obvious that taking the time to master MI skills is important if you are going to maximise the benefits of MI for your clients and keep 'true' to the techniques. We have established that skilled application of MI would potentially increase the likelihood of your clients achieving their behaviour change goals. The strength of MI is undoubtedly in working with ambivalence or resistance to change and many of the MI techniques we have covered could form part of an MI toolkit for coaching your clients through this. Building a productive and empathetic coaching relationship which values the 'spirit of MI' and appreciates the autonomy of the client, has the potential grow your clients' intrinsic motivation and make their behaviour change a reality.

Five questions for further reflection

1. **How could MI be adapted to work with highly productive employees as well as those who are struggling?**

MI's core skills are effective at eliciting commitment to change in any population and are not specific to working with resistant or struggling groups. An experienced coach will be able to support clients in eliciting desired goals and the need for behaviour change across any context or level of professional responsibility.

2. **Which of the MI techniques do you feel would be most challenging to deliver in line with the true 'spirit of MI'?**

As with many interpersonal coaching strategies, delivering the intervention effectively can depend on the response and engagement of the client. Engaged clients who are invested in their coaching sessions may move very rapidly towards behaviour change, whereas others may show evidence of choosing to remain 'stuck' and ambivalent. This needs skilful navigation by the coach to move the client past sustain talk and towards change talk. The effective coach needs to work hard to establish a collaborative coaching relationship and when that has been built, then the MI techniques are likely to be more effective. The approaches which involve scaling (The Readiness Ruler) or information delivery (elicit-provide-elicit) can be most difficult to deliver as it can be tempting to use them in a formulaic way, without the collaboration and reflection which might increase the traction of the techniques.

3. **How might cultural differences influence MI?**

Language-use and wording choices can mask many different underlying and implicit differences in readiness for change. It is essential to prioritise reflective listening so that it is clear that coach and client are working from the same point of reference and communicating with mutual understanding. Coaches should pay particular attention to the coherence between verbal and non-verbal signals from clients, particularly when working with non-native speakers. When verbal and non-verbal signals show a mismatch, then it may be an indicator that the client's word choices do not tell the whole story.

4. **Are there other approaches which could be combined with MI to increase the efficacy of the coaching style?**

Research has suggested that MI may work particularly well with cognitive behavioural coaching and mindfulness (Minzlaff, 2019), but there is a need for further research in this area to answer this question fully.

5. **What kind of issues are most suited to MI?**

The heritage of MI is in working with health motivation and substance misuse. MI may have particular strength in health coaching, but preliminary research findings reviewed in this chapter do suggest that it is suitable for use in organisational and employment settings.

Acronyms

EARS = elaboration, affirmations, reflections, summaries

EPE = elicit-provide-elicit

HAART = highly active anti-retroviral therapy

MEMS = medication event monitoring systems

MI = motivational interviewing

MITI = motivational interviewing treatment integrity

OARS = open questions, affirmations, reflections, summaries

OEP = Otago exercise programme

RCT = randomized controlled trial

ROI = return on investment

RR = relative risk

RTW = return to work

SDT = self-determination theory

TTM = transtheoretical model

Suggested reading

Anstiss, T. (2020) Chapter 11: Affirmations, Reflections and Summaries. In: J. Passmore (Ed) *The Coach's Handbook*. Taylor Francis: London

Anstiss. T. & *Passmore, J. (2013) Motivational Interviewing. In J. Passmore, D.B. Peterson and T. Freire (Eds) Wiley Blackwell Handbook of the Psychology of Coaching & Mentoring*. Chichester: Wiley, pp339–364.

Miller, W. R. & Rollnick, S. (2009) Ten things that motivational interviewing is not. *Behavioural and Cognitive Psychotherapy*, **37** (2) 129–140.

Miller, W. R. & Rollnick, S. (2012) *Motivational Interviewing: Helping people change* (3rd edition). New York, NY: Guilford Press.

Passmore, J. (2014) Motivational Interviewing. In: J. Passmore (Ed) *Mastery in Coaching*. London: Kogan, pp283–311.

References

Aanesen, F., Berg, R., Løchting, I., Tingulstad, A., Eik, H., Storheim, K., Grotle, M. & Øiestad, B. E. (2021) Motivational interviewing and return to work for people with musculoskeletal disorders: a systematic mapping review. *Journal of Occupational Rehabilitation*, **31** (1) 63–71.

Anstiss, T. & Passmore, J. (2013) Motivational Interviewing. In: J. Passmore, D.B. Peterson and T. Freire (Eds) Wiley Blackwell *Handbook of the Psychology of Coaching and Mentoring*. Chichester: Wiley, pp339–364.

Anstiss, T. (2020) Chapter 11: Affirmations, Reflections and Summaries in Coaching. In: J. Passmore (Ed) *The Coach's Handbook*. London: Taylor Francis.

Arkowitz, H., Miller, W.R., Westra, H. & Rollnick, S. (2008) Motivational interviewing in the treatment of psychological problems: Conclusions and future directions. In: *Motivational Interviewing in the Treatment of Psychological Problems*. New York, NY: Guilford Press, pp324–341.

Britt, E., Sawatzky, R. & Swibaker, K. (2018) Motivational interviewing to promote employment. *Journal of Employment Counseling*, **55** (4) 176–189.

Bus, K., Peyer, K. L., Bai, Y., Ellingson, L.D. & Welk, G.J. (2018) Comparison of in-person and online motivational interviewing-based health coaching. *Health Promotion Practice*, **19** (4) 513–521.

Deci, E.L. & Ryan, R.M. (1985) *Intrinsic Motivation and Self-determination in Human Behaviour*. New York: Plenum Press.

Deci, E.L. & Ryan, R.M. (2012) Self-determination theory in health care and its relations to motivational interviewing: a few comments. *International Journal of Behavioral Nutrition and Physical Activity*, **9** (1) 24.

DiClemente, C.C., Prochaska, J.O., Fairhurst, S.K., Velicer, W.F., Velasquez, M.M. & Rossi, J.S. (1991) The process of smoking cessation: An analysis of precontemplation, contemplation, and preparation stages of change. *Journal of Consulting and Clinical Psychology*, **59** (2) 295–304.

DiClemente, C.C. & Velasquez, M.M. (1985) Processes and stages of change: Coping and competence in smoking behavior change. In: *Coping and Substance Abuse*. London: Academic Press, pp319–342.

Ellingson, L.D., Lansing, J.E., DeShaw, K.J., Peyer, K.L., Bai, Y., Perez, M., Phillips, L.A. & Welk, G.J. (2019) Evaluating motivational interviewing and habit formation to enhance the effect of activity trackers on healthy adults' activity levels: randomized intervention. *JMIR MHealth and UHealth*, **7** (2), e10988.

Foldal, V.S., Solbjør, M., Standal, M.I., Fors, E.A., Hagen, R., Bagøien, G., Johnsen, R., Hara, K. W., Fossen, H., Løchting, I., Eik, H., Grotle, M. & Aasdahl, L. (2021) Barriers and facilitators for implementing motivational interviewing as a return to work intervention in a norwegian social insurance setting: a mixed methods process evaluation. *Journal of Occupational Rehabilitation*. Available online at: https://doi.org/10.1007/s10926-021-09964-9. Accessed 17 July 2021.

Ghizzardi, G., Arrigoni, C., Dellafiore, F., Vellone, E. & Caruso, R. (2021) Efficacy of motivational interviewing on enhancing self-care behaviors among patients with chronic heart failure: A systematic review and meta-analysis of randomized controlled trials. *Heart Failure Reviews*. Available online at: https://doi.org/10.1007/s10741-021-10110-z. Accessed 17 July 2021.

Goddard, A.M. & Morrow, D. (2015) Assessing the impact of motivational-interviewing via co-active life coaching on engagement in physical activity. *International Journal of Evidence Based Coaching and Mentoring*, **13** (2) 101–122.

Grimolizzi-Jensen, C.J. (2018) Organizational change: effect of motivational interviewing on readiness to change. *Journal of Change Management*, **18** (1) 54–69.

Gross, D.P., Park, J., Rayani, F., Norris, C.M. & Esmail, S. (2017) Motivational interviewing improves sustainable return to work in injured workers after rehabilitation: a cluster randomized controlled trial. *Archives of Physical Medicine and Rehabilitation*, **98** (12) 2355–2363.

Harakas, P. (2013) Resistance, motivational interviewing, and executive coaching. Consulting Psychology Journal: Practice and Research, **65** (2) 108–127.

Kouwenhoven-Pasmooij, T.A., Robroek, S.J., Nieboer, D., Helmhout, P.H., Wery, M.F., Hunink, M.M. & Burdorf, A. (2018) Quality of motivational interviewing matters: the effect on participation in health-promotion activities in a cluster randomized controlled trial. *Scandinavian Journal of Work, Environment & Health*, **44** (4) 414–422.

Lindson, N., Thompson, T. P., Ferrey, A., Lambert, J. D. & Aveyard, P. (2019) Motivational interviewing for smoking cessation. *Cochrane Database of Systematic Reviews*, 7. Available online at: https://doi.org/10.1002/14651858.CD006936.pub4. Accessed 17 July 2021.

Madson, M.B., Lane, C. & Noble, J.J. (2012) Delivering quality motivational interviewing training: a survey of MI trainers. *Motivational Interviewing: Training, Research, Implementation, Practice*, **1** (1) 16–24.

Magill, M., Apodaca, T. R., Borsari, B., Gaume, J., Hoadley, A., Gordon, R.E.F., Tonigan, J.S. & Moyers, T. (2018) A meta-analysis of motivational interviewing process: Technical, relational, and conditional process models of change. *Journal of Consulting and Clinical Psychology*, **86** (2) 140–157.

Magill, M., Gaume, J., Apodaca, T. R., Walthers, J., Mastroleo, N. R., Borsari, B. & Longabaugh, R. (2014) The Technical hypothesis of motivational interviewing: a meta-analysis of MI's key causal model. *Journal of Consulting and Clinical Psychology*, **82** (6) 973–983.

Magill, M. & Hallgren, K. A. (2019) Mechanisms of behavior change in motivational interviewing: do we understand how MI works? *Current Opinion in Psychology*, **30**, 1–5. Available online at: https://doi.org/10.1016/j.copsyc.2018.12.010 Accessed 17 July 2021.

Magnussen, L., Strand, L., Skouen, J. & Eriksen, H. (2007) Motivating disability pensioners with back pain to return to work: a randomized controlled trial. *Journal of Rehabilitation Medicine*, **39** (1) 81–87.

Meinecke, A. L. & Kauffeld, S. (2019) Engaging the hearts and minds of followers: leader empathy and language style matching during appraisal interviews. *Journal of Business and Psychology*, **34**(4), 485–501. https://doi.org/10.1007/s10869-018-9554-9

Michaelis, M., Witte (née Farian), C., Schüle, B., Frick, K. & Rieger, M. A. (2021) Can motivational interviewing make a difference in supporting employees to deal with elevated blood pressure? a feasibility study at the workplace. *International Journal of Environmental Research and Public Health*, **18** (8) 4179.

Miller, W. R. & Rollnick, S. (2009) Ten things that motivational interviewing is not. *Behavioural and Cognitive Psychotherapy*, **37** (2) 129–140.

Miller, W. R. & Rollnick, S. (2012) *Motivational Interviewing: Helping people change* (3rd edition). New York, NY: Guilford Press.

Miller, W. R. & Rose, G. S. (2009) Toward a theory of motivational interviewing. *American Psychologist*, **64** (6) 527–537.

Minzlaff, K. A. (2019) Organisational coaching: Integrating motivational interviewing and mindfulness with cognitive behavioural coaching. *Coaching: An International Journal of Theory, Research and Practice*, **12** (1) 15–28.

Moyers, T. B., Manuel, J. K. & Ernst, D. (2014) *Motivational Interviewing Treatment Integrity Coding Manual 4.1 (MITI 4.2)*. Available online at: http://www.micardiff.co.uk/resources/2)%20 MITI4.2%20Coding%20Manual.pdf Accessed 17 July 2021.

Moyers, T. B., Rowell, L. N., Manuel, J. K., Ernst, D. & Houck, J. M. (2016) The motivational interviewing treatment integrity code (MITI 4): rationale, preliminary reliability and validity. *Journal of Substance Abuse Treatment*, **65**, 36–42.

Nigg, C. R., Harmon, B., Jiang, Y., Martin Ginis, K. A., Motl, R. W. & Dishman, R. K. (2019) Temporal sequencing of physical activity change constructs within the transtheoretical model. *Psychology of Sport and Exercise*, **45**, 101557.

Pace, B. T., Dembe, A., Soma, C. S., Baldwin, S. A., Atkins, D. C. & Imel, Z. E. (2017) A multivariate meta-analysis of motivational interviewing process and outcome. *Psychology of Addictive Behaviors*, **31** (5) 524–533.

Palacio, A., Garay, D., Langer, B., Taylor, J., Wood, B. A. & Tamariz, L. (2016) Motivational interviewing improves medication adherence: a systematic review and meta-analysis. *Journal of General Internal Medicine*, **31** (8) 929–940.

Park, J., Esmail, S., Rayani, F., Norris, C. M. & Gross, D. P. (2018) Motivational interviewing for workers with disabling musculoskeletal disorders: results of a cluster randomized control trial. *Journal of Occupational Rehabilitation*, **28** (2) 252–264.

Passmore, J. (2011a) MI techniques: Reflective listening. *The Coaching Psychologist*, **7** (1) 49–52.

Passmore, J. (2011b) MI techniques: balance sheet. *The Coaching Psychologist*, **7** (2) 151–153.

Passmore, J. (2012a) MI techniques: recognising change talk. *The Coaching Psychologist*, **8** (2) 107–111.

Passmore, J. (2012b) MI techniques — typical day. *The Coaching Psychologist*, **8** (1) 50–52.

Passmore, J. (2013) MI techniques: agenda mapping. *The Coaching Psychologist*, **9** (1)32–35.

Pedersen, C., Halvari, H., Solstad, B. E. & Bentzen, M. (2019) Longitudinal trajectories of physical activity among employees participating in a worksite health promotion intervention: A latent class growth approach. *Psychology of Sport and Exercise*, **43**, 311–320.

Prochaska, J. O. & DiClemente, C. C. (1983) Stages and processes of self-change of smoking: Toward an integrative model of change. *Journal of Consulting and Clinical Psychology*, **51** (3) 390–395.

Prochaska, J. O. & Velicer, W. F. (1997) The transtheoretical model of health behavior change. *American Journal of Health Promotion*, **12** (1) 38–48.

Rochat, S. (2019) Effects of motivational interviewing training in career counseling: a pilot study. *Journal of Career Development*, **46** (3) 280–294.

Rollnick, S., Heather, N. & Bell, A. (1992) Negotiating behaviour change in medical settings: the development of brief motivational interviewing. *Journal of Mental Health*, **1** (1) 25–37.

Ryan, R.M. & Deci, E.L. (2000a) Self-determination theory and the facilitation of intrinsic motivation, social development, and well-being. *American Psychologist*, **55** (1) 68–78.

Ryan, R.M. & Deci, E.L. (2000b) Intrinsic and extrinsic motivations: classic definitions and new directions. *Contemporary Educational Psychology*, **25** (1) 54–67.

Ryan, R.M. & Deci, E.L. (2008) A self-determination theory approach to psychotherapy: the motivational basis for effective change. *Canadian Psychology/Psychologie Canadienne*, **49** (3) 186–193.

van Dongen, J.M., Coffeng, J.K., van Wier, M. F., Boot, C.R.L., Hendriksen, I.J.M., van Mechelen, W., Bongers, P.M., van der Beek, A.J., Bosmans, J.E. & van Tulder, M.W. (2017) The cost-effectiveness and return-on-investment of a combined social and physical environmental intervention in office employees. *Health Education Research*, **32** (5) 384–398.

Vansteenkiste, M. & Sheldon, K. M. (2006) There's nothing more practical than a good theory: Integrating motivational interviewing and self-determination theory. *British Journal of Clinical Psychology*, **45** (1) 63–82.

Villarosa-Hurlocker, M.C., O'Sickey, A.J., Houck, J.M. & Moyers, T.B. (2019) Examining the influence of active ingredients of motivational interviewing on client change talk. *Journal of Substance Abuse Treatment*, **96**, 39–45.

Zomahoun, H.T.V., Guénette, L., Grégoire, J.-P., Lauzier, S., Lawani, A.M., Ferdynus, C., Huiart, L. & Moisan, J. (2017) Effectiveness of motivational interviewing interventions on medication adherence in adults with chronic diseases: a systematic review and meta-analysis. *International Journal of Epidemiology*, **46** (2) 589–602.

Chapter 12
Third-Generation Coaching: Theory, research and practice

Reinhard Stelter

Introduction

Third-generation coaching describes a developmental step that goes beyond earlier forms of coaching. Coaching needs to be developed further because of rapid changes and growing complexity within all areas of society and its organizations. Although coaching practices are often a mixture of approaches, methods and techniques, third-generation coaching marks a major shift in the relationship between the dialogical partners based on *moments of symmetry*, with a strong focus on shared meaning-making and collaborative value reflections.

Originally, the coach worked as a facilitator by more or less exclusively asking questions as a way to help clients reflect on their challenges and to enable new perspectives on their problems. By contrast, a third-generation coach acts as a co-reflecting partner and thus adopts a more active and collaborative position as a fellow human companion through *withness-thinking* (Shotter, 2006) and by sharing his or her own thoughts and reflections with the client. Pausing and lingering in the dialogue opens new possibilities for fundamental self-insights (Stelter, 2019). Third-generation coaching indicates an intentional shift for the coach, away from more or less exclusively asking questions towards a collaborative meta-dialogue. Third-generation coaching can be an integrated part of other approaches. One key question remains unanswered: will more reflective and collaborative approaches inspired by third-generation coaching be more dominant in the future coaching scene (see Greif, 2014)? Furthermore, the idea of meta-dialogue might be most interesting and can even be connected to cognitive behavioural coaching, which also encourages meta conversations, conversations not just about what to do, but what I think, feel, and do.

Theoretical foundations

The fundamental idea behind third-generation coaching has been the awareness of rapid social change and its impact on both professional and civil life. The acronym VUCA draws attention to the challenges of our time: volatility, uncertainty, complexity, ambiguity. Sharma & Sharma (2019, p151) wrote:

> 'In today's volatile, complex and challenging times, organisational focus on employees requires a paradigm shift.'

This paradigm shift is the basic driver for the promotion of third-generation coaching, which builds on and partly includes practices from all three coaching generations.

First generation coaching has its roots in sports. Its focus is on setting goals and solving specific problems. However, to work towards clear goals is increasingly difficult in a VUCA world. The coaching literature contains growing criticism of such a narrow goal perspective (see David *et al*, 2013; Ordóñez *et al*, 2009). The focus on goals and objectives can lock a person into a particular and sometimes narrow lookout; ultimately, this represents the polar opposite of the purpose of a fruitful and developmental dialogue, which invites new horizons and enables novel perspectives. Therefore, first-generation coaching approaches will have reduced impact on future dialogue practices.

Second-generation coaching revolves around possible solutions and appreciative dialogues. It is rooted in systemic (Hawkins & Turner, 2019), constructionist/constructivist (Pavlović, 2021) and appreciative (Orem *et al*, 2009) theory and practice. This type of coaching offers a useful ground for our work as coaches and has a future in dialogue practice. However, times have changed, and we need to broaden our understanding of coaching fundamentally. It is becoming increasingly important for both individuals and organizations to focus on purpose, meaning-making and values as the foundation for their way of acting in today's challenging times.

The objective of third-generation coaching is to expand the theoretical foundation of coaching and to invite practitioners to enrich their practice with a collaborative perspective, where coaching client(s) and coach interact as co-reflective partners – as fellow human companions (Stelter, 2016a). Stelter (2014a; 2014b) introduced the term *third-generation coaching* as the underlying inspiration for a range of different dialogue forms that incorporate changes in society and organizational life at large. Third-generation coaching will be used here as the term that describes the point of departure for the continuing development and renewal of coaching in theory and practice. With its special awareness of the coaching client's current professional and/or personal challenges – often related to organizational and social changes – coaching inspired by third-generation approaches places particular emphasis on values and narrative co-creation and minimizes the emphasis on often short-sighted goals and pure performance optimization. The Danish psychology professor Svend Brinkmann (2017) challenged the agenda of performance optimization by lending a hand to people who are willing to do anything to keep up with development and who are thus at risk of burning out. His work offers an alternative. And he has a point! As long as coaches offer to help their clients pursue the ill-conceived desire to 'keep up' at all costs, they should be sacked, as Brinkmann suggested as one of his precepts. This narrow focus on goals and performance no longer seems helpful, also in light of the world's growing complexity and unpredictability. We need to rediscover *the art of lingering in dialogue* (see more in Stelter, 2019) – for our own sake and for the sake of those around us! The shift away from a narrow focus on performance optimization towards seeing human interaction entirely as a matter of collaborative meaning-making is the driver of the agenda of third-generation coaching.

Third-generation coaching in a nutshell

The following presentation will focus on the key elements of third-generation coaching, which Stelter (2019) also defined as a 'transformative dialogue'.

Self and identity are the focus of transformation

The coaching client experiences *transformation* via the intensive co-reflective process with the coach. The term *transformation* is connected to self and identity, concepts that have changed due to the rapid societal changes. Self and identity have become key psychological issues in the late modern or postmodern society we live in. In third-generation coaching two central perspectives of self and identity are merged to present an integral whole:

- *Self and identity as relational*: Gergen (2009), a social constructionist, has set the stage for a new understanding of individuals as *relational beings*. Gergen defines mental discourses – which is what coaching is about – as originating in human relationships, as a function in the service of relationships and as an action within relationships. Third-generation coaching is a process in the service of a relationship where both parties act as collaborative and co-reflecting partners.

- *Self and identity possessing a sensual and existential dimension*: the word *identity* comes from the Latin word *idem*, meaning 'the same'. Individuals are sensually anchored in their *lived* body. Our intentional and sensual orientation towards the environment let us experience the world as consistent. Individuals strive for *stability and consistency* (Stelter, 2014 a). Our actions are implicitly, and sometimes even explicitly, driven by personal values and beliefs, such as freedom, courage, goodness etc. Values are beliefs linked inextricably to affect and they guide our actions (Schwartz, 2012). Values serve as a key anchor for our identity. For the coach, it is important to develop a sensibility for the coaching client's life world via empathy, resonating and withness-thinking. (More about this in the Practice section of this chapter).

The three central guiding concepts of third-generation coaching

In the following, I address three aspects of the coaching dialogue that can help to expand the client's reflective space. These three aspects are essential features in my understanding of third-generation coaching (see also Stelter, 2014a; 2014b):

1. Value focus
2. Opportunities for meaning-making
3. The narrative-collaborative perspective

Value focus

The ultimate objective of third-generation coaching is to facilitate and build a foundation for leadership, communication, and cooperation, not by focusing on specific goals but by reflecting on key values as important landmarks for guiding our actions and navigating in life.

This value-focused coaching process is inspired by *protreptics*, a form of meta-coaching (re-) articulated by the Danish philosopher and leadership theorist Ole Fogh Kirkeby (2009). Translating the term from classical Greek, it describes the art of *turning oneself or others to the core of human existence*. Protreptics is a method for self-reflection and dialogical guidance that has been used in the Greek executive academies for generals and leaders since 500 BCE. Protreptics is a form of philosophical coaching that is focused exclusively on reflections on values not on specific situations or actions. The dialogue between coach and client tends towards symmetry, meaning that both parties are equally engaged in the abstract reflection on specific values or terms, such as 'responsibility', 'freedom', 'care' etc. Unlike conventional (exclusively asymmetrical) coaching dialogues, where the coach adopts a neutral position in relation to the client's challenge or problem, these value-driven dialogues essentially strive for a growing degree of symmetry: coach and client have a shared interest in examining specific values, because these values are of universal relevance to all human beings (see also Stelter, 2016b). After these value-oriented reflections, the consideration of potential consequences for one's future actions may move the dialogue back to a more specific coaching agenda.

Opportunities for meaning-making

Meaning-making is considered one of the most important means of facilitating the coaching dialogue (Stelter, 2007, 2014). Meaning is fundamental because we attribute particular values to our experiences, acts, interactions with others and personal and professional lives. Things become meaningful when we understand how we feel, think and act, for example by telling stories about ourselves and the world we live in. After surviving Nazi concentration camps, the existential psychiatrist Victor Frankl (1988) worked intensively with this concept. Finding and fulfilling meaning is the basic striving of any human being. Meaning-making is a holistic way of integrating past and present experiences as well as ideas about what the future might bring. Meaning develops in the interaction between action, sensation, reflection, and speech.

Meaning-making marks the interaction between sensual and relational processes, which are integrated in the dialogue practice. The distinction that is drawn between these two aspects of meaning-making in the following is purely analytical:

1. One point of departure for the coaching intervention is the *coaching client's sensory experience and personal meaning-making*. Here, the coaching dialogue is inspired by a phenomenological-existentialist approach. Together with the coach, the client seeks to understand his or her subjective reality or subjective perceptions and experiences of the context and culture he or she lives in. The focus is on the implicit and often sensory-bodily dimensions of certain situations, actions, or individuals. This perspective may shed light on essential and existentially meaningful experiences and values of past memories – especially uplifting moments – and of what feels right and important to oneself. The process of experiential meaning-making builds a link to practice, habits and routines that are embedded in the flow of action. Immersing oneself in the practice and reliving practices sensorially will often provide a source of new insight for the client into the things we 'just do' without really thinking about them. This sensory awareness that we strive to articulate helps us to understand the inherent meaning of our practices.

2. The second essential point of departure for collaborative coaching dialogue is how meaning is shaped in a *shared process of co-reflection between both coach and client*. In this sense, the coaching dialogue is inspired by relational and constructionist approaches. The coaching client projects certain self-perceived realities from the outside world into the coaching context. The coach is involved in the dialogue as a reflective partner who offers new voices in relation to the presented reality: voices of empathy, of understanding, of his or her own memories, of associations, of reformulation etc. In doing so, the coach takes part in the shared process of meaning-making that will enable the coaching client to see his or her world in a new and, hopefully, more uplifting light.

The narrative-collaborative perspective

The following presents my understanding of the narrative-collaborative perspective as well as its role in stimulating the reflective space in the coaching dialogue. The concept of narrativity and narrative psychology can be seen as an extension of the social constructionist perspective. I see this as a new way to integrate experiential and subjective-existential approaches with relational-constructionist approaches. This is also my own fundamental orientation, a view that regards the two ways as integrated aspects of the coaching dialogue. Other researchers who have similarly sought to integrate the embodied-experimental concept with the relational-discursive concept include Crossley (2003), Shotter & Lannaman (2002), Stam (2001) and Sampson (1996). They all saw the potential in relating phenomenological thinking with social constructionist thinking, which is also the ambition of the author. This is very different from adopting a naturalist perspective, for example by viewing personality as something that is anchored in a more or less stable character feature. Instead, the goal is a culturally oriented form of psychology where experiences and feelings are used to shape narratives with personal and shared values, individually as well as together with others. As Bruner (1990, p29) stated:

> '[Values] become incorporated in one's self-identity and, at the
> same time, they locate one in a culture.'

Telling each other stories and developing and exchanging stories and narratives, whether in a coach-client relationship or in a group context, are crucial activities for social meaning-making; a person's anchorage in a cultural context is always framed by specific values and meaning. Bruner (2006, p14) emphasized the importance of storytelling:

> 'The principal way in which our minds, our "realities", get shaped to
> the patterns of daily cultural life is through the stories we tell, listen
> to, and read – true or fictional. We "become" active participants
> in our culture mainly through the narratives we share in order to
> "make sense" of what is happening around us, what has happened,
> and what may happen.'

Narratives structure events and order them in a timeline. They make stories – the source of meaning-making – coherent and, as a result, make life meaningful. Narratives give rise to temporal coherence and shape our perception of events, acts, others, and ourselves as sensible and meaningful. The plot in any story frames the development of an inner structure and drama (Sarbin, 1986). By telling and listening to stories, we make our lives meaningful.

These three themes should be understood as a necessary theoretical basis and set of guidelines for creating a new dialogue culture. The coach's key question is, 'How do I generate meaning, explore values and formulate and reformulate narratives in the dialogue?' The later practice section presents some ideas and guidelines for how to develop concrete dialogue skills as a third-generation coach or as an initiator of and partner in fruitful transformative dialogues. I will examine and outline how these theoretically anchored basic themes can unfold in practice in the actual relationship with and among the clients.

Research evidence

As third-generation coaching is not a closed system but based on narrative, collaborative, reflective and existential theory and practice, the search for and documentation of theoretical and scientific evidence is nearly impossible to cover fully in this chapter. Furthermore, the understanding and terminology of third-generation coaching were initiated by the author only about a decade ago (Stelter & Law, 2010; Stelter, 2014a; 2014b), which naturally limits the amount of research related to this approach. However, different studies will be presented below that are based on main assumptions and ideas of third-generation coaching.

Some of the key theoretical sources of third-generation coaching will be in focus, and afterwards, we will take a closer look at some empirical studies based on the ideas of third-generation coaching.

Narrative research and practice

There is a rich literature in this field, originally inspired by narrative therapy (White & Epston, 1990). In the field of coaching, there is a growing interest in narrative approaches (Drake, 2015; Drake & Stelter, 2014; Laurence, 2018). Linell (2010), a researcher and therapist, has based her work on post-structural theory inspired by Butler, Foucault, Deleuxe and others who question the assumption of a deep and universal structure underlying language, culture, and subjectivity. The poststructuralist awareness is focused on the notion of differences, the proliferation of discourses and deconstruction. From a post-structural perspective, the researcher is not 'outside' the research as in early positivism; due to this inside position, post-structural research is conducted in a qualitative and contextualized manner. Davies (2000) describes the researcher's engagement with the fleeting reflexive spaces of thought that position 'agency' within the play of discourses. Dwyer and Emerald (2016, p5) describe how 'narrative work is typically within a transactional frame – focused on the way knowledge is created in social settings, whether that is in the interactions between the researcher and participants and/or between participants and others'. From that position, research evidence is often based on in-depth investigation of one's own or others' practice. In a single case study, Stelter (2015) investigated the transformational process of a woman who sought coaching with the aim of losing weight. Because she already knew the author's approach, the specific coaching for weight loss was less about strict behavioural guidelines and more about supporting the client to re-author specific situations and life events to empower her to live differently. Drake (2008) wrote about the *era of the artisan*: a post-professional era in which coaches are seen as master craftspeople skilled in an applied art, an approach to research and practice that is closely related to the actual practice, where coaches are seen as reflective or scientific practitioners (see also Lane & Corrie, 2006; Stelter, 2014, Chapter 6). From this perspective, the concept of *evidence* must be defined in a different way than in natural or medical sciences (Drake, 2009; Stelter, 2014, Chapter 6). Another example of a more artisanal approach to narrative research is a study by de Ronde (2019), who explored the theme of multi-voicedness in the search of the path of life. In his coaching practice, de Ronde searched for working methods that contribute to the exploration of multiple perspectives in which we live, and which provide support for dealing with the life questions we may grapple with. As human beings, we not only live in an ambiguous world but also have to deal with an ambiguous self. The article described a narrative method based on the archetypal biblical story of the prodigal son. By retelling this story three times as three symbolic stories, namely that of the youngest son, the oldest son and the father, the participants were invited to probe their lives from different vantage points and accept all their inner voices. Here, we again become aware of the objectives of narrative approaches that focus on deconstructing the subject's incriminating stories by supporting the capacity of re-authoring and empowerment (see also de Ronde, 2018; Swart, 2013; 2019).

A different approach to working with narratives was presented by Kerr and colleagues (2019). The purpose of their paper was to construct a conceptual framework for investigating the reconstruction of narrative identity in mental health recovery from a complexity perspective. This conceptual framework provides the foundation for developing a health boardgame to facilitate narrative identity reconstruction. As the authors wrote, the significance of the paper is that it provides a way of integrating concepts and theories with the common theme of adaptive growth (non-linear phenomena) in narrative identity reconstruction during mental health recovery and, further, creates a framework for assisting clients, in a practice-based way, to author their preferred narrative identity. This is important, as narrative identity reconstruction is a key task in recovery. Following Nurser and colleagues (2018), recovery is narrative in character. Creating individual recovery stories aligned with wellbeing and positive identity is central to mental health recovery. Based on their theoretical and practical models, Kerr and colleagues developed a boardgame designed to facilitate people's narrative identity reconstruction in recovery. The boardgame was intended to be used as a tool in connection with narrative coaching. The boardgame (titled 'Heroes and heroines: The recovery journey boardgame') is an immersive role-playing experience designed to be a 'crucible' for adaptive growth in recovery. Using a narrative coaching treatment approach aligned with complex change processes inherent in adaptive growth, provided an integrated framework that may be of value for understanding and facilitating narrative identity reconstruction as part of psychological wellbeing in recovery.

Wang and colleagues (2017) have presented a narrative-based coaching study that explored undergraduate students' experiences of developing mindful agency as a learning disposition, their perceived growth and change as learners and the possible impact of coaching on the students' learning and personal growth. The coaching supported the students' ability to foster positive self-identities and become more reflective, mindful, and self-determined (see also Wang, 2018).

The narrative approach was also included in a coaching study by Yip and colleagues (2020), who focused on the transition processes of new leaders, which requires identity work. The authors presented a framework of coaching principles and narrative practices inspired by Drake (2015) and Stelter (2014) (see also Drake & Stelter, 2014) that can support leaders through the identity transition processes of separation, liminality, and the integration of a new leader identity. In doing so, this paper provided actionable practices for coaching new leaders as well as directions for research on coaching and leadership development.

Grecco (2020) presented a doctoral study with a narrative coaching approach including 31 undergraduate students aimed at helping the participants develop a better understanding of their own narratives. The results of the study suggest that using philosophical coaching approaches, such as narrative based coaching (NBC), to enhance students' narratives can be beneficial to overall wellbeing, thus supporting the presence of coaching centres on university campuses to boost students' potential both inside and outside the classroom (see also Paaske et al, 2015).

A growing field of interest with some relationship to third-generation coaching is narrative medicine (Charon, 2006). This approach places a high priority on listening to the patients' story to gain a better understanding of their health issues, general outlook, and personal considerations in regard to illness and death, with the purpose of seeing the whole person behind the symptoms and the specific diagnosis. Narrative medicine thus places special emphasis on listening to the patient but also to stories in novels, or other forms of fiction, and essays which patients and health professionals use to make sense of their current life situation (see Fernandes, 2015).

Collaborative research and practice

A second perspective in third-generation coaching is on collaborative theory and practice, an approach that is applied in therapy, learning, organizational development, and coaching. It is important to mention that there is a form of fluid interconnectedness between narrative and collaborative approaches (see, eg, Madsen, 2016; Monk & Gerhart, 2001; Stelter, 2014a). The research design applied is mainly in-depth and qualitatively oriented.

One example of a collaborative coaching study was presented by Lee Keenan (2020), who applied a qualitative microanalytic approach to the study of coaching interactions for the purpose of understanding the character of collaborative discourse between cooperating teachers (CTs) and preservice teachers (PTs) in practice-based teacher preparation programmes. This study illuminated the complex social and discursive dance embedded within collaborative interactions. It showed how collaborative interactions developed from the strategic repositioning of social roles, which created space for authentic problem-posing by both the CT and the PT, and the co-construction of teaching events, which supported more specific planning toward future lessons. Further collaborative coaching studies carried out in different professional contexts were presented by Burley and Pomphrey (2011), Houchens and colleagues (2017), Roman and Woods (2018) and Tweedie and colleagues (2019).

Collaborative coaching approaches are often included in a broader learning context. In their paper, Jewett and MacPhee (2012) provided an account of coaching elements that were included in an existing graduate literacy course. Here, they described the responses of experienced and less experienced teachers as they began to add collaborative peer coaching to their teaching identities.

Reflective and existential approaches in research and practice

In comparison to third-generation coaching, reflective and existential approaches adopt a different epistemological stance by focusing on the individual's existential challenges that are worthwhile to reflect on as part of an in-depth coaching dialogue. The approach is based on phenomenological philosophy and existentialist psychology. Unlike collaborative theory, which is based on the co-created interrelatedness between both parties, the focus of an existential practice is on ongoing in-depth work with personal experiences and reflections that may have a genuine impact on the client. Both existential-phenomenological and collaborative approaches are based on a constructivist paradigm (Charreire Petit & Huault, 2008). Reflective and existential approaches are influenced by a philosophical mindset that favours research, often based on theoretical studies and a qualitative research design (see, eg, Floridi 2013; Hansen, 2016; Courant, 2020).

Studies with direct reference to third-generation coaching

During recent years, third-generation coaching has been the chosen intervention in several different empirical studies. As the promotor of this approach, the author has conducted several studies to document the value and effectiveness of the approach:

Stelter *et al* (2011) reported a mixed-method study that investigated the influence of narrative-collaborative group/third-generation coaching on career development, self-reflection and the general functioning of young sports talents with the aim of achieving integration of their sports careers, educational demands and private lives. This third-generation coaching intervention was conducted over eight sessions of 1.5 hours over a period of three months. In an extended version, Stelter (2014) presented the data material, which then also included a follow-up study (five months after intervention), based on both quantitative and qualitative material. The randomized controlled design was based on 77 participants (using a questionnaire measuring recovery/stress, motivation, and action control). A qualitative interview study included six participants. The group coaching intervention had a significant effect on the scores for social recovery and general wellbeing. One of the central findings was on the improvement in social recovery, a construct in the questionnaire that reflected a return to a higher level of social functioning and the participants' growing awareness and inclusion of others in their life. The findings showed significant improvements among the subjects who participated in group coaching. Figure 12.1 illustrates how the 12-week-long coaching intervention influenced the level of social recovery; this positive effect was also present in comparisons between the situation before the intervention and the situation five months after its completion. However, no significant improvement was found from the completion of the intervention to the measurement five months later.

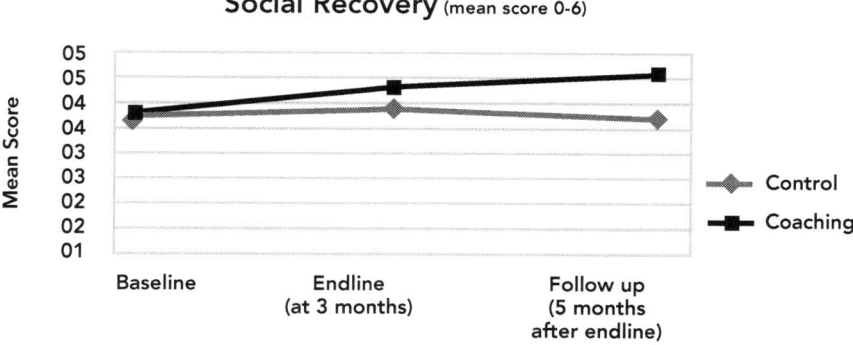

Figure 12.1: Influence of 12-week-long coaching intervention on social recovery

Summary of results:
Before intervention to end of intervention: *positive effect*

Adjusted for baseline scores, the coaching group had 0.381 higher social recovery scores after 12 weeks compared to control group. Effect size was medium (r=0.24, p=0.038).

Before intervention to follow-up: *positive effect*

Adjusted for baseline scores, the coaching group had 0.584 higher social recovery scores at follow-up compared to the control group. Effect size was moderate (r=0.275, p=0.035).

End of intervention to follow-up: *no effect*

Adjusted for Week 12 scores, the coaching group had 0.359 insignificant (p=0.247) higher social recovery scores at follow-up compared to the control group. Effect size was low (r=0.163) and insignificant (p=0.247).

Similar positive effects were found for *general wellbeing*. In the final evaluation at the end of the course of sessions, many participants stated that their behaviour had changed: they had begun to include some of the group members as clients, also outside the coaching context. Some of them also modified the way they related to team or club mates and became more interested in cooperating with the sports coach in their club in a new way. These changes clearly reflect the essence of social recovery.

The qualitative study showed that group coaching participants considered the shared process of meaning-making especially valuable. Third-generation group coaching can be understood as a community psychological intervention that helps to support the development of durable social networks and the increase of social capital. As the final theoretical cornerstone, the following can be highlighted: the social processes that have led to social recovery and which were the result of collaborative meaning-making in communities of practice led to the accumulation of social capital – a central concept that explains how people can cooperate successfully in society and certain social settings and attain a greater sense of social integration and satisfaction. Social capital is a theoretical concept considered to be useful for understanding the importance of social relationships and the formation of civil society. Bourdieu (1983, p248) defined social capital as:

> *'the aggregate of the actual or potential resources which are linked*
> *to possession of a durable network of more or less institutionalized*
> *relationships of mutual acquaintance or recognition'.*

The development of social capital is a key benefit of this highly collaborative approach, which is the main characteristic of third-generation coaching, especially when conducted in a group setting. Stelter and collaborators have conducted several studies fundamentally based on third-generation group coaching, some in the form of case studies (Stelter, 2014; Hansen *et al*, 2019), some with a strong community orientation (Ryom *et al*, 2017; Ryom *et al*, 2020) and some with a focus on health and lifestyle change (Stelter & Andersen, 2018; De Dominicis *et al*, submitted).

Other researchers have been inspired by the third-generation coaching approach: Godskesena & Kobayashi (2016) reported a study of individual coaching conducted as a mix of second- and third-generation coaching carried out by an external coach as a new pedagogical element that can impact doctoral students' sense of progress in doctoral education. The study used a mixed-method approach drawing on quantitative and qualitative data from the evaluation of a project on coaching doctoral students. It explored how coaching can contribute to the doctoral students' development of a broad set of personal competences and suggests that coaching may work to engender self-management and improve relational competences. The analysis of the participants' self-reported gains from coaching showed that doctoral students experience coaching as an effective method for supporting the doctoral study process. This study also provided preliminary empirical evidence that coaching of doctoral students can facilitate the doctoral study process, giving the doctoral students an enhanced sense of progress and the perceived ability to change their study behaviour in a positive direction.

As mentioned in earlier examples, third-generation coaching inspired the choice of coaching approach in other studies. One final example that will be mentioned here is the qualitative health coaching study by Knudsen and colleagues (2018), who highlighted the value for patients with cystic fibrosis of telling their individual stories. The young adults included in the intervention rarely spoke to others about their situation and thus valued the opportunity of opening up to a professional coach about their life and concerns. A close, trustful, and supportive relationship with the coach were of major importance for them.

Practice

Third-generation coaching practice is not manual-based. Hence, the dialogue between coach and client is more of an art, based on the coach's *relational capacity* and the safety and depth developed in the mutual relationship between both parties.

Relational attitude

The *relational attitude of the coach* is what counts. The following terms might help to illustrate the spirit of the relationship with and among the client(s) (see also Stelter, 2014; 2016a; 2019):

- *Sensitive responsiveness*: The collaborative practice of third-generation coaching facilitates an entirely new conversation culture, where one listens to the other and in turn strives to inspire the other with one's own thoughts and reflections on a particular story or description that one of the participants presented. It is a mutuality that Wittgenstein (1953, p122) described as 'seeing connections'. Listening is more than simply understanding what was said. Listening is not just about absorbing information but involves making meaning for oneself as a listener and inviting the other into the reflections it gives rise to.
- *Relational attunement* and *resonance*: Both terms give association to the world of music. Musicians playing together tune into each other. They relate to a common rhythm and melodic figure. Their tunes and

melodies match each other. Similarly, in a third-generation dialogue, when listening to someone's story, the coach will pay attention to him/herself and will then – initially, often implicitly – begin to relate to the client's story by tuning into it from the basis of his or her own sensations and meaning-making. In this way, the conversation partner's story or challenge 'becomes one's own'. Relational attunement can be describe as a shared or co-created articulation, where a sensation, a sensory impression or a theme is addressed collectively, and where the participants achieve a meeting or encounter. To describe this state, I adopted the term *resonance*, which the German sociologist Hartmut Rosa (2019) used to indicate a necessary change of focus and awareness towards a better society. By adjusting Rosa's term to the coaching dialogue, we can describe the coach as the other's *tuning fork*, as the coach tunes into the 'tone' of their clients. The goal is to develop a sense of *presence* and *attunement* where both parties constantly strive to be in resonance with one another. This is the objective of third-generation coaching, but it will certainly not be a permanent state. There will be moments of 'dissonance' where coach and client(s) do not fully understand each other. To achieve relational attunement and resonance should be a main ambition for the dialogue.

■ *Withness-thinking*: relational attunement is achieved by means of a special form of co-thinking, which Shotter (2006) calls withness-thinking or withness-talk. It is based on the coach's passion to immerse him/herself in the narrator's situation, allowing him/herself to be gripped by it and linking the narrator's story to his or her own life, experiences and thoughts while listening. Shotter (2006, p600) describes withness-thinking as a way of being with a strong element of sensual and bodily presence:

> 'Withness (dialogic)-talk/thinking occurs in those reflective interactions that involve our coming into living, interactive contact with an other's living being, with their utterances, with their bodily expressions, with their words, their "works". It is a meeting of outsides, of surfaces, of two kinds of "flesh" (Merleau-Ponty, 1968), such that they come into "touch" or "contact" with each other. ... In the interplay of living moments intertwining with each other, new possibilities of relation are engendered, new interconnections are made, new 'shapes' of experience can emerge'.

Withness-thinking becomes a shared process of knowledge production between the clients. In a mutual process of withness-thinking and presence, the conversation becomes a dynamic dialogue between both parties or – if it takes place in a group – among the clients.

Approaching the practice of third-generation coaching

Third-generation coaching is inspired by both systemic, collaborative, narrative, and reflective practices. The essential objective for a coaching dialogue aimed at change must be to initiate a *shift in perspective* or work towards *transformation*, where clients see themselves or the reality around them in a new light. A closer look at some specific methods or approaches to the dialogue might help to illustrate this objective.

Circular questioning

Circular questions are a central 'invention' of systemic theory and practice, an approach first applied in family therapy (see Tomm, 1988). Circular questions break with the linear mode, which means operating on the underlying assumption of a clear timeline or a cause-and-effect link. Linear questions are perfectly fine to use, especially in the beginning of the session, when the coach needs to understand the client's context, the persons involved and the client's basic perception of the situation. Circular questions invite the client to view things differently, to see the world from different angles and new perspectives. Circular questions help the client to explore and discover several and often unusual perceptions of reality, including the realities of others in the client's workplace or other people's positions in relation to a particular event. By asking circular questions the coach also influences the client's way of reflecting on reality, for example through hypothetical questions, a special type of circular question that challenges a particular perception and allows for other, novel perceptions of reality. The coach presents a hypothetical question based on a specific new picture of reality and thus invites the client to experiment and play with this reality and how it might impact the client's perception of reality. Circular questions appear unusual because they often are slightly provocative. Below are some examples of circular questions:

- What happened with you before you decided to introduce XY?
- What would your co-workers mention as their reason for doing things the way they did?
- Let's say that the challenge you face had been dealt with; who would be the first to notice that?
- What would be different if you were the person to make the final decision?
- If you were the fly on the wall, what would you focus on from the first moment?
- If you were to ask your colleague about this challenge, what would her answer be?
- If the problem had been solved, what would be different about the way you get up in the morning, go to work, enter your workplace, perceive your colleagues and so forth?

Externalization

The main mantra for understanding externalizing conversations comes from the narrative practitioners and therapists Michael White and David Epston (1990):

'The problem is the problem, the person is not the problem.'

In many cases it is clear that clients have internalized their problem, as if it stems from their own personality features or character. In an externalizing conversation, clients are invited to tell their story from a different – externalized – angle. Externalization offers the client a new perspective by providing an alternative way of viewing and talking about the problem (White, 2004). The conversation begins by the coach asking the client to name the problem, for example, 'the work overload'. By re-authoring the story with the problem as the actor, clients can see and perceive their situation in a new light, without blaming themselves or seeing themselves as the cause of all their problems. Externalizing conversations empower clients by distinguishing the person from the problem, on the one hand, and strengthening their focus on dealing with the problems and challenges in a new way.

Statement of position map

To support the client in his or her self-concept, narrative co-creative practice uses a so-called statement of position map, which adds depth to the collaborative dialogue between coach and client. Narrative theory speaks of 'thickening the story'. The statement of position map is used to address a specific problem in the following way (see Table 12.1).

Table 12.1: Statement of position map (Stelter, 2019, p99)

Naming
- What would you call the problem you are describing? Could you give the problem a name?

Effects
- How does [name of the problem] affect you? And others?
- How does it affect the way you and others act?

Evaluation
- How do you feel about the effects of [name of the problem] on you?
- How do you like it?
- Why?
- Could there be a positive side to it?

Justification – the person's values
- Do you have a sense of why you feel that way about it?
- Why are you not happy with it? [This would be a good time to ask about values]
- Is there any aspect of it that you are happy with? What is your wish for your situation and your problem?
- In what way does your assessment of the situation differ from the way others see it?

Co-creating dialogues – generating moments of symmetry

Narrative, collaborative, and co-creative practices employ different strategies to establish a community attitude between coach and client(s). This collaborative stance is especially powerful in group coaching sessions, where the coach functions both as driver of the session and as an involved co-participant. The most co-creative activity in the coaching dialogue is when the coach acts as a fellow human companion (Stelter, 2016a), accompanying the client on his or her journey, while the two interlocutors position themselves in a mutual relationship that generates *moments of symmetry*. This is a new and innovative feature of third-generation coaching that may also be helpful in other everyday professional dialogues, where one part actively adopts a co-creative position in relation to a possible colleague or staff member with the purpose of supporting and optimizing the reflective process. In group or team dialogues, any group member can adopt the role of co-active partner. Moments of symmetry can occur when the coach or a group member shares reflections on specific descriptions, statements, feelings, or thoughts from the focus person. This should be done in a non-judgmental way. It is an attitude of resonance, where the reaction to the focus person's contribution may be inspired by the following questions:

- What kinds of skills, talents or qualities do you value as you listen to the focus person?
- What kind of pictures or metaphors come to mind as you listen to the focus person?
- How does what you have heard relate to your own life, experiences, or specific values?
- Based on what you have heard, do you feel inspired to do something in your life differently?

Receiving and giving gifts

This metaphor goes back to the South-African coach and organisational developer Chené Swart (2013, p168), who wrote:

> 'When listening to a story teller, narrative practitioners are always aware that they are not only witnessing a story, but in the listening their lives are also touched by the story of the other. This point of being moved and touched by the story being listened to, I have come to call gifts. Gifts can be learnings from a story, a reminder of my own values and beliefs which I may have forgotten, a challenge to my own beliefs and ideas about something, an experience of not being alone in my own struggles and thoughts, and so forth.'

In terms of how people talk about things, narrative practice distinguishes between two fundamental perspectives:

1. *Landscapes of action* include specific activities or ways of doing things.
2. *Landscapes of identity* include all issues concerning specific personal beliefs, attitudes, values, dreams, intentions, expectations and so forth.

When the coach or coaching group member relates to the focus person, they react to these two landscapes – often with particular emphasis on one of them – by responding, as an active listener, to what the focus person said. Listeners can react by either *receiving a gift* from the focus person or by *giving a gift* (see also Stelter, 2019).

■ 'While listening to you I notice the strength and courage you have shown in the situation, and I feel an energy raising in myself to deal with a challenge I am recently faced with.' This is an example of receiving a gift in relation to the listener's own landscape of action, where the listener finally gets the energy to act.

■ 'When I listen to you and hear what you have done for these people, I can only express my deepest respect.' This is an example of *giving a gift* in regard to the focus *landscape of action*, which has an impact on the listener's *landscape of identity* ('deepest respect').

The following figure (Figure 12.2) illustrates how the coach, or a coaching group member, can respond to the focus person by receiving or giving gifts:

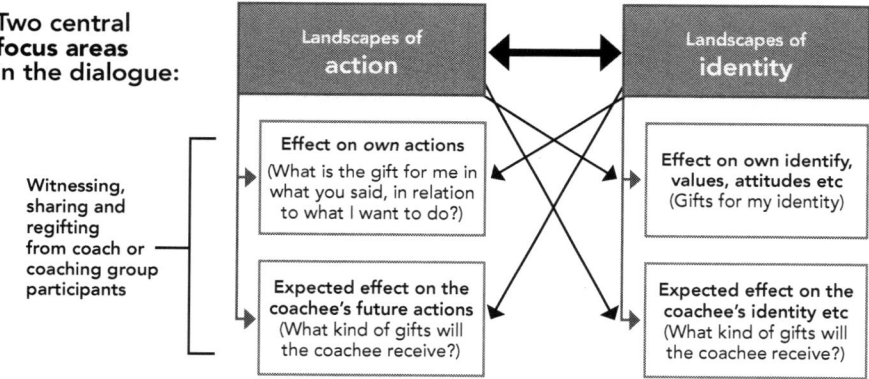

Figure 12.2: Giving and receiving gifts (see also Stelter, 2019, p104)

Focusing on values

The deeper reflective and existentially based dimension can move into the centre of the dialogue when coach and client involve each other in value reflections. In the dialogue with or among clients (in group or team coaching), the focus will sometimes turn to abstract terms (see, for example, the statement of giving a gift in the previous paragraph, where 'respect' was mentioned as being central to the listener).

The coach can direct focus towards a specific central value by asking the client:

- What does *respect* mean to you?
- When did you learn something about *respect*?
- What types of feelings and thoughts come up when you relate *respect* to a person or situation?
- Is there a person in your life who represents *respect* to you?
- How can *respect* be related to and distinguished from similar terms (such as honesty, trustworthiness and so forth)?
- What would be the opposite of *respect*?
- What kind of aura or appearance do you associated with the word *respect*?
- What is the purpose of *respect*?
- How would your work unit or organisation look when *respect* is the key driver?

Reflecting on values often goes deeper than a normal conversation, which is bound to a specific situation. An abstract reflection relates to something fundamental, which may turn out to be central to the client. Because it is abstract and thus universally human, a value reflection facilitates a *moment of symmetry* between client and coach more than a dialogue where the client's specific challenge is in focus. Value reflections are fundamentally liberating. After having a deep reflection on *respect*, the term takes on a life of its own in the client's world and thus prepares the client to act whenever 'respect' implicitly comes into the centre of the situation as the right way to act.

Conclusion

Third-generation coaching is not based on one single approach; it is a wide-ranging and seminal understanding of coaching unfolded in a specific form and relational attitude. What is common across different third-generation coaching approaches is the objective of providing a *reflective space* for meaning-making and maintaining a focus on values, which goes beyond the narrow focus on the attainment of predefined goals. The major driver for promoting third-generation coaching is the acceleration processes in our hypercomplex society, its organizations, workplaces, and life in general. There is a growing need to find anchor holds by developing social capital, interrelatedness, solidarity, and shared values. The most prominent feature of third-generation coaching is the effort to achieve *moments of symmetry* in the dialogue between coach and client, an attempt that resonates with special qualities in group or team coaching contexts. Moments of symmetry create an atmosphere of sharing and collaboration and a space of co-reflection that lays the ground for deep reflections on human existence as the foundation for our actions in the world. The motto of coaching is 'in true dialogue, both sides are willing to change', inspired by the Buddhist monk and peace activist Thich Nhat Hanh.

Five questions for reflection

1. **What do you see as the most prominent challenges in our society, our organizations, our working life and personal life that might have an impact on coaching?**

Surprisingly, there is very little attention on societal changes in the coaching literature. Earlier on, coaching has been connected to the world of sports. However, by the end of the 20th century, coaching was applied more and more in organisational life. What happened? An explanation can be traced back to the changes in society and organisational life.

2. **What do you see as the most valuable dialogue qualities of a coach?**

Coaching (and therapy) research has clearly documented that relational qualities are essential in a satisfying and efficient dialogues. Some of the suggestions in this chapter might strengthen your focus on these dialogue features.

3. **How can the three key theoretical aspects – value focus, opportunities for meaning-making and the narrative collaborative perspective – inspire your coaching practice?**

Third generation coaching highlights these three dimensions as essential. They are the foundation for a dialogue that goes beyond goals and beyond an understanding that the coach is a more or less neutral facilitator of the dialogue.

4. **How might some of the studies presented in the research section lay the ground for your work as a reflective practitioner in coaching?**

Being a reflective practitioner should be the coach's main ambition. That means you start to make use of the research at hand and try to adapt theory and empirical results as useful inspiration in your own practice. Furthermore, you can start to develop your own small studies, i.e. by writing a logbook based on reflections about your practice.

5. **Based on what you have previously read about coaching and neuroscience in the earlier chapters of this book, what points might lend support to the relational attitude recommended in this chapter?**

The mirror neurons are what pops up in my mind. I first thought to include them in this chapter. After having read this book in detail, I am sure you will be able to come with many more reflections.

Suggested reading

Drake, D. & Stelter, R. (2014) Narrative coaching. In: J. Passmore (Ed) *Mastery in Coaching: A complete psychological toolkit for advanced coaching*. London: Kogan Page, pp65–94.

Stelter, R. (2014) *A Guide to Third-Generation Coaching: Narrative-collaborative theory and practice*. Springer Science + Business Media.

Stelter, R. *(2014) Third-generation coaching: Striving towards value-oriented and collaborative dialogues*. International Coaching Psychology Review, **9** (1) 33–48.

Stelter R. (2016a) The coach as a fellow human companion. In: L. van Zyl, M. Stande and A. Odendaal (Eds) *Coaching Psychology: Meta-theoretical perspectives and applications in multicultural contexts*. New York, NY: Springer, pp47–66.

Stelter, R. (2016b) Working with values in coaching. In: T. Bachkirova, G. Spence and D. Drake (Eds) *The SAGE Handbook of Coaching*. London: Sage Publications.

Stelter, R. (2019) *The Art of Dialogue in Coaching: Towards transformative exchange*. London: Routledge.

References

Brinkmann, S. (2017) *Stand Firm: Resisting the self-improvement craze*. Cambridge: Polity Press.

Bruner, J. (1990) *Acts of Meaning*. Cambridge, MA: Harvard University Press.

Bruner, J. (2006) Culture, mind and narrative. In: J. Bruner, C. F. Feldman, M. Hermansen and J. Mollin (Eds) *Narrative Learning and Culture* (New social science monographs, pp13–24). Copenhagen: Copenhagen Business School.

Burley, S. & Pomphrey, C. (2011) *Mentoring and coaching in schools: Professional learning through collaborative inquiry*. London: Taylor & Francis.

Charon, R. (2006) *Narrative Medicine: Honoring the stories of illness*. Oxford: Oxford University Press.

Charreire Petit, S. & Huault, I. (2008) From practice-based knowledge to the practice of research: Revisiting constructivist research works on knowledge. *Management Learning*, **39** (1) 73–91.

Cook, J. (2016) Collaborative action coaching for leaders: A way of enabling transfer and sustainability of learning for all external coaches? *International Journal of Evidence Based Coaching and Mentoring*, **10**, 76–83.

Courant, E. (2020) *Cultivating Character: The practical application of virtue ethics theory through philosophical coaching*. Michigan: ProQuest Dissertations Publishing.

Crossley, M. (2000) *Introducing Narrative Psychology*. Milton Keynes: Open University Press.

David, S., Clutterbuck, D. & Megginson, D. (Eds) (2013) *Beyond Goals: Effective strategies for coaching and mentoring*. Aldershot: Gower.

Davies, B. (2000) *A Body of Writing*. Maryland: AltaMira Press.

De Dominicis, Elsborg, S.P., Andersen, V. & Stelter, R. (submitted) Group coaching for healthy lifestyle for menopausal women: a randomized experiment.

de Ronde, M. (2018) Walking in a fairy tale forest in search of a second primitivity with the help of Little Red Riding Hood. *British Journal of Guidance & Counselling*, **46** (3) 315–325.

de Ronde, M. (2019) Renewal and multi-voicedness: in search of narrative conscience. British Journal of Guidance & Counselling, 47(2) 157–167.

Drake, D. (2008) Finding our way home: Coaching's search for identity in a new era. Coaching: An International Journal of Theory, Research & Practice, **1** (1) 16–27.

Drake, D. (2009) Evidence is a verb: A relational approach to knowledge and mastery in coaching. International *Journal of Evidence Based Coaching and Mentoring*, **7** (1) 1–12.

Drake, D. (2015) *Narrative Coaching: Bringing our new stories to life*. Petaluma, CA: CNC Press.

Drake, D. & Stelter, R. (2014) Narrative coaching. In: J. Passmore (Ed) *Mastery in Coaching: A complete psychological toolkit for advanced coaching*. London: KoganPage, pp65–94.

Dwyer, R. & Emerald, E. (2016) Narrative research in practice: navigating the terrain. In: *Narrative Research in Practice*. Singapore: Springer, pp1–25.

Fernandes, I. (2015) *Creative Dialogues: Narrative and medicine*. Cambridge: Cambridge Scholars Publishing.

Floridi, L. (2013) What is a philosophical question? *Metaphilosophy*, **44** (3) 195–221.

Frankl, V.E. (1988) *The Will to Meaning. Foundations and applications of logotherapy*. New York, NY: New American Library.

Grecco, C. (2020) *Perceptions of Narrative Based Coaching Among Undergraduate Students at Middle Tennessee State University*. Michigan: ProQuest Dissertations Publishing.

Gergen, K. J. (2009) *Relational Being: Beyond self and community*. Oxford: Oxford University Press.

Godskesen, M. & Kobayashi, S. (2016) Coaching doctoral students: A means to enhance progress and support self-organisation in doctoral education. *Studies in Continuing Education*, **38** (2) 145–161.

Greif, S. (2014) Coaching und Wissenschaft: Geschichte einer schwierigen Beziehung. [Coaching and science: The story of a difficult relationship]. *Organisationsberatung, Supervision, Coaching*, **21**, 295–311.

Hawkins, P. & Turner, E. (2019) *Systemic Coaching: Delivering value beyond the individual*. London: Taylor & Francis.

Hansen, F.T. (2016) Socratic wonder as a way to Aletheia in qualitative research and action research. HASER. *Revista Internacional de Filosofía Aplicada*, **7**, 51–88.

Hansen, T., Jensen, C.S., Nielsen, A.S. & Stelter, R. (2019) 'Jeg ved godt, hvad jeg burde gøre, jeg kan bare ikke': Sundere livsstil gennem narrativ-samskabende coaching ['I know what I'm supposed to do, I just can't': Healthier lifestyle through narrative-co-creative coaching]. *Coaching Psykologi: The Danish Journal of Coaching Psychology*, 8 (1) [3630].

Houchens, G., Stewart, T. & Jennings, S. (2017) Enhancing instructional leadership through collaborative coaching: A multi-case study. *International Journal of Mentoring and Coaching in Education*, **6** (1) 34–49.

Jewett, P. & MacPhee, D. (2012) A dialogic conception of learning: collaborative peer coaching. *International Journal of Mentoring and Coaching in Education*, **1** (1) 12–23.

Kerr, D., Deane, F. & Crowe, T. (2019) Narrative identity reconstruction as adaptive growth during mental health recovery: A narrative coaching boardgame approach. *Frontiers in Psychology*, **10**, article 994. Available online at: https://doi.org/10.3389/fpsyg.2019.00994 Accessed 17 July 2021.

Kirkeby, O.F. (2009) *The New Protreptic: The Concept and the Art*. Copenhagen: Copenhagen Business School Press.

Knudsen, K., Boisen, K., Katzenstein, T., Mortensen, L., Pressler, T., Skov, M. & Jarden, M. (2018) Living with cystic fibrosis: a qualitative study of a life coaching intervention. *Patient Preference and Adherence*, **12**, 585–594.

Lane, D.A. & Corrie, S. (2006) *The Modern Scientist-Practitioner: A guide to practice in psychology*. London: Routledge.

LeeKeenan, K. (2020) 'We're just building!': a study of collaborative coaching interactions. *International Journal of Mentoring and Coaching in Education*, **9** (3) 239–255.

Lawrence, P. (2018) A narrative approach to coaching multiple selves. *International Journal of Evidence Based Coaching and Mentoring*, **16** (2) 32–41.

Linnell, S. (2010) *Art Psychotherapy and Narrative Therapy: An account of practitioner research*. Sharjah, UAE: Bentham Science Publishers.

Madsen, W. (2016) Narrative approaches to organizational development: A case study of implementation of collaborative helping. *Family Process*, **55** (2) 253–269.

Monk, G. & Gehart, D. (2003) Sociopolitical activist or conversational partner? Distinguishing the position of the therapist in narrative and collaborative therapies. *Family Process*, **42** (1) 19–30.

Nurser, K., Rushworth, I., Shakespeare, T. & Williams, D. (2018) Personal storytelling in mental health recovery. *Mental Health Review Journal*, **23**, 25–36.

Ordóñez, L.D., Schweitzer, M.E., Galinsky, A.E. & Bazerman, M.H. (2009) Goals gone wild: The systematic side effects of overprescribing goal setting. *Academy of Management Perspectives*, **23** (1) 6–16.

Orem, S., Binkert, L.J. & Clancy, A.L. (2009) *Appreciative Coaching: A positive process for change.* San Francisco, CA: Jossey-Bass.

Paaske Nielsen, L. & Stelter, R. (2015) Motivation til studiegennemførsel: Er coaching svaret? [Motivation for completing studies: Is coaching the answer?] *Coaching Psykologi: Danish Journal of Coaching Psychology*, **4**, 1. Available online at: http://dx.doi.org/10.5278/ojs.cp.v4i1.1346 Accessed 17 July 2021.

Pavlović, J. (2021) *Coaching Psychology – Constructivist Approaches.* London: Routledge.

Romano, M. & Woods, J. (2018) Collaborative coaching with Early Head Start teachers using responsive communication strategies. *Topics in Early Childhood Special Education*, **38** (1) 30–41.

Rosa, H. (2019) *Resonance: A sociology of our relationship to the world.* Cambridge: Polity Press.

Ryom, K., Andersen, M.M. & Stelter, R. (2017) Coaching at-risk youth in a school within a socially challenging environment. *Improving Schools*, **20** (2) 143–160.

Ryom, K., Wikman, J. & Stelter, R. (2020) Supporting self-concept in school settings targeting migrant background boys. *Scandinavian Journal of Educational Research*, 1–17. Available online at: https://doi.org/10.1080/00313831.2020.1739136 Accessed 17 July 2021.

Sarbin, T. R. (Ed) (1986) *Narrative Psychology: The storied nature of human conduct.* Westport, CT: Praeger.

Sampson, E. E. (1996) Establishing embodiment in psychology. *Theory & Psychology*, **6**, 601–624.

Schwartz, S. H. (2012) An overview of the Schwartz theory of basic values. *Psychology and Culture*, **2** (1). Available online at: https://doi.org/10.9707/2307-0919.1116 Accessed 17 July 2021.

Shotter, J. (2006) Understanding process from within: An argument for withness-thinking. *Organizational Studies*, **27** (5) 585–602.

Shotter, J. & Lannamann, J.W. (2002) The situation of social constructionism: Its 'imprisonment' within the ritual of theory – criticism – and-debate. *Theory & Psychology*, **12** (5) 577–609.

Stam, H. (2001) Social constructionism and its critics. *Theory & Psychology*, **11** (3) 291–296.

Stelter, R. (2007) Coaching: A process of personal and social meaning making. *International Coaching Psychology Review*, **2** (2) 191–201.

Stelter, R. (2014a) *A Guide to Third Generation Coaching: Narrative-collaborative theory and practice.* New York, NY: Springer Science + Business Media.

Stelter, R. (2014b) Third-generation coaching: Striving towards value-oriented and collaborative dialogues. *International Coaching Psychology Review*, **9** (1) 51–66.

Stelter, R. (2015) 'I tried so many diets, now I want to do it differently': A single case study on coaching for weight loss. *International Journal of Qualitative Studies on Health and Wellbeing*, **10**, [26925]. Available online at: https://doi.org/10.3402/qhw.v10.26925 Accessed 17 July 2021.

Stelter R. (2016a) The coach as a fellow human companion. In: L. van Zyl, M. Stander and A. Odendaal (Eds) *Coaching Psychology: Meta-theoretical perspectives and applications in multicultural contexts.* New York, NY: Springer, Cham.

Stelter, R. (2016b) Working with values in coaching. In: T. Bachkirova, G. Spence and D. Drake (Eds) *The SAGE Handbook of Coaching.* Newbury Park, CA: Sage Publications.

Stelter, R. (2019) *The art of dialogue in coaching: Towards transformative exchange.* London: Routledge.

Stelter, R. & Law, H. (2010) Coaching: Narrative-collaborative practice. *International Coaching Psychology Review*, **5** (2) 152–164.

Stelter, R., Nielsen, G. & Wikman, J. (2011) Narrative-collaborative group coaching develops social capital: A randomised control trial and further implications of the social impact of the intervention. *Coaching: An International Journal of Theory, Research & Practice*, **4** (2) 123–137.

Stelter, R. & Andersen, V. (2018) Coaching for health and lifestyle change: Theory and guidelines for interacting and reflecting with women about their challenges and aspirations. *International Coaching Psychology Review*, **13** (1) 61–71.

Sharma, A. & Sharma, L. (2019) VUCA World: The road ahead for HR. *NHRD Network Journal*, **12** (2) 151–158.

Swart, C. (2013) *Re-Authoring the World: The narrative lens and practices for organisations, communities and individuals*. Johannesburg: Knowres Publishing.

Swart, C. (2019) Transforming organisations through the re-authoring lens and practices. In: J. Chlopczyk and C. Erlach (Eds) *Transforming Organizations: Management for professionals*. New York, NY: Springer.

Tomm, K. (1988) Interventive interviewing: Part III: Intending to ask lineal, circular, strategic, or reflexive questions? *Family Process*, **27** (1) 1–15.

Tweedie, K., Yerrell, J. & Crozier, K. (2019) Collaborative coaching and learning in midwifery clinical placements. *British Journal of Midwifery*, **27** (5) 324–329.

Wang, Q. (2018) The place of coaching psychology in learning. In: *Coaching Psychology for Learning* (1st edition). London: Routledge, pp60–88.

Wang, Q, Law, H.C., Li, Y., Xu, Z. & Pang, W. (2017) Awareness and awakening: A narrative-oriented inquiry of undergraduate students' development of mindful agency in China. *Frontiers in Psychologoy*, **8**, 2036. Available online at: https://doi.org/10.3389/fpsyg.2017.02036 Accessed 17 July 2021.

White, M. (2004) Narrative practice and the unpacking of identity conclusions. In: M. White (Ed) *Narrative Practice and Exotic Lives: Resurrecting diversity in everyday life*. Dulwich Centre Publications, pp119–148.

White, M. & Epston, D. (1990) *Narrative Means to Therapeutic Ends*. London: Norton & Company.

Wittgenstein, L. (1953) *Philosophical Investigations*. Hoboken, NJ: Blackwell.

Yip, J., Trainor, L., Black, H., Soto-Torres, L. & Reichard, R. (2019) Coaching new leaders: A relational process of integrating multiple identities. *Academy of Management Learning & Education*, 19 (4). Available online at: https://doi.org/10.5465/amle.2017.0449 Accessed 17 July 2021.